Your Literacy Standards C... at a Glance

Indexes Cross-Referencing Your State Standards with the Common Core appear at the front of the book.

Specific strands and standards are listed for each state.

Each state and grade level is listed at the top for easy reference.

The gist of each standard is succinctly summarized.

This column shows where to find instructional guidance for each standard.

Indexes Cross-Referencing Your State Standards

Alaska, Grade 3

Alaska Strand/Standard	Focus of Alaska Standard	For More Information
Reading Literature		
RL.1	Ask and answer questions to demonstrate understanding of a text, referring explicitly to the text as the basis for the answers	R1 pp. 6–11
RL.2	Determine the author's central message, lesson, or moral, and explain how it is conveyed through key details; summarize stories	R2 pp. 12–17
RL.3	Describe characters in a story and explain how their actions contribute to the sequence of events	R3 pp. 18–23
RL.4	Determine the meaning of words and phrases as they are used in a text, distinguishing literal from nonliteral language	R4 pp. 24–29
RL.5	Refer to parts of stories, dramas, and poems when writing or speaking about a text, using terms such as chapter, scene, and stanza; describe how each successive part builds on earlier sections	R5 pp. 30–35
RL.6	Distinguish their own point of view from that of the narrator or those of the characters	R6 pp. 36–41
RL.7	Explain how specific elements of a text's illustrations contribute to what is conveyed by the words in a story	R7 pp. 42–47
RL.8	NA	
RL.9	Compare and contrast the themes, settings, and plots of stories written by the same author about the same or similar characters	R9 pp. 54–59
RL.10	Read literature of appropriate complexity independently with proficiency	R10 pp. 60–65
Reading Informational Text		
RI.1	Ask and answer questions to demonstrate understanding of a text, referring explicitly to the text as the basis for the answers	R1 pp. 6–11
RI.2	Determine the main idea of a text; recount the key details and explain how they support the main idea	R2 pp. 12–17
RI.3	Describe the relationship between a series of historical events, scientific ideas or concepts, or steps in technical procedures in a text	R3 pp. 18–23
RI.4	Determine the meaning of general academic and domain-specific words and phrases in a text	R4 pp. 24–29
RI.5	Use text features and search tools to locate information on a topic efficiently	R5 pp. 30–35
RI.6	Determine author's purpose; distinguish own point of view from that of the author of a text	R6 pp. 36–41
RI.7	Use information from illustrations and the words in a text to demonstrate understanding of the text	R7 pp. 42–47
RI.8	Describe the logical connection between particular sentences and paragraphs in a text	R8 pp. 48–53
RI.9	Compare and contrast the most important points and key details presented by two texts on the same topic	R9 pp. 54–59
RI.10	Read and comprehend appropriately complex informational texts independently and proficiently	R10 pp. 60–65

(Continued)

Alaska Strand/Standard	Focus of Alaska Standard	For More Information
Reading Foundational Skills		
RF.3	Phonics: Know and apply grade-level phonics and word analysis skills in decoding words	RF3 pp. 214–219
RF.4	Fluency: Read grade-level texts with sufficient accuracy and fluency to support comprehension	RF4 pp. 220–225
Writing		
W.1	Write opinion pieces on topics or texts, supporting a point of view with fact- or text-based reasons	W1 pp. 70–75
W.2	Write informative/explanatory texts to examine a topic and convey ideas and information clearly	W2 pp. 76–81
W.3	Write narrative writing to develop real or imagined experiences or events using effective technique and clear event sequences	W3 pp. 82–87
W.4	Produce writing in which the development and organization are appropriate to the task and purpose	W4 pp. 88–93
W.5	Develop and strengthen writing as needed by planning, revising, and editing	W5 pp. 94–99
W.6	Use technology to produce and publish writing	W6 pp. 100–105
W.7	Conduct short research projects that build knowledge about a topic	W7 pp. 106–111
W.8	Recall information from experiences or gather information from print and digital sources	W8 pp. 112–117
W.9	NA	
W.10	Write routinely over shorter and extended time frames	W10 pp. 124–129
Speaking and Listening		
SL.1	Engage effectively in a range of collaborative discussions with diverse partners, building on others' ideas and expressing their own clearly	SL1 pp. 134–139
SL.2	Determine the main ideas and supporting details of a text read aloud or information presented in diverse media and formats	SL2 pp. 140–145
SL.3	Ask and answer questions about information from a speaker, offering appropriate elaboration and detail	SL3 pp. 146–151
SL.4	Report on a topic or text, tell a story, or recount an experience with appropriate facts and relevant details	SL4 pp. 152–157
SL.5	Create audio recordings of stories or poems, demonstrating fluent reading; add visual displays when appropriate	SL5 pp. 158–163
SL.6	Speak in complete sentences when appropriate to task and situation in order to provide requested detail or clarification	SL6 pp. 164–169
Language		
L.1	Demonstrate command of the conventions of standard English grammar and usage when writing or speaking	L1 pp. 174–179
L.2	Demonstrate command of the conventions of standard English capitalization, punctuation, and spelling when writing	L2 pp. 180–185
L.3	Use knowledge of language and its conventions when writing, speaking, reading, or listening	L3 pp. 186–191
L.4	Determine or clarify the meaning of unknown and multiple-meaning words and phrases, choosing flexibly from an array of strategies	L4 pp. 192–197
L.5	Demonstrate understanding of word relationships and nuances in word meanings	L5 pp. 198–203
L.6	Acquire and use accurately conversational, general academic, and domain-specific words and phrases	L6 pp. 204–209

Shaded bands highlight the overarching strands.

Each standard under the strand is specifically called out.

Each section begins with a restatement of the official anchor standards as they appear in the actual Common Core State Standards document.

College and Career Readiness Anchor Standards for
Reading K–12

The 3–5 Reading Standards outlined on the following pages define what students should understand and be able to do by the end of each grade. Here on this page we present the College and Career Readiness (CCR) anchor standards for K–12 so you can see how students in grades 3–5 work toward the same goals as a high school senior: it's a universal, K–12 vision. The CCR anchor standards and the grade-specific standards correspond to one another by numbers 1–10. They are necessary complements: the former providing broad standards, the latter providing additional specificity. Together, they define the skills and understandings that all students must eventually demonstrate.

Key Ideas and Details

1. Read closely to determine what the text says explicitly and to make logical inferences from it; cite specific textual evidence when writing or speaking to support conclusions drawn from the text.
2. Determine central ideas or themes of a text and analyze their development; summarize the key supporting details and ideas.
3. Analyze how and why individuals, events, and ideas develop and interact over the course of a text.

Craft and Structure

4. Interpret words and phrases as they are used in a text, including determining technical, connotative, and figurative meanings, and analyze how specific word choices shape meaning or tone.
5. Analyze the structure of texts, including how specific sentences, paragraphs, and larger portions of the text (e.g., a section, chapter, scene, or stanza) relate to each other and the whole.
6. Assess how point of view or purpose shapes the content and style of a text.

Integration of Knowledge and Ideas

7. Integrate and evaluate content presented in diverse media and formats, including visually and quantitatively, as well as in words.*
8. Delineate and evaluate the argument and specific claims in a text, including the validity of the reasoning as well as the relevance and sufficiency of the evidence.
9. Analyze how two or more texts address similar themes or topics in order to build knowledge or to compare the approaches the authors take.

Range of Reading and Level of Text Complexity

10. Read and comprehend complex literary and informational texts independently and proficiently.

Note on Range and Content of Student Reading

To build a foundation for college and career readiness, students must read widely and deeply from among a broad range of high-quality, increasingly challenging literary and informational texts. Through extensive reading of stories, dramas, poems, and myths from diverse cultures and different time periods, students gain literary and cultural knowledge as well as familiarity with various text structures and elements. By reading texts in history/social studies, science, and other disciplines, students build a foundation of knowledge in these fields that will also give them the background to be better readers in all content areas. Students can only gain this foundation when the curriculum is intentionally and coherently structured to develop rich content knowledge within and across grades. Students also acquire the habits of reading independently and closely, which are essential to their future success.

*Please consult the full Common Core State Standards document (and all updates and appendices) at http://www.corestandards.org/ELA-Literacy. See "Research to Build Knowledge" in the Writing section and "Comprehension and Collaboration" in the Speaking and Listening section for additional standards relevant to gathering, assessing, and applying information from print and digital sources.

College and Career Readiness Anchor Standards for
Reading K–12

The College and Career Readiness (CCR) anchor standards are the same for K–12. The guiding principle here is that the core reading skills should not change as students advance; rather, the level at which they learn and can perform these skills should increase in complexity as students move from one grade to the next. However, for grades 3–5, we have to recognize that the standards were back mapped from the secondary grades—the authors envisioned what college students needed and then wrote standards, working their way down the grades. Thus, as you use this book remember that children in grades 3–5 can't just "jump over" developmental milestones in an ambitious attempt toward an anchor standard. There are certain life and learning experiences they need to have, and certain concepts they need to learn, before they are capable of handling many complex academic skills in a meaningful way. The anchor standards nonetheless are goal posts to work toward. As you read the "gist" of the standards on the following pages, remember they represent what our 3–5 students will *grow into* during each year and deepen later in middle school and high school.

Key Ideas and Details

This first strand of reading standards emphasizes students' ability to identify key ideas and themes in a text, whether literary, informational, primary, or foundational; whether print, graphic, quantitative, or mixed media. The focus of this first set of standards in on *reading to understand*, during which students focus on *what* the text says. The premise is that students cannot delve into the deeper (implicit) meaning of any text if they cannot first grasp the surface (explicit) meaning of that text. Beyond merely identifying these ideas, readers must learn to see how these ideas and themes, or the story's characters and events, develop and evolve over the course of a text. Such reading demands that students know how to identify, evaluate, assess, and analyze the elements of a text for their importance, function, and meaning within the text.

Craft and Structure

The second set of standards builds on the first, focusing not on *what* the text says but *how* it says it, the emphasis here being on analyzing how texts are made to serve a function or achieve a purpose. These standards ask readers to examine the choices the author makes in terms of words, sentence, and paragraph structure and how these choices contribute to the meaning of the text and the author's larger purpose. Inherent in the study of craft and structure is how these items interact with and influence the ideas and details outlined in the first three standards.

Integration of Knowledge and Ideas

This third strand might be summed up as: *reading to extend or deepen* one's knowledge of a subject by comparing what a range of sources have said about it over time and across different media. In addition, these standards emphasize the importance of being able to read the arguments; that is, they look at how to identify the claims the texts make and evaluate the evidence used to support those claims regardless of the media. Finally, these standards ask students to analyze the choice of means and medium the author chooses and the effect those choices have on ideas and details. Thus, if a writer integrates words, images, and video in a mixed-media text, readers should be able to examine how and why the author did that in terms of stylistic and rhetorical purposes.

Range of Reading and Level of Text Complexity

The Common Core State Standards document itself offers the most useful explanation of what this last standard means in a footnote titled "Note of range and content of student reading," which accompanies the reading standards:

To become college and career ready, students must grapple with works of exceptional craft and thought whose range extends across genres, cultures, and centuries. Such works offer profound insights into the human condition and serve as models for students' own thinking and writing. Along with high-quality contemporary works, these texts should be chosen from among seminal U.S. documents, the classics of American literature, and the timeless dramas of Shakespeare. Through wide and deep reading of literature and literary nonfiction of steadily increasing sophistication, students gain a reservoir of literary and cultural knowledge, references, and images; the ability to evaluate intricate arguments; and the capacity to surmount the challenges posed by complex texts. (CCSS, 2010, p. 35)

On the facing page, a user-friendly "translation" of each standard gives you a fuller sense of the big picture and big objectives as you consider how it relates to your state's standards.

Bold type spotlighting what's different across grade spans specifically identifies what students must learn within each grade.

On this page you'll find accessible translations of the standards at your left so you can better grasp what they mean.

The emphasis now is on what students should do, utilizing the same grade-level structure at your left.

Built-in tabs facilitate navigation.

The actual CCSS anchor standard is included for easy reference.

The specific strand situates you within the larger context of the standards.

Comprehension questions are included for helping students master thinking moves and skills behind each standard; all can be adapted to a range of class texts and topics or to needs specific to your particular state standards.

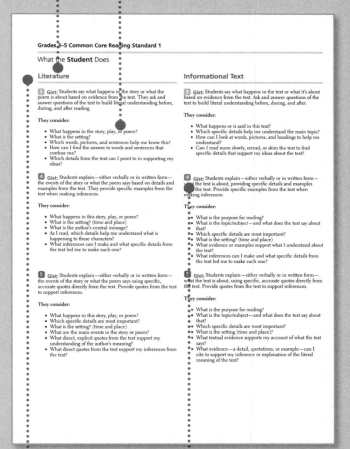

Horizontal and vertical views enable you to consider how the standards change across grade levels.

Standards for each discipline are featured on a single page for easy planning.

The right-hand page utilizes the very same grade-level format to provide two distinct visual paths for understanding the standards.

"Gist" sections provide plain-English synopses of the standards so you can put them to immediate use.

Featured on a separate page are specific teaching techniques for realizing each standard. Applicable to all subjects across grades 3–5, these strategies focus on what works in the classroom.

Common Core Reading Standard 1

What the **Teacher** Does

To teach students how to "read closely":

- Think aloud your close reading process as you share fiction and informational short texts and picture books. When reading shared novels as a class, plan ahead a chapter opening or passage you want to model with. Track thinking with sticky notes placed directly on the text, big chart paper and/or highlighting, displaying text on a screen.
- Pose questions about the text's words, actions, and details that require students to look closely. Don't do the answering for them!
- Display a text via tablet or computer and ask students to select specific words, sentences, or paragraphs they think are essential; ask students to explain how it contributes to the meaning of the larger text.
- Draw students' attention to text features and structures, and think aloud how you combine information in these elements to understand the page/section/text as a whole.
- Provide short pieces of text for students to practice "reading closely" for specific purposes.
- Have students respond to their reading and their thinking about texts. This could be accomplished in response journals or other reading notebooks.

To teach students how to ask and answer questions to demonstrate understanding:

- Using picture books, ask a question and think aloud how it helped you understand. For example, when a fiction reader muses, *"I wonder why she acted that way towards him?"* it puts the reader on high alert, looking for the answer in the text. Readers of nonfiction also pose questions when their comprehension falters or as a way to cement understandings, sentence by sentence. For example, *"What does hibernation mean? I sort of think it has something to do with winter, but I'll read on to see if the author explains it."*
- Use chart paper to record students' questions about a shared text as you read. Then, after reading, go back and answer these questions. Encourage students to pose analytical (how, why) questions along with literal (who, what, where, when) questions. Code if questions were answered literally (L), inferentially (I), or not answered at all (NA).
- Over time, help students grasp that readers pose questions before reading (What's my purpose for reading this?), during reading (What's with all the descriptions

of sunlight in each chapter?), and after reading (What did the main character finally learn?).

- Have students practice posing questions on their own (independently). Students can annotate on the text where they have questions. Have students share them with a partner or the class.

To develop students' ability to determine "what the text says explicitly," "refer to details and examples in a text," and "quote accurately from a text":

- In a series of lessons and using various texts, write *text-dependent* questions on sticky notes or annotate in the margins. Model how to find the answers to the questions posed. Annotate in the margins the exact words where questions are answered.
- Provide students with a copy of a sample text and circulate, coaching as they highlight *specific* details and annotate their thinking. Remind them to "say what it says"—not what they think it means.
- Photocopy and distribute short pieces of text and highlighter markers, and instruct students to highlight sections of the text to show where questions you pose are answered explicitly (or literally). Compare findings as a class.
- Using whiteboards, have students highlight quotes from a text to use as evidence when explaining what the text is about.
- Provide graphic organizers for students to write their questions and then record details, examples, and quotes.

To teach students how to "draw inferences from the text":

- Choose texts to read aloud and plan where you will model inferring. Think aloud how you make inferences, and tie these inferences back to specific words and phrases in the text.
- Have students use two different colored highlighters to code where information in the text is answered literally or explicitly and another color to show where it's answered inferentially. Annotate how the text led to inferences.

To help your English language learners, try this:

- Confer with students and have them read aloud a portion of the text. Then stop and have them tell you what questions they have about what they've read.

 For graphic organizer templates, see online resources at **resources.corwin.com/literacycompanion3-5.**

Preparing to Teach

Standard: _____

Preparing the Classroom	Preparing the Mindset

Preparing the Texts to Use	Preparing to Differentiate

Connections to Other Standards:

In this worksheet, you record ideas for turning the standard into instruction. Notice there's a place for jotting which lessons or texts from other standards you might adapt and re-teach in connection with this standard, because the goal is to integrate several standards.

A dedicated academic vocabulary section offers a quick-reference glossary of key words and phrases for each standard.

In this worksheet, you think about how to address the standard in a variety of instructional formats. Record initial plans for whole class lessons, think-alouds, read-alouds, small-group practice, and projects that get students doing the work of learning, and independent practice/conferring.

Common Core Reading Standard 1

Academic Vocabulary: Key Words and Phrases

Cite specific textual evidence: Students should be able to quote a specific passage from the text to support all claims, assertions, or arguments about what a text means or says. Evidence comes from within the text itself, not from the reader's opinion or experience.

Demonstrate understanding of a text: Readers take a group of details (different findings, series of events, related examples) and draw from them an insight or understanding about their meaning or importance within the passage of the text as a whole.

Drawing inferences: To understand the text by generalizing, deducing, and concluding from reasoning and evidence that is not presented literally or explicitly. These conclusions are based on textual clues.

Explicitly: Clearly stated in great or precise detail; may pertain to factual information or literal meaning, though this is not necessarily always the case.

Informational text: These include nonfiction texts from a range of sources and written for a variety of purposes; everything from essays to advertisements, historical documents to op-ed pieces. Informational texts include written arguments as well as infographics.

Key details: Parts of a text that support the main idea, and enable the reader to draw conclusions and infer what the text or a portion of a text is about.

Literature: Fiction, poetry, drama, graphic stories, but also artworks by distinguished painters, sculptors, or photographers.

Logical inferences (drawn from the text): To infer, readers add what they *learned* from the text to what they already *know* about the subject; however, for an inference to be "logical," it must be based on evidence *from the text*.

Quote accurately: "Lifting lines" directly from the text or copying specific sections of the text to demonstrate understanding. All claims, assertions, or arguments about what a text means or says require specific examples from the text.

Read closely (aka close reading): Reading that emphasizes not only surface details but the deeper meanings and larger connotations between words, sentences, and the full text; also demands scrutiny of craft, including arguments and style used by the author.

Text: In its broadest meaning, a text is whatever one is trying to read: a poem, essay, drama, story, or article; in its most modern sense, a text can also be an image, an artwork, speech, or multimedia format such as a website, film, or social media message such as a tweet.

Textual evidence: Not all evidence is created equal; students need to choose those pieces of evidence (words, phrases, passages illustrations) that provide the best proof of what they are asserting about the text.

Notes

Planning to Teach

Standard: _____

Whole Class

Small Group

Individual Practice/Conferring

Clearly worded entries decode each word or phrase according to the particular way it is used in a given standard.

Example of a Filled-in Worksheet: Fifth Grade

This is a place to think about books (or book bundles), other texts, and a range of levels.

Think through room arrangement ideas (e.g., Will the students be working in groups?) and the tools and materials you will need.

Here, note ways to intellectually and emotionally engage your students for the standard.

Preparing to Teach

Standard: Reading Standard 6

Preparing the Classroom

Space for a meeting area

Reading response journals

Clipboards or lapboards if necessary

Easel and chart paper

Markers, colored highlighters, sticky notes

Graphic organizers

Interactive whiteboard

Document camera

Preparing the Mindset

Get students' candid response to the books we've read aloud thus far—did they like them or not? Have them share reasons why, using this activity to demonstrate how their point of view influences how they describe them. Bring in published book reviews. Be sure to engage boys and girls who love sports with POV on the latest sports game (college, professional, or school).

Preparing the Texts to Use

<u>Books:</u> Read either R. J. Palacio's *Wonder* or *Because of Mr. Terupt* by Rob Buyea as a read-aloud or anchor text; use several Capstone-Picture Window Books, including *Believe Me, Goldilocks Rocks! The Story of the Three Bears as Told by Baby Bear* and *No Lie, I Acted Like a Beast! The Story of Beauty and the Beast as Told by the Beast* by Nancy Loewen; Trisha Speed Shaskan's *Honestly, Red Riding Hood Was Rotten! The Story of Little Red Riding Hood as Told by the Wolf*; the Three Little Pigs books that offer different POV; Michael Teague's *Dear Mr Larue* books—also great for POV

<u>Magazines/short passages:</u> Sports commentaries in local paper—make copies for independent work

<u>Online resources:</u> Editorials from papers around the country; book reviews (*New York Times*, Amazon)

Preparing to Differentiate

Multiple copies of books for small group—the fairy tale books; also have the original fairy tales

Graphic organizer—two column for the different points of view

Books written from first- and third-person viewpoints to reinforce

Books with easily recognized points of view

Connections to Other Standards:

Reading Standards 1 and 3: Key Ideas and Details

Reading Standard 9: Analyze how two texts address the same topic or theme

Reading Standard 10: Read, read, read!

Writing Standard 1: Write opinion pieces supporting a point of view

Speaking and Listening 1: Conversations and collaborations

List skills, texts, and ideas for foregrounding or reinforcing other ELA standards.

Here, consider texts that are accessible, different supplies, differentiation.

Example of a Filled-in Worksheet: Third Grade

Preparing to Teach

Standard: *Reading Standard 3*

Preparing the Classroom

Whole-class meeting area
Writers notebooks or journals; writing folders
Clipboards or lapboards if necessary
Easel chart paper
Sticky notes, colored highlighters
Drawing paper so that students can sketch setting
Writing paper, staplers, paperclips, etc.
Graphic organizers
Interactive whiteboard and document camera
Rubrics or checklists
Expectations
Computers, printer

Preparing the Mindset

Prior to starting this unit read numerous narratives. As a class, chart the main problems, characters and events.

Discuss how personal narratives are different from fictional stories.

Tell stories of your own life and *why* they're important to you.

Have students begin a list of true stories about their lives.

Provide numerous opportunities for students to share their stories with others *before* they begin to write them.

Preparing the Texts to Use

Photocopy the short student/mentor texts in Bernabei and Reimer's *Fun-Size Academic Writing for Serious Learning*. Invite students to bring in mentor texts to share, too.

Narrative picture books. Patricia Polacco, Cynthia Rylant

Night Driving or *Today I'm Going Fishing with My Dad* or *Fireflies* by Julie Brinkloe

<u>Online Resources</u>: Online books—both animated and texts; graphic organizers, story organizers

Preparing to Differentiate

Short pieces of narrative text at appropriate reading level

Apps to use on the iPad or computers

Short movies or animated books that can be stopped and discussed

Graphic organizers, especially story boards

Opportunities to "talk out" their stories first

Connections to Other Standards:

Writing Standard 4: Production and Distribution of Writing
Writing Standard 5: Writing Process
Writing Standard 1: Write Routinely
Reading Standards 1-3: Key Ideas and Details
Speaking and Listening Standard 1
Language Standards 1-3

Example of a Filled-in Worksheet: Fifth Grade

What lessons will you
do as a whole class?

Planning to Teach

Standard: *Reading Standard 6*

Whole Class

Wonder or *Because of Mr. Terupt:* Read aloud a chapter, record what students notice on chart paper—character's traits and how POV influences the narration. Discuss *author's* POV and *narrator's or characters'* POV.

Read aloud two versions of same fairy tale. Students do two-column chart on how the different narrators explained events.

Possible focus questions:

Who is telling the story? Why do you think this character was chosen by the author?

How does this narrator explain events? Why? What's his/her angle?

If another character told the story how would she describe the events?

Small Group

Groups fill-out two-column charts as they read fairy tale books—plan on about 5 groups.

Advanced students read a short story at an upper level instead for additional challenge (any of the *Guys Read* books by John Scieszka, as well as short stories by Avi).

Individual Practice/Conferring

Using copied sports columns from different papers (the *Denver Post* for the Broncos and the *Kansas City* paper for the Chiefs) have students choose an important event from each and write these on different colored sticky notes. Then place these on a class Venn diagram to see how the articles and the columnists see things the same and some differently. Confer with students as they work.

Hold individual conferences with Stephen, Miranda, and Xavier during independent reading time and have students explain the POV and what they notice about it.

Have students respond to reading. Question: *What do all effective points of view have in common? Name three attributes and explain why you think so.* Write back to them or meet with them one-on-one to discuss their thinking.

How will you deliver individual
instruction? How will you record
conferences? Check in with
students?

This section is for you to plan what types of
grouping you will use. Needs-based groups?
Remediation? Extensions? Guided reading
groups? Book clubs or literature circles?

Example of a Filled-in Worksheet: Third Grade

Planning to Teach

Standard: Reading Standard 6

Whole Class

Read and discuss numerous narratives
Chart characters, plot events, setting
Share personal stories
Model how to create a story map—using a shared text
With each stage of the writing process work as a whole class (mini-lessons)

- Topic
- Characters
- Setting
- Sequencing events
- The "problem"

- Dialogue
- Adding description—especially to the character
- Using words to signify order of events (temporal words)
- Endings

Small Group

Have students create a story map of a shared text.

Have students share their own story maps with groups.

Pull together needs groups for each stage of the writing process—rehearsing, drafting, revising, editing. These groups could be for students who need more explicit instruction or for a group of students working at the advanced level who would benefit from sharing with others.

Have peer conferences.

Individual Practice/Conferring

Confer with students throughout the writing process. Use conferences to identify students with similar needs to pull together as a group. In each conference, be sure to teach the writer one thing he needs. Remember to keep track of conferences—both student strengths and what was taught.

As a unit of study, students write a personal narrative with the focus being Why is it important? Why do I want to tell it?

YOUR LITERACY STANDARDS COMPANION, GRADES 3–5

What They Mean and How to Teach Them

Leslie Blauman

with Jim Burke

resources.corwin.com/literacycompanion3-5

Name: _____

Department: _____

Learning Team: _____

CORWIN
A SAGE Publishing Company

FOR INFORMATION:

Corwin
A SAGE Company
2455 Teller Road
Thousand Oaks, California 91320
(800) 233-9936
www.corwin.com

SAGE Publications Ltd.
1 Oliver's Yard
55 City Road
London EC1Y 1SP
United Kingdom

SAGE Publications India Pvt. Ltd.
B 1/I 1 Mohan Cooperative Industrial Area
Mathura Road, New Delhi 110 044
India

SAGE Publications Asia-Pacific Pte. Ltd.
3 Church Street
#10-04 Samsung Hub
Singapore 049483

Publisher and Senior Program Director: Lisa Luedeke
Senior Acquisitions Editor: Wendy Murray
Editorial Development Manager: Julie Nemer
Editorial Assistant: Nicole Shade
Production Editor: Melanie Birdsall
Copy Editors: Amy Rosenstein and Deanna Noga
Typesetter: C&M Digitals (P) Ltd.
Proofreaders: Victoria Reed-Castro and Alison Syring
Cover Designer: Scott Van Atta
Interior Designer: Auburn Associates, Inc.
Marketing Manager: Rebecca Eaton

Printed in the United States of America

ISBN 978-1-5063-8700-0

This book is printed on acid-free paper.

SUSTAINABLE FORESTRY INITIATIVE
Certified Chain of Custody
Promoting Sustainable Forestry
www.sfiprogram.org
SFI-01268
SFI label applies to text stock

17 18 19 20 21 10 9 8 7 6 5 4 3 2 1

Contents

Visit the companion website at
resources.corwin.com/literacycompanion3-5
for downloadable versions of the
Indexes Cross-Referencing Your State Standards and additional resources.

Note: For the complete Common Core State Standards document, please visit corestandards.org.

Preface

The standards offer us all a tremendous opportunity to help our students learn what they need to know for success in school and life, but using them requires a lot of something we as teachers have very little of: *time*. Standards demand that we find more time for students to learn in school—more time to think, practice, collaborate, and reflect. And we have to find more time as teachers to plan and teach, to learn the related language and instructional moves implicit in the standards.

With an all too keen sense of my own limited time, I began to create a version of the Common Core State Standards that better met my needs, one I could keep by my side and reference quickly when planning, writing, or participating in meetings related to the Common Core standards. When teachers saw it, they wanted their own copies, and the result was *The Common Core Companion*—one for grades 6–8 and another for 9–12, which were both published in 2013.

What's the big idea behind *Your Literacy Standards Companion*? It's inefficient for us all across the nation to spend time deciphering what our specific state standards say and digesting what they mean for teaching and learning, so I created the *Companion* to do that for you. With this book at your side, you can reclaim hours of time to do the most important work: develop your instructional ideas (and the standards themselves) into rich, engaging learning experiences for our students that meet the standards' higher expectations.

Because I often work with literacy coordinators who are responsible for all students in their district, I wanted these *Companion* books to be K–12, districtwide, and school-wide tools. That way teachers and administrators could hit the ground running as they implemented the standards and envisioned professional development that would support all teachers. But I had one problem: I was not an elementary school teacher. For teachers in grades K–2, I thought of Sharon Taberski, an exemplary teacher and guide to teachers around the country.

When it came to someone in grades 3–5, I did not have to think long about whom to ask, for in those grades, all roads lead to Leslie Blauman. While there is so much to recommend Leslie, especially her work as a literacy coordinator and a demonstration teacher at the Public Education & Business Coalition, it is her 30 years of hands-on experience in the classroom that make her uniquely qualified for this project—and her dedication to kids! This grades 3–5 version retains many of the formatting features that have worked so well with middle and high school teachers. But Leslie made it her own, pumping up the volume of teaching ideas. She knew what you would want, what you need.

So without further ado, and with deepest gratitude for all she has taught me through the process of writing this book, I introduce you to *Your Literacy Standards Companion, Grades 3–5*. If you're looking for someone to help you understand and, more important, *use* the state standards in your classroom, you have come to the right place, for with Leslie Blauman, you are in good hands. Trust her to help you create exemplary standards-aligned 3–5 literacy instruction that will allow you to be the teacher you have been and are capable of becoming.

—Jim Burke

Introduction

Turning Standards Into Daily Teaching

Thank you for making me go to school.

—August Pullman (*Wonder*, Palacio, 2012)

An excellent education should not be an accident; it should be a right, though nowhere in the United States Constitution or any of our other founding documents do we find that right listed. The Common Core State Standards address that omission and challenge us all—administrators and teachers, parents and children, politicians and the public at large, professors and student teachers—to commit ourselves anew to the success of our children and our country.

This is how Jim Burke opened the grades 6–12 and 9–12 versions of *The Common Core Companion*, the four-volume ELA series he conceived of for Corwin Literacy in 2013. In the 3 years since these books were published, they have been so-called "evergreen" bestsellers, selling more copies each year, because they help educators everywhere get the important work done of transforming standards into daily learning outcomes. A series for Common Core Mathematics Companion also thrives. Here's the interesting thing: Corwin sales data showed robust book sales in states that never even adopted the Common Core State Standards (CCSS), which means educators were purchasing the CCSS books to help them refresh or reimagine their own state standards. As a teacher, this doesn't surprise me, because we educators are an enterprising lot, forever rolling up our sleeves and adapting things to suit our needs. Perhaps more important, it speaks to the nature of well-thought-out standards.

Corwin Literacy saw this market need and decided to issue this new version, *Your Literacy Standards Companion*, complete with indexes for each state that opted out of the CCSS, to make it easier for users to go right to the pages most aligned to their state's standards. The following states have indexes beginning on page I-1:

Alaska	Florida
Arizona	Georgia
Arkansas	Indiana
Colorado	Iowa

Kansas

Louisiana

Maryland

Minnesota

Mississippi

Missouri

Nebraska

New Jersey

Oklahoma

Pennsylvania

South Carolina

Tennessee

Utah

Virginia

West Virginia

I am a full-time fourth-grade teacher and bring to this book my expertise as an intermediate-grade teacher who has also worn other hats of district literacy coordinator, PEBC (Public Education and Business Coalition) Lab teacher, and literacy consultant, spending time in classrooms in just about all 50 states. As a teacher, I can look down the hall at third grade, and up the hall to fifth grade, to help you know and name what the standards are asking of intermediate-grade teachers in particular.

As I write this revised introduction, I could tell you all sorts of stories about implementing the standards or how students, parents, and administrators responded to the testing, but the biggest takeaway in the years since the CCSS were enacted is that my students, and maybe all students, *can* rise to the challenge of becoming accomplished readers, writers, and thinkers. The biggest change that the CCSS nudged me to make? I am teaching students to cite evidence in a more deliberate way since implementing the standards. Students write more about their reading in more detail with specific examples from text to support their thinking. Overall, I think that is a positive change!

Whether you are in a place using the CCSS or your own state's standards, the important thing is to translate the standards into learning outcomes in age-appropriate, best-practice ways. That's why I'm so gratified when teachers who have used this book say to me how much they love the What the Student Does and What the Teacher Does pages most. Anyone can sit at a computer and find lists of standards, but what makes *Your Literacy Standards Companion* special is that it helps educators confirm the daily practices that have the most impact on student learning.

As I think is the case in designing state standards, the authors of the Common Core State Standards focus on the "what," and leave it to the capable practitioners to design the teaching and learning that will get students *to* the goals:

By emphasizing required achievements, the Standards leave room for teachers, curriculum developers, and states to determine how those goals should be reached and what additional topics should be addressed. Thus, the standards do not mandate such things as a particular writing process or the full range of metacognitive strategies that students may need to monitor and direct their thinking and learning. Teachers are thus free to provide students with whatever tools and knowledge their professional judgment and experience identify as most helpful for meeting the goals set out in the standards. (National Governors Association Center for Best Practices [NGA Center] & Council of Chief State School Officers [CCSSO], 2010)

The standards also uphold and advance the strong research base for how learners learn and progress. Students become better readers when they *read*. They become better writers when they *write*. Digging into the CCSS, you find that Reading Standard 10 requires that students read. Writing Standard 10 stipulates that students write for a variety of purposes over an extended time. And don't we want our students—of all ages—doing lots of actual reading and writing and *thinking*? Here are a few sentences from the standards that should woo any of us:

> Students who meet the Standards readily undertake close, attentive reading that is at the heart of understanding and enjoying complex works of literature. They habitually perform the critical reading necessary to pick carefully through the staggering amount of information available today in print and digitally. They actively seek the wide, deep, and thoughtful engagement with high quality literary and informational texts that builds knowledge, enlarges experience, and broadens worldviews. (NGA Center & CCSSO, 2010, p. 3)

And you know what? This is what students want, too! They don't want canned lessons, teachers reading from scripts, random worksheets tied to a commercial program or downloaded off the Internet. They want to *engage*. It doesn't matter about socioeconomics, or race, or whatever factors you want to insert here: kids of all ages want, almost clamor for, the same thing. They want rigor and choice and someone who helps them think and learn and communicate with others. They want someone who listens to them, validates where they are, and then moves them forward.

Our students want us teachers to bring texts, rich discussions, complex ideas, and emotions into their lives in the safety of the classroom culture. Last year I read R. J. Palacio's novel *Wonder* aloud to the class. I looked up after I'd read the final sentence in one of the last chapters to see more than half the class in tears. Then the tears turned to cheers at how the protagonist overcame such incredible odds. This is a book that unfolds gradually, but without spoiling it, the main character, August, is unlike any other child, and my students empathize with him because he's ostracized due to genetics giving him the short straw. The principal is presenting year-end awards and uses Henry Ward Beecher's words on greatness. "'Greatness,' wrote Beecher, 'lies not in being strong, but in the right using of strength. . . . He is the greatest whose strength carries up the most hearts.'" As the principal finishes, the last sentence reads, "So will August Pullman please come up here to receive this award?" My students understood—Auggie's quiet greatness, his outlook on life, his perseverance all prevailed. And they had lived with August throughout the adversity.

This book will stay with my students. The story, the lessons, the empathy. This is one of many powerful books we read from a list that could go on and on. But they will remember Auggie Pullman perhaps most of all. "Thank you for making me go to school," Auggie said.

I want all our students to say that—*every day*! And I believe that the Common Core standards can create the kind of conditions in our classrooms that lead students to say that, to revere school. The standards are "bookish" and "intellectual," and, despite or because of their rigor, they're about ensuring students' engagement.

So before I move on to an overview of how this book is organized, I want to give you a metaphor of how I envision this book serving you. Jim Burke uses a metaphor of a compass in his introduction of *Your Literacy Standards Companion*, a wonderful metaphor.

For this book, I offer you this image:

Source: Courtesy of clipart.com.

The image was sent by a friend of mine as I was working on the final section of this book, with a brief note, "The silhouetted hands made me think of students leaning in with raised hands. With the standards, aren't all students supposed to be thinking and participating?"

Bingo. I had my metaphor. The standards and in turn the suggestions in this book are a mere outline of how you might begin. The book allows you to color, contour, and add texture to the teaching and learning that I charcoal-outlined in these pages.

A Brief Orientation to *Your Literacy Standards Companion, Grades 3–5*

When I was asked to write *Your Literacy Standards Companion, Grades 3–5*, I was thrilled to follow Jim Burke's design and the standard his first two books set. He envisioned this series and blazed the trail, with the help of teachers, curriculum supervisors, and superintendents with whom he has worked around the country.

Jim's words in his orientation are applicable to the elementary setting, too:

As is true for all of us, administrators have come to the job of leading with their sense of what their role is or should be; past experience, along with their training and education, has given them this orientation. Now administrators and teachers such as yourself find their role being redefined, the demands on them and their time being dramatically restructured, often in ways that cause some sense of disorientation, as if all your previous experience, all your knowledge, was suddenly suspect, leaving you to navigate this new era without a working compass. Eventually, as we know, we get our bearings, find the star by which we might chart our course, and realize that much of what we already know and value does still, in fact, apply to the task at hand, that it certainly need not be tossed overboard.

So in other words, "we don't toss out the baby with the bathwater." This book is for you, whether you are an administrator or teacher, district curriculum supervisor, professor, or student teacher training to join in the education field. The goal is to understand and make better use of the standards themselves and to plan for how to implement them in the classroom using *best instructional practices*.

In addition to the new Indexes Cross-Referencing Your State Standards, key features of this revised *Your Literacy Standards Companion* include the following:

A one-page overview of *all* the anchor standards. Designed for quick reference or self-assessment, this one-page document offers a one-stop place to see all the English Language Arts Common Core Standards. In addition to using this to quickly check the Common Core anchor standards, grade-level teachers or the whole faculty might use them to evaluate which standards they know and are addressing effectively and which ones they need to learn and teach.

Side-by-side anchor standards translation. The CCSS College Readiness anchor standards for each category—reading, foundational skills, writing, speaking and listening, and language—appear in a two-page spread with the original Common Core anchor standards on the left and, on the right, their matching translations in language that is more accessible to those on the run or new to literacy instruction.

A new user-friendly format for each standard. Instead of the two reading standard domains—literature and informational text—spread throughout the CCSS document, here you will find the first reading standard for grades 3–5 and the two different domains all on one page. This allows you to use *Your Literacy Standards Companion* to see at a glance what Reading Standard 1 looks like in grades 3–5 across literature and informational texts. The design makes it easy to look at how the standard plays out across grade levels, so you can plan with teachers just how to increase complexity as students move from grade to grade.

Parallel translation/what the student does. Each standard opens to a two-page spread that has the original Common Core standards on the left and a parallel translation of each standard mirrored on the right-hand page in more accessible language (referred to as the "Gist") so you can concentrate on how to *teach* in ways that meet the CCSS instead of how to understand them. These Gist pages align themselves with the original Common Core, so you can move between the two without turning a page as you think about what they mean and how to teach them. Also, beneath each translation of a standard appears a list of *They Consider*. These are brief practical questions that will help students "crack open" the thinking and comprehension skills being asked of them. Ultimately, students pose these questions for themselves—both unconsciously and deliberately—as they engage in the endeavor. But because metacognition is something children grow into, you can use these questions as comprehension questions to pose to students after you model how to approach them. The goal is to provide ample practice with these questions so that students *internalize* them and own them as readers, writers, and thinkers. So be sure to incorporate them into the fabric of your instruction each and every day, having students talking, listening, and writing off them.

Instructional techniques/what the teacher does. In the "What the Teacher Does" pages, you will find a great many suggestions. Although I don't always say "Put your students in groups" or "Put your students in pairs," I can't emphasize enough that the goal is to demonstrate less and have students *do* more. Periodically you will see references to online resources that provide graphic organizers, visuals, book lists, and other tools that support the teaching of the standard.

Preparing to teach templates. These templates serve as reminders, too, that teachers should be considering all these kinds of work every day when they plan. This page is divided into five sections—a place for you to plan, make notes, and so on. Examples of how it might look are shown in the beginning of the book. The sections are as follows:

- **Preparing the Classroom:** Where you can consider room arrangement (e.g., Will the students be working in groups? Do you have an area where you can meet with a group of students? A place for large group activities?) and the physical tools and materials you will need. For example, chart paper, graphic organizers, or multiple copies of material.
- **Preparing the Mindset:** Here is where you brainstorm ways to intellectually ready and engage your students for the standard.
- **Preparing the Texts to Use:** A place to think about books (or book bundles), magazines, short passages or mentor texts, online resources, and so on that you could use for this standard.
- **Preparing to Differentiate:** This is for you to think about your learners who need additional support. You might consider texts that are accessible, different supplies, and

differentiation. You may choose to differentiate and include how you will extend the lesson for students working at the upper level.

- **Connections to Other Standards:** A place to draw your own connections between the standard in question and other standards.

As you use these pages, they should become a resource for future lessons and a record of instruction. They are also beneficial for collaboration with colleagues.

Academic vocabulary: Key words and phrases. Each standard comes with a unique glossary since words used in more than one standard have a unique meaning in each. Any word or phrase that seemed a source of possible confusion is defined in detail.

Planning to teach templates. This is another template for you to record your notes and your planning. This page is divided into three sections: **Whole Class, Small Group,** and **Individual Practice/Conferring.** These templates serve as reminders that you should be considering these kinds of work every day when you plan.

How to Use This Book

Every school, district, instructional team, or teacher will pick up *Your Literacy Standards Companion* and have different ideas about how to use it as a tool. And, of course, there is no one right way to use it. Here are some possible ways, which you should adapt, adopt, or avoid as you see fit:

- Provide all teachers on a grade-level team or school with a copy to establish a common text to work from throughout their planning and instructional design work.
- Use it in tandem with the K–2 version by Sharon Taberski to dig into the standards in a whole-school initiative.
- Use it along with the K–2, 6–8, and 9–12 volumes for district-level planning and professional development work.
- Bring your *Companion* to all meetings for quick reference or planning with colleagues in your school or on your grade-level team.
- Use your *Companion* to aid in the transition from what you were doing to what you will be doing, treating the planning pages that accompany each standard as a place to note what you do or which standard corresponds with one of your district or state standards you are trying to adapt to the Common Core.
- Use your *Companion* as a resource for revisiting your curriculum plans in Year 2 (or beyond!) of implementing the standards to help you develop, refine, and deepen instruction.
- Begin or end meetings with a brief but carefully planned sample lesson based on a teaching idea in this book. Ask one or more colleagues in the school to present at the next meeting on how it might apply to other grade levels.
- Use the *Companion* in conjunction with your professional learning community to add further cohesion and consistency between all your ideas and plans.

References

National Governors Association Center for Best Practices & Council of Chief State School Officers. (2010). *Common Core State Standards English language arts & literacy in history/social studies, science, and technical subjects.* Washington, DC: Authors.

Palacio, R. J. (2012). *Wonder.* New York, NY: Random House.

Pearson, P. D. (2013). Research foundations of the Common Core State Standards in English language arts. In S. Neuman & L. Gambrell (Eds.), *Quality reading instruction in the age of Common Core Standards* (pp. 237–262). Newark, DE: International Reading Association.

Key Principles and Additional Teaching Strategies for

English Language Learners 3–5

You may have students who are English language learners in your classroom. Some of these students may be new to English, having just emigrated from another country where English is not the primary language, and others may have started learning English in kindergarten and first grade. Whether the English language learners have just started learning English or have developed some proficiency in English, they have unique needs from native English speakers.

To help you meet their needs, you'll find suggestions for each standard at the end of the "What the Teacher Does" pages. Here, I supplement these instructional ideas with additional background, the stages of language acquisition, and the implications for differentiated scaffolding that will be most effective.

Focus on Acquisition

The students in our grades 3–5 classrooms, both native-English-speaking students and English language learners (ELLs), are learning language. In many respects they are remarkably the same in their quest and language acquisition. Both groups of children are rapidly developing their vocabularies, using language to communicate, and learning about academic language and formal English.

However, there is a difference between native-English-speaking students and ELLs. ELLs are acquiring a *second* language when they learn English at school; they already have their primary language, with which they communicate at home and in the community. Thus, many of these children are fluent in their first language, an important point to remember so that our mindset as teachers isn't that all these kids are struggling learners overall.

We learn language through two processes. One process is called *acquisition*, and the other process is called *language learning*. Language acquisition is "picking up" a language. Language learning is what we experience when we take a class in a foreign language.

In our classrooms, we want to focus on the natural process of "picking up" a language. Thus, for both native-English-speaking students and ELL students, this book is filled with strategies and lessons to teach the standards through natural, motivating, and supportive teaching.

Consider the Five Stages

To understand the best ways to help your ELLs and to differentiate instruction based on their language acquisition needs, it is important to understand that not all children learning English need the same scaffolds, the same types of instruction, or the same performance tasks. What they need depends on which stage of language acquisition they are in. While people don't fit into boxes and language learning is a fluid process, it truly

Source: Contributed by Nancy Akhavan.

helps to understand the five stages of language acquisition and assess where your students are so you can tailor instruction based on their language needs. These five stages, as described in the following chart on page xxviii, are preproduction, early production, speech emergence, intermediate fluency, and advanced fluency (Haynes & Zacarian, 2010; Krashen, 1982/2009, 2003; Krashen & Terrell, 1983).

It is also important to note that students acquire language in a natural order (Krashen, 1982/2009, 2003; Peregoy & Boyle, 1997). The key idea behind this natural order idea is that students won't learn English in the order that you teach it but, rather, in the natural way that the brain learns language. In other words, you can't force students to learn a grammar rule by teaching it explicitly, but you can ensure students acquire English rapidly by providing engaging, language-rich, supportive, culturally respectful, and meaningful classroom experiences in English (Akhavan, 2006; Hoover & Patton, 2005).

Understand the Needs of Long-Term ELLs

The general amount of time it takes to become proficient in a second language is about four to seven years; for some students it takes longer (up to 10 years) and for others, they never reach proficiency (Hakuta, 2000). Students who enter upper grades, middle school, and high school having started learning English in kindergarten or first grade—but not reaching proficiency—are considered long-term English learners. Long-term English learners comprise those students who are designated as still learning English after five or more years of enrollment in U.S. schools (Callahan, 2005). It is important to understand the different needs of the students in your classroom learning English. If a student has been learning English for more than five years and is not making progress in English proficiency, he needs continued support and scaffolded language and content lessons. Often, it is hard to discern that these students are not making progress in language acquisition because they may speak English well. Speaking English well, and having good interpersonal communication skills, doesn't mean that the student has academic language skills.

Offer Collaborative Activities

To support language acquisition, it is important to provide learning activities that encourage ELLs to work together with native English speakers to give them opportunities to talk, think, read, and write in English. It is also important to take into consideration the prior knowledge of the ELLs and preview, or frontload, information, ideas, and activities with them in small groups before they join the whole group for a lesson in English. This frontloading in small-group discussion gives ELLs the opportunity to develop knowledge about a subject, discuss the topic in a "safe" setting where they can question, and even use their primary language to discuss the lesson so that they have a foundation before receiving the main lesson in English.

Check the Clarity of Your Lessons

Making your lessons understandable to ELLs is the most important thing you can do to help these students be successful in your classroom. Making "input" comprehensible will help your students participate in lessons, help them understand what is going on in the classroom, and encourage them to speak in English, as appropriate (Krashen, 2003). You need to provide comprehensible lessons that scaffold the language learner. Scaffolds can include pictures, objects, media from the Internet, and other realia, as they powerfully contextualize what you are saying, making it comprehensible and concrete.

Speak Clearly and at an Appropriate Pace

It also helps to slow down your speech rate and to repeat what you are saying to give students learning English "clues" about what you are teaching and time to process. This is not only true for students new to English; it is also true for students who seem to be proficient because they can speak well in English but who may not have yet developed academic language.

Attune Your Teaching and Learning Expectations to the Stages of Language Acquisition

Language-appropriate, culturally relevant instruction and instruction with high expectations for learning can support students as they learn English. The following chart explains the five stages of language acquisition and highlights learner characteristics at each stage. You can best support language acquisition by matching your expectations for student production and interaction in English with the stages that your students are in as evidenced by their oral and written work.

Unfortunately, many students remain in the Intermediate and Early Advanced stages for their entire school careers, never reaching full English proficiency. These students are considered long-term English learners and struggle in content-area classes. This is why it is so important to know and understand the five stages of language acquisition so you can differentiate instruction based on students' needs.

The Five Stages of Language Acquisition: What to Expect of Students

Stage	Student Characteristics	Time Frame	Appropriate Instructional Activities
Preproduction	Student is silent and doesn't speak. They may parrot English speakers. They will listen a lot and may be able to copy words from the board. They can understand gestures and movements (i.e., they can nod yes or no).	0–6 months	Ask students to point, touch, or use gestures. Provide listening experiences without the expectation to talk in English. Build vocabulary through physical response (i.e., having students act out words and phrases). Pair student with a primary language student.
Early Production	Student can speak in one- or two-word chunks and phrases. They may use memorized phrases but will not always be correct (e.g., *May I get a drink of water?*). Can produce short sentences with present tense verbs.	6 months to 1 year	Ask yes or no, either/or, and who and what questions. Provide comprehensible listening activities. Use pictures, language frames, sentence starters, and simplified content through picture books and modified texts. Build vocabulary through pictures and realia.
Speech Emergence	Student can speak in simple sentences. Can understand a lot of what is said. Makes grammatical errors in speaking and writing. May pronounce words incorrectly.	1–3 years	Involve students in short conversations in small groups with other students. Provide short or modified texts. Use graphic organizers and word banks. Provide writing activities through response journals or short writing assignments. Provide contextualized support for content work. Develop vocabulary through matching activities and lessons that develop conceptual understanding.

Stage	Student Characteristics	Time Frame	Appropriate Instructional Activities
Intermediate Fluency	Student comprehends basic communication well but may not understand academic and content lessons. Makes few grammatical errors when speaking but may make errors when writing, especially with academic writing. Students will use more complex language and can participate in class with teacher support.	3–5 years	Provide longer writing assignments. Engage students in group work, project-based lessons, and relevant instruction. Provide instruction in grammar and language conventions as related to student needs (e.g., assess student needs by examining writing journals and reading records). Provide English language development lessons in vocabulary, content, and grammar tailored to student needs. Many students remain in the Intermediate and Early Advanced stages for their entire school careers, never reaching full English proficiency. These students are considered long-term English learners and struggle in content-area classes.
Advanced Fluency	Students are near-native in their ability to speak and use English in content areas or with academic language. They will need continued support with academic language to continue acquiring language and conventions in academic domains.	4–7 years, or longer	Provide rich and engaging instruction based on standards and grade-level content expectations. Continue to contextualize language and content. Provide English language development tailored to student needs. Many students remain in the Intermediate and Early Advanced stages for their entire school careers, never reaching full English proficiency. These students are considered long-term English learners and struggle in content-area classes.

References

Akhavan, N. (2006). *Help! My kids don't all speak English: How to set up a language workshop in your linguistically diverse classroom.* Portsmouth, NH: Heinemann.

Callahan, R. M. (2005). Tracking and high school English learners: Limiting opportunity to learn. *American Educational Research Journal, 42*(2), 305–328. Retrieved from http://search.proquest.com/docview/200368076?accountid=10349.

Hakuta, K. (2000). *How long does it take English learners to attain proficiency?* Berkeley: University of California Linguistic Minority Research Institute. Retrieved from http://escholarship.org/uc/item/13w7m06g.

Haynes, J., & Zacarian, D. (2010). *Teaching English language learners: Across the content areas.* Alexandria, VA: ASCD.

Hoover, J., & Patton, J. (2005). Differentiating curriculum and instruction for English-language learners with special needs. *Intervention in School and Clinic, 40*(4), 231–235.

Krashen, S. D. (1982/2009). *Principles and practice in second language acquisition.* Retrieved from http://www.sdkrashen.com/content/books/principles_and_practice.pdf.

Krashen, S. (2003). *Explorations in language acquisition and use: The Taipei lectures.* Portsmouth, NH: Heinemann.

Krashen, S. D., & Terrell, D. (1983). *The natural approach: Language acquisition in the classroom.* Hayward, CA: Alemany Press.

Peregoy, S. F., & Boyle O. F. (1997). *Reading, writing and learning in ESL: A resource book for K–12 teachers* (2nd ed.). New York, NY: Longman.

Quick Reference: Common Core State Standards, K–12 English Language Arts

Reading

Key Ideas and Details

1. Read closely to determine what the text says explicitly and to make logical inferences from it; cite specific textual evidence when writing or speaking to support conclusions drawn from the text.

2. Determine central ideas or themes of a text and analyze their development; summarize the key supporting details and ideas.

3. Analyze how and why individuals, events, and ideas develop and interact over the course of a text.

Craft and Structure

4. Interpret words and phrases as they are used in a text, including determining technical, connotative, and figurative meanings, and analyze how specific word choices shape meaning or tone.

5. Analyze the structure of texts, including how specific sentences, paragraphs, and larger portions of the text (e.g., a section, chapter, scene, or stanza) relate to each other and the whole.

6. Assess how point of view or purpose shapes the content and style of a text.

Integration of Knowledge and Ideas

7. Integrate and evaluate content presented in diverse media and formats, including visually and quantitatively, as well as in words.

8. Delineate and evaluate the argument and specific claims in a text, including the validity of the reasoning as well as the relevance and sufficiency of the evidence.

9. Analyze how two or more texts address similar themes or topics in order to build knowledge or to compare the approaches the authors take.

Range of Reading and Level of Text Complexity

10. Read and comprehend complex literary and informational texts independently and proficiently.

Writing

Text Types and Purposes*

1. Write arguments to support claims in an analysis of substantive topics or texts, using valid reasoning and relevant and sufficient evidence.

2. Write informative/explanatory texts to examine and convey complex ideas and information clearly and accurately through the effective selection, organization, and analysis of content.

3. Write narratives to develop real or imagined experiences or events using effective technique, well-chosen details, and well-structured event sequences.

Production and Distribution of Writing

4. Produce clear and coherent writing in which the development, organization, and style are appropriate to task, purpose, and audience.

5. Develop and strengthen writing as needed by planning, revising, editing, rewriting, or trying a new approach.

6. Use technology, including the Internet, to produce and publish writing and to interact and collaborate with others.

Research to Build and Present Knowledge

7. Conduct short as well as more sustained research projects based on focused questions, demonstrating understanding of the subject under investigation.

8. Gather relevant information from multiple print and digital sources, assess the credibility and accuracy of each source, and integrate the information while avoiding plagiarism.

9. Draw evidence from literary or informational texts to support analysis, reflection, and research.

Range of Writing

10. Write routinely over extended time frames (time for research, reflection, and revision) and shorter time frames (a single sitting or a day or two) for a range of tasks, purposes, and audiences.

Speaking and Listening

Comprehension and Collaboration

1. Prepare for and participate effectively in a range of conversations and collaborations with diverse partners, building on others' ideas and expressing their own clearly and persuasively.

2. Integrate and evaluate information presented in diverse media and formats, including visually, quantitatively, and orally.

3. Evaluate a speaker's point of view, reasoning, and use of evidence and rhetoric.

Presentation of Knowledge and Ideas

4. Present information, findings, and supporting evidence such that listeners can follow the line of reasoning and the organization, development, and style are appropriate to task, purpose, and audience.

5. Make strategic use of digital media and visual displays of data to express information and enhance understanding of presentations.

6. Adapt speech to a variety of contexts and communicative tasks, demonstrating command of formal English when indicated or appropriate.

Language

Conventions of Standard English

1. Demonstrate command of the conventions of standard English grammar and usage when writing or speaking.

2. Demonstrate command of the conventions of standard English capitalization, punctuation, and spelling when writing.

Knowledge of Language

3. Apply knowledge of language to understand how language functions in different contexts, to make effective choices for meaning or style, and to comprehend more fully when reading or listening.

Vocabulary Acquisition and Use

4. Determine or clarify the meaning of unknown and multiple-meaning words and phrases by using context clues, analyzing meaningful word parts, and consulting general and specialized reference materials, as appropriate.

5. Demonstrate understanding of figurative language, word relationships, and nuances in word meanings.

6. Acquire and use accurately a range of general academic and domain-specific words and phrases sufficient for reading, writing, speaking, and listening at the college and career readiness level; demonstrate independence in gathering vocabulary knowledge when encountering an unknown term important to comprehension or expression.

Source: Designed by Jim Burke. Visit www.englishcompanion.com for more information.

Note: For the complete Common Core State Standards document, please visit corestandards.org.

* These broad types of writing include many subgenres. See Appendix A in the Common Core State Standards for definitions of key writing types.

Indexes Cross-Referencing Your State Standards

 Available for download at **resources.corwin.com/literacycompanion3-5**

Alaska, Grade 3

Alaska Strand/Standard	Focus of Alaska Standard	For More Information
Reading Literature		
RL.1	Ask and answer questions to demonstrate understanding of a text, referring explicitly to the text as the basis for the answers	R1 pp. 6–11
RL.2	Determine the author's central message, lesson, or moral, and explain how it is conveyed through key details; summarize stories	R2 pp. 12–17
RL.3	Describe characters in a story and explain how their actions contribute to the sequence of events	R3 pp. 18–23
RL.4	Determine the meaning of words and phrases as they are used in a text, distinguishing literal from nonliteral language	R4 pp. 24–29
RL.5	Refer to parts of stories, dramas, and poems when writing or speaking about a text, using terms such as chapter, scene, and stanza; describe how each successive part builds on earlier sections	R5 pp. 30–35
RL.6	Distinguish their own point of view from that of the narrator or those of the characters	R6 pp. 36–41
RL.7	Explain how specific elements of a text's illustrations contribute to what is conveyed by the words in a story	R7 pp. 42–47
RL.8	NA	
RL.9	Compare and contrast the themes, settings, and plots of stories written by the same author about the same or similar characters	R9 pp. 54–59
RL.10	Read literature of appropriate complexity independently with proficiency	R10 pp. 60–65
Reading Informational Text		
RI.1	Ask and answer questions to demonstrate understanding of a text, referring explicitly to the text as the basis for the answers	R1 pp. 6–11
RI.2	Determine the main idea of a text; recount the key details and explain how they support the main idea	R2 pp. 12–17
RI.3	Describe the relationship between a series of historical events, scientific ideas or concepts, or steps in technical procedures in a text	R3 pp. 18–23
RI.4	Determine the meaning of general academic and domain-specific words and phrases in a text	R4 pp. 24–29
RI.5	Use text features and search tools to locate information on a topic efficiently	R5 pp. 30–35
RI.6	Determine author's purpose; distinguish own point of view from that of the author of a text	R6 pp. 36–41
RI.7	Use information from illustrations and the words in a text to demonstrate understanding of the text	R7 pp. 42–47
RI.8	Describe the logical connection between particular sentences and paragraphs in a text	R8 pp. 48–53
RI.9	Compare and contrast the most important points and key details presented by two texts on the same topic	R9 pp. 54–59
RI.10	Read and comprehend appropriately complex informational texts independently and proficiently	R10 pp. 60–65

(Continued)

Alaska Strand/Standard	Focus of Alaska Standard	For More Information
Reading Foundational Skills		
RF.3	Phonics: Know and apply grade-level phonics and word analysis skills in decoding words	RF3 pp. 214–219
RF.4	Fluency: Read grade-level texts with sufficient accuracy and fluency to support comprehension	RF4 pp. 220–225
Writing		
W.1	Write opinion pieces on topics or texts, supporting a point of view with fact- or text-based reasons	W1 pp. 70–75
W.2	Write informative/explanatory texts to examine a topic and convey ideas and information clearly	W2 pp. 76–81
W.3	Write narrative writing to develop real or imagined experiences or events using effective technique and clear event sequences	W3 pp. 82–87
W.4	Produce writing in which the development and organization are appropriate to the task and purpose	W4 pp. 88–93
W.5	Develop and strengthen writing as needed by planning, revising, and editing	W5 pp. 94–99
W.6	Use technology to produce and publish writing	W6 pp. 100–105
W.7	Conduct short research projects that build knowledge about a topic	W7 pp. 106–111
W.8	Recall information from experiences or gather information from print and digital sources	W8 pp. 112–117
W.9	NA	
W.10	Write routinely over shorter and extended time frames	W10 pp. 124–129
Speaking and Listening		
SL.1	Engage effectively in a range of collaborative discussions with diverse partners, building on others' ideas and expressing their own clearly	SL1 pp. 134–139
SL.2	Determine the main ideas and supporting details of a text read aloud or information presented in diverse media and formats	SL2 pp. 140–145
SL.3	Ask and answer questions about information from a speaker, offering appropriate elaboration and detail	SL3 pp. 146–151
SL.4	Report on a topic or text, tell a story, or recount an experience with appropriate facts and relevant details	SL4 pp. 152–157
SL.5	Create audio recordings of stories or poems, demonstrating fluent reading; add visual displays when appropriate	SL5 pp. 158–163
SL.6	Speak in complete sentences when appropriate to task and situation in order to provide requested detail or clarification	SL6 pp. 164–169
Language		
L.1	Demonstrate command of the conventions of standard English grammar and usage when writing or speaking	L1 pp. 174–179
L.2	Demonstrate command of the conventions of standard English capitalization, punctuation, and spelling when writing	L2 pp. 180–185
L.3	Use knowledge of language and its conventions when writing, speaking, reading, or listening	L3 pp. 186–191
L.4	Determine or clarify the meaning of unknown and multiple-meaning words and phrases, choosing flexibly from an array of strategies	L4 pp. 192–197
L.5	Demonstrate understanding of word relationships and nuances in word meanings	L5 pp. 198–203
L.6	Acquire and use accurately conversational, general academic, and domain-specific words and phrases	L6 pp. 204–209

Alaska, Grade 4

Alaska Strand/Standard	Focus of Alaska Standard	For More Information
Reading Literature		
RL.1	Refer to details and examples in a text when explaining what the text says explicitly and when drawing inferences	R1 pp. 6–11
RL.2	Determine a theme or author's message of a story, drama, or poem using details from the text as support; summarize the text	R2 pp. 12–17
RL.3	Describe in depth a character, setting, or event in a story or drama, drawing on specific details in the text	R3 pp. 18–23
RL.4	Determine the meaning of words and phrases as they are used in a text	R4 pp. 24–29
RL.5	Explain the major differences between poems, drama, and prose; refer to structural elements when writing or speaking about a text	R5 pp. 30–35
RL.6	Compare and contrast the point of view from which different stories are narrated, including how the use of first or third person can change the way a reader might see characters or events described	R6 pp. 36–41
RL.7	Make connections between the text of a story or drama and a visual or oral representation of the text	R7 pp. 42–47
RL.8	NA	
RL.9	Compare and contrast the treatment of similar themes and plots and patterns of events in literature	R9 pp. 54–59
RL.10	Read literature of appropriate complexity independently with proficiency	R10 pp. 60–65
Reading Informational Text		
RI.1	Locate explicit information in the text to explain what the text says explicitly and when drawing inferences from the text	R1 pp. 6–11
RI.2	Determine the main idea of a text and explain how it is supported by key details; paraphrase or summarize key ideas, events, or procedures	R2 pp. 12–17
RI.3	Explain relationships among events, procedures, ideas, or concepts in a historical, scientific, or technical text	R3 pp. 18–23
RI.4	Determine the meaning of general academic and domain-specific words and phrases in a text	R4 pp. 24–29
RI.5	Describe the overall structure of events, ideas, concepts, or information in a text	R5 pp. 30–35
RI.6	Determine author's purpose; compare and contrast a firsthand and secondhand account of the same event or topic	R6 pp. 36–41
RI.7	Interpret information presented visually, orally, or quantitatively, and explain how it contributes to an understanding of the text	R7 pp. 42–47
RI.8	Explain how an author uses reasons and evidence to support particular points in a text	R8 pp. 48–53
RI.9	Integrate information from two texts on the same topic in order to write or speak about the subject	R9 pp. 54–59
RI.10	Read and comprehend appropriately complex informational texts independently and proficiently	R10 pp. 60–65
Reading Foundational Skills		
RF.3	Phonics: Know and apply grade-level phonics and word analysis skills in decoding words	RF3 pp. 214–219
RF.4	Fluency: Read grade-level texts with sufficient accuracy and fluency to support comprehension	RF4 pp. 220–225
Writing		
W.1	Write opinion pieces on topics or texts, supporting a point of view with fact- or text-based reasons and information	W1 pp. 70–75
W.2	Write informative/explanatory texts to examine a topic and convey ideas and information clearly	W2 pp. 76–81
W.3	Use narrative writing to develop real or imagined experiences or events using effective techniques and clear event sequences	W3 pp. 82–87
W.4	Produce writing in which the development and organization are appropriate to the task, purpose, and audience	W4 pp. 88–93
W.5	Develop and strengthen writing as needed by planning, revising, and editing	W5 pp. 94–99

(Continued)

Alaska Strand/Standard	Focus of Alaska Standard	For More Information
Writing		
W.6	Use technology to produce and publish writing; demonstrate keyboarding skills	W6 pp. 100–105
W.7	Conduct short research projects that build knowledge through investigation of different aspects of a topic	W7 pp. 106–111
W.8	Recall information from experiences or gather information from print and digital sources	W8 pp. 112–117
W.9	Draw evidence from literary or informational texts to support analysis, reflection, and research	W9 pp. 118–123
W.10	Write routinely over shorter and extended time frames	W10 pp. 124–129
Speaking and Listening		
SL.1	Engage effectively in a range of collaborative discussions with diverse partners, building on others' ideas and expressing their own clearly	SL1 pp. 134–139
SL.2	Paraphrase portions of a text read aloud or information presented in diverse media and formats	SL2 pp. 140–145
SL.3	Identify the reasons and evidence a speaker provides to support particular points	SL3 pp. 146–151
SL.4	Report on a topic or text, tell a story, or recount an experience using appropriate facts and details to support main ideas or themes	SL4 pp. 152–157
SL.5	Add audio recordings and visual displays to presentations when appropriate to enhance the development of main ideas or themes	SL5 pp. 158–163
SL.6	Differentiate between contexts that call for formal English and situations where informal discourse is appropriate; use formal English when appropriate to task and situation	SL6 pp. 164–169
Language		
L.1	Demonstrate command of the conventions of standard English grammar and usage when writing or speaking	L1 pp. 174–179
L.2	Demonstrate command of the conventions of standard English capitalization, punctuation, and spelling when writing	L2 pp. 180–185
L.3	Use knowledge of language and its conventions when writing, speaking, reading, or listening	L3 pp. 186–191
L.4	Determine or clarify the meaning of unknown and multiple-meaning words and phrases, choosing flexibly from an array of strategies	L4 pp. 192–197
L.5	Demonstrate understanding of figurative language, word relationships, and nuances in word meanings	L5 pp. 198–203
L.6	Acquire and use accurately general academic and domain-specific words and phrases	L6 pp. 204–209

Alaska, Grade 5

Alaska Strand/Standard	Focus of Alaska Standard	For More Information
Reading Literature		
RL.1	Locate explicit information and quote accurately from a text when explaining what the text says explicitly and when drawing inferences from the text	R1 pp. 6–11
RL.2	Determine a theme or author's message or purpose of a story, drama, or poem using details in the text for support; summarize the text	R2 pp. 12–17
RL.3	Compare and contrast two or more characters, settings, or events in a story or drama, drawing on specific details in the text	R3 pp. 18–23
RL.4	Determine the meaning of words and phrases as they are used in a text, including figurative language	R4 pp. 24–29
RL.5	Explain how a series of chapters, scenes, or stanzas fits together to provide the overall structure of a story, drama, or poem	R5 pp. 30–35
RL.6	Describe how a narrator's or speaker's point of view influences how events are described	R6 pp. 36–41
RL.7	Analyze how visual and multimedia elements contribute to the meaning, tone, or beauty of a text	R7 pp. 42–47
RL.8	NA	

Alaska Strand/Standard	Focus of Alaska Standard	For More Information
Reading Literature		
RL.9	Compare and contrast stories in the same genre on their approaches to similar themes and plot development	R9 pp. 54–59
RL.10	Read literature of appropriate complexity independently with proficiency	R10 pp. 60–65
Reading Informational Text		
RI.1	Locate explicit information to explain what the text says explicitly and to support inferences drawn from the text	R1 pp. 6–11
RI.2	Determine the main ideas of a text and explain how they are supported by key details; summarize the text	R2 pp. 12–17
RI.3	Explain the relationships or interactions between two or more individuals, events, ideas, or concepts in a text, based on specific information in the text	R3 pp. 18–23
RI.4	Determine the meaning of general academic and domain-specific words and phrases in a text	R4 pp. 24–29
RI.5	Compare and contrast the overall structure of events, ideas, concepts, or information in two or more texts	R5 pp. 30–35
RI.6	Determine author's purpose; analyze multiple accounts of the same event or topic, noting important similarities and differences in the point of view they represent	R6 pp. 36–41
RI.7	Draw on information from multiple sources, demonstrating the ability to locate an answer to a question quickly or solve a problem efficiently	R7 pp. 42–47
RI.8	Explain how an author uses reasons and evidence to support particular points in a text	R8 pp. 48–53
RI.9	Integrate information from several texts on the same topic in order to write or speak about the subject	R9 pp. 54–59
RI.10	Read and comprehend appropriately complex informational texts independently and proficiently	R10 pp. 60–65
Reading Foundational Skills		
RF.3	Phonics: Know and apply grade-level phonics and word analysis skills in decoding words	RF3 pp. 214–219
RF.4	Fluency: Read grade-level texts with sufficient accuracy and fluency to support comprehension	RF4 pp. 220–225
Writing		
W.1	Write opinion pieces on topics or texts, supporting a point of view with fact- or text-based reasons and information	W1 pp. 70–75
W.2	Write informative/explanatory texts to examine a topic and convey ideas and information clearly	W2 pp. 76–81
W.3	Use narrative writing to develop real or imagined experiences or events using effective techniques and clear event sequences	W3 pp. 82–87
W.4	Produce writing in which the development and organization are appropriate to the task, purpose, and audience	W4 pp. 88–93
W.5	Develop and strengthen writing as needed by planning, revising, editing, rewriting, or trying a new approach	W5 pp. 94–99
W.6	Use technology to produce and publish writing; demonstrate keyboarding skills	W6 pp. 100–105
W.7	Conduct short research projects that use several sources to build knowledge through investigation of different aspects of a topic	W7 pp. 106–111
W.8	Recall information from experiences or gather information from print and digital sources	W8 pp. 112–117
W.9	Draw evidence from literary or informational texts to support analysis, reflection, and research	W9 pp. 118–123
W.10	Write routinely over shorter and extended time frames	W10 pp. 124–129
Speaking and Listening		
SL.1	Engage effectively in a range of collaborative discussions with diverse partners, building on others' ideas and expressing their own clearly	SL1 pp. 134–139
SL.2	Summarize a written text read aloud or information presented in diverse media and formats	SL2 pp. 140–145
SL.3	Summarize points a speaker makes and explain how each claim is supported by reasons and evidence	SL3 pp. 146–151
SL.4	Report on a topic or text or present an opinion, using appropriate facts and details to support main ideas and themes	SL4 pp. 152–157

(Continued)

Alaska Strand/Standard	Focus of Alaska Standard	For More Information
Speaking and Listening		
SL.5	Include multimedia components and visual displays in presentations when appropriate to enhance the development of main ideas or themes	SL5 pp. 158–163
SL.6	Adapt speech to a variety of contexts, using formal English when appropriate to task and situation	SL6 pp. 164–169
Language		
L.1	Demonstrate command of the conventions of standard English grammar and usage when writing or speaking	L1 pp. 174–179
L.2	Demonstrate command of the conventions of standard English capitalization, punctuation, and spelling when writing	L2 pp. 180–185
L.3	Use knowledge of language and its conventions when writing, speaking, reading, or listening	L3 pp. 186–191
L.4	Determine or clarify the meaning of unknown and multiple-meaning words and phrases, choosing flexibly from an array of strategies	L4 pp. 192–197
L.5	Demonstrate understanding of figurative language, word relationships, and nuances in word meanings	L5 pp. 198–203
L.6	Acquire and use accurately general academic and domain-specific words and phrases	L6 pp. 204–209

Arizona, Grade 3

Arizona Strand/Standard	Focus of Arizona Standard	For More Information
Reading Literature		
RL.1	Ask and answer questions to demonstrate understanding of a text, referring explicitly to the text as the basis for the answers	R1 pp. 6–11
RL.2	Recount stories from diverse cultures, determine their central message, lesson, or moral, and explain how it is conveyed	R2 pp. 12–17
RL.3	Describe characters in a story and explain how their actions contribute to the sequence of events	R3 pp. 18–23
RL.4	Determine the meaning of words and phrases as they are used in a text, distinguishing literal from nonliteral language	R4 pp. 24–29
RL.5	Refer to parts of stories, dramas, and poems when writing or speaking about a text, using terms such as chapter, scene, and stanza; describe how each successive part builds on earlier sections	R5 pp. 30–35
RL.6	Distinguish their own point of view from that of the narrator or those of the characters	R6 pp. 36–41
RL.7	Explain how specific elements of a text's illustrations contribute to what is conveyed by the words in a story	R7 pp. 42–47
RL.8	NA	
RL.9	Compare and contrast the themes, settings, and plots of stories written by the same author about the same or similar characters	R9 pp. 54–59
RL.10	Read literature of appropriate complexity independently with proficiency	R10 pp. 60–65
Reading Informational Text		
RI.1	Ask and answer questions to demonstrate understanding of a text, referring explicitly to the text as the basis for understanding	R1 pp. 6–11
RI.2	Determine the main idea of a text; recount the key details and explain how they support the main idea	R2 pp. 12–17
RI.3	Describe the relationship between a series of historical events, scientific ideas or concepts, or steps in technical procedures in a text	R3 pp. 18–23
RI.4	Determine the meaning of general academic and domain-specific words and phrases in a text	R4 pp. 24–29
RI.5	Use text features and search tools to locate information on a topic efficiently	R5 pp. 30–35
RI.6	Distinguish own point of view from that of the author of a text	R6 pp. 36–41

Arizona Strand/Standard	Focus of Arizona Standard	For More Information
Reading Informational Text		
RI.7	Use information from illustrations and the words in a text to demonstrate understanding of the text	R7 pp. 42–47
RI.8	Describe the logical connection between particular sentences and paragraphs in a text	R8 pp. 48–53
RI.9	Compare and contrast the most important points and key details presented by two texts on the same topic	R9 pp. 54–59
RI.10	Read and comprehend appropriately complex informational texts independently and proficiently	R10 pp. 60–65
Reading Foundational Skills		
RF.3	Phonics: Know and apply grade-level phonics and word analysis skills in decoding words	RF3 pp. 214–219
RF.4	Fluency: Read grade-level texts with sufficient accuracy and fluency to support comprehension	RF4 pp. 220–225
Writing		
W.1	Write opinion pieces on topics or texts, supporting a point of view with reasons	W1 pp. 70–75
W.2	Write informative/explanatory texts to examine a topic and convey ideas and information clearly	W2 pp. 76–81
W.3	Write narratives to develop real or imagined experiences or events using effective technique, descriptive details, and clear event sequences	W3 pp. 82–87
W.4	Produce writing in which the development and organization are appropriate to the task and purpose	W4 pp. 88–93
W.5	Develop and strengthen writing as needed by planning, revising, and editing	W5 pp. 94–99
W.6	Use technology to produce and publish writing	W6 pp. 100–105
W.7	Conduct short research projects that build knowledge about a topic	W7 pp. 106–111
W.8	Recall information from experiences or gather information from print and digital sources	W8 pp. 112–117
W.9	NA	
W.10	Write routinely over shorter and extended time frames	W10 pp. 124–129
Speaking and Listening		
SL.1	Engage effectively in a range of collaborative discussions with diverse partners, building on others' ideas and expressing their own clearly	SL1 pp. 134–139
SL.2	Determine the main ideas and supporting details of a text read aloud or information presented in diverse media and formats	SL2 pp. 140–145
SL.3	Ask and answer questions about information from a speaker, offering appropriate elaboration and detail	SL3 pp. 146–151
SL.4	Report on a topic or text, tell a story, or recount an experience with appropriate facts and relevant details	SL4 pp. 152–157
SL.5	Create audio recordings of stories or poems, demonstrating fluent reading; add visual displays when appropriate	SL5 pp. 158–163
SL.6	Speak in complete sentences when appropriate to task and situation in order to provide requested detail or clarification	SL6 pp. 164–169
Language		
L.1	Demonstrate command of the conventions of standard English grammar and usage when writing or speaking	L1 pp. 174–179
L.2	Demonstrate command of the conventions of standard English capitalization, punctuation, and spelling when writing	L2 pp. 180–185
L.3	Use knowledge of language and its conventions when writing, speaking, reading, or listening	L3 pp. 186–191
L.4	Determine or clarify the meaning of unknown and multiple-meaning words and phrases, choosing flexibly from an array of strategies	L4 pp. 192–197
L.5	Demonstrate understanding of word relationships and nuances in word meanings	L5 pp. 198–203
L.6	Acquire and use accurately conversational, general academic, and domain-specific words and phrases	L6 pp. 204–209

Arizona, Grade 4

Arizona Strand/Standard	Focus of Arizona Standard	For More Information
Reading Literature		
RL.1	Refer to details and examples in a text when explaining what the text says explicitly and when drawing inferences	R1 pp. 6–11
RL.2	Determine a theme of a story, drama, or poem from details in the text; summarize the text	R2 pp. 12–17
RL.3	Describe in depth a character, setting, or event in a story or drama, drawing on specific details in the text	R3 pp. 18–23
RL.4	Determine the meaning of words and phrases as they are used in a text	R4 pp. 24–29
RL.5	Explain the major differences between poems, drama, and prose; refer to structural elements when writing or speaking about a text	R5 pp. 30–35
RL.6	Compare and contrast the point of view from which different stories are narrated, including the difference between first- and third-person narratives	R6 pp. 36–41
RL.7	Make connections between the text of a story or drama and a visual or oral representation of the text	R7 pp. 42–47
RL.8	NA	
RL.9	Compare and contrast the treatment of similar themes and topics and patterns of events in stories and traditional literature from different cultures	R9 pp. 54–59
RL.10	Read literature of appropriate complexity independently with proficiency	R10 pp. 60–65
Reading Informational Text		
RI.1	Refer to details and examples in a text when explaining what the text says explicitly and when drawing inferences from the text	R1 pp. 6–11
RI.2	Determine the main idea of a text and explain how it is supported by key details; summarize the text	R2 pp. 12–17
RI.3	Explain events, procedures, ideas, or concepts in a historical, scientific, or technical text	R3 pp. 18–23
RI.4	Determine the meaning of general academic and domain-specific words and phrases in a text	R4 pp. 24–29
RI.5	Describe the overall structure of events, ideas, concepts, or information in a text	R5 pp. 30–35
RI.6	Compare and contrast a firsthand and secondhand account of the same event or topic	R6 pp. 36–41
RI.7	Interpret information presented visually, orally, or quantitatively, and explain how it contributes to an understanding of the text	R7 pp. 42–47
RI.8	Explain how an author uses reasons and evidence to support particular points in a text	R8 pp. 48–53
RI.9	Integrate information from two texts on the same topic in order to write or speak about the subject	R9 pp. 54–59
RI.10	Read and comprehend appropriately complex informational texts independently and proficiently	R10 pp. 60–65
Reading Foundational Skills		
RF.3	Phonics: Know and apply grade-level phonics and word analysis skills in decoding words	RF3 pp. 214–219
RF.4	Fluency: Read grade-level texts with sufficient accuracy and fluency to support comprehension	RF4 pp. 220–225
Writing		
W.1	Write opinion pieces on topics or texts, supporting a point of view with reasons and information	W1 pp. 70–75
W.2	Write informative/explanatory texts to examine a topic and convey ideas and information clearly	W2 pp. 76–81
W.3	Write narratives to develop real or imagined experiences or events using effective technique, descriptive details, and clear event sequences	W3 pp. 82–87
W.4	Produce writing in which the development and organization are appropriate to the task, purpose, and audience	W4 pp. 88–93
W.5	Develop and strengthen writing as needed by planning, revising, and editing	W5 pp. 94–99
W.6	Use technology to produce and publish writing; demonstrate keyboarding skills	W6 pp. 100–105
W.7	Conduct short research projects that build knowledge through investigation of different aspects of a topic	W7 pp. 106–111
W.8	Recall information from experiences or gather information from print and digital sources	W8 pp. 112–117
W.9	Draw evidence from literary or informational texts to support analysis, reflection, and research	W9 pp. 118–123
W.10	Write routinely over shorter and extended time frames	W10 pp. 124–129

Arizona Strand/Standard	Focus of Arizona Standard	For More Information
Speaking and Listening		
SL.1	Engage effectively in a range of collaborative discussions with diverse partners, building on others' ideas and expressing their own clearly	SL1 pp. 134–139
SL.2	Paraphrase portions of a text read aloud or information presented in diverse media and formats	SL2 pp. 140–145
SL.3	Identify the reasons and evidence a speaker provides to support particular points	SL3 pp. 146–151
SL.4	Report on a topic or text, tell a story, or recount an experience with appropriate facts and details to support main ideas or themes	SL4 pp. 152–157
SL.5	Add audio recordings and visual displays to presentations when appropriate to enhance the development of main ideas or themes	SL5 pp. 158–163
SL.6	Differentiate between contexts that call for formal English and situations where informal discourse is appropriate; use formal English when appropriate to task and situation	SL6 pp. 164–169
Language		
L.1	Demonstrate command of the conventions of standard English grammar and usage when writing or speaking	L1 pp. 174–179
L.2	Demonstrate command of the conventions of standard English capitalization, punctuation, and spelling when writing	L2 pp. 180–185
L.3	Use knowledge of language and its conventions when writing, speaking, reading, or listening	L3 pp. 186–191
L.4	Determine or clarify the meaning of unknown and multiple-meaning words and phrases, choosing flexibly from an array of strategies	L4 pp. 192–197
L.5	Demonstrate understanding of figurative language, word relationships, and nuances in word meanings	L5 pp. 198–203
L.6	Acquire and use accurately general academic and domain-specific words and phrases	L6 pp. 204–209

Arizona, Grade 5

Arizona Strand/Standard	Focus of Arizona Standard	For More Information
Reading Literature		
RL.1	Quote accurately from a text when explaining what the text says explicitly and when drawing inferences from the text	R1 pp. 6–11
RL.2	Determine a theme of a story, drama, or poem from details in the text; summarize the text	R2 pp. 12–17
RL.3	Compare and contrast two or more characters, settings, or events in a story or drama, drawing on specific details in the text	R3 pp. 18–23
RL.4	Determine the meaning of words and phrases as they are used in a text, including figurative language	R4 pp. 24–29
RL.5	Explain how a series of chapters, scenes, or stanzas fits together to provide the overall structure of a story, drama, or poem	R5 pp. 30–35
RL.6	Describe how a narrator's or speaker's point of view influences how events are described	R6 pp. 36–41
RL.7	Analyze how visual and multimedia elements contribute to the meaning, tone, or beauty of a text	R7 pp. 42–47
RL.8	NA	
RL.9	Compare and contrast stories in the same genre on their approaches to similar themes and topics	R9 pp. 54–59
RL.10	Read literature of appropriate complexity independently with proficiency	R10 pp. 60–65
Reading Informational Text		
RI.1	Quote accurately from a text when explaining what the text says explicitly and when drawing inferences from the text	R1 pp. 6–11
RI.2	Determine two or more main ideas of a text and explain how they are supported by key details; summarize the text	R2 pp. 12–17

(Continued)

Arizona Strand/Standard	Focus of Arizona Standard	For More Information
Reading Informational Text		
RI.3	Explain the relationships or interactions between two or more individuals, events, ideas, or concepts in a text, based on specific information in the text	R3 pp. 18–23
RI.4	Determine the meaning of general academic and domain-specific words and phrases in a text	R4 pp. 24–29
RI.5	Compare and contrast the overall structure of events, ideas, concepts, or information in two or more texts	R5 pp. 30–35
RI.6	Analyze multiple accounts of the same event or topic, noting important similarities and differences in the point of view they represent	R6 pp. 36–41
RI.7	Draw on information from multiple sources, demonstrating the ability to locate an answer to a question quickly or solve a problem efficiently	R7 pp. 42–47
RI.8	Explain how an author uses reasons and evidence to support particular points in a text	R8 pp. 48–53
RI.9	Integrate information from several texts on the same topic in order to write or speak about the subject	R9 pp. 54–59
RI.10	Read and comprehend appropriately complex informational texts independently and proficiently	R10 pp. 60–65
Reading Foundational Skills		
RF.3	Phonics: Know and apply grade-level phonics and word analysis skills in decoding words	RF3 pp. 214–219
RF.4	Fluency: Read grade-level texts with sufficient accuracy and fluency to support comprehension	RF4 pp. 220–225
Writing		
W.1	Write opinion pieces on topics or texts, supporting a point of view with reasons and information	W1 pp. 70–75
W.2	Write informative/explanatory texts to examine a topic and convey ideas and information clearly	W2 pp. 76–81
W.3	Write narratives to develop real or imagined experiences or events using effective technique, descriptive details, and clear event sequences	W3 pp. 82–87
W.4	Produce writing in which the development and organization are appropriate to the task, purpose, and audience	W4 pp. 88–93
W.5	Develop and strengthen writing as needed by planning, revising, editing, rewriting, or trying a new approach	W5 pp. 94–99
W.6	Use technology to produce and publish writing; demonstrate keyboarding skills	W6 pp. 100–105
W.7	Conduct short research projects that use several sources to build knowledge through investigation of different aspects of a topic	W7 pp. 106–111
W.8	Recall information from experiences or gather information from print and digital sources	W8 pp. 112–117
W.9	Draw evidence from literary or informational texts to support analysis, reflection, and research	W9 pp. 118–123
W.10	Write routinely over shorter and extended time frames	W10 pp. 124–129
Speaking and Listening		
SL.1	Engage effectively in a range of collaborative discussions with diverse partners, building on others' ideas and expressing their own clearly	SL1 pp. 134–139
SL.2	Summarize a written text read aloud or information presented in diverse media and formats	SL2 pp. 140–145
SL.3	Summarize points a speaker makes and explain how each claim is supported by reasons and evidence	SL3 pp. 146–151
SL.4	Report on a topic or text or present an opinion, using appropriate facts and details to support main ideas and themes	SL4 pp. 152–157
SL.5	Include multimedia components and visual displays in presentations when appropriate to enhance the development of main ideas or themes	SL5 pp. 158–163
SL.6	Adapt speech to a variety of contexts, using formal English when appropriate to task and situation	SL6 pp. 164–169
Language		
L.1	Demonstrate command of the conventions of standard English grammar and usage when writing or speaking	L1 pp. 174–179
L.2	Demonstrate command of the conventions of standard English capitalization, punctuation, and spelling when writing	L2 pp. 180–185
L.3	Use knowledge of language and its conventions when writing, speaking, reading, or listening	L3 pp. 186–191

Arizona Strand/Standard	Focus of Arizona Standard	For More Information
Language		
L.4	Determine or clarify the meaning of unknown and multiple-meaning words and phrases, choosing flexibly from an array of strategies	L4 pp. 192–197
L.5	Demonstrate understanding of figurative language, word relationships, and nuances in word meanings	L5 pp. 198–203
L.6	Acquire and use accurately general academic and domain-specific words and phrases	L6 pp. 204–209

Arkansas, Grade 3

Arkansas Strand/Standard	Focus of Arkansas Standard	For More Information
Reading Literature		
RL.1	Ask and answer questions to demonstrate understanding of a text, referring explicitly to the text as the basis for the answers	R1 pp. 6–11
RL.2	Recount stories, including fables and folktales from diverse cultures, and determine their central message, lesson, or moral, and explain how it is conveyed	R2 pp. 12–17
RL.3	Describe characters in a story and explain how their actions contribute to the sequence of events	R3 pp. 18–23
RL.4	Determine the meaning of words and phrases as they are used in a text, distinguishing literal from nonliteral language	R4 pp. 24–29
RL.5	Refer to parts of stories, dramas, and poems when writing or speaking about a text, using terms such as chapter, scene, and stanza; describe how each successive part builds on earlier sections	R5 pp. 30–35
RL.6	Distinguish their own perspective from that of the narrator or those of the characters, distinguishing the difference between first- and third-person point-of-view narrations	R6 pp. 36–41
RL.7	Explain how specific elements of a text's illustrations contribute to what is conveyed by the words in a story	R7 pp. 42–47
RL.8	NA	
RL.9	Compare and contrast the themes, settings, and plots of stories written by the same author about the same or similar characters	R9 pp. 54–59
RL.10	Read literature of appropriate complexity independently with proficiency	R10 pp. 60–65
Reading Informational Text		
RI.1	Ask and answer questions to demonstrate understanding of a text, referring explicitly to the text as the basis for understanding	R1 pp. 6–11
RI.2	Determine the main idea of a text; recount the key details and explain how they support the main idea	R2 pp. 12–17
RI.3	Describe the connection between a series of historical events, scientific ideas or concepts, or steps in technical procedures in a text	R3 pp. 18–23
RI.4	Determine the meaning of general academic and domain-specific words and phrases in a text	R4 pp. 24–29
RI.5	Use text features and search tools to locate information on a topic efficiently	R5 pp. 30–35
RI.6	Distinguish own perspective from that of the author of a text	R6 pp. 36–41
RI.7	Use information from illustrations and the words in a text to demonstrate understanding of the text	R7 pp. 42–47
RI.8	Describe the logical connection between particular sentences and paragraphs in a text	R8 pp. 48–53
RI.9	Compare and contrast the most important points presented by two texts on the same topic	R9 pp. 54–59
RI.10	Read and comprehend appropriately complex informational texts independently and proficiently	R10 pp. 60–65
Reading Foundational Skills		
RF.3	Phonics: Know and apply grade-level phonics and word analysis skills in decoding words	RF3 pp. 214–219
RF.4	Fluency: Read grade-level texts with sufficient accuracy and fluency to support comprehension	RF4 pp. 220–225

(Continued)

Arkansas Strand/Standard	Focus of Arkansas Standard	For More Information
Writing		
W.1	Write opinion pieces on topics or texts, supporting a point of view with reasons	W1 pp. 70–75
W.2	Write informative/explanatory texts to examine a topic and convey ideas and information clearly	W2 pp. 76–81
W.3	Write narratives to develop real or imagined experiences or events using effective technique, descriptive details, and clear event sequences	W3 pp. 82–87
W.4	Produce writing in which the development and organization are appropriate to the task and purpose	W4 pp. 88–93
W.5	Develop and strengthen writing as needed by planning, revising, and editing	W5 pp. 94–99
W.6	Use technology to produce and publish writing	W6 pp. 100–105
W.7	Conduct short research projects that build knowledge about a topic	W7 pp. 106–111
W.8	Recall information from experiences or gather information from print and digital sources	W8 pp. 112–117
W.9	NA	
W.10	Write routinely over shorter and extended time frames	W10 pp. 124–129
Speaking and Listening		
SL.1	Engage effectively in a range of collaborative discussions with diverse partners, building on others' ideas and expressing their own clearly	SL1 pp. 134–139
SL.2	Determine the main ideas and supporting details of information that is gained by means other than reading	SL2 pp. 140–145
SL.3	Ask and answer questions in order to clarify comprehension, offering appropriate elaboration and detail	SL3 pp. 146–151
SL.4	Report on a topic or text, tell a story, or recount an experience with appropriate facts and relevant details	SL4 pp. 152–157
SL.5	Create audio recordings of stories or poems, reading at a fluent pace; add visual displays when appropriate to emphasize or enhance certain elements	SL5 pp. 158–163
SL.6	Speak in complete sentences when appropriate to task and situation in order to provide requested detail or clarification	SL6 pp. 164–169
Language		
L.1	Demonstrate command of the conventions of standard English grammar and usage when writing or speaking	L1 pp. 174–179
L.2	Demonstrate command of the conventions of standard English capitalization, punctuation, and spelling when writing	L2 pp. 180–185
L.3	Use knowledge of language and its conventions when writing, speaking, reading, or listening	L3 pp. 186–191
L.4	Determine or clarify the meaning of unknown and multiple-meaning words and phrases, choosing flexibly from an array of strategies	L4 pp. 192–197
L.5	Demonstrate understanding of figurative language, word relationships, and nuances in word meanings	L5 pp. 198–203
L.6	Acquire and use accurately conversational, general academic, and domain-specific words and phrases	L6 pp. 204–209

Arkansas, Grade 4

Arkansas Strand/Standard	Focus of Arkansas Standard	For More Information
Reading Literature		
RL.1	Refer to details and examples in a text when explaining what the text says explicitly and when drawing inferences	R1 pp. 6–11
RL.2	Determine a theme of a story, drama, or poem from details in the text; summarize the text	R2 pp. 12–17

Arkansas Strand/Standard	Focus of Arkansas Standard	For More Information
Reading Literature		
RL.3	Describe in depth a character, setting, or event in a story or drama, drawing on specific details in the text	R3 pp. 18–23
RL.4	Determine the meaning of words and phrases as they are used in a text, including figurative language	R4 pp. 24–29
RL.5	Compare and contrast the structural elements of poems, drama, and prose	R5 pp. 30–35
RL.6	Compare and contrast the point of view from which different stories are narrated, including the difference between first- and third-person narratives	R6 pp. 36–41
RL.7	Analyze the similarities and differences between the text of a story or drama and a visual or oral presentation of the same text	R7 pp. 42–47
RL.8	NA	
RL.9	Compare and contrast the treatment of similar themes and topics and patterns of events in stories and traditional literature from different cultures	R9 pp. 54–59
RL.10	Read literature of appropriate complexity independently with proficiency	R10 pp. 60–65
Reading Informational Text		
RI.1	Refer to details and examples in a text when explaining what the text says explicitly and when drawing inferences from the text	R1 pp. 6–11
RI.2	Determine the main idea of a text and explain how it is supported by key details; provide a summary	R2 pp. 12–17
RI.3	Explain events, procedures, ideas, or concepts in a historical, scientific, or technical text	R3 pp. 18–23
RI.4	Determine the meaning of general academic and domain-specific words and phrases in a text	R4 pp. 24–29
RI.5	Describe the overall structure of events, ideas, concepts, or information in a text	R5 pp. 30–35
RI.6	Compare and contrast a firsthand and secondhand account of the same event or topic	R6 pp. 36–41
RI.7	Interpret information presented visually, orally, or quantitatively, and explain how it contributes to an understanding of the text	R7 pp. 42–47
RI.8	Explain how an author uses reasons and evidence to support particular points in a text	R8 pp. 48–53
RI.9	Integrate information from two texts on the same topic in order to write or speak about the subject	R9 pp. 54–59
RI.10	Read and comprehend appropriately complex informational texts independently and proficiently	R10 pp. 60–65
Reading Foundational Skills		
RF.3	Phonics: Know and apply grade-level phonics and word analysis skills in decoding words	RF3 pp. 214–219
RF.4	Fluency: Read grade-level texts with sufficient accuracy and fluency to support comprehension	RF4 pp. 220–225
Writing		
W.1	Write opinion pieces on topics or texts, supporting a point of view with reasons and information	W1 pp. 70–75
W.2	Write informative/explanatory texts to examine a topic and convey ideas and information clearly	W2 pp. 76–81
W.3	Write narratives to develop real or imagined experiences or events using effective technique, descriptive details, and clear event sequences	W3 pp. 82–87
W.4	Produce writing in which the development and organization are appropriate to the task and purpose	W4 pp. 88–93
W.5	Develop and strengthen writing as needed by planning, revising, and editing	W5 pp. 94–99
W.6	Use technology to produce and publish writing; demonstrate keyboarding skills	W6 pp. 100–105
W.7	Conduct short research projects that build knowledge through investigation of different aspects of a topic	W7 pp. 106–111
W.8	Recall information from experiences or gather information from print and digital sources	W8 pp. 112–117
W.9	Draw evidence from literary or informational texts to support analysis, reflection, and research	W9 pp. 118–123
W.10	Write routinely over shorter and extended time frames	W10 pp. 124–129
Speaking and Listening		
SL.1	Engage effectively in a range of collaborative discussions with diverse partners, building on others' ideas and expressing their own clearly	SL1 pp. 134–139
SL.2	Paraphrase portions of information gained by means other than reading	SL2 pp. 140–145

(Continued)

Arkansas Strand/Standard	Focus of Arkansas Standard	For More Information
Speaking and Listening		
SL.3	Identify the reasons and evidence a speaker provides to support particular points	SL3 pp. 146–151
SL.4	Report on a topic or text, tell a story, or recount an experience to support main ideas or themes	SL4 pp. 152–157
SL.5	Add audio recordings and visual displays to presentations when appropriate to enhance the development of main ideas or themes	SL5 pp. 158–163
SL.6	Use standard English when speaking, differentiating between contexts that call for formal English and situations where informal discourse is appropriate	SL6 pp. 164–169
Language		
L.1	Demonstrate command of the conventions of standard English grammar and usage when writing or speaking	L1 pp. 174–179
L.2	Demonstrate command of the conventions of standard English capitalization, punctuation, and spelling when writing	L2 pp. 180–185
L.3	Use knowledge of language and its conventions when writing, speaking, reading, or listening	L3 pp. 186–191
L.4	Determine or clarify the meaning of unknown and multiple-meaning words and phrases, choosing flexibly from an array of strategies	L4 pp. 192–197
L.5	Demonstrate understanding of figurative language, word relationships, and nuances in word meanings	L5 pp. 198–203
L.6	Acquire and use accurately general academic and domain-specific words and phrases	L6 pp. 204–209

Arkansas, Grade 5

Arkansas Strand/Standard	Focus of Arkansas Standard	For More Information
Reading Literature		
RL.1	Quote accurately from a text when explaining what the text says explicitly and when drawing inferences from the text	R1 pp. 6–11
RL.2	Determine a theme of a story, drama, or poem from details in the text; summarize the text	R2 pp. 12–17
RL.3	Compare and contrast two or more characters, settings, or events in a story or drama, drawing on specific details in the text	R3 pp. 18–23
RL.4	Determine the meaning of words and phrases as they are used in a text, including figurative language	R4 pp. 24–29
RL.5	Explain how a series of chapters, scenes, or stanzas fits together to provide the overall structure of a story, drama, or poem	R5 pp. 30–35
RL.6	Describe how a narrator's or speaker's point of view influences how events are described	R6 pp. 36–41
RL.7	Analyze how multimedia elements contribute to the meaning, tone, or beauty of a text	R7 pp. 42–47
RL.8	NA	
RL.9	Compare and contrast stories in the same genre on their approaches to similar themes and topics	R9 pp. 54–59
RL.10	Read literature of appropriate complexity independently with proficiency	R10 pp. 60–65
Reading Informational Text		
RI.1	Quote accurately from a text when explaining what the text says explicitly and when drawing inferences from the text	R1 pp. 6–11
RI.2	Determine the main idea of a text and explain how it is supported by key details; provide a summary	R2 pp. 12–17
RI.3	Explain the relationships or interactions between two or more individuals, events, ideas, or concepts in a text, based on specific information in the text	R3 pp. 18–23
RI.4	Determine the meaning of general academic and domain-specific words and phrases in a text	R4 pp. 24–29
RI.5	Compare and contrast the overall structure of events, ideas, concepts, or information in two or more texts	R5 pp. 30–35

Arkansas Strand/Standard	Focus of Arkansas Standard	For More Information
Reading Informational Text		
RI.6	Analyze multiple accounts of the same event or topic, noting important similarities and differences in the point of view they represent	R6 pp. 36–41
RI.7	Draw on information from multiple sources, demonstrating the ability to locate an answer to a question quickly or solve a problem efficiently	R7 pp. 42–47
RI.8	Explain how an author uses reasons and evidence to support particular points in a text	R8 pp. 48–53
RI.9	Integrate information from several texts on the same topic in order to write or speak about the subject	R9 pp. 54–59
RI.10	Read and comprehend appropriately complex informational texts independently and proficiently	R10 pp. 60–65
Reading Foundational Skills		
RF.3	Phonics: Know and apply grade-level phonics and word analysis skills in decoding words	RF3 pp. 214–219
RF.4	Fluency: Read grade-level texts with sufficient accuracy and fluency to support comprehension	RF4 pp. 220–225
Writing		
W.1	Write opinion pieces on topics or texts, supporting a point of view with reasons and information	W1 pp. 70–75
W.2	Write informative/explanatory texts to examine a topic and convey ideas and information clearly	W2 pp. 76–81
W.3	Write narratives to develop real or imagined experiences or events using effective technique, descriptive details, and clear event sequences	W3 pp. 82–87
W.4	Produce writing in which the development and organization are appropriate to the task, purpose, and audience	W4 pp. 88–93
W.5	Develop and strengthen writing as needed by planning, revising, editing, rewriting, or trying a new approach	W5 pp. 94–99
W.6	Use technology to produce and publish writing; demonstrate keyboarding skills	W6 pp. 100–105
W.7	Conduct short research projects that use several sources to build knowledge through investigation of different aspects of a topic	W7 pp. 106–111
W.8	Recall information from experiences or gather information from print and digital sources	W8 pp. 112–117
W.9	Draw evidence from literary or informational texts to support analysis, reflection, and research	W9 pp. 118–123
W.10	Write routinely over shorter and extended time frames	W10 pp. 124–129
Speaking and Listening		
SL.1	Engage effectively in a range of collaborative discussions with diverse partners, building on others' ideas and expressing their own clearly	SL1 pp. 134–139
SL.2	Summarize information gained by means other than reading	SL2 pp. 140–145
SL.3	Summarize points a speaker makes and explain how each claim is supported by reasons and evidence	SL3 pp. 146–151
SL.4	Report on a topic or text or present an opinion, using appropriate facts and details to support main ideas and themes	SL4 pp. 152–157
SL.5	Include multimedia components and visual displays in presentations when appropriate to enhance the development of main ideas or themes	SL5 pp. 158–163
SL.6	Adapt speech to a variety of contexts, using formal English when appropriate to task and situation	SL6 pp. 164–169
Language		
L.1	Demonstrate command of the conventions of standard English grammar and usage when writing or speaking	L1 pp. 174–179
L.2	Demonstrate command of the conventions of standard English capitalization, punctuation, and spelling when writing	L2 pp. 180–185
L.3	Use knowledge of language and its conventions when writing, speaking, reading, or listening	L3 pp. 186–191
L.4	Determine or clarify the meaning of unknown and multiple-meaning words and phrases, choosing flexibly from an array of strategies	L4 pp. 192–197
L.5	Demonstrate understanding of figurative language, word relationships, and nuances in word meanings	L5 pp. 198–203
L.6	Acquire and use accurately general academic and domain-specific words and phrases	L6 pp. 204–209

Colorado, Grade 3

Colorado Strand/Standard	Focus of Colorado Standard	For More Information
Oral Expression and Listening		
1	Oral communication is used both formally and informally	SL4 pp. 152–157 SL5 pp. 158–163 SL6 pp. 164–169
2	Successful group activities need the cooperation of everyone	SL1 pp. 134–139 SL2 pp. 140–145 SL3 pp. 146–151
Reading for All Purposes		
1	Strategies are used to make meaning of various types of literary genres	R1 pp. 6–11 R2 pp. 12–17 R3 pp. 18–23 R4 pp. 24–29 R5 pp. 30–35 R6 pp. 36–41 R7 pp. 42–47 R9 pp. 54–59 R10 pp. 60–65 RF4 pp. 220–225
2	Comprehension strategies are necessary when reading informational or persuasive text	R1 pp. 6–11 R2 pp. 12–17 R3 pp. 18–23 R4 pp. 24–29 R5 pp. 30–35 R6 pp. 36–41 R7 pp. 42–47 R8 pp. 48–53 R9 pp. 54–59 R10 pp. 60–65 RF4 pp. 220–225
3	Increasing word understanding, word use, and word relationships increases vocabulary	RF3 pp. 214–219 RF4 pp. 220–225 L4 pp. 192–197 L5 pp. 198–203 L6 pp. 204–209
Writing and Composition		
1	A writing process is used to plan, draft, and write a variety of literary genres	W1 pp. 70–75 W3 pp. 82–87
2	A writing process is used to plan, draft, and write a variety of informational texts	W2 pp. 76–81
3	Correct grammar, capitalization, punctuation, and spelling are used when writing	W4 pp. 88–93 W5 pp. 94–99 W6 pp. 100–105 L1 pp. 174–179 L2 pp. 180–185 L3 pp. 186–191
Research and Reasoning		
1	Researching a topic and sharing findings are often done with others	W7 pp. 106–111 W8 pp. 112–117
2	Inferences and points of view exist	NA

Colorado, Grade 4

Colorado Strand/Standard	Focus of Colorado Standard	For More Information
Oral Expression and Listening		
1	A clear communication plan is necessary to effectively deliver and receive information	SL1 pp. 134–139 SL2 pp. 140–145 SL3 pp. 146–151 SL4 pp. 152–157 SL5 pp. 158–163 SL6 pp. 164–169
Reading for All Purposes		
1	Comprehension and fluency matter when reading literary texts in a fluent way	R1 pp. 6–11 R2 pp. 12–17 R3 pp. 18–23 R4 pp. 24–29 R5 pp. 30–35 R6 pp. 36–41 R7 pp. 42–47 R9 pp. 54–59 R10 pp. 60–65 RF4 pp. 220–225
2	Comprehension and fluency matter when reading informational and persuasive texts in a fluent way	R1 pp. 6–11 R2 pp. 12–17 R3 pp. 18–23 R4 pp. 24–29 R5 pp. 30–35 R6 pp. 36–41 R7 pp. 42–47 R8 pp. 48–53 R9 pp. 54–59 R10 pp. 60–65
3	Knowledge of complex orthography, morphology, and word relationships to decode multisyllabic words contributes to better reading skills	RF3 pp. 214–219 RF4 pp. 220–225 L4 pp. 192–197 L5 pp. 198–203 L6 pp. 204–209
Writing and Composition		
1	The recursive writing process is used to create a variety of literary genres for an intended audience	W3 pp. 82–87
2	Informational and persuasive texts use the recursive writing process	W1 pp. 70–75 W2 pp. 76–81
3	Correct sentence formation, grammar, punctuation, capitalization, and spelling are applied to make the meaning clear to the reader	W4 pp. 88–93 W5 pp. 94–99 W6 pp. 100–105 L1 pp. 174–179 L2 pp. 180–185 L3 pp. 186–191
Research and Reasoning		
1	Comprehending new information for research is a process undertaken with discipline both alone and in groups	W7 pp. 106–111 W8 pp. 112–117 W9 pp. 118–123
2	Identifying implications, concepts, and ideas enriches reasoning skills	SL3 pp. 146–151

Colorado, Grade 5

Colorado Strand/Standard	Focus of Colorado Standard	For More Information
Oral Expression and Listening		
1	Effective communication requires speakers to express an opinion, provide information, describe a process, and persuade an audience	SL4 pp. 152–157 SL5 pp. 158–163 SL6 pp. 164–169
2	Listening strategies are techniques that contribute to understanding different situations and serving different purposes	SL1 pp. 134–139 SL2 pp. 140–145 SL3 pp. 146–151
Reading for All Purposes		
1	Literary texts are understood and interpreted using a range of strategies	R1 pp. 6–11 R2 pp. 12–17 R3 pp. 18–23 R4 pp. 24–29 R5 pp. 30–35 R6 pp. 36–41 R7 pp. 42–47 R9 pp. 54–59 R10 pp. 60–65
2	Ideas found in a variety of informational texts need to be compared and understood	R1 pp. 6–11 R2 pp. 12–17 R3 pp. 18–23 R4 pp. 24–29 R5 pp. 30–35 R6 pp. 36–41 R7 pp. 42–47 R8 pp. 48–53 R9 pp. 54–59 R10 pp. 60–65
3	Knowledge of morphology and word relationships matters when reading	RF3 pp. 214–219 RF4 pp. 220–225 L3 pp. 186–191 L4 pp. 192–197
Writing and Composition		
1	The recursive writing process contributes to the creative and unique literary genres for a variety of audiences and purposes	W3 pp. 82–87
2	The recursive writing process creates stronger informational and persuasive texts for a variety of audiences and purposes	W1 pp. 70–75 W2 pp. 76–81
3	Conventions apply consistently when evaluating written texts	W4 pp. 88–93 W5 pp. 94–99 W6 pp. 100–105 L1 pp. 174–179 L2 pp. 180–185
Research and Reasoning		
1	High-quality research requires information that is organized and presented with documentation	W7 pp. 106–111 W8 pp. 112–117
2	Identifying and evaluating concepts and ideas have implications and consequences	W9 pp. 118–123

Florida, Grade 3

Florida Strand/Standard	Focus of Florida Standard	For More Information
Reading Literature		
RL.1.1	Ask and answer questions to demonstrate understanding of a text, referring explicitly to the text as the basis for the answers	R1 pp. 6–11
RL.1.2	Recount stories from diverse cultures, determine their central message, lesson, or moral, and explain how it is conveyed	R2 pp. 12–17
RL.1.3	Describe characters in a story and explain how their actions contribute to the sequence of events	R3 pp. 18–23
RL.2.4	Determine the meaning of words and phrases as they are used in a text, distinguishing literal from nonliteral language	R4 pp. 24–29
RL.2.5	Refer to parts of stories, dramas, and poems when writing or speaking about a text, using terms such as chapter, scene, and stanza; describe how each successive part builds on earlier sections	R5 pp. 30–35
RL.2.6	Distinguish their own point of view from that of the narrator or those of the characters	R6 pp. 36–41
RL.3.7	Explain how specific elements of a text's illustrations contribute to what is conveyed by the words in a story	R7 pp. 42–47
RL.3.9	Compare and contrast the themes, settings, and plots of stories written by the same author about the same or similar characters	R9 pp. 54–59
RL.4.10	Read literature of appropriate complexity independently with proficiency	R10 pp. 60–65
Reading Informational Text		
RI.1.1	Ask and answer questions to demonstrate understanding of a text, referring explicitly to the text as the basis for the answers	R1 pp. 6–11
RI.1.2	Determine the main idea of a text; recount the key details and explain how they support the main idea	R2 pp. 12–17
RI.1.3	Describe the relationship between a series of historical events, scientific ideas or concepts, or steps in technical procedures in a text	R3 pp. 18–23
RI.2.4	Determine the meaning of general academic and domain-specific words and phrases in a text	R4 pp. 24–29
RI.2.5	Use text features and search tools to locate information on a topic efficiently	R5 pp. 30–35
RI.2.6	Distinguish own point of view from that of the author of a text	R6 pp. 36–41
RI.3.7	Use information from illustrations and the words in a text to demonstrate understanding of the text	R7 pp. 42–47
RI.3.8	Describe the logical connection between particular sentences and paragraphs in a text	R8 pp. 48–53
RI.3.9	Compare and contrast the most important points and key details presented by two texts on the same topic	R9 pp. 54–59
RI.4.10	Read and comprehend appropriately complex informational texts independently and proficiently	R10 pp. 60–65
Reading Foundational Skills		
RF.3.3	Phonics: Know and apply grade-level phonics and word analysis skills in decoding words	RF3 pp. 214–219
RF.4.4	Fluency: Read grade-level texts with sufficient accuracy and fluency to support comprehension	RF4 pp. 220–225
Writing		
W.1.1	Write opinion pieces on topics or texts, supporting a point of view with reasons	W1 pp. 70–75
W.1.2	Write informative/explanatory texts to examine a topic and convey ideas and information clearly	W2 pp. 76–81
W.1.3	Write narratives to develop real or imagined experiences or events using effective technique, descriptive details, and clear event sequences	W3 pp. 82–87
W.2.4	Produce writing in which the development and organization are appropriate to the task and purpose	W4 pp. 88–93
W.2.5	Develop and strengthen writing as needed by planning, revising, and editing	W5 pp. 94–99
W.2.6	Use technology to produce and publish writing	W6 pp. 100–105

(Continued)

Florida Strand/Standard	Focus of Florida Standard	For More Information
Writing		
W.3.7	Conduct short research projects that build knowledge about a topic	W7 pp. 106–111
W.3.8	Recall information from experiences or gather information from print and digital sources	W8 pp. 112–117
W.4.10	Write routinely over shorter and extended time frames	W10 pp. 124–129
Speaking and Listening		
SL.1.1	Engage effectively in a range of collaborative discussions with diverse partners, building on others' ideas and expressing their own clearly	SL1 pp. 134–139
SL.1.2	Determine the main ideas and supporting details of a text read aloud or information presented in diverse media and formats	SL2 pp. 140–145
SL.1.3	Ask and answer questions about information from a speaker, offering appropriate elaboration and detail	SL3 pp. 146–151
SL.2.4	Report on a topic or text, tell a story, or recount an experience with appropriate facts and relevant details	SL4 pp. 152–157
SL.5	Demonstrate fluent reading; add visual displays and audio recordings when appropriate	SL5 pp. 158–163
SL.2.6	Speak in complete sentences when appropriate to task and situation in order to provide requested detail or clarification	SL6 pp. 164–169
Language		
L.1.1	Demonstrate command of the conventions of standard English grammar and usage when writing or speaking	L1 pp. 174–179
L.1.2	Demonstrate command of the conventions of standard English capitalization, punctuation, and spelling when writing	L2 pp. 180–185
L.2.3	Use knowledge of language and its conventions when writing, speaking, reading, or listening	L3 pp. 186–191
L.3.4	Determine or clarify the meaning of unknown and multiple-meaning words and phrases, choosing flexibly from an array of strategies	L4 pp. 192–197
L.3.5	Demonstrate understanding of word relationships and nuances in word meanings	L5 pp. 198–203
L.3.6	Acquire and use accurately conversational, general academic, and domain-specific words and phrases	L6 pp. 204–209

Florida, Grade 4

Florida Strand/Standard	Focus of Florida Standard	For More Information
Reading Literature		
RL.1.1	Refer to details and examples in a text when explaining what the text says explicitly and when drawing inferences	R1 pp. 6–11
RL.1.2	Determine a theme of a story, drama, or poem from details in the text; summarize the text	R2 pp. 12–17
RL.1.3	Describe in depth a character, setting, or event in a story or drama, drawing on specific details in the text	R3 pp. 18–23
RL.2.4	Determine the meaning of words and phrases as they are used in a text	R4 pp. 24–29
RL.2.5	Explain the major differences between poems, drama, and prose; refer to structural elements when writing or speaking about a text	R5 pp. 30–35
RL.2.6	Compare and contrast the point of view from which different stories are narrated, including the difference between first- and third-person narratives	R6 pp. 36–41
RL.3.7	Make connections between the text of a story or drama and a visual or oral representation of the text	R7 pp. 42–47

Florida Strand/Standard	Focus of Florida Standard	For More Information
Reading Literature		
RL.3.9	Compare and contrast the treatment of similar themes and topics and patterns of events in stories and traditional literature from different cultures	R9 pp. 54–59
RL.4.10	Read literature of appropriate complexity independently with proficiency	R10 pp. 60–65
Reading Informational Text		
RI.1.1	Refer to details and examples in a text when explaining what the text says explicitly and when drawing inferences from the text	R1 pp. 6–11
RI.1.2	Determine the main idea of a text and explain how it is supported by key details; summarize the text	R2 pp. 12–17
RI.1.3	Explain events, procedures, ideas, or concepts in a historical, scientific, or technical text	R3 pp. 18–23
RI.2.4	Determine the meaning of general academic and domain-specific words and phrases in a text	R4 pp. 24–29
RI.2.5	Describe the overall structure of events, ideas, concepts, or information in a text	R5 pp. 30–35
RI.2.6	Compare and contrast a firsthand and secondhand account of the same event or topic	R6 pp. 36–41
RI.3.7	Interpret information presented visually, orally, or quantitatively, and explain how it contributes to an understanding of the text	R7 pp. 42–47
RI.3.8	Explain how an author uses reasons and evidence to support particular points in a text	R8 pp. 48–53
RI.3.9	Integrate information from two texts on the same topic in order to write or speak about the subject	R9 pp. 54–59
RI.4.10	Read and comprehend appropriately complex informational texts independently and proficiently	R10 pp. 60–65
Reading Foundational Skills		
RF.3.3	Phonics: Know and apply grade-level phonics and word analysis skills in decoding words	RF3 pp. 214–219
RF.4.4	Fluency: Read grade-level texts with sufficient accuracy and fluency to support comprehension	RF4 pp. 220–225
Writing		
W.1.1	Write opinion pieces on topics or texts, supporting a point of view with reasons and information	W1 pp. 70–75
W.1.2	Write informative/explanatory texts to examine a topic and convey ideas and information clearly	W2 pp. 76–81
W.1.3	Write narratives to develop real or imagined experiences or events using effective technique, descriptive details, and clear event sequences	W3 pp. 82–87
W.2.4	Produce writing in which the development and organization are appropriate to the task, purpose, and audience	W4 pp. 88–93
W.2.5	Develop and strengthen writing as needed by planning, revising, and editing	W5 pp. 94–99
W.2.6	Use technology to produce and publish writing; demonstrate keyboarding skills	W6 pp. 100–105
W.3.7	Conduct short research projects that build knowledge through investigation of different aspects of a topic	W7 pp. 106–111
W.3.8	Recall information from experiences or gather information from print and digital sources	W8 pp. 112–117
W.3.9	Draw evidence from literary or informational texts to support analysis, reflection, and research	W9 pp. 118–123
W.4.10	Write routinely over shorter and extended time frames	W10 pp. 124–129
Speaking and Listening		
SL.1.1	Engage effectively in a range of collaborative discussions with diverse partners, building on others' ideas and expressing their own clearly	SL1 pp. 134–139
SL.1.2	Paraphrase portions of a text read aloud or information presented in diverse media and formats	SL2 pp. 140–145
SL.1.3	Identify the reasons and evidence a speaker provides to support particular points	SL3 pp. 146–151
SL.2.4	Report on a topic or text, tell a story, or recount an experience with appropriate facts and details to support main ideas or themes	SL4 pp. 152–157
SL.2.5	Add audio recordings and visual displays to presentations when appropriate to enhance the development of main ideas or themes	SL5 pp. 158–163
SL.2.6	Differentiate between contexts that call for formal English and situations where informal discourse is appropriate; use formal English when appropriate to task and situation	SL6 pp. 164–169

(Continued)

Florida Strand/Standard	Focus of Florida Standard	For More Information
Language		
L.1.1	Demonstrate command of the conventions of standard English grammar and usage when writing or speaking	L1 pp. 174–179
L.1.2	Demonstrate command of the conventions of standard English capitalization, punctuation, and spelling when writing	L2 pp. 180–185
L.2.3	Use knowledge of language and its conventions when writing, speaking, reading, or listening	L3 pp. 186–191
L.3.4	Determine or clarify the meaning of unknown and multiple-meaning words and phrases, choosing flexibly from an array of strategies	L4 pp. 192–197
L.3.5	Demonstrate understanding of word relationships and nuances in word meanings	L5 pp. 198–203
L.3.6	Acquire and use accurately general academic and domain-specific words and phrases	L6 pp. 204–209

Florida, Grade 5

Florida Strand/Standard	Focus of Florida Standard	For More Information
Reading Literature		
RL.1.1	Quote accurately from a text when explaining what the text says explicitly and when drawing inferences from the text	R1 pp. 6–11
RL.1.2	Determine a theme of a story, drama, or poem from details in the text; summarize the text	R2 pp. 12–17
RL.1.3	Compare and contrast two or more characters, settings, or events in a story or drama, drawing on specific details in the text	R3 pp. 18–23
RL.2.4	Determine the meaning of words and phrases as they are used in a text, including figurative language	R4 pp. 24–29
RL.2.5	Explain how a series of chapters, scenes, or stanzas fits together to provide the overall structure of a story, drama, or poem	R5 pp. 30–35
RL.2.6	Describe how a narrator's or speaker's point of view influences how events are described	R6 pp. 36–41
RL.3.7	Analyze how visual and multimedia elements contribute to the meaning, tone, or beauty of a text	R7 pp. 42–47
RL.3.9	Compare and contrast stories in the same genre on their approaches to similar themes and topics	R9 pp. 54–59
RL.4.10	Read literature of appropriate complexity independently with proficiency	R10 pp. 60–65
Reading Informational Text		
RI.1.1	Quote accurately from a text when explaining what the text says explicitly and when drawing inferences from the text	R1 pp. 6–11
RI.1.2	Determine two or more main ideas of a text and explain how they are supported by key details; summarize the text	R2 pp. 12–17
RI.1.3	Explain the relationships or interactions between two or more individuals, events, ideas, or concepts in a text, based on specific information in the text	R3 pp. 18–23
RI.2.4	Determine the meaning of general academic and domain-specific words and phrases in a text	R4 pp. 24–29
RI.2.5	Compare and contrast the overall structure of events, ideas, concepts, or information in two or more texts	R5 pp. 30–35
RI.2.6	Analyze multiple accounts of the same event or topic, noting important similarities and differences in the point of view they represent	R6 pp. 36–41
RI.3.7	Draw on information from multiple sources, demonstrating the ability to locate an answer to a question quickly or solve a problem efficiently	R7 pp. 42–47

Florida Strand/Standard	Focus of Florida Standard	For More Information
Reading Informational Text		
RI.3.8	Explain how an author uses reasons and evidence to support particular points in a text	R8 pp. 48–53
RI.3.9	Integrate information from several texts on the same topic in order to write or speak about the subject	R9 pp. 54–59
RI.4.10	Read and comprehend appropriately complex informational texts independently and proficiently	R10 pp. 60–65
Reading Foundational Skills		
RF.3.3	Phonics: Know and apply grade-level phonics and word analysis skills in decoding words	RF3 pp. 214–219
RF.4.4	Fluency: Read grade-level texts with sufficient accuracy and fluency to support comprehension	RF4 pp. 220–225
Writing		
W.1.1	Write opinion pieces on topics or texts, supporting a point of view with reasons and information	W1 pp. 70–75
W.1.2	Write informative/explanatory texts to examine a topic and convey ideas and information clearly	W2 pp. 76–81
W.1.3	Write narratives to develop real or imagined experiences or events using effective technique, descriptive details, and clear event sequences	W3 pp. 82–87
W.2.4	Produce writing in which the development and organization are appropriate to the task, purpose, and audience	W4 pp. 88–93
W.2.5	Develop and strengthen writing as needed by planning, revising, editing, rewriting, or trying a new approach	W5 pp. 94–99
W.2.6	Use technology to produce and publish writing; demonstrate keyboarding skills	W6 pp. 100–105
W.3.7	Conduct short research projects that use several sources to build knowledge through investigation of different aspects of a topic	W7 pp. 106–111
W.3.8	Recall information from experiences or gather information from print and digital sources	W8 pp. 112–117
W.3.9	Draw evidence from literary or informational texts to support analysis, reflection, and research	W9 pp. 118–123
W.4.10	Write routinely over shorter and extended time frames	W10 pp. 124–129
Speaking and Listening		
SL.1.1	Engage effectively in a range of collaborative discussions with diverse partners, building on others' ideas and expressing their own clearly	SL1 pp. 134–139
SL.1.2	Summarize a written text read aloud or information presented in diverse media and formats	SL2 pp. 140–145
SL.1.3	Summarize points a speaker makes and explain how each claim is supported by reasons and evidence	SL3 pp. 146–151
SL.2.4	Report on a topic or text or present an opinion, using appropriate facts and details to support main ideas and themes	SL4 pp. 152–157
SL.2.5	Include multimedia components and visual displays in presentations when appropriate to enhance the development of main ideas or themes	SL5 pp. 158–163
SL.2.6	Adapt speech to a variety of contexts, using formal English when appropriate to task and situation	SL6 pp. 164–169
Language		
L.1.1	Demonstrate command of the conventions of standard English grammar and usage when writing or speaking	L1 pp. 174–179
L.1.2	Demonstrate command of the conventions of standard English capitalization, punctuation, and spelling when writing	L2 pp. 180–185
L.2.3	Use knowledge of language and its conventions when writing, speaking, reading, or listening	L3 pp. 186–191
L.3.4	Determine or clarify the meaning of unknown and multiple-meaning words and phrases, choosing flexibly from an array of strategies	L4 pp. 192–197
L.3.5	Demonstrate understanding of figurative language, word relationships, and nuances in word meanings	L5 pp. 198–203
L.3.6	Acquire and use accurately general academic and domain-specific words and phrases	L6 pp. 204–209

Georgia, Grade 3

Georgia Strand/Standard	Focus of Georgia Standard	For More Information
Reading Literature		
RL.1	Ask and answer questions to demonstrate understanding of a text, referring explicitly to the text as the basis for the answers	R1 pp. 6–11
RL.2	Recount stories from diverse cultures, determine their central message, lesson, or moral, and explain how it is conveyed	R2 pp. 12–17
RL.3	Describe characters in a story and explain how their actions contribute to the sequence of events	R3 pp. 18–23
RL.4	Determine the meaning of words and phrases both literal and nonliteral as they are used in a text	R4 pp. 24–29
RL.5	Refer to parts of stories, dramas, and poems when writing or speaking about a text, using terms such as chapter, scene, and stanza; describe how each successive part builds on earlier sections	R5 pp. 30–35
RL.6	Distinguish their own point of view from that of the narrator or those of the characters	R6 pp. 36–41
RL.7	Explain how specific elements of a text's illustrations contribute to what is conveyed by the words in a story	R7 pp. 42–47
RL.8	NA	
RL.9	Compare and contrast the themes, settings, and plots of stories written by the same author about the same or similar characters	R9 pp. 54–59
RL.10	Read literature of appropriate complexity independently with proficiency	R10 pp. 60–65
Reading Informational Text		
RI.1	Ask and answer questions to demonstrate understanding of a text, referring explicitly to the text as the basis for the answers	R1 pp. 6–11
RI.2	Determine the main idea of a text; recount the key details and explain how they support the main idea	R2 pp. 12–17
RI.3	Describe the relationship between a series of historical events, scientific ideas or concepts, or steps in technical procedures in a text	R3 pp. 18–23
RI.4	Determine the meaning of general academic and domain-specific words and phrases in a text	R4 pp. 24–29
RI.5	Use text features and search tools to locate information on a topic efficiently	R5 pp. 30–35
RI.6	Distinguish own point of view from that of the author of a text	R6 pp. 36–41
RI.7	Use information from illustrations and the words in a text to demonstrate understanding of the text	R7 pp. 42–47
RI.8	Describe the logical connection between particular sentences and paragraphs in a text	R8 pp. 48–53
RI.9	Compare and contrast the most important points and key details presented by two texts on the same topic	R9 pp. 54–59
RI.10	Read and comprehend appropriately complex informational texts independently and proficiently	R10 pp. 60–65
Reading Foundational Skills		
RF.3	Phonics: Know and apply grade-level phonics and word analysis skills in decoding words	RF3 pp. 214–219
RF.4	Fluency: Read grade-level texts with sufficient accuracy and fluency to support comprehension	RF4 pp. 220–225
Writing		
W.1	Write opinion pieces on topics or texts, supporting a point of view with reasons	W1 pp. 70–75
W.2	Write informative/explanatory texts to examine a topic and convey ideas and information clearly	W2 pp. 76–81
W.3	Write narratives to develop real or imagined experiences or events using effective technique, descriptive details, and clear event sequences	W3 pp. 82–87
W.4	Produce writing in which the development and organization are appropriate to the task and purpose	W4 pp. 88–93
W.5	Develop and strengthen writing as needed by planning, revising, and editing	W5 pp. 94–99
W.6	Use technology to produce and publish writing	W6 pp. 100–105
W.7	Conduct short research projects that build knowledge about a topic	W7 pp. 106–111
W.8	Recall information from experiences or gather information from print and digital sources	W8 pp. 112–117
W.9	NA	
W.10	Write routinely over shorter and extended time frames	W10 pp. 124–129

Georgia Strand/Standard	Focus of Georgia Standard	For More Information
Speaking and Listening		
SL.1	Engage effectively in a range of collaborative discussions with diverse partners, building on others' ideas and expressing their own clearly	SL1 pp. 134–139
SL.2	Determine the main ideas and supporting details of a text read aloud or information presented in diverse media and formats	SL2 pp. 140–145
SL.3	Ask and answer questions about information from a speaker, offering appropriate elaboration and detail	SL3 pp. 146–151
SL.4	Report on a topic or text, tell a story, or recount an experience with appropriate facts and relevant details	SL4 pp. 152–157
SL.5	Create audio recordings of stories or poems, demonstrating fluent reading; add visual displays when appropriate	SL5 pp. 158–163
SL.6	Speak in complete sentences when appropriate to task and situation in order to provide requested detail or clarification	SL6 pp. 164–169
Language		
L.1	Demonstrate command of the conventions of standard English grammar and usage when writing or speaking	L1 pp. 174–179
L.2	Demonstrate command of the conventions of standard English capitalization, punctuation, and spelling when writing	L2 pp. 180–185
L.3	Use knowledge of language and its conventions when writing, speaking, reading, or listening	L3 pp. 186–191
L.4	Determine or clarify the meaning of unknown and multiple-meaning words and phrases, choosing flexibly from an array of strategies	L4 pp. 192–197
L.5	Demonstrate understanding of word relationships and nuances in word meanings	L5 pp. 198–203
L.6	Acquire and use accurately conversational, general academic, and domain-specific words and phrases	L6 pp. 204–209

Georgia, Grade 4

Georgia Strand/Standard	Focus of Georgia Standard	For More Information
Reading Literature		
RL.1	Refer to details and examples in a text when explaining what the text says explicitly and when drawing inferences	R1 pp. 6–11
RL.2	Determine a theme of a story, drama, or poem from details in the text; summarize the text	R2 pp. 12–17
RL.3	Describe in depth a character, setting, or event in a story or drama, drawing on specific details in the text	R3 pp. 18–23
RL.4	Determine the meaning of words and phrases as they are used in a text	R4 pp. 24–29
RL.5	Explain the major differences between poems, drama, and prose; refer to structural elements when writing or speaking about a text	R5 pp. 30–35
RL.6	Compare and contrast the point of view from which different stories are narrated, including the difference between first- and third-person narratives	R6 pp. 36–41
RL.7	Make connections between the text of a story or drama and a visual or oral representation of the text identifying similarities and differences	R7 pp. 42–47
RL.8	NA	
RL.9	Compare and contrast the treatment of similar themes and topics and patterns of events in stories and traditional literature from different cultures	R9 pp. 54–59
RL.10	Read literature of appropriate complexity independently with proficiency	R10 pp. 60–65

(Continued)

Georgia Strand/Standard	Focus of Georgia Standard	For More Information
Reading Informational Text		
RI.1	Refer to details and examples in a text when explaining what the text says explicitly and when drawing inferences from the text	R1 pp. 6–11
RI.2	Determine the main idea of a text and explain how it is supported by key details; summarize the text	R2 pp. 12–17
RI.3	Explain events, procedures, ideas, or concepts in a historical, scientific, or technical text	R3 pp. 18–23
RI.4	Determine the meaning of general academic and domain-specific words and phrases in a text	R4 pp. 24–29
RI.5	Describe the overall structure of events, ideas, concepts, or information in a text	R5 pp. 30–35
RI.6	Compare and contrast a firsthand and secondhand account of the same event or topic	R6 pp. 36–41
RI.7	Interpret information presented visually, orally, or quantitatively, and explain how it contributes to an understanding of the text	R7 pp. 42–47
RI.8	Explain how an author uses reasons and evidence to support particular points in a text	R8 pp. 48–53
RI.9	Integrate information from two texts on the same topic in order to write or speak about the subject	R9 pp. 54–59
RI.10	Read and comprehend appropriately complex informational texts independently and proficiently	R10 pp. 60–65
Reading Foundational Skills		
RF.3	Phonics: Know and apply grade-level phonics and word analysis skills in decoding words	RF3 pp. 214–219
RF.4	Fluency: Read grade-level texts with sufficient accuracy and fluency to support comprehension	RF4 pp. 220–225
Writing		
W.1	Write opinion pieces on topics or texts, supporting a point of view with reasons and information	W1 pp. 70–75
W.2	Write informative/explanatory texts to examine a topic and convey ideas and information clearly	W2 pp. 76–81
W.3	Write narratives to develop real or imagined experiences or events using effective technique, descriptive details, and clear event sequences	W3 pp. 82–87
W.4	Produce writing in which the development and organization are appropriate to the task, purpose, and audience	W4 pp. 88–93
W.5	Develop and strengthen writing as needed by planning, revising, and editing	W5 pp. 94–99
W.6	Use technology to produce and publish writing; demonstrate keyboarding skills	W6 pp. 100–105
W.7	Conduct short research projects that build knowledge through investigation of different aspects of a topic	W7 pp. 106–111
W.8	Recall information from experiences or gather information from print and digital sources	W8 pp. 112–117
W.9	Draw evidence from literary or informational texts to support analysis, reflection, and research	W9 pp. 118–123
W.10	Write routinely over shorter and extended time frames	W10 pp. 124–129
Speaking and Listening		
SL.1	Engage effectively in a range of collaborative discussions with diverse partners, building on others' ideas and expressing their own clearly	SL1 pp. 134–139
SL.2	Paraphrase portions of a text read aloud or information presented in diverse media and formats	SL2 pp. 140–145
SL.3	Identify the reasons and evidence a speaker provides to support particular points	SL3 pp. 146–151
SL.4	Report on a topic or text, tell a story, or recount an experience with appropriate facts and details to support main ideas or themes	SL4 pp. 152–157
SL.5	Add audio recordings and visual displays to presentations when appropriate to enhance the development of main ideas or themes	SL5 pp. 158–163
SL.6	Differentiate between contexts that call for formal English and situations where informal discourse is appropriate; use formal English when appropriate to task and situation	SL6 pp. 164–169
Language		
L.1	Demonstrate command of the conventions of standard English grammar and usage when writing or speaking	L1 pp. 174–179
L.2	Demonstrate command of the conventions of standard English capitalization, punctuation, and spelling when writing	L2 pp. 180–185
L.3	Use knowledge of language and its conventions when writing, speaking, reading, or listening	L3 pp. 186–191

Georgia Strand/Standard	Focus of Georgia Standard	For More Information
Language		
L.4	Determine or clarify the meaning of unknown and multiple-meaning words and phrases, choosing flexibly from an array of strategies	L4 pp. 192–197
L.5	Demonstrate understanding of figurative language, word relationships, and nuances in word meanings	L5 pp. 198–203
L.6	Acquire and use accurately general academic and domain-specific words and phrases	L6 pp. 204–209

Georgia, Grade 5

Georgia Strand/Standard	Focus of Georgia Standard	For More Information
Reading Literature		
RL.1	Quote accurately from a text when explaining what the text says explicitly and when drawing inferences from the text	R1 pp. 6–11
RL.2	Determine a theme of a story, drama, or poem from details in the text; summarize the text	R2 pp. 12–17
RL.3	Compare and contrast two or more characters, settings, or events in a story or drama, drawing on specific details in the text	R3 pp. 18–23
RL.4	Determine the meaning of words and phrases as they are used in a text, including figurative language	R4 pp. 24–29
RL.5	Explain how a series of chapters, scenes, or stanzas fits together to provide the overall structure of a story, drama, or poem	R5 pp. 30–35
RL.6	Describe how a narrator's or speaker's point of view influences how events are described	R6 pp. 36–41
RL.7	Analyze how visual and multimedia elements contribute to the meaning, tone, or beauty of a text	R7 pp. 42–47
RL.8	NA	
RL.9	Compare and contrast stories in the same genre on their approaches to similar themes and topics	R9 pp. 54–59
RL.10	Read literature of appropriate complexity independently with proficiency	R10 pp. 60–65
Reading Informational Text		
RI.1	Quote accurately from a text when explaining what the text says explicitly and when drawing inferences from the text	R1 pp. 6–11
RI.2	Determine two or more main ideas of a text and explain how they are supported by key details; summarize the text	R2 pp. 12–17
RI.3	Explain the relationships or interactions between two or more individuals, events, ideas, or concepts in a text, based on specific information in the text	R3 pp. 18–23
RI.4	Determine the meaning of general academic and domain-specific words and phrases in a text	R4 pp. 24–29
RI.5	Compare and contrast the overall structure of events, ideas, concepts, or information in two or more texts	R5 pp. 30–35
RI.6	Analyze multiple accounts of the same event or topic, noting important similarities and differences in the point of view they represent	R6 pp. 36–41
RI.7	Draw on information from multiple sources, demonstrating the ability to locate an answer to a question quickly or solve a problem efficiently	R7 pp. 42–47
RI.8	Explain how an author uses reasons and evidence to support particular points in a text	R8 pp. 48–53
RI.9	Integrate information from several texts on the same topic in order to write or speak about the subject	R9 pp. 54–59
RI.10	Read and comprehend appropriately complex informational texts independently and proficiently	R10 pp. 60–65

(Continued)

Georgia Strand/Standard	Focus of Georgia Standard	For More Information
Reading Foundational Skills		
RF.3	Phonics: Know and apply grade-level phonics and word analysis skills in decoding words	RF3 pp. 214–219
RF.4	Fluency: Read grade-level texts with sufficient accuracy and fluency to support comprehension	RF4 pp. 220–225
Writing		
W.1	Write opinion pieces on topics or texts, supporting a point of view with reasons and information	W1 pp. 70–75
W.2	Write informative/explanatory texts to examine a topic and convey ideas and information clearly	W2 pp. 76–81
W.3	Write narratives to develop real or imagined experiences or events using effective technique, descriptive details, and clear event sequences	W3 pp. 82–87
W.4	Produce writing in which the development and organization are appropriate to the task, purpose, and audience	W4 pp. 88–93
W.5	Develop and strengthen writing as needed by planning, revising, editing, rewriting, or trying a new approach	W5 pp. 94–99
W.6	Use technology to produce and publish writing; demonstrate keyboarding skills	W6 pp. 100–105
W.7	Conduct short research projects that use several sources to build knowledge through investigation of different aspects of a topic	W7 pp. 106–111
W.8	Recall information from experiences or gather information from print and digital sources	W8 pp. 112–117
W.9	Draw evidence from literary or informational texts to support analysis, reflection, and research	W9 pp. 118–123
W.10	Write routinely over shorter and extended time frames	W10 pp. 124–129
Speaking and Listening		
SL.1	Engage effectively in a range of collaborative discussions with diverse partners, building on others' ideas and expressing their own clearly	SL1 pp. 134–139
SL.2	Summarize a written text read aloud or information presented in diverse media and formats	SL2 pp. 140–145
SL.3	Summarize points a speaker makes and explain how each claim is supported by reasons and evidence	SL3 pp. 146–151
SL.4	Report on a topic or text or present an opinion, using appropriate facts and details to support main ideas and themes	SL4 pp. 152–157
SL.5	Include multimedia components and visual displays in presentations when appropriate to enhance the development of main ideas or themes	SL5 pp. 158–163
SL.6	Adapt speech to a variety of contexts, using formal English when appropriate to task and situation	SL6 pp. 164–169
Language		
L.1	Demonstrate command of the conventions of standard English grammar and usage when writing or speaking	L1 pp. 174–179
L.2	Demonstrate command of the conventions of standard English capitalization, punctuation, and spelling when writing	L2 pp. 180–185
L.3	Use knowledge of language and its conventions when writing, speaking, reading, or listening	L3 pp. 186–191
L.4	Determine or clarify the meaning of unknown and multiple-meaning words and phrases, choosing flexibly from an array of strategies	L4 pp. 192–197
L.5	Demonstrate understanding of figurative language, word relationships, and nuances in word meanings	L5 pp. 198–203
L.6	Acquire and use accurately general academic and domain-specific words and phrases	L6 pp. 204–209

Indiana, Grade 3

Indiana Strand/Standard	Focus of Indiana Standard	For More Information
Reading Foundational Skills		
RF.4	Phonics: Know and apply grade-level phonics and word analysis skills in decoding words	RF3 pp. 214–219
RF.5	Fluency: Read level-appropriate texts smoothly and accurately and with expression	RF4 pp. 220–225
Reading Literature		
RL.1	Read and comprehend a variety of literature that is level-appropriate	R10 pp. 60–65
RL.2.1	Ask and answer questions to demonstrate understanding of a text, referring explicitly to the text as the basis for the answers	R1 pp. 6–11
RL.2.2	Recount stories from diverse cultures, determine their central message, lesson, or moral, and explain how it is conveyed	R2 pp. 12–17
RL.2.3	Describe characters in a story and explain how their actions contribute to the sequence of events	R3 pp. 18–23
RL.3.1	Refer to parts of stories, dramas, and poems when writing or speaking about a text, using terms such as chapter, scene, and stanza; describe how each successive part builds on earlier sections	R5 pp. 30–35
RL.3.2	Distinguish personal point of view from that of the narrator or those of the characters	R6 pp. 36–41
RL.4.1	Explain how specific elements of a text's illustrations contribute to what is conveyed by the words in a story	R7 pp. 42–47
RL.4.2	Compare and contrast the themes, settings, and plots of stories written by the same author about the same or similar characters	R9 pp. 54–59
Reading Nonfiction Text		
RN.1	Read and comprehend a variety of level-appropriate nonfiction texts	R10 pp. 60–65
RN.2.1	Ask and answer questions to demonstrate understanding of a text, referring explicitly to the text as the basis for the answers	R1 pp. 6–11
RN.2.2	Determine the main idea of a text; recount the key details and explain how they support the main idea	R2 pp. 12–17
RN.2.3	Describe the relationship between a series of historical events, scientific ideas or concepts, or steps in technical procedures in a text	R3 pp. 18–23
RN.3.1	Use text features and search tools to locate information on a topic efficiently	R5 pp. 30–35
RN.3.2	Identify how a nonfiction can be structured to compare and contrast, describe a procedure, and explain a cause-effect relationship	R5 pp. 30–35
RN.3.3	Distinguish own point of view from that of the author of a text	R6 pp. 36–41
RN.4.1	Distinguish between fact and opinion; explain how the author uses facts to support specific points in a text	R8 pp. 48–53
RN.4.2	Compare and contrast the most important points presented by two texts on the same topic	R9 pp. 54–59
Reading Vocabulary		
RV.1	Acquire and use accurately conversational, general academic, and domain-specific words and phrases	L6 pp. 204–209
RV2.1	Use context clues to determine the meaning of unknown words	L4 pp. 192–197
RV2.2	Identify relationships among words	L5 pp. 198–203
RV.2.4	Use a known word as a clue to the meaning of an unknown word with the same root	L4 pp. 192–197
RV.2.5	Consult reference materials to determine the meaning of words and phrases	L4 pp. 192–197
RV.3.1	Determine how the author uses words and phrases to provide meaning, distinguishing literal from nonliteral language	R4 pp. 24–29 L5 pp. 198–203
RV.3.2	Determine the meanings of general academic and content-specific words and phrases in a nonfiction text	R4 pp. 24–29 L6 pp. 204–209
RV.3.3	Recognize the meanings of idioms in context	L5 pp. 198–203

(Continued)

Indiana Strand/Standard	Focus of Indiana Standard	For More Information
Writing		
W.1	Write routinely for specific purposes and audiences	W10 pp. 124–129
W.2	Demonstrate the ability to write legibly	NA
W.3.1	Write persuasive compositions in a variety of forms	W1 pp. 70–75
W.3.2	Write informative compositions on a variety of topics	W2 pp. 76–81
W.3.3	Write narrative compositions in a variety of forms	W3 pp. 82–87
W.4	Generate a draft; revise to improve writing using appropriate reference materials; edit writing for format and conventions; use technology to produce and publish writing	W5 pp. 94–99 W6 pp. 100–105 L2 pp. 180–185
W.5	Conduct short research on a topic; locate information in reference sources; record information in own words; present information	W7 pp. 106–111 W8 pp. 112–117
W.6.1	Demonstrate command of the conventions of English grammar and usage	L1 pp. 174–179
W.6.2	Demonstrate a command of capitalization, punctuation, and spelling	L2 pp. 180–185
Speaking and Listening		
SL.1	Listen actively and communicate effectively	SL1 pp. 134–139 SL2 pp. 140–145 SL3 pp. 146–151
SL.2.1	Engage in collaborative discussions, building on other's ideas and expressing personal ideas clearly	SL1 pp. 134–139
SL.2.2	Explore ideas under discussion by drawing on readings and other information	SL1 pp. 134–139
SL.2.3	Demonstrate knowledge and use of agreed-upon rules for discussions	SL1 pp. 134–139
SL.2.4	Ask questions to check understanding of information presented	SL3 pp. 146–151
SL.2.5	Explain personal ideas and understanding in reference to the discussion	SL1 pp. 134–139
SL.3.1	Retell, paraphrase, and explain main ideas and details in text read aloud or information presented in diverse media	SL2 pp. 140–145
SL.3.2	Ask and answer questions about information from a speaker	SL3 pp. 146–151
SL.4.1	Using appropriate language, report on a topic or a text, or present an organized narrative with descriptive details; speak clearly at an understandable pace	SL4 pp. 152–157 SL6 pp. 164–169
SL4.2	Create oral presentations that maintain a clear focus, using various media when appropriate	SL5 pp. 158–163

Indiana, Grade 4

Indiana Strand/Standard	Focus of Indiana Standard	For More Information
Reading Foundational Skills		
RF.4	Phonics: Know and apply grade-level phonics and word analysis skills in decoding words	RF3 pp. 214–219
RF.5	Fluency: Read level-appropriate texts smoothly and accurately and with expression	RF4 pp. 220–225
Reading Literature		
RL.1	Read and comprehend a variety of literature that is level-appropriate	R10 pp. 60–65
RL.2.1	Refer to details and examples in a text when explaining what the text says explicitly and when drawing inferences	R1 pp. 6–11
RL.2.2	Paraphrase or retell the main events in a story; identify the theme and provide evidence for the interpretation	R2 pp. 12–17
RL.2.3	Describe a character, setting, or event in a story or drama, drawing on specific details in the text	R3 pp. 18–23
RL.3.1	Explain the major differences between poems, drama, and prose; refer to structural elements when writing or speaking about a text	R5 pp. 30–35
RL.3.2	Compare and contrast the point of view from which different stories are narrated, including the difference between first- and third-person narratives	R6 pp. 36–41
RL.4.1	Describe how visuals and multimedia can enhance the meaning of a text	R7 pp. 42–47
RL.4.2	Compare and contrast the treatment of similar themes and topics and patterns of events in stories and traditional literature from different cultures	R9 pp. 54–59

Indiana Strand/Standard	Focus of Indiana Standard	For More Information
Reading Nonfiction Text		
RN.1	Read and comprehend a variety of level-appropriate nonfiction texts	R10 pp. 60–65
RN.2.1	Refer to details and examples in a text when explaining what the text says explicitly and when drawing inferences from the text	R1 pp. 6–11
RN.2.2	Determine the main idea of a text and explain how it is supported by key details; summarize the text	R2 pp. 12–17
RN.2.3	Explain the relationship between events, procedures, ideas, or concepts in a historical, scientific, or technical text	R3 pp. 18–23
RN.3.1	Apply knowledge of text features to locate information and gain meaning from a text	R5 pp. 30–35
RN.3.2	Describe the organizational structure of events, ideas, concepts, or information in a text	R5 pp. 30–35
RN.3.3	Compare and contrast a firsthand and secondhand account of the same event or topic	R6 pp. 36–41
RN.4.1	Distinguish between fact and opinion; explain how an author uses reasons and evidence to support particular points in a text	R8 pp. 48–53
RN.4.2	Combine information from two texts on the same topic in order to demonstrate knowledge about the subject	R9 pp. 54–59
Reading Vocabulary		
RV.1	Acquire and use accurately conversational, general academic, and domain-specific words and phrases	L6 pp. 204–209
RV2.1	Use context clues to determine the meaning of unknown words	L4 pp. 192–197
RV2.2	Identify relationships among words	L5 pp. 198–203
RV.2.4	Apply knowledge or word structure, known words, and word patterns to determine meaning	L4 pp. 192–197
RV.2.5	Consult reference materials to clarify the meaning of words and phrases	L4 pp. 192–197
RV.3.1	Determine how words and phrases provide meaning to works of literature	R4 pp. 24–29 L5 pp. 198–203
RV.3.2	Determine the meanings of general academic and content-specific words and phrases in a nonfiction text	R4 pp. 24–29 L6 pp. 204–209
RV.3.3	Explain the meanings of proverbs, adages, and idioms in context	L5 pp. 198–203
Writing		
W.1	Write routinely for specific purposes and audiences	W10 pp. 124–129
W.2	Demonstrate the ability to write legibly	NA
W.3.1	Write persuasive compositions in a variety of forms	W1 pp. 70–75
W.3.2	Write informative compositions on a variety of topics	W2 pp. 76–81
W.3.3	Write narrative compositions in a variety of forms	W3 pp. 82–87
W.4	Generate a draft; revise to improve writing using appropriate reference materials; edit writing for format and conventions; use technology to produce and publish writing	W5 pp. 94–99 W6 pp. 100–105 L2 pp. 180–185
W.5	Conduct short research on a topic; locate information and determine reliability; summarize and organize information in own words; present information	W7 pp. 106–111 W8 pp. 112–117
W.6.1	Demonstrate command of the conventions of English grammar and usage	L1 pp. 174–179
W.6.2	Demonstrate a command of capitalization, punctuation, and spelling	L2 pp. 180–185
Speaking and Listening		
SL.1	Listen actively and communicate effectively	SL1 pp. 134–139 SL2 pp. 140–145 SL3 pp. 146–151
SL.2.1	Engage in collaborative discussions, building on other's ideas and expressing personal ideas clearly	SL1 pp. 134–139
SL.2.2	Explore ideas under discussion by drawing on readings and other information	SL1 pp. 134–139
SL.2.3	Demonstrate knowledge and use of agreed-upon rules for discussions	SL1 pp. 134–139
SL.2.4	Pose and respond to specific questions to clarify or follow up on information	SL3 pp. 146–151
SL.2.5	Review the key ideas expressed and explain personal ideas in reference to the discussion	SL1 pp. 134–139

(Continued)

Indiana Strand/Standard	Focus of Indiana Standard	For More Information
Speaking and Listening		
SL.3.1	Summarize major ideas and supportive evidence from a text read aloud or information presented in diverse media and formats	SL2 pp. 140–145
SL.3.2	Identify and use evidence a speaker provides to support particular points	SL3 pp. 146–151
SL.4.1	Using appropriate language, report on a topic or a text, or present an organized narrative with descriptive details; speak clearly and concisely at an understandable pace	SL4 pp. 152–157 SL6 pp. 164–169
SL4.2	Create oral presentations that maintain a clear focus, using various media when appropriate	SL5 pp. 158–163

Indiana, Grade 5

Indiana Strand/Standard	Focus of Indiana Standard	For More Information
Reading Foundational Skills		
RF.4	Phonics: Know and apply grade-level phonics and word analysis skills in decoding words	RF3 pp. 214–219
RF.5	Fluency: Read level-appropriate texts smoothly and accurately and with expression	RF4 pp. 220–225
Reading Literature		
RL.1	Read and comprehend a variety of literature that is level-appropriate	R10 pp. 60–65
RL.2.1	Quote accurately from a text when explaining what the text says explicitly and when drawing inferences from the text	R1 pp. 6–11
RL.2.2	Determine a theme of a story, drama, or poem from details in the text; summarize the text	R2 pp. 12–17
RL.2.3	Describe two or more characters, settings, or events in a story or drama, drawing on specific details in the text	R3 pp. 18–23
RL.3.1	Explain how a series of chapters, scenes, or stanzas fits together to provide the overall structure of a story, drama, or poem	R5 pp. 30–35
RL.3.2	Describe how a narrator's or speaker's point of view influences how events are described	R6 pp. 36–41
RL.4.1	Analyze how visual and multimedia elements contribute to the meaning, tone, or beauty of a text	R7 pp. 42–47
RL.4.2	Compare and contrast stories in the same genre on their approaches to similar themes and topics	R9 pp. 54–59
Reading Nonfiction Text		
RN.1	Read and comprehend a variety of level-appropriate nonfiction texts	R10 pp. 60–65
RN.2.1	Quote accurately from a text when explaining what the text says explicitly and when drawing inferences from the text	R1 pp. 6–11
RN.2.2	Determine two or more main ideas of a text and explain how they are supported by key details; summarize the text	R2 pp. 12–17
RN.2.3	Explain the relationships or interactions between two or more individuals, events, ideas, or concepts in a text, based on specific information in the text	R3 pp. 18–23
RN.3.1	Apply knowledge of text features to locate information and gain meaning from a text, or solve a problem	R5 pp. 30–35
RN.3.2	Compare and contrast the organizational structure of events, ideas, concepts, or information in two or more texts	R5 pp. 30–35
RN.3.3	Analyze multiple accounts of the same event or topic, noting important similarities and differences in the point of view they represent	R6 pp. 36–41
RN.4.1	Explain how an author uses reasons and evidence to support particular points in a text	R8 pp. 48–53
RN.4.2	Combine information from several texts on the same topic in order to write or speak about the subject	R9 pp. 54–59
Reading Vocabulary		
RV.1	Acquire and use accurately conversational, general academic, and domain-specific words and phrases	L6 pp. 204–209
RV2.1	Select and apply context clues to determine the meaning of unknown words	L4 pp. 192–197
RV2.2	Identify relationships among words	L5 pp. 198–203
RV.2.4	Apply knowledge or word structure, known words, and word patterns to determine meaning	L4 pp. 192–197

Indiana Strand/Standard	Focus of Indiana Standard	For More Information
Reading Vocabulary		
RV.2.5	Consult reference materials to clarify the meaning of words and phrases	L4 pp. 192–197
RV.3.1	Determine how words and phrases provide meaning to works of literature	R4 pp. 24–29 L5 pp. 198–203
RV.3.2	Determine the meanings of general academic and content-specific words and phrases in a nonfiction text	R4 pp. 24–29 L6 pp. 204–209
RV.3.3	Analyze the meanings of proverbs, adages, and idioms in context	L5 pp. 198–203
Writing		
W.1	Write routinely for specific purposes and audiences	W10 pp. 124–129
W.2	Demonstrate the ability to write legibly	NA
W.3.1	Write persuasive compositions in a variety of forms	W1 pp. 70–75
W.3.2	Write informative compositions on a variety of topics	W2 pp. 76–81
W.3.3	Write narrative compositions in a variety of forms	W3 pp. 82–87
W.4	Generate a draft; revise to improve writing using appropriate reference materials; edit writing for format and conventions; use technology to produce and publish writing	W5 pp. 94–99 W6 pp. 100–105 L2 pp. 180–185
W.5	Conduct short research assignments on a topic; locate information and determine reliability; summarize and organize information in own words; present information	W7 pp. 106–111 W8 pp. 112–117
W.6.1	Demonstrate command of the conventions of English grammar and usage	L1 pp. 174–179
W.6.2	Demonstrate a command of capitalization, punctuation, and spelling	L2 pp. 180–185
Speaking and Listening		
SL.1	Listen actively and communicate effectively	SL1 pp. 134–139 SL2 pp. 140–145 SL3 pp. 146–151
SL.2.1	Engage in collaborative discussions, building on other's ideas and expressing personal ideas clearly	SL1 pp. 134–139
SL.2.2	Reflect on and contribute to ideas under discussion by drawing on readings and other information	SL1 pp. 134–139
SL.2.3	Establish and follow agreed-upon rules for discussions	SL1 pp. 134–139
SL.2.4	Pose and respond to specific questions by making comments that contribute to discussion and elaborate on the remarks of others	SL3 pp. 146–151
SL.2.5	Review the key ideas expressed and draw conclusions in reference to information gained from the discussions	SL1 pp. 134–139
SL.3.1	Summarize or respond to a written text read aloud or information presented in diverse media and formats	SL2 pp. 140–145
SL.3.2	Summarize points a speaker makes as they relate to main idea and supporting details and demonstrate how each claim is supported by reasons and evidence	SL3 pp. 146–151
SL.4.1	Using appropriate language, present information on a topic or a text in an organized manner, using appropriate structure, with relevant details; speak clearly and concisely at an understandable pace	SL4 pp. 152–157 SL6 pp. 164–169
SL4.2	Create presentations that include multimedia components and visual displays when appropriate	SL5 pp. 158–163

Iowa, Grade 3

Iowa Strand/Standard	Focus of Iowa Standard	For More Information
Reading Literature		
RL.1	Ask and answer questions to demonstrate understanding of a text, referring explicitly to the text as the basis for the answers	R1 pp. 6–11
RL.2	Recount stories from diverse cultures, determine their central message, lesson, or moral, and explain how it is conveyed	R2 pp. 12–17

(Continued)

Iowa Strand/Standard	Focus of Iowa Standard	For More Information
Reading Literature		
RL.3	Describe characters in a story and explain how their actions contribute to the sequence of events	R3 pp. 18–23
RL.4	Determine the meaning of words and phrases as they are used in a text, distinguishing literal from nonliteral language	R4 pp. 24–29
RL.5	Refer to parts of stories, dramas, and poems when writing or speaking about a text, using terms such as chapter, scene, and stanza; describe how each successive part builds on earlier sections	R5 pp. 30–35
RL.6	Distinguish their own point of view from that of the narrator or those of the characters	R6 pp. 36–41
RL.7	Explain how specific elements of a text's illustrations contribute to what is conveyed by the words in a story	R7 pp. 42–47
RL.8	NA	
RL.9	Compare and contrast the themes, settings, and plots of stories written by the same author about the same or similar characters	R9 pp. 54–59
RL.10	Read literature of appropriate complexity independently with proficiency	R10 pp. 60–65
Reading Informational Text		
RI.1	Ask and answer questions to demonstrate understanding of a text, referring explicitly to the text as the basis for the answers	R1 pp. 6–11
RI.2	Determine the main idea of a text; recount the key details and explain how they support the main idea	R2 pp. 12–17
RI.3	Describe the relationship between a series of historical events, scientific ideas or concepts, or steps in technical procedures in a text	R3 pp. 18–23
RI.4	Determine the meaning of general academic and domain-specific words and phrases in a text	R4 pp. 24–29
RI.5	Use text features and search tools to locate information on a topic efficiently	R5 pp. 30–35
RI.6	Distinguish own point of view from that of the author of a text	R6 pp. 36–41
RI.7	Use information from illustrations and the words in a text to demonstrate understanding of the text	R7 pp. 42–47
RI.8	Describe the logical connection between particular sentences and paragraphs in a text	R8 pp. 48–53
RI.9	Compare and contrast the most important points and key details presented by two texts on the same topic	R9 pp. 54–59
RI.10	Read and comprehend appropriately complex informational texts independently and proficiently	R10 pp. 60–65
Reading Foundational Skills		
RF.3	Phonics: Know and apply grade-level phonics and word analysis skills in decoding words	RF3 pp. 214–219
RF.4	Fluency: Read grade-level texts with sufficient accuracy and fluency to support comprehension	RF4 pp. 220–225
Writing		
W.1	Write opinion pieces on topics or texts, supporting a point of view with reasons	W1 pp. 70–75
W.2	Write informative/explanatory texts to examine a topic and convey ideas and information clearly	W2 pp. 76–81
W.3	Write narratives to develop real or imagined experiences or events using effective technique, descriptive details, and clear event sequences	W3 pp. 82–87
W.4	Produce writing in which the development and organization are appropriate to the task and purpose	W4 pp. 88–93
W.5	Develop and strengthen writing as needed by planning, revising, and editing	W5 pp. 94–99
W.6	Use technology to produce and publish writing	W6 pp. 100–105
W.7	Conduct short research projects that build knowledge about a topic	W7 pp. 106–111
W.8	Recall information from experiences or gather information from print and digital sources	W8 pp. 112–117
W.9	NA	
W.10	Write routinely over shorter and extended time frames	W10 pp. 124–129
Speaking and Listening		
SL.1	Engage effectively in a range of collaborative discussions with diverse partners, building on others' ideas and expressing their own clearly	SL1 pp. 134–139
SL.2	Determine the main ideas and supporting details of a text read aloud or information presented in diverse media and formats	SL2 pp. 140–145

Iowa Strand/Standard	Focus of Iowa Standard	For More Information
Speaking and Listening		
SL.3	Ask and answer questions about information from a speaker, offering appropriate elaboration and detail	SL3 pp. 146–151
SL.4	Report on a topic or text, tell a story, or recount an experience with appropriate facts and relevant details	SL4 pp. 152–157
SL.5	Create audio recordings of stories or poems, demonstrating fluent reading; add visual displays when appropriate	SL5 pp. 158–163
SL.6	Speak in complete sentences when appropriate to task and situation in order to provide requested detail or clarification	SL6 pp. 164–169
Language		
L.1	Demonstrate command of the conventions of standard English grammar and usage when writing or speaking	L1 pp. 174–179
L.2	Demonstrate command of the conventions of standard English capitalization, punctuation, and spelling when writing	L2 pp. 180–185
L.3	Use knowledge of language and its conventions when writing, speaking, reading, or listening	L3 pp. 186–191
L.4	Determine or clarify the meaning of unknown and multiple-meaning words and phrases, choosing flexibly from an array of strategies	L4 pp. 192–197
L.5	Demonstrate understanding of word relationships and nuances in word meanings	L5 pp. 198–203
L.6	Acquire and use accurately conversational, general academic, and domain-specific words and phrases	L6 pp. 204–209

Iowa, Grade 4

Iowa Strand/Standard	Focus of Iowa Standard	For More Information
Reading Literature		
RL.1	Refer to details and examples in a text when explaining what the text says explicitly and when drawing inferences	R1 pp. 6–11
RL.2	Determine a theme of a story, drama, or poem from details in the text; summarize the text	R2 pp. 12–17
RL.3	Describe in depth a character, setting, or event in a story or drama, drawing on specific details in the text	R3 pp. 18–23
RL.4	Determine the meaning of words and phrases as they are used in a text	R4 pp. 24–29
RL.5	Explain the major differences between poems, drama, and prose; refer to structural elements when writing or speaking about a text	R5 pp. 30–35
RL.6	Compare and contrast the point of view from which different stories are narrated, including the difference between first- and third-person narratives	R6 pp. 36–41
RL.7	Make connections between the text of a story or drama and a visual or oral representation of the text	R7 pp. 42–47
RL.8	NA	
RL.9	Compare and contrast the treatment of similar themes and topics and patterns of events in stories and traditional literature from different cultures	R9 pp. 54–59
RL.10	Read literature of appropriate complexity independently with proficiency	R10 pp. 60–65
Reading Informational Text		
RI.1	Refer to details and examples in a text when explaining what the text says explicitly and when drawing inferences from the text	R1 pp. 6–11
RI.2	Determine the main idea of a text and explain how it is supported by key details; summarize the text	R2 pp. 12–17
RI.3	Explain events, procedures, ideas, or concepts in a historical, scientific, or technical text	R3 pp. 18–23
RI.4	Determine the meaning of general academic and domain-specific words and phrases in a text	R4 pp. 24–29
RI.5	Describe the overall structure of events, ideas, concepts, or information in a text	R5 pp. 30–35

(Continued)

Iowa Strand/Standard	Focus of Iowa Standard	For More Information
Reading Informational Text		
RI.6	Compare and contrast a firsthand and secondhand account of the same event or topic	R6 pp. 36–41
RI.7	Interpret information presented visually, orally, or quantitatively, and explain how it contributes to an understanding of the text	R7 pp. 42–47
RI.8	Explain how an author uses reasons and evidence to support particular points in a text	R8 pp. 48–53
RI.9	Integrate information from two texts on the same topic in order to write or speak about the subject	R9 pp. 54–59
RI.10	Read and comprehend appropriately complex informational texts independently and proficiently	R10 pp. 60–65
Reading Foundational Skills		
RF.3	Phonics: Know and apply grade-level phonics and word analysis skills in decoding words	RF3 pp. 214–219
RF.4	Fluency: Read grade-level texts with sufficient accuracy and fluency to support comprehension	RF4 pp. 220–225
Writing		
W.1	Write opinion pieces on topics or texts, supporting a point of view with reasons and information	W1 pp. 70–75
W.2	Write informative/explanatory texts to examine a topic and convey ideas and information clearly	W2 pp. 76–81
W.3	Write narratives to develop real or imagined experiences or events using effective technique, descriptive details, and clear event sequences	W3 pp. 82–87
W.4	Produce writing in which the development and organization are appropriate to the task, purpose, and audience	W4 pp. 88–93
W.5	Develop and strengthen writing as needed by planning, revising, and editing	W5 pp. 94–99
W.6	Use technology to produce and publish writing; demonstrate keyboarding skills	W6 pp. 100–105
W.7	Conduct short research projects that build knowledge through investigation of different aspects of a topic	W7 pp. 106–111
W.8	Recall information from experiences or gather information from print and digital sources	W8 pp. 112–117
W.9	Draw evidence from literary or informational texts to support analysis, reflection, and research	W9 pp. 118–123
W.10	Write routinely over shorter and extended time frames	W10 pp. 124–129
Speaking and Listening		
SL.1	Engage effectively in a range of collaborative discussions with diverse partners, building on others' ideas and expressing their own clearly	SL1 pp. 134–139
SL.2	Paraphrase portions of a text read aloud or information presented in diverse media and formats	SL2 pp. 140–145
SL.3	Identify the reasons and evidence a speaker provides to support particular points	SL3 pp. 146–151
SL.4	Report on a topic or text, tell a story, or recount an experience with appropriate facts and details to support main ideas or themes	SL4 pp. 152–157
SL.5	Add audio recordings and visual displays to presentations when appropriate to enhance the development of main ideas or themes	SL5 pp. 158–163
SL.6	Differentiate between contexts that call for formal English and situations where informal discourse is appropriate; use formal English when appropriate to task and situation	SL6 pp. 164–169
Language		
L.1	Demonstrate command of the conventions of standard English grammar and usage when writing or speaking	L1 pp. 174–179
L.2	Demonstrate command of the conventions of standard English capitalization, punctuation, and spelling when writing	L2 pp. 180–185
L.3	Use knowledge of language and its conventions when writing, speaking, reading, or listening	L3 pp. 186–191
L.4	Determine or clarify the meaning of unknown and multiple-meaning words and phrases, choosing flexibly from an array of strategies	L4 pp. 192–197
L.5	Demonstrate understanding of figurative language, word relationships, and nuances in word meanings	L5 pp. 198–203
L.6	Acquire and use accurately general academic and domain-specific words and phrases	L6 pp. 204–209

Iowa, Grade 5

Iowa Strand/Standard	Focus of Iowa Standard	For More Information
Reading Literature		
RL.1	Quote accurately from a text when explaining what the text says explicitly and when drawing inferences from the text	R1 pp. 6–11
RL.2	Determine a theme of a story, drama, or poem from details in the text; summarize the text	R2 pp. 12–17
RL.3	Compare and contrast two or more characters, settings, or events in a story or drama, drawing on specific details in the text	R3 pp. 18–23
RL.4	Determine the meaning of words and phrases as they are used in a text, including figurative language	R4 pp. 24–29
RL.5	Explain how a series of chapters, scenes, or stanzas fits together to provide the overall structure of a story, drama, or poem	R5 pp. 30–35
RL.6	Describe how a narrator's or speaker's point of view influences how events are described	R6 pp. 36–41
RL.7	Analyze how visual and multimedia elements contribute to the meaning, tone, or beauty of a text	R7 pp. 42–47
RL.8	NA	
RL.9	Compare and contrast stories in the same genre on their approaches to similar themes and topics	R9 pp. 54–59
RL.10	Read literature of appropriate complexity independently with proficiency	R10 pp. 60–65
Reading Informational Text		
RI.1	Quote accurately from a text when explaining what the text says explicitly and when drawing inferences from the text	R1 pp. 6–11
RI.2	Determine two or more main ideas of a text and explain how they are supported by key details; summarize the text	R2 pp. 12–17
RI.3	Explain the relationships or interactions between two or more individuals, events, ideas, or concepts in a text, based on specific information in the text	R3 pp. 18–23
RI.4	Determine the meaning of general academic and domain-specific words and phrases in a text	R4 pp. 24–29
RI.5	Compare and contrast the overall structure of events, ideas, concepts, or information in two or more texts	R5 pp. 30–35
RI.6	Analyze multiple accounts of the same event or topic, noting important similarities and differences in the point of view they represent	R6 pp. 36–41
RI.7	Draw on information from multiple sources, demonstrating the ability to locate an answer to a question quickly or solve a problem efficiently	R7 pp. 42–47
RI.8	Explain how an author uses reasons and evidence to support particular points in a text	R8 pp. 48–53
RI.9	Integrate information from several texts on the same topic in order to write or speak about the subject	R9 pp. 54–59
RI.10	Read and comprehend appropriately complex informational texts independently and proficiently	R10 pp. 60–65
Reading Foundational Skills		
RF.3	Phonics: Know and apply grade-level phonics and word analysis skills in decoding words	RF3 pp. 214–219
RF.4	Fluency: Read grade-level texts with sufficient accuracy and fluency to support comprehension	RF4 pp. 220–225

(Continued)

Iowa Strand/Standard	Focus of Iowa Standard	For More Information
Writing		
W.1	Write opinion pieces on topics or texts, supporting a point of view with reasons and information	W1 pp. 70–75
W.2	Write informative/explanatory texts to examine a topic and convey ideas and information clearly	W2 pp. 76–81
W.3	Write narratives to develop real or imagined experiences or events using effective technique, descriptive details, and clear event sequences	W3 pp. 82–87
W.4	Produce writing in which the development and organization are appropriate to the task, purpose, and audience	W4 pp. 88–93
W.5	Develop and strengthen writing as needed by planning, revising, editing, rewriting, or trying a new approach	W5 pp. 94–99
W.6	Use technology to produce and publish writing; demonstrate keyboarding skills	W6 pp. 100–105
W.7	Conduct short research projects that use several sources to build knowledge through investigation of different aspects of a topic	W7 pp. 106–111
W.8	Recall information from experiences or gather information from print and digital sources	W8 pp. 112–117
W.9	Draw evidence from literary or informational texts to support analysis, reflection, and research	W9 pp. 118–123
W.10	Write routinely over shorter and extended time frames	W10 pp. 124–129
Speaking and Listening		
SL.1	Engage effectively in a range of collaborative discussions with diverse partners, building on others' ideas and expressing their own clearly	SL1 pp. 134–139
SL.2	Summarize a written text read aloud or information presented in diverse media and formats	SL2 pp. 140–145
SL.3	Summarize points a speaker makes and explain how each claim is supported by reasons and evidence	SL3 pp. 146–151
SL.4	Report on a topic or text or present an opinion, using appropriate facts and details to support main ideas and themes	SL4 pp. 152–157
SL.5	Include multimedia components and visual displays in presentations when appropriate to enhance the development of main ideas or themes	SL5 pp. 158–163
SL.6	Adapt speech to a variety of contexts, using formal English when appropriate to task and situation	SL6 pp. 164–169
Language		
L.1	Demonstrate command of the conventions of standard English grammar and usage when writing or speaking	L1 pp. 174–179
L.2	Demonstrate command of the conventions of standard English capitalization, punctuation, and spelling when writing	L2 pp. 180–185
L.3	Use knowledge of language and its conventions when writing, speaking, reading, or listening	L3 pp. 186–191
L.4	Determine or clarify the meaning of unknown and multiple-meaning words and phrases, choosing flexibly from an array of strategies	L4 pp. 192–197
L.5	Demonstrate understanding of figurative language, word relationships, and nuances in word meanings	L5 pp. 198–203
L.6	Acquire and use accurately general academic and domain-specific words and phrases	L6 pp. 204–209

Kansas, Grade 3

Kansas Strand/Standard	Focus of Kansas Standard	For More Information
Reading Literature		
RL.1	Ask and answer questions to demonstrate understanding of a text, referring explicitly to the text as the basis for the answers	R1 pp. 6–11
RL.2	Recount stories from diverse cultures, determine their central message, lesson, or moral, and explain how it is conveyed	R2 pp. 12–17
RL.3	Describe characters in a story and explain how their actions contribute to the sequence of events	R3 pp. 18–23
RL.4	Determine the meaning of words and phrases as they are used in a text, distinguishing literal from nonliteral language	R4 pp. 24–29
RL.5	Refer to parts of stories, dramas, and poems when writing or speaking about a text, using terms such as chapter, scene, and stanza; describe how each successive part builds on earlier sections	R5 pp. 30–35
RL.6	Distinguish their own point of view from that of the narrator or those of the characters	R6 pp. 36–41
RL.7	Explain how specific elements of a text's illustrations contribute to what is conveyed by the words in a story	R7 pp. 42–47
RL.8	NA	
RL.9	Compare and contrast the themes, settings, and plots of stories written by the same author about the same or similar characters	R9 pp. 54–59
RL.10	Read literature of appropriate complexity independently with proficiency	R10 pp. 60–65
Reading Informational Text		
RI.1	Ask and answer questions to demonstrate understanding of a text, referring explicitly to the text as the basis for the answers	R1 pp. 6–11
RI.2	Determine the main idea of a text; recount the key details and explain how they support the main idea	R2 pp. 12–17
RI.3	Describe the relationship between a series of historical events, scientific ideas or concepts, or steps in technical procedures in a text	R3 pp. 18–23
RI.4	Determine the meaning of general academic and domain-specific words and phrases in a text	R4 pp. 24–29
RI.5	Use text features and search tools to locate information on a topic efficiently	R5 pp. 30–35
RI.6	Distinguish own point of view from that of the author of a text	R6 pp. 36–41
RI.7	Use information from illustrations and the words in a text to demonstrate understanding of the text	R7 pp. 42–47
RI.8	Describe the logical connection between particular sentences and paragraphs in a text	R8 pp. 48–53
RI.9	Compare and contrast the most important points and key details presented by two texts on the same topic	R9 pp. 54–59
RI.10	Read and comprehend appropriately complex informational texts independently and proficiently	R10 pp. 60–65
Reading Foundational Skills		
RF.3	Phonics: Know and apply grade-level phonics and word analysis skills in decoding words	RF3 pp. 214–219
RF.4	Fluency: Read grade-level texts with sufficient accuracy and fluency to support comprehension	RF4 pp. 220–225
Writing		
W.1	Write opinion pieces on topics or texts, supporting a point of view with reasons	W1 pp. 70–75
W.2	Write informative/explanatory texts to examine a topic and convey ideas and information clearly	W2 pp. 76–81
W.3	Write narratives to develop real or imagined experiences or events using effective technique, descriptive details, and clear event sequences	W3 pp. 82–87
W.4	Produce writing in which the development and organization are appropriate to the task and purpose	W4 pp. 88–93
W.5	Develop and strengthen writing as needed by planning, revising, and editing	W5 pp. 94–99
W.6	Use technology to produce and publish writing	W6 pp. 100–105
W.7	Conduct short research projects that build knowledge about a topic	W7 pp. 106–111
W.8	Recall information from experiences or gather information from print and digital sources	W8 pp. 112–117

(Continued)

Kansas Strand/Standard	Focus of Kansas Standard	For More Information
Writing		
W.9	NA	
W.10	Write routinely over shorter and extended time frames	W10 pp. 124–129
Speaking and Listening		
SL.1	Engage effectively in a range of collaborative discussions with diverse partners, building on others' ideas and expressing their own clearly	SL1 pp. 134–139
SL.2	Determine the main ideas and supporting details of a text read aloud or information presented in diverse media and formats	SL2 pp. 140–145
SL.3	Ask and answer questions about information from a speaker, offering appropriate elaboration and detail	SL3 pp. 146–151
SL.4	Report on a topic or text, tell a story, or recount an experience with appropriate facts and relevant details	SL4 pp. 152–157
SL.5	Create audio recordings of stories or poems, demonstrating fluent reading; add visual displays when appropriate	SL5 pp. 158–163
SL.6	Speak in complete sentences when appropriate to task and situation in order to provide requested detail or clarification	SL6 pp. 164–169
Language		
L.1	Demonstrate command of the conventions of standard English grammar and usage when writing or speaking	L1 pp. 174–179
L.2	Demonstrate command of the conventions of standard English capitalization, punctuation, and spelling when writing	L2 pp. 180–185
L.3	Use knowledge of language and its conventions when writing, speaking, reading, or listening	L3 pp. 186–191
L.4	Determine or clarify the meaning of unknown and multiple-meaning words and phrases, choosing flexibly from an array of strategies	L4 pp. 192–197
L.5	Demonstrate understanding of word relationships and nuances in word meanings	L5 pp. 198–203
L.6	Acquire and use accurately conversational, general academic, and domain-specific words and phrases	L6 pp. 204–209

Kansas, Grade 4

Kansas Strand/Standard	Focus of Kansas Standard	For More Information
Reading Literature		
RL.1	Refer to details and examples in a text when explaining what the text says explicitly and when drawing inferences	R1 pp. 6–11
RL.2	Determine a theme of a story, drama, or poem from details in the text; summarize the text	R2 pp. 12–17
RL.3	Describe in depth a character, setting, or event in a story or drama, drawing on specific details in the text	R3 pp. 18–23
RL.4	Determine the meaning of words and phrases as they are used in a text	R4 pp. 24–29
RL.5	Explain the major differences between poems, drama, and prose; refer to structural elements when writing or speaking about a text	R5 pp. 30–35
RL.6	Compare and contrast the point of view from which different stories are narrated, including the difference between first- and third-person narratives	R6 pp. 36–41
RL.7	Make connections between the text of a story or drama and a visual or oral representation of the text	R7 pp. 42–47
RL.8	NA	
RL.9	Compare and contrast the treatment of similar themes and topics and patterns of events in stories and traditional literature from different cultures	R9 pp. 54–59
RL.10	Read literature of appropriate complexity independently with proficiency	R10 pp. 60–65

Kansas Strand/Standard	Focus of Kansas Standard	For More Information
Reading Informational Text		
RI.1	Refer to details and examples in a text when explaining what the text says explicitly and when drawing inferences from the text	R1 pp. 6–11
RI.2	Determine the main idea of a text and explain how it is supported by key details; summarize the text	R2 pp. 12–17
RI.3	Explain events, procedures, ideas, or concepts in a historical, scientific, or technical text	R3 pp. 18–23
RI.4	Determine the meaning of general academic and domain-specific words and phrases in a text	R4 pp. 24–29
RI.5	Describe the overall structure of events, ideas, concepts, or information in a text	R5 pp. 30–35
RI.6	Compare and contrast a firsthand and secondhand account of the same event or topic	R6 pp. 36–41
RI.7	Interpret information presented visually, orally, or quantitatively, and explain how it contributes to an understanding of the text	R7 pp. 42–47
RI.8	Explain how an author uses reasons and evidence to support particular points in a text	R8 pp. 48–53
RI.9	Integrate information from two texts on the same topic in order to write or speak about the subject	R9 pp. 54–59
RI.10	Read and comprehend appropriately complex informational texts independently and proficiently	R10 pp. 60–65
Reading Foundational Skills		
RF.3	Phonics: Know and apply grade-level phonics and word analysis skills in decoding words	RF3 pp. 214–219
RF.4	Fluency: Read grade-level texts with sufficient accuracy and fluency to support comprehension	RF4 pp. 220–225
Writing		
W.1	Write opinion pieces on topics or texts, supporting a point of view with reasons and information	W1 pp. 70–75
W.2	Write informative/explanatory texts to examine a topic and convey ideas and information clearly	W2 pp. 76–81
W.3	Write narratives to develop real or imagined experiences or events using effective technique, descriptive details, and clear event sequences	W3 pp. 82–87
W.4	Produce writing in which the development and organization are appropriate to the task, purpose, and audience	W4 pp. 88–93
W.5	Develop and strengthen writing as needed by planning, revising, and editing	W5 pp. 94–99
W.6	Use technology to produce and publish writing; demonstrate keyboarding skills	W6 pp. 100–105
W.7	Conduct short research projects that build knowledge through investigation of different aspects of a topic	W7 pp. 106–111
W.8	Recall information from experiences or gather information from print and digital sources	W8 pp. 112–117
W.9	Draw evidence from literary or informational texts to support analysis, reflection, and research	W9 pp. 118–123
W.10	Write routinely over shorter and extended time frames	W10 pp. 124–129
Speaking and Listening		
SL.1	Engage effectively in a range of collaborative discussions with diverse partners, building on others' ideas and expressing their own clearly	SL1 pp. 134–139
SL.2	Paraphrase portions of a text read aloud or information presented in diverse media and formats	SL2 pp. 140–145
SL.3	Identify the reasons and evidence a speaker provides to support particular points	SL3 pp. 146–151
SL.4	Report on a topic or text, tell a story, or recount an experience with appropriate facts and details to support main ideas or themes	SL4 pp. 152–157
SL.5	Add audio recordings and visual displays to presentations when appropriate to enhance the development of main ideas or themes	SL5 pp. 158–163
SL.6	Differentiate between contexts that call for formal English and situations where informal discourse is appropriate; use formal English when appropriate to task and situation	SL6 pp. 164–169
Language		
L.1	Demonstrate command of the conventions of standard English grammar and usage when writing or speaking	L1 pp. 174–179
L.2	Demonstrate command of the conventions of standard English capitalization, punctuation, and spelling when writing	L2 pp. 180–185
L.3	Use knowledge of language and its conventions when writing, speaking, reading, or listening	L3 pp. 186–191

(Continued)

Kansas Strand/Standard	Focus of Kansas Standard	For More Information
Language		
L.4	Determine or clarify the meaning of unknown and multiple-meaning words and phrases, choosing flexibly from an array of strategies	L4 pp. 192–197
L.5	Demonstrate understanding of figurative language, word relationships, and nuances in word meanings	L5 pp. 198–203
L.6	Acquire and use accurately general academic and domain-specific words and phrases	L6 pp. 204–209

Kansas, Grade 5

Kansas Strand/Standard	Focus of Kansas Standard	For More Information
Reading Literature		
RL.1	Quote accurately from a text when explaining what the text says explicitly and when drawing inferences from the text	R1 pp. 6–11
RL.2	Determine a theme of a story, drama, or poem from details in the text; summarize the text	R2 pp. 12–17
RL.3	Compare and contrast two or more characters, settings, or events in a story or drama, drawing on specific details in the text	R3 pp. 18–23
RL.4	Determine the meaning of words and phrases as they are used in a text, including figurative language	R4 pp. 24–29
RL.5	Explain how a series of chapters, scenes, or stanzas fits together to provide the overall structure of a story, drama, or poem	R5 pp. 30–35
RL.6	Describe how a narrator's or speaker's point of view influences how events are described	R6 pp. 36–41
RL.7	Analyze how visual and multimedia elements contribute to the meaning, tone, or beauty of a text	R7 pp. 42–47
RL.8	NA	
RL.9	Compare and contrast stories in the same genre on their approaches to similar themes and topics	R9 pp. 54–59
RL.10	Read literature of appropriate complexity independently with proficiency	R10 pp. 60–65
Reading Informational Text		
RI.1	Quote accurately from a text when explaining what the text says explicitly and when drawing inferences from the text	R1 pp. 6–11
RI.2	Determine two or more main ideas of a text and explain how they are supported by key details; summarize the text	R2 pp. 12–17
RI.3	Explain the relationships or interactions between two or more individuals, events, ideas, or concepts in a text, based on specific information in the text	R3 pp. 18–23
RI.4	Determine the meaning of general academic and domain-specific words and phrases in a text	R4 pp. 24–29
RI.5	Compare and contrast the overall structure of events, ideas, concepts, or information in two or more texts	R5 pp. 30–35
RI.6	Analyze multiple accounts of the same event or topic, noting important similarities and differences in the point of view they represent	R6 pp. 36–41
RI.7	Draw on information from multiple sources, demonstrating the ability to locate an answer to a question quickly or solve a problem efficiently	R7 pp. 42–47
RI.8	Explain how an author uses reasons and evidence to support particular points in a text	R8 pp. 48–53
RI.9	Integrate information from several texts on the same topic in order to write or speak about the subject	R9 pp. 54–59
RI.10	Read and comprehend appropriately complex informational texts independently and proficiently	R10 pp. 60–65

Kansas Strand/Standard	Focus of Kansas Standard	For More Information
Reading Foundational Skills		
RF.3	Phonics: Know and apply grade-level phonics and word analysis skills in decoding words	RF3 pp. 214–219
RF.4	Fluency: Read grade-level texts with sufficient accuracy and fluency to support comprehension	RF4 pp. 220–225
Writing		
W.1	Write opinion pieces on topics or texts, supporting a point of view with reasons and information	W1 pp. 70–75
W.2	Write informative/explanatory texts to examine a topic and convey ideas and information clearly	W2 pp. 76–81
W.3	Write narratives to develop real or imagined experiences or events using effective technique, descriptive details, and clear event sequences	W3 pp. 82–87
W.4	Produce writing in which the development and organization are appropriate to the task, purpose, and audience	W4 pp. 88–93
W.5	Develop and strengthen writing as needed by planning, revising, editing, rewriting, or trying a new approach	W5 pp. 94–99
W.6	Use technology to produce and publish writing; demonstrate keyboarding skills	W6 pp. 100–105
W.7	Conduct short research projects that use several sources to build knowledge through investigation of different aspects of a topic	W7 pp. 106–111
W.8	Recall information from experiences or gather information from print and digital sources	W8 pp. 112–117
W.9	Draw evidence from literary or informational texts to support analysis, reflection, and research	W9 pp. 118–123
W.10	Write routinely over shorter and extended time frames	W10 pp. 124–129
Speaking and Listening		
SL.1	Engage effectively in a range of collaborative discussions with diverse partners, building on others' ideas and expressing their own clearly	SL1 pp. 134–139
SL.2	Summarize a written text read aloud or information presented in diverse media and formats	SL2 pp. 140–145
SL.3	Summarize points a speaker makes and explain how each claim is supported by reasons and evidence	SL3 pp. 146–151
SL.4	Report on a topic or text or present an opinion, using appropriate facts and details to support main ideas and themes	SL4 pp. 152–157
SL.5	Include multimedia components and visual displays in presentations when appropriate to enhance the development of main ideas or themes	SL5 pp. 158–163
SL.6	Adapt speech to a variety of contexts, using formal English when appropriate to task and situation	SL6 pp. 164–169
Language		
L.1	Demonstrate command of the conventions of standard English grammar and usage when writing or speaking	L1 pp. 174–179
L.2	Demonstrate command of the conventions of standard English capitalization, punctuation, and spelling when writing	L2 pp. 180–185
L.3	Use knowledge of language and its conventions when writing, speaking, reading, or listening	L3 pp. 186–191
L.4	Determine or clarify the meaning of unknown and multiple-meaning words and phrases, choosing flexibly from an array of strategies	L4 pp. 192–197
L.5	Demonstrate understanding of figurative language, word relationships, and nuances in word meanings	L5 pp. 198–203
L.6	Acquire and use accurately general academic and domain-specific words and phrases	L6 pp. 204–209

Louisiana, Grade 3

Louisiana Strand/Standard	Focus of Louisiana Standard	For More Information
Reading Literature		
RL.1	Ask and answer questions to demonstrate understanding of a text, referring explicitly to the text as the basis for the answers	R1 pp. 6–11
RL.2	Recount stories from diverse cultures, determine their central message, lesson, or moral, and explain how it is conveyed	R2 pp. 12–17
RL.3	Describe characters in a story and explain how their actions contribute to the sequence of events	R3 pp. 18–23
RL.4	Determine the meaning of words and phrases as they are used in a text, distinguishing literal from nonliteral language	R4 pp. 24–29
RL.5	Refer to parts of stories, dramas, and poems when writing or speaking about a text, using terms such as chapter, scene, and stanza; describe how each successive part builds on earlier sections	R5 pp. 30–35
RL.6	Distinguish the student's point of view from that of the narrator or those of the characters	R6 pp. 36–41
RL.7	Explain how specific aspects of a text's illustrations contribute to what is conveyed by the words in a story	R7 pp. 42–47
RL.8	NA	
RL.9	Compare and contrast the themes, settings, and plots of stories written by the same author about the same or similar characters	R9 pp. 54–59
RL.10	Read literature of appropriate complexity independently with proficiency	R10 pp. 60–65
Reading Informational Text		
RI.1	Ask and answer questions to demonstrate understanding of a text, referring explicitly to the text as the basis for the answers	R1 pp. 6–11
RI.2	Determine the main idea of a text; recount the key details and explain how they support the main idea	R2 pp. 12–17
RI.3	Describe the relationship between a series of historical events, scientific ideas or concepts, or steps in technical procedures in a text	R3 pp. 18–23
RI.4	Determine the meaning of general academic and domain-specific words and phrases in a text	R4 pp. 24–29
RI.5	Use text features and search tools to locate information on a topic efficiently	R5 pp. 30–35
RI.6	Distinguish the student's point of view from that of the author of a text	R6 pp. 36–41
RI.7	Use information from illustrations and the words in a text to demonstrate understanding of the text	R7 pp. 42–47
RI.8	Describe the logical connection between particular sentences and paragraphs in a text	R8 pp. 48–53
RI.9	Compare and contrast the most important points and key details presented by two texts on the same topic	R9 pp. 54–59
RI.10	Read and comprehend appropriately complex informational texts independently and proficiently	R10 pp. 60–65
Reading Foundational Skills		
RF.3	Phonics: Know and apply grade-level phonics and word analysis skills in decoding words	RF3 pp. 214–219
RF.4	Fluency: Read grade-level texts with sufficient accuracy and fluency to support comprehension	RF4 pp. 220–225
Writing		
W.1	Write opinion pieces on topics or texts, supporting a point of view with reasons	W1 pp. 70–75
W.2	Write informative/explanatory texts to examine a topic and convey ideas and information clearly	W2 pp. 76–81
W.3	Write narratives to develop real or imagined experiences or events using effective technique, descriptive details, and clear event sequences	W3 pp. 82–87
W.4	Produce writing in which the development and organization are appropriate to the task and purpose	W4 pp. 88–93
W.5	Develop and strengthen writing as needed by planning, revising, and editing	W5 pp. 94–99
W.6	Produce and publish writing, using technology	W6 pp. 100–105
W.7	Conduct short research projects that build knowledge about a topic	W7 pp. 106–111
W.8	Recall information from experiences or gather information from print and digital sources	W8 pp. 112–117

Louisiana Strand/Standard	Focus of Louisiana Standard	For More Information
Writing		
W.9	NA	
W.10	Write routinely over shorter and extended time frames	W10 pp. 124–129
Speaking and Listening		
SL.1	Engage effectively in a range of collaborative discussions with diverse partners, building on others' ideas and expressing their own clearly	SL1 pp. 134–139
SL.2	Determine the main ideas and supporting details of a text read aloud or information presented in diverse media and formats	SL2 pp. 140–145
SL.3	Ask and answer questions about information from a speaker, offering appropriate elaboration and detail	SL3 pp. 146–151
SL.4	Report on a topic or text, tell a story, or recount an experience with appropriate facts and relevant details	SL4 pp. 152–157
SL.5	Create audio recordings of stories or poems, demonstrating fluent reading; add visual displays when appropriate	SL5 pp. 158–163
SL.6	Speak in complete sentences when appropriate to task, audience, and situation in order to provide requested detail or clarification	SL6 pp. 164–169
Language		
L.1	Demonstrate command of the conventions of standard English grammar and usage when writing or speaking	L1 pp. 174–179
L.2	Demonstrate command of the conventions of standard English capitalization, punctuation, and spelling when writing	L2 pp. 180–185
L.3	Use knowledge of language and its conventions when writing, speaking, reading, or listening	L3 pp. 186–191
L.4	Determine or clarify the meaning of unknown and multiple-meaning words and phrases, choosing flexibly from an array of strategies	L4 pp. 192–197
L.5	Demonstrate understanding of word relationships and nuances in word meanings	L5 pp. 198–203
L.6	Acquire and use accurately conversational, general academic, and domain-specific words and phrases	L6 pp. 204–209

Louisiana, Grade 4

Louisiana Strand/Standard	Focus of Louisiana Standard	For More Information
Reading Literature		
RL.1	Refer to details and examples in a text when explaining what the text says explicitly and when drawing inferences	R1 pp. 6–11
RL.2	Determine a theme of a story, drama, or poem from details in the text; summarize the text	R2 pp. 12–17
RL.3	Describe in depth a character, setting, or event in a story or drama, drawing on specific details in the text	R3 pp. 18–23
RL.4	Determine the meaning of words and phrases as they are used in a text	R4 pp. 24–29
RL.5	Explain the major differences between poems, drama, and prose; refer to structural elements when writing or speaking about a text	R5 pp. 30–35
RL.6	Compare and contrast the point of view from which different stories are narrated, including the difference between first- and third-person narratives	R6 pp. 36–41
RL.7	Make connections between the text of a story or drama and a visual or oral representation of the text	R7 pp. 42–47
RL.8	NA	
RL.9	Compare and contrast the treatment of similar themes and topics and patterns of events in stories and traditional literature from different cultures	R9 pp. 54–59
RL.10	Read literature of appropriate complexity independently with proficiency	R10 pp. 60–65

(Continued)

Louisiana Strand/Standard	Focus of Louisiana Standard	For More Information
Reading Informational Text		
RI.1	Refer to details and examples in a text when explaining what the text says explicitly and when drawing inferences from the text	R1 pp. 6–11
RI.2	Determine the main idea of a text and explain how it is supported by key details; summarize the text	R2 pp. 12–17
RI.3	Explain events, procedures, ideas, or concepts in a historical, scientific, or technical text	R3 pp. 18–23
RI.4	Determine the meaning of general academic and domain-specific words and phrases in a text	R4 pp. 24–29
RI.5	Describe the overall structure of events, ideas, concepts, or information in a text	R5 pp. 30–35
RI.6	Compare and contrast a firsthand and secondhand account of the same event or topic	R6 pp. 36–41
RI.7	Interpret information presented visually, orally, or quantitatively, and explain how it contributes to an understanding of the text	R7 pp. 42–47
RI.8	Explain how an author uses reasons and evidence to support particular points in a text	R8 pp. 48–53
RI.9	Integrate information from two texts on the same topic in order to write or speak about the subject	R9 pp. 54–59
RI.10	Read and comprehend appropriately complex informational texts independently and proficiently	R10 pp. 60–65
Reading Foundational Skills		
RF.3	Phonics: Know and apply grade-level phonics and word analysis skills in decoding words	RF3 pp. 214–219
RF.4	Fluency: Read grade-level texts with sufficient accuracy and fluency to support comprehension	RF4 pp. 220–225
Writing		
W.1	Write opinion pieces on topics or texts, supporting a point of view with reasons and information	W1 pp. 70–75
W.2	Write informative/explanatory texts to examine a topic and convey ideas and information clearly	W2 pp. 76–81
W.3	Write narratives to develop real or imagined experiences or events using effective technique, descriptive details, and clear event sequences	W3 pp. 82–87
W.4	Produce writing in which the development and organization are appropriate to the task, purpose, and audience	W4 pp. 88–93
W.5	Develop and strengthen writing as needed by planning, revising, and editing	W5 pp. 94–99
W.6	Produce and publish writing, using technology	W6 pp. 100–105
W.7	Conduct short research projects that build knowledge through investigation of different aspects of a topic	W7 pp. 106–111
W.8	Recall information from experiences or gather information from print and digital sources	W8 pp. 112–117
W.9	Draw evidence from literary or informational texts to support analysis, reflection, and research	W9 pp. 118–123
W.10	Write routinely over shorter and extended time frames	W10 pp. 124–129
Speaking and Listening		
SL.1	Engage effectively in a range of collaborative discussions with diverse partners, building on others' ideas and expressing their own clearly	SL1 pp. 134–139
SL.2	Paraphrase portions of a text read aloud or information presented in diverse media and formats	SL2 pp. 140–145
SL.3	Identify the reasons and evidence a speaker provides to support particular points	SL3 pp. 146–151
SL.4	Report on a topic or text, tell a story, or recount an experience with appropriate facts and details to support main ideas or themes	SL4 pp. 152–157
SL.5	Add audio recordings and visual displays to presentations when appropriate to enhance the development of main ideas or themes	SL5 pp. 158–163
SL.6	Differentiate between contexts that call for formal English and situations where informal discourse is appropriate; use formal English when appropriate to task, audience, and situation	SL6 pp. 164–169
Language		
L.1	Demonstrate command of the conventions of standard English grammar and usage when writing or speaking	L1 pp. 174–179
L.2	Demonstrate command of the conventions of standard English capitalization, punctuation, and spelling when writing	L2 pp. 180–185
L.3	Use knowledge of language and its conventions when writing, speaking, reading, or listening	L3 pp. 186–191

Louisiana Strand/Standard	Focus of Louisiana Standard	For More Information
Language		
L.4	Determine or clarify the meaning of unknown and multiple-meaning words and phrases, choosing flexibly from an array of strategies	L4 pp. 192–197
L.5	Demonstrate understanding of figurative language, word relationships, and nuances in word meanings	L5 pp. 198–203
L.6	Acquire and use accurately general academic and domain-specific words and phrases	L6 pp. 204–209

Louisiana, Grade 5

Louisiana Strand/Standard	Focus of Louisiana Standard	For More Information
Reading Literature		
RL.1	Quote accurately from a text when explaining what the text says explicitly and when drawing inferences from the text	R1 pp. 6–11
RL.2	Determine a theme of a story, drama, or poem from details in the text; summarize the text	R2 pp. 12–17
RL.3	Compare and contrast two or more characters, settings, or events in a story or drama, drawing on specific details in the text	R3 pp. 18–23
RL.4	Determine the meaning of words and phrases as they are used in a text, including figurative language	R4 pp. 24–29
RL.5	Explain how a series of chapters, scenes, or stanzas fits together to provide the overall structure of a story, drama, or poem	R5 pp. 30–35
RL.6	Describe how a narrator's or speaker's point of view influences how events are described	R6 pp. 36–41
RL.7	Analyze how visual and multimedia elements contribute to the meaning, tone, or beauty of a text	R7 pp. 42–47
RL.8	NA	
RL.9	Compare and contrast stories in the same genre on their approaches to similar themes and topics	R9 pp. 54–59
RL.10	Read literature of appropriate complexity independently with proficiency	R10 pp. 60–65
Reading Informational Text		
RI.1	Quote accurately from a text when explaining what the text says explicitly and when drawing inferences from the text	R1 pp. 6–11
RI.2	Determine two or more main ideas of a text and explain how they are supported by key details; summarize the text	R2 pp. 12–17
RI.3	Explain the relationships or interactions between two or more individuals, events, ideas, or concepts in a text, based on specific information in the text	R3 pp. 18–23
RI.4	Determine the meaning of general academic and domain-specific words and phrases in a text	R4 pp. 24–29
RI.5	Compare and contrast the overall structure of events, ideas, concepts, or information in two or more texts	R5 pp. 30–35
RI.6	Analyze multiple accounts of the same event or topic, noting important similarities and differences in the point of view they represent	R6 pp. 36–41
RI.7	Utilize information from multiple sources, demonstrating the ability to locate an answer to a question quickly or solve a problem efficiently	R7 pp. 42–47
RI.8	Explain how an author uses reasons and evidence to support particular points in a text	R8 pp. 48–53
RI.9	Integrate information from several texts on the same topic in order to write or speak about the subject	R9 pp. 54–59
RI.10	Read and comprehend appropriately complex informational texts independently and proficiently	R10 pp. 60–65

(Continued)

Louisiana Strand/Standard	Focus of Louisiana Standard	For More Information
Reading Foundational Skills		
RF.3	Phonics: Know and apply grade-level phonics and word analysis skills in decoding words	RF3 pp. 214–219
RF.4	Fluency: Read grade-level texts with sufficient accuracy and fluency to support comprehension	RF4 pp. 220–225
Writing		
W.1	Write opinion pieces on topics or texts, supporting a point of view with reasons and information	W1 pp. 70–75
W.2	Write informative/explanatory texts to examine a topic and convey ideas and information clearly	W2 pp. 76–81
W.3	Write narratives to develop real or imagined experiences or events using effective technique, descriptive details, and clear event sequences	W3 pp. 82–87
W.4	Produce writing in which the development and organization are appropriate to the task, purpose, and audience	W4 pp. 88–93
W.5	Develop and strengthen writing as needed by planning, revising, editing, rewriting, or trying a new approach	W5 pp. 94–99
W.6	Produce and publish writing, using technology	W6 pp. 100–105
W.7	Conduct short research projects that use several sources to build knowledge through investigation of different aspects of a topic	W7 pp. 106–111
W.8	Recall information from experiences or gather information from print and digital sources	W8 pp. 112–117
W.9	Draw evidence from literary or informational texts to support analysis, reflection, and research	W9 pp. 118–123
W.10	Write routinely over shorter and extended time frames	W10 pp. 124–129
Speaking and Listening		
SL.1	Engage effectively in a range of collaborative discussions with diverse partners, building on others' ideas and expressing their own clearly	SL1 pp. 134–139
SL.2	Summarize a written text read aloud or information presented in diverse media and formats	SL2 pp. 140–145
SL.3	Summarize points a speaker makes and explain how each claim is supported by reasons and evidence	SL3 pp. 146–151
SL.4	Report on a topic or text or present an opinion, using appropriate facts and details to support main ideas and themes	SL4 pp. 152–157
SL.5	Include multimedia components and visual displays in presentations when appropriate to enhance the development of main ideas or themes	SL5 pp. 158–163
SL.6	Adapt speech to a variety of contexts, using formal English when appropriate to task, audience, and situation	SL6 pp. 164–169
Language		
L.1	Demonstrate command of the conventions of standard English grammar and usage when writing or speaking	L1 pp. 174–179
L.2	Demonstrate command of the conventions of standard English capitalization, punctuation, and spelling when writing	L2 pp. 180–185
L.3	Use knowledge of language and its conventions when writing, speaking, reading, or listening	L3 pp. 186–191
L.4	Determine or clarify the meaning of unknown and multiple-meaning words and phrases, choosing flexibly from an array of strategies	L4 pp. 192–197
L.5	Demonstrate understanding of figurative language, word relationships, and nuances in word meanings	L5 pp. 198–203
L.6	Acquire and use accurately general academic and domain-specific words and phrases	L6 pp. 204–209

Maryland, Grade 3

Maryland Strand/Standard	Focus of Maryland Standard	For More Information
Reading Literature		
RL.1	Ask and answer questions to demonstrate understanding of a text, referring explicitly to the text as the basis for the answers	R1 pp. 6–11
RL.2	Recount stories from diverse cultures, determine their central message, lesson, or moral, and explain how it is conveyed	R2 pp. 12–17
RL.3	Describe characters in a story and explain how their actions contribute to the sequence of events	R3 pp. 18–23
RL.4	Determine the meaning of words and phrases as they are used in a text, distinguishing literal from nonliteral language	R4 pp. 24–29
RL.5	Refer to parts of stories, dramas, and poems when writing or speaking about a text, using terms such as chapter, scene, and stanza; describe how each successive part builds on earlier sections	R5 pp. 30–35
RL.6	Distinguish their own point of view from that of the narrator or those of the characters	R6 pp. 36–41
RL.7	Explain how specific elements of a text's illustrations contribute to what is conveyed by the words in a story	R7 pp. 42–47
RL.8	NA	
RL.9	Compare and contrast the themes, settings, and plots of stories written by the same author about the same or similar characters	R9 pp. 54–59
RL.10	Read literature of appropriate complexity independently with proficiency	R10 pp. 60–65
Reading Informational Text		
RI.1	Ask and answer questions to demonstrate understanding of a text, referring explicitly to the text as the basis for the answers	R1 pp. 6–11
RI.2	Determine the main idea of a text; recount the key details and explain how they support the main idea	R2 pp. 12–17
RI.3	Describe the relationship between a series of historical events, scientific ideas or concepts, or steps in technical procedures in a text	R3 pp. 18–23
RI.4	Determine the meaning of general academic and domain-specific words and phrases in a text	R4 pp. 24–29
RI.5	Use text features and search tools to locate information on a topic efficiently	R5 pp. 30–35
RI.6	Distinguish own point of view from that of the author of a text	R6 pp. 36–41
RI.7	Use information from illustrations and the words in a text to demonstrate understanding of the text	R7 pp. 42–47
RI.8	Describe the logical connection between particular sentences and paragraphs in a text	R8 pp. 48–53
RI.9	Compare and contrast the most important points and key details presented by two texts on the same topic	R9 pp. 54–59
RI.10	Read and comprehend appropriately complex informational texts independently and proficiently	R10 pp. 60–65
Reading Foundational Skills		
RF.3	Phonics: Know and apply grade-level phonics and word analysis skills in decoding words	RF3 pp. 214–219
RF.4	Fluency: Read grade-level texts with sufficient accuracy and fluency to support comprehension	RF4 pp. 220–225
Writing		
W.1	Write opinion pieces on topics or texts, supporting a point of view with reasons	W1 pp. 70–75
W.2	Write informative/explanatory texts to examine a topic and convey ideas and information clearly	W2 pp. 76–81
W.3	Write narratives to develop real or imagined experiences or events using effective technique, descriptive details, and clear event sequences	W3 pp. 82–87
W.4	Produce writing in which the development and organization are appropriate to the task and purpose	W4 pp. 88–93
W.5	Develop and strengthen writing as needed by planning, revising, and editing	W5 pp. 94–99
W.6	Use technology to produce and publish writing	W6 pp. 100–105
W.7	Conduct short research projects that build knowledge about a topic	W7 pp. 106–111

(Continued)

Maryland Strand/Standard	Focus of Maryland Standard	For More Information
Writing		
W.8	Recall information from experiences or gather information from print and digital sources	W8 pp. 112–117
W.9	NA	
W.10	Write routinely over shorter and extended time frames	W10 pp. 124–129
Speaking and Listening		
SL.1	Engage effectively in a range of collaborative discussions with diverse partners, building on others' ideas and expressing their own clearly	SL1 pp. 134–139
SL.2	Determine the main ideas and supporting details of a text read aloud or information presented in diverse media and formats	SL2 pp. 140–145
SL.3	Ask and answer questions about information from a speaker, offering appropriate elaboration and detail	SL3 pp. 146–151
SL.4	Report on a topic or text, tell a story, or recount an experience with appropriate facts and relevant details	SL4 pp. 152–157
SL.5	Create audio recordings of stories or poems, demonstrating fluent reading; add visual displays when appropriate	SL5 pp. 158–163
SL.6	Speak in complete sentences when appropriate to task and situation in order to provide requested detail or clarification	SL6 pp. 164–169
Language		
L.1	Demonstrate command of the conventions of standard English grammar and usage when writing or speaking	L1 pp. 174–179
L.2	Demonstrate command of the conventions of standard English capitalization, punctuation, and spelling when writing	L2 pp. 180–185
L.3	Use knowledge of language and its conventions when writing, speaking, reading, or listening	L3 pp. 186–191
L.4	Determine or clarify the meaning of unknown and multiple-meaning words and phrases, choosing flexibly from an array of strategies	L4 pp. 192–197
L.5	Demonstrate understanding of word relationships and nuances in word meanings	L5 pp. 198–203
L.6	Acquire and use accurately conversational, general academic, and domain-specific words and phrases	L6 pp. 204–209

Maryland, Grade 4

Maryland Strand/Standard	Focus of Maryland Standard	For More Information
Reading Literature		
RL.1	Refer to details and examples in a text when explaining what the text says explicitly and when drawing inferences	R1 pp. 6–11
RL.2	Determine a theme of a story, drama, or poem from details in the text; summarize the text	R2 pp. 12–17
RL.3	Describe in depth a character, setting, or event in a story or drama, drawing on specific details in the text	R3 pp. 18–23
RL.4	Determine the meaning of words and phrases as they are used in a text	R4 pp. 24–29
RL.5	Explain the major differences between poems, drama, and prose; refer to structural elements when writing or speaking about a text	R5 pp. 30–35
RL.6	Compare and contrast the point of view from which different stories are narrated, including the difference between first- and third-person narratives	R6 pp. 36–41
RL.7	Make connections between the text of a story or drama and a visual or oral representation of the text	R7 pp. 42–47
RL.8	NA	
RL.9	Compare and contrast the treatment of similar themes and topics and patterns of events in stories and traditional literature from different cultures	R9 pp. 54–59
RL.10	Read literature of appropriate complexity independently with proficiency	R10 pp. 60–65

Maryland Strand/Standard	Focus of Maryland Standard	For More Information
Reading Informational Text		
RI.1	Refer to details and examples in a text when explaining what the text says explicitly and when drawing inferences from the text	R1 pp. 6–11
RI.2	Determine the main idea of a text and explain how it is supported by key details; summarize the text	R2 pp. 12–17
RI.3	Explain events, procedures, ideas, or concepts in a historical, scientific, or technical text	R3 pp. 18–23
RI.4	Determine the meaning of general academic and domain-specific words and phrases in a text	R4 pp. 24–29
RI.5	Describe the overall structure of events, ideas, concepts, or information in a text	R5 pp. 30–35
RI.6	Compare and contrast a firsthand and secondhand account of the same event or topic	R6 pp. 36–41
RI.7	Interpret information presented visually, orally, or quantitatively, and explain how it contributes to an understanding of the text	R7 pp. 42–47
RI.8	Explain how an author uses reasons and evidence to support particular points in a text	R8 pp. 48–53
RI.9	Integrate information from two texts on the same topic in order to write or speak about the subject	R9 pp. 54–59
RI.10	Read and comprehend appropriately complex informational texts independently and proficiently	R10 pp. 60–65
Reading Foundational Skills		
RF.3	Phonics: Know and apply grade-level phonics and word analysis skills in decoding words	RF3 pp. 214–219
RF.4	Fluency: Read grade-level texts with sufficient accuracy and fluency to support comprehension	RF4 pp. 220–225
Writing		
W.1	Write opinion pieces on topics or texts, supporting a point of view with reasons and information	W1 pp. 70–75
W.2	Write informative/explanatory texts to examine a topic and convey ideas and information clearly	W2 pp. 76–81
W.3	Write narratives to develop real or imagined experiences or events using effective technique, descriptive details, and clear event sequences	W3 pp. 82–87
W.4	Produce writing in which the development and organization are appropriate to the task, purpose, and audience	W4 pp. 88–93
W.5	Develop and strengthen writing as needed by planning, revising, and editing	W5 pp. 94–99
W.6	Use technology to produce and publish writing; demonstrate keyboarding skills	W6 pp. 100–105
W.7	Conduct short research projects that build knowledge through investigation of different aspects of a topic	W7 pp. 106–111
W.8	Recall information from experiences or gather information from print and digital sources	W8 pp. 112–117
W.9	Draw evidence from literary or informational texts to support analysis, reflection, and research	W9 pp. 118–123
W.10	Write routinely over shorter and extended time frames	W10 pp. 124–129
Speaking and Listening		
SL.1	Engage effectively in a range of collaborative discussions with diverse partners, building on others' ideas and expressing their own clearly	SL1 pp. 134–139
SL.2	Paraphrase portions of a text read aloud or information presented in diverse media and formats	SL2 pp. 140–145
SL.3	Identify the reasons and evidence a speaker provides to support particular points	SL3 pp. 146–151
SL.4	Report on a topic or text, tell a story, or recount an experience with appropriate facts and details to support main ideas or themes	SL4 pp. 152–157
SL.5	Add audio recordings and visual displays to presentations when appropriate to enhance the development of main ideas or themes	SL5 pp. 158–163
SL.6	Differentiate between contexts that call for formal English and situations where informal discourse is appropriate; use formal English when appropriate to task and situation	SL6 pp. 164–169
Language		
L.1	Demonstrate command of the conventions of standard English grammar and usage when writing or speaking	L1 pp. 174–179
L.2	Demonstrate command of the conventions of standard English capitalization, punctuation, and spelling when writing	L2 pp. 180–185
L.3	Use knowledge of language and its conventions when writing, speaking, reading, or listening	L3 pp. 186–191

(Continued)

Maryland Strand/Standard	Focus of Maryland Standard	For More Information
Language		
L.4	Determine or clarify the meaning of unknown and multiple-meaning words and phrases, choosing flexibly from an array of strategies	L4 pp. 192–197
L.5	Demonstrate understanding of figurative language, word relationships, and nuances in word meanings	L5 pp. 198–203
L.6	Acquire and use accurately general academic and domain-specific words and phrases	L6 pp. 204–209

Maryland, Grade 5

Maryland Strand/Standard	Focus of Maryland Standard	For More Information
Reading Literature		
RL.1	Quote accurately from a text when explaining what the text says explicitly and when drawing inferences from the text	R1 pp. 6–11
RL.2	Determine a theme of a story, drama, or poem from details in the text; summarize the text	R2 pp. 12–17
RL.3	Compare and contrast two or more characters, settings, or events in a story or drama, drawing on specific details in the text	R3 pp. 18–23
RL.4	Determine the meaning of words and phrases as they are used in a text, including figurative language	R4 pp. 24–29
RL.5	Explain how a series of chapters, scenes, or stanzas fits together to provide the overall structure of a story, drama, or poem	R5 pp. 30–35
RL.6	Describe how a narrator's or speaker's point of view influences how events are described	R6 pp. 36–41
RL.7	Analyze how visual and multimedia elements contribute to the meaning, tone, or beauty of a text	R7 pp. 42–47
RL.8	NA	
RL.9	Compare and contrast stories in the same genre on their approaches to similar themes and topics	R9 pp. 54–59
RL.10	Read literature of appropriate complexity independently with proficiency	R10 pp. 60–65
Reading Informational Text		
RI.1	Quote accurately from a text when explaining what the text says explicitly and when drawing inferences from the text	R1 pp. 6–11
RI.2	Determine two or more main ideas of a text and explain how they are supported by key details; summarize the text	R2 pp. 12–17
RI.3	Explain the relationships or interactions between two or more individuals, events, ideas, or concepts in a text, based on specific information in the text	R3 pp. 18–23
RI.4	Determine the meaning of general academic and domain-specific words and phrases in a text	R4 pp. 24–29
RI.5	Compare and contrast the overall structure of events, ideas, concepts, or information in two or more texts	R5 pp. 30–35
RI.6	Analyze multiple accounts of the same event or topic, noting important similarities and differences in the point of view they represent	R6 pp. 36–41
RI.7	Draw on information from multiple sources, demonstrating the ability to locate an answer to a question quickly or solve a problem efficiently	R7 pp. 42–47
RI.8	Explain how an author uses reasons and evidence to support particular points in a text	R8 pp. 48–53
RI.9	Integrate information from several texts on the same topic in order to write or speak about the subject	R9 pp. 54–59
RI.10	Read and comprehend appropriately complex informational texts independently and proficiently	R10 pp. 60–65
Reading Foundational Skills		
RF.3	Phonics: Know and apply grade-level phonics and word analysis skills in decoding words	RF3 pp. 214–219
RF.4	Fluency: Read grade-level texts with sufficient accuracy and fluency to support comprehension	RF4 pp. 220–225

Maryland Strand/Standard	Focus of Maryland Standard	For More Information
Writing		
W.1	Write opinion pieces on topics or texts, supporting a point of view with reasons and information	W1 pp. 70–75
W.2	Write informative/explanatory texts to examine a topic and convey ideas and information clearly	W2 pp. 76–81
W.3	Write narratives to develop real or imagined experiences or events using effective technique, descriptive details, and clear event sequences	W3 pp. 82–87
W.4	Produce writing in which the development and organization are appropriate to the task, purpose, and audience	W4 pp. 88–93
W.5	Develop and strengthen writing as needed by planning, revising, editing, rewriting, or trying a new approach	W5 pp. 94–99
W.6	Use technology to produce and publish writing; demonstrate keyboarding skills	W6 pp. 100–105
W.7	Conduct short research projects that use several sources to build knowledge through investigation of different aspects of a topic	W7 pp. 106–111
W.8	Recall information from experiences or gather information from print and digital sources	W8 pp. 112–117
W.9	Draw evidence from literary or informational texts to support analysis, reflection, and research	W9 pp. 118–123
W.10	Write routinely over shorter and extended time frames	W10 pp. 124–129
Speaking and Listening		
SL.1	Engage effectively in a range of collaborative discussions with diverse partners, building on others' ideas and expressing their own clearly	SL1 pp. 134–139
SL.2	Summarize a written text read aloud or information presented in diverse media and formats	SL2 pp. 140–145
SL.3	Summarize points a speaker makes and explain how each claim is supported by reasons and evidence	SL3 pp. 146–151
SL.4	Report on a topic or text or present an opinion, using appropriate facts and details to support main ideas and themes	SL4 pp. 152–157
SL.5	Include multimedia components and visual displays in presentations when appropriate to enhance the development of main ideas or themes	SL5 pp. 158–163
SL.6	Adapt speech to a variety of contexts, using formal English when appropriate to task and situation	SL6 pp. 164–169
Language		
L.1	Demonstrate command of the conventions of standard English grammar and usage when writing or speaking	L1 pp. 174–179
L.2	Demonstrate command of the conventions of standard English capitalization, punctuation, and spelling when writing	L2 pp. 180–185
L.3	Use knowledge of language and its conventions when writing, speaking, reading, or listening	L3 pp. 186–191
L.4	Determine or clarify the meaning of unknown and multiple-meaning words and phrases, choosing flexibly from an array of strategies	L4 pp. 192–197
L.5	Demonstrate understanding of figurative language, word relationships, and nuances in word meanings	L5 pp. 198–203
L.6	Acquire and use accurately general academic and domain-specific words and phrases	L6 pp. 204–209

Minnesota, Grade 3

Minnesota Strand/Standard	Focus of Minnesota Standard	For More Information
Reading Literature		
1.1.1	Ask and answer questions to demonstrate understanding of a text, referring explicitly to the text as the basis for the answers	R1 pp. 6–11
1.2.2	Recount stories from diverse cultures, determine their central message, lesson, or moral, and explain how it is conveyed	R2 pp. 12–17
1.3.3	Describe characters in a story and explain how their actions contribute to the sequence of events	R3 pp. 18–23

(Continued)

Minnesota Strand/Standard	Focus of Minnesota Standard	For More Information
Reading Literature		
1.4.4	Determine the meaning of words and phrases as they are used in a text, distinguishing literal from nonliteral language	R4 pp. 24–29
1.5.5	Refer to parts of stories, dramas, and poems when writing or speaking about a text, using terms such as chapter, scene, and stanza; describe how each successive part builds on earlier sections	R5 pp. 30–35
1.6.6	Distinguish their own point of view from that of the narrator or those of the characters	R6 pp. 36–41
1.7.7	Explain how specific elements of a text's illustrations contribute to what is conveyed by the words in a story	R7 pp. 42–47
1.8.8	NA	
1.9.9	Compare and contrast the themes, settings, and plots of stories written by the same author about the same or similar characters	R9 pp. 54–59
1.10.10	Read literature of appropriate complexity independently with proficiency	R10 pp. 60–65
Reading Informational Text		
2.1.1	Ask and answer questions to demonstrate understanding of a text, referring explicitly to the text as the basis for the answers	R1 pp. 6–11
2.2.2	Determine the main idea of a text; recount the key details and explain how they support the main idea	R2 pp. 12–17
2.3.3	Describe the relationship between a series of historical events, scientific ideas or concepts, or steps in technical procedures in a text	R3 pp. 18–23
2.4.4	Determine the meaning of general academic and domain-specific words and phrases in a text	R4 pp. 24–29
2.5.5	Use text features and search tools to locate information on a topic efficiently	R5 pp. 30–35
2.6.6	Distinguish own point of view from that of the author of a text	R6 pp. 36–41
2.7.7	Use information from illustrations and the words in a text to demonstrate understanding of the text	R7 pp. 42–47
2.8.8	Describe the logical connection between particular sentences and paragraphs in a text	R8 pp. 48–53
2.9.9	Compare and contrast the most important points and key details presented by two texts on the same topic	R9 pp. 54–59
2.10.10	Read and comprehend appropriately complex informational texts independently and proficiently	R10 pp. 60–65
Reading Foundational Skills		
3.1.3	Phonics: Know and apply grade-level phonics and word analysis skills in decoding words	RF3 pp. 214–219
3.1.4	Fluency: Read grade-level texts with sufficient accuracy and fluency to support comprehension	RF4 pp. 220–225
Writing		
6.1.1	Write opinion pieces on topics or texts, supporting a point of view with reasons	W1 pp. 70–75
6.2.2	Write informative/explanatory texts to examine a topic and convey ideas and information clearly	W2 pp. 76–81
6.3.3	Write narratives to develop real or imagined experiences or events using effective technique, descriptive details, and clear event sequences	W3 pp. 82–87
6.4.4	Produce writing in which the development and organization are appropriate to the task and purpose	W4 pp. 88–93
6.5.5	Develop and strengthen writing as needed by planning, revising, and editing	W5 pp. 94–99
6.6.6	Use technology to produce and publish writing	W6 pp. 100–105
6.7.7	Conduct short research projects that build knowledge about a topic	W7 pp. 106–111
6.8.8	Recall information from experiences or gather information from print and digital sources	W8 pp. 112–117
6.9.9	NA	
6.10.10	Write routinely over shorter and extended time frames	W10 pp. 124–129
Speaking, Viewing, Listening, and Media Literacy		
8.1.1	Engage effectively in a range of collaborative discussions with diverse partners, building on others' ideas and expressing their own clearly	SL1 pp. 134–139
8.2.2	Determine the main ideas and supporting details of a text read aloud or information presented in diverse media and formats	SL2 pp. 140–145
8.3.3	Ask and answer questions about information from a speaker, offering appropriate elaboration and detail	SL3 pp. 146–151

Minnesota Strand/Standard	Focus of Minnesota Standard	For More Information
Speaking, Viewing, Listening, and Media Literacy		
8.4.4	Report on a topic or text, tell a story, or recount an experience with appropriate facts and relevant details	SL4 pp. 152–157
8.5.5	Create audio recordings of stories or poems, demonstrating fluent reading; add visual displays when appropriate	SL5 pp. 158–163
8.6.6	Speak in complete sentences when appropriate to task and situation in order to provide requested detail or clarification	SL6 pp. 164–169
8.7.7	Distinguish among, understand, and use different types of print, digital, and multimodal media	NA
8.8.8	Create a multimedia work for a specific purpose	NA
Language		
10.1.1	Demonstrate command of the conventions of standard English grammar and usage when writing or speaking	L1 pp. 174–179
10.2.2	Demonstrate command of the conventions of standard English capitalization, punctuation, and spelling when writing	L2 pp. 180–185
10.3.3	Use knowledge of language and its conventions when writing, speaking, reading, or listening	L3 pp. 186–191
10.4.4	Determine or clarify the meaning of unknown and multiple-meaning words and phrases, choosing flexibly from an array of strategies	L4 pp. 192–197
10.5.5	Demonstrate understanding of word relationships and nuances in word meanings	L5 pp. 198–203
10.6.6	Acquire and use accurately conversational, general academic, and domain-specific words and phrases	L6 pp. 204–209

Minnesota, Grade 4

Minnesota Strand/Standard	Focus of Minnesota Standard	For More Information
Reading Literature		
1.1.1	Refer to details and examples in a text when explaining what the text says explicitly and when drawing inferences	R1 pp. 6–11
1.2.2	Determine a theme of a story, drama, or poem from details in the text; summarize the text	R2 pp. 12–17
1.3.3	Describe in depth a character, setting, or event in a story or drama, drawing on specific details in the text	R3 pp. 18–23
1.4.4	Determine the meaning of words and phrases as they are used in a text	R4 pp. 24–29
1.5.5	Explain the major differences between poems, drama, and prose; refer to structural elements when writing or speaking about a text	R5 pp. 30–35
1.6.6	Compare and contrast the point of view from which different stories are narrated, including the difference between first- and third-person narratives	R6 pp. 36–41
1.7.7	Make connections between the text of a story or drama and a visual or oral representation of the text	R7 pp. 42–47
1.8.8	NA	
1.9.9	Compare and contrast the treatment of similar themes and topics and patterns of events in stories and traditional literature from different cultures	R9 pp. 54–59
1.10.10	Read literature of appropriate complexity independently with proficiency	R10 pp. 60–65
Reading Informational Text		
2.1.1	Refer to details and examples in a text when explaining what the text says explicitly and when drawing inferences from the text	R1 pp. 6–11
2.2.2	Determine the main idea of a text and explain how it is supported by key details; summarize the text	R2 pp. 12–17
2.3.3	Explain events, procedures, ideas, or concepts in a historical, scientific, or technical text	R3 pp. 18–23
2.4.4	Determine the meaning of general academic and domain-specific words and phrases in a text	R4 pp. 24–29

(Continued)

Minnesota Strand/Standard	Focus of Minnesota Standard	For More Information
Reading Informational Text		
2.5.5	Describe the overall structure of events, ideas, concepts, or information in a text	R5 pp. 30–35
2.6.6	Compare and contrast a firsthand and secondhand account of the same event or topic	R6 pp. 36–41
2.7.7	Interpret information presented visually, orally, or quantitatively, and explain how it contributes to an understanding of the text	R7 pp. 42–47
2.8.8	Explain how an author uses reasons and evidence to support particular points in a text	R8 pp. 48–53
2.9.9	Integrate information from two texts on the same topic in order to write or speak about the subject	R9 pp. 54–59
2.10.10	Read and comprehend appropriately complex informational texts independently and proficiently	R10 pp. 60–65
Reading Foundational Skills		
3.1.3	Phonics: Know and apply grade-level phonics and word analysis skills in decoding words	RF3 pp. 214–219
3.1.4	Fluency: Read grade-level texts with sufficient accuracy and fluency to support comprehension	RF4 pp. 220–225
Writing		
6.1.1	Write opinion pieces on topics or texts, supporting a point of view with reasons and information	W1 pp. 70–75
6.2.2	Write informative/explanatory texts to examine a topic and convey ideas and information clearly	W2 pp. 76–81
6.3.3	Write narratives to develop real or imagined experiences or events using effective technique, descriptive details, and clear event sequences	W3 pp. 82–87
6.4.4	Produce writing in which the development and organization are appropriate to the task, purpose, and audience	W4 pp. 88–93
6.5.5	Develop and strengthen writing as needed by planning, revising, and editing	W5 pp. 94–99
6.6.6	Use technology to produce and publish writing; demonstrate keyboarding skills	W6 pp. 100–105
6.7.7	Conduct short research projects that build knowledge through investigation of different aspects of a topic	W7 pp. 106–111
6.8.8	Recall information from experiences or gather information from print and digital sources	W8 pp. 112–117
6.9.9	Draw evidence from literary or informational texts to support analysis, reflection, and research	W9 pp. 118–123
6.10.10	Write routinely over shorter and extended time frames	W10 pp. 124–129
Speaking, Viewing, Listening, and Media Literacy		
8.1.1	Engage effectively in a range of collaborative discussions with diverse partners, building on others' ideas and expressing their own clearly	SL1 pp. 134–139
8.2.2	Paraphrase portions of a text read aloud or information presented in diverse media and formats	SL2 pp. 140–145
8.3.3	Identify the reasons and evidence a speaker provides to support particular points	SL3 pp. 146–151
8.4.4	Report on a topic or text, tell a story, or recount an experience with appropriate facts and details to support main ideas or themes	SL4 pp. 152–157
8.5.5	Add audio recordings and visual displays to presentations when appropriate to enhance the development of main ideas or themes	SL5 pp. 158–163
8.6.6	Differentiate between contexts that call for formal English and situations where informal discourse is appropriate; use formal English when appropriate to task and situation	SL6 pp. 164–169
8.7.7	Distinguish among, understand, and use different types of print, digital, and multimodal media	NA
8.8.8	Create a multimedia work for a specific purpose	NA
Language		
10.1.1	Demonstrate command of the conventions of standard English grammar and usage when writing or speaking	L1 pp. 174–179
10.2.2	Demonstrate command of the conventions of standard English capitalization, punctuation, and spelling when writing	L2 pp. 180–185
10.3.3	Use knowledge of language and its conventions when writing, speaking, reading, or listening	L3 pp. 186–191
10.4.4	Determine or clarify the meaning of unknown and multiple-meaning words and phrases, choosing flexibly from an array of strategies	L4 pp. 192–197
10.5.5	Demonstrate understanding of figurative language, word relationships, and nuances in word meanings	L5 pp. 198–203
10.6.6	Acquire and use accurately general academic and domain-specific words and phrases	L6 pp. 204–209

Minnesota, Grade 5

Minnesota Strand/Standard	Focus of Minnesota Standard	For More Information
Reading Literature		
1.1.1	Quote accurately from a text when explaining what the text says explicitly and when drawing inferences from the text	R1 pp. 6–11
1.2.2	Determine a theme of a story, drama, or poem from details in the text; summarize the text	R2 pp. 12–17
1.3.3	Compare and contrast two or more characters, settings, or events in a story or drama, drawing on specific details in the text	R3 pp. 18–23
1.4.4	Determine the meaning of words and phrases as they are used in a text, including figurative language	R4 pp. 24–29
1.5.5	Explain how a series of chapters, scenes, or stanzas fits together to provide the overall structure of a story, drama, or poem	R5 pp. 30–35
1.6.6	Describe how a narrator's or speaker's point of view influences how events are described	R6 pp. 36–41
1.7.7	Analyze how visual and multimedia elements contribute to the meaning, tone, or beauty of a text	R7 pp. 42–47
1.8.8	NA	
1.9.9	Compare and contrast stories in the same genre on their approaches to similar themes and topics	R9 pp. 54–59
1.10.10	Read literature of appropriate complexity independently with proficiency	R10 pp. 60–65
Reading Informational Text		
2.1.1	Quote accurately from a text when explaining what the text says explicitly and when drawing inferences from the text	R1 pp. 6–11
2.2.2	Determine two or more main ideas of a text and explain how they are supported by key details; summarize the text	R2 pp. 12–17
2.3.3	Explain the relationships or interactions between two or more individuals, events, ideas, or concepts in a text, based on specific information in the text	R3 pp. 18–23
2.4.4	Determine the meaning of general academic and domain-specific words and phrases in a text	R4 pp. 24–29
2.5.5	Compare and contrast the overall structure of events, ideas, concepts, or information in two or more texts	R5 pp. 30–35
2.6.6	Analyze multiple accounts of the same event or topic, noting important similarities and differences in the point of view they represent	R6 pp. 36–41
2.7.7	Draw on information from multiple sources, demonstrating the ability to locate an answer to a question quickly or solve a problem efficiently	R7 pp. 42–47
2.8.8	Explain how an author uses reasons and evidence to support particular points in a text	R8 pp. 48–53
2.9.9	Integrate information from several texts on the same topic in order to write or speak about the subject	R9 pp. 54–59
2.10.10	Read and comprehend appropriately complex informational texts independently and proficiently	R10 pp. 60–65
Reading Foundational Skills		
3.1.3	Phonics: Know and apply grade-level phonics and word analysis skills in decoding words	RF3 pp. 214–219
3.1.4	Fluency: Read grade-level texts with sufficient accuracy and fluency to support comprehension	RF4 pp. 220–225
Writing		
6.1.1	Write opinion pieces on topics or texts, supporting a point of view with reasons and information	W1 pp. 70–75
6.2.2	Write informative/explanatory texts to examine a topic and convey ideas and information clearly	W2 pp. 76–81
6.3.3	Write narratives to develop real or imagined experiences or events using effective technique, descriptive details, and clear event sequences	W3 pp. 82–87
6.4.4	Produce writing in which the development and organization are appropriate to the task, purpose, and audience	W4 pp. 88–93
6.5.5	Develop and strengthen writing as needed by planning, revising, editing, rewriting, or trying a new approach	W5 pp. 94–99
6.6.6	Use technology to produce and publish writing; demonstrate keyboarding skills	W6 pp. 100–105
6.7.7	Conduct short research projects that use several sources to build knowledge through investigation of different aspects of a topic	W7 pp. 106–111

(Continued)

Minnesota Strand/Standard	Focus of Minnesota Standard	For More Information
Writing		
6.8.8	Recall information from experiences or gather information from print and digital sources	W8 pp. 112–117
6.9.9	Draw evidence from literary or informational texts to support analysis, reflection, and research	W9 pp. 118–123
6.10.10	Write routinely over shorter and extended time frames	W10 pp. 124–129
Speaking, Viewing, Listening, and Media Literacy		
8.1.1	Engage effectively in a range of collaborative discussions with diverse partners, building on others' ideas and expressing their own clearly	SL1 pp. 134–139
8.2.2	Summarize a written text read aloud or information presented in diverse media and formats	SL2 pp. 140–145
8.3.3	Summarize points a speaker makes and explain how each claim is supported by reasons and evidence	SL3 pp. 146–151
8.4.4	Report on a topic or text or present an opinion, using appropriate facts and details to support main ideas and themes	SL4 pp. 152–157
8.5.5	Include multimedia components and visual displays in presentations when appropriate to enhance the development of main ideas or themes	SL5 pp. 158–163
8.6.6	Adapt speech to a variety of contexts, using formal English when appropriate to task and situation	SL6 pp. 164–169
8.7.7	Distinguish among, understand, and use different types of print, digital, and multimodal media	NA
8.8.8	Create a multimedia work for a specific purpose	NA
Language		
10.1.1	Demonstrate command of the conventions of standard English grammar and usage when writing or speaking	L1 pp. 174–179
10.2.2	Demonstrate command of the conventions of standard English capitalization, punctuation, and spelling when writing	L2 pp. 180–185
10.3.3	Use knowledge of language and its conventions when writing, speaking, reading, or listening	L3 pp. 186–191
10.4.4	Determine or clarify the meaning of unknown and multiple-meaning words and phrases, choosing flexibly from an array of strategies	L4 pp. 192–197
10.5.5	Demonstrate understanding of figurative language, word relationships, and nuances in word meanings	L5 pp. 198–203
10.6.6	Acquire and use accurately general academic and domain-specific words and phrases	L6 pp. 204–209

Mississippi, Grade 3

Mississippi Strand/Standard	Focus of Mississippi Standard	For More Information
Reading Literature		
RL.1	Ask and answer questions to demonstrate understanding of a text, referring explicitly to the text as the basis for the answers	R1 pp. 6–11
RL.2	Recount stories from diverse cultures, determine their central message, lesson, or moral, and explain how it is conveyed	R2 pp. 12–17
RL.3	Describe characters in a story and explain how their actions contribute to the sequence of events	R3 pp. 18–23
RL.4	Determine the meaning of words and phrases as they are used in a text, distinguishing literal from nonliteral language	R4 pp. 24–29
RL.5	Refer to parts of stories, dramas, and poems when writing or speaking about a text, using terms such as chapter, scene, and stanza; describe how each successive part builds on earlier sections	R5 pp. 30–35
RL.6	Distinguish their own point of view from that of the narrator or those of the characters	R6 pp. 36–41
RL.7	Explain how specific elements of a text's illustrations contribute to what is conveyed by the words in a story	R7 pp. 42–47
RL.8	NA	
RL.9	Compare and contrast the themes, settings, and plots of stories written by the same author about the same or similar characters	R9 pp. 54–59
RL.10	Read literature of appropriate complexity independently with proficiency	R10 pp. 60–65

Mississippi Strand/Standard	Focus of Mississippi Standard	For More Information
Reading Informational Text		
RI.1	Ask and answer questions to demonstrate understanding of a text, referring explicitly to the text as the basis for the answers	R1 pp. 6–11
RI.2	Determine the main idea of a text; recount the key details and explain how they support the main idea	R2 pp. 12–17
RI.3	Describe the relationship between a series of historical events, scientific ideas or concepts, or steps in technical procedures in a text	R3 pp. 18–23
RI.4	Determine the meaning of general academic and domain-specific words and phrases in a text	R4 pp. 24–29
RI.5	Use text features and search tools to locate information on a topic efficiently	R5 pp. 30–35
RI.6	Distinguish own point of view from that of the author of a text	R6 pp. 36–41
RI.7	Use information from illustrations and the words in a text to demonstrate understanding of the text	R7 pp. 42–47
RI.8	Describe the logical connection between particular sentences and paragraphs in a text	R8 pp. 48–53
RI.9	Compare and contrast the most important points and key details presented by two texts on the same topic	R9 pp. 54–59
RI.10	Read and comprehend appropriately complex informational texts independently and proficiently	R10 pp. 60–65
Reading Foundational Skills		
RF.3	Phonics: Know and apply grade-level phonics and word analysis skills in decoding words	RF3 pp. 214–219
RF.4	Fluency: Read grade-level texts with sufficient accuracy and fluency to support comprehension	RF4 pp. 220–225
Writing		
W.1	Write opinion pieces on topics or texts, supporting a point of view with reasons	W1 pp. 70–75
W.2	Write informative/explanatory texts to examine a topic and convey ideas and information clearly	W2 pp. 76–81
W.3	Write narratives to develop real or imagined experiences or events using effective technique, descriptive details, and clear event sequences	W3 pp. 82–87
W.4	Produce writing in which the development and organization are appropriate to the task and purpose	W4 pp. 88–93
W.5	Develop and strengthen writing as needed by planning, revising, and editing	W5 pp. 94–99
W.6	Use technology to produce and publish writing	W6 pp. 100–105
W.7	Conduct short research projects that build knowledge about a topic	W7 pp. 106–111
W.8	Recall information from experiences or gather information from print and digital sources	W8 pp. 112–117
W.9	NA	
W.10	Write routinely over shorter and extended time frames	W10 pp. 124–129
Speaking and Listening		
SL.1	Engage effectively in a range of collaborative discussions with diverse partners, building on others' ideas and expressing their own clearly	SL1 pp. 134–139
SL.2	Determine the main ideas and supporting details of a text read aloud or information presented in diverse media and formats	SL2 pp. 140–145
SL.3	Ask and answer questions about information from a speaker, offering appropriate elaboration and detail	SL3 pp. 146–151
SL.4	Report on a topic or text, tell a story, or recount an experience with appropriate facts and relevant details	SL4 pp. 152–157
SL.5	Create audio recordings of stories or poems, demonstrating fluent reading; add visual displays when appropriate	SL5 pp. 158–163
SL.6	Speak in complete sentences when appropriate to task and situation in order to provide requested detail or clarification	SL6 pp. 164–169
Language		
L.1	Demonstrate command of the conventions of standard English grammar and usage when writing or speaking	L1 pp. 174–179
L.2	Demonstrate command of the conventions of standard English capitalization, punctuation, and spelling when writing	L2 pp. 180–185

(Continued)

Mississippi Strand/Standard	Focus of Mississippi Standard	For More Information
Language		
L.3	Use knowledge of language and its conventions when writing, speaking, reading, or listening	L3 pp. 186–191
L.4	Determine or clarify the meaning of unknown and multiple-meaning words and phrases, choosing flexibly from an array of strategies	L4 pp. 192–197
L.5	Demonstrate understanding of word relationships and nuances in word meanings	L5 pp. 198–203
L.6	Acquire and use accurately conversational, general academic, and domain-specific words and phrases	L6 pp. 204–209

Mississippi, Grade 4

Mississippi Strand/Standard	Focus of Mississippi Standard	For More Information
Reading Literature		
RL.1	Refer to details and examples in a text when explaining what the text says explicitly and when drawing inferences	R1 pp. 6–11
RL.2	Determine a theme of a story, drama, or poem from details in the text; summarize the text	R2 pp. 12–17
RL.3	Describe in depth a character, setting, or event in a story or drama, drawing on specific details in the text	R3 pp. 18–23
RL.4	Determine the meaning of words and phrases as they are used in a text	R4 pp. 24–29
RL.5	Explain the major differences between poems, drama, and prose; refer to structural elements when writing or speaking about a text	R5 pp. 30–35
RL.6	Compare and contrast the point of view from which different stories are narrated, including the difference between first- and third-person narratives	R6 pp. 36–41
RL.7	Make connections between the text of a story or drama and a visual or oral representation of the text	R7 pp. 42–47
RL.8	NA	
RL.9	Compare and contrast the treatment of similar themes and topics and patterns of events in stories and traditional literature from different cultures	R9 pp. 54–59
RL.10	Read literature of appropriate complexity independently with proficiency	R10 pp. 60–65
Reading Informational Text		
RI.1	Refer to details and examples in a text when explaining what the text says explicitly and when drawing inferences from the text	R1 pp. 6–11
RI.2	Determine the main idea of a text and explain how it is supported by key details; summarize the text	R2 pp. 12–17
RI.3	Explain events, procedures, ideas, or concepts in a historical, scientific, or technical text	R3 pp. 18–23
RI.4	Determine the meaning of general academic and domain-specific words and phrases in a text	R4 pp. 24–29
RI.5	Describe the overall structure of events, ideas, concepts, or information in a text	R5 pp. 30–35
RI.6	Compare and contrast a firsthand and secondhand account of the same event or topic	R6 pp. 36–41
RI.7	Interpret information presented visually, orally, or quantitatively, and explain how it contributes to an understanding of the text	R7 pp. 42–47
RI.8	Explain how an author uses reasons and evidence to support particular points in a text	R8 pp. 48–53
RI.9	Integrate information from two texts on the same topic in order to write or speak about the subject	R9 pp. 54–59
RI.10	Read and comprehend appropriately complex informational texts independently and proficiently	R10 pp. 60–65
Reading Foundational Skills		
RF.3	Phonics: Know and apply grade-level phonics and word analysis skills in decoding words	RF3 pp. 214–219
RF.4	Fluency: Read grade-level texts with sufficient accuracy and fluency to support comprehension	RF4 pp. 220–225
Writing		
W.1	Write opinion pieces on topics or texts, supporting a point of view with reasons and information	W1 pp. 70–75
W.2	Write informative/explanatory texts to examine a topic and convey ideas and information clearly	W2 pp. 76–81

Mississippi Strand/Standard	Focus of Mississippi Standard	For More Information
Writing		
W.3	Write narratives to develop real or imagined experiences or events using effective technique, descriptive details, and clear event sequences	W3 pp. 82–87
W.4	Produce writing in which the development and organization are appropriate to the task, purpose, and audience	W4 pp. 88–93
W.5	Develop and strengthen writing as needed by planning, revising, and editing	W5 pp. 94–99
W.6	Use technology to produce and publish writing; demonstrate keyboarding skills	W6 pp. 100–105
W.7	Conduct short research projects that build knowledge through investigation of different aspects of a topic	W7 pp. 106–111
W.8	Recall information from experiences or gather information from print and digital sources	W8 pp. 112–117
W.9	Draw evidence from literary or informational texts to support analysis, reflection, and research	W9 pp. 118–123
W.10	Write routinely over shorter and extended time frames	W10 pp. 124–129
Speaking and Listening		
SL.1	Engage effectively in a range of collaborative discussions with diverse partners, building on others' ideas and expressing their own clearly	SL1 pp. 134–139
SL.2	Paraphrase portions of a text read aloud or information presented in diverse media and formats	SL2 pp. 140–145
SL.3	Identify the reasons and evidence a speaker provides to support particular points	SL3 pp. 146–151
SL.4	Report on a topic or text, tell a story, or recount an experience with appropriate facts and details to support main ideas or themes	SL4 pp. 152–157
SL.5	Add audio recordings and visual displays to presentations when appropriate to enhance the development of main ideas or themes	SL5 pp. 158–163
SL.6	Differentiate between contexts that call for formal English and situations where informal discourse is appropriate; use formal English when appropriate to task and situation	SL6 pp. 164–169
Language		
L.1	Demonstrate command of the conventions of standard English grammar and usage when writing or speaking	L1 pp. 174–179
L.2	Demonstrate command of the conventions of standard English capitalization, punctuation, and spelling when writing	L2 pp. 180–185
L.3	Use knowledge of language and its conventions when writing, speaking, reading, or listening	L3 pp. 186–191
L.4	Determine or clarify the meaning of unknown and multiple-meaning words and phrases, choosing flexibly from an array of strategies	L4 pp. 192–197
L.5	Demonstrate understanding of figurative language, word relationships, and nuances in word meanings	L5 pp. 198–203
L.6	Acquire and use accurately general academic and domain-specific words and phrases	L6 pp. 204–209

Mississippi, Grade 5

Mississippi Strand/Standard	Focus of Mississippi Standard	For More Information
Reading Literature		
RL.1	Quote accurately from a text when explaining what the text says explicitly and when drawing inferences from the text	R1 pp. 6–11
RL.2	Determine a theme of a story, drama, or poem from details in the text; summarize the text	R2 pp. 12–17
RL.3	Compare and contrast two or more characters, settings, or events in a story or drama, drawing on specific details in the text	R3 pp. 18–23
RL.4	Determine the meaning of words and phrases as they are used in a text, including figurative language	R4 pp. 24–29
RL.5	Explain how a series of chapters, scenes, or stanzas fits together to provide the overall structure of a story, drama, or poem	R5 pp. 30–35

(Continued)

Mississippi Strand/Standard	Focus of Mississippi Standard	For More Information
Reading Literature		
RL.6	Describe how a narrator's or speaker's point of view influences how events are described	R6 pp. 36–41
RL.7	Analyze how visual and multimedia elements contribute to the meaning, tone, or beauty of a text	R7 pp. 42–47
RL.8	NA	
RL.9	Compare and contrast stories in the same genre on their approaches to similar themes and topics	R9 pp. 54–59
RL.10	Read literature of appropriate complexity independently with proficiency	R10 pp. 60–65
Reading Informational Text		
RI.1	Quote accurately from a text when explaining what the text says explicitly and when drawing inferences from the text	R1 pp. 6–11
RI.2	Determine two or more main ideas of a text and explain how they are supported by key details; summarize the text	R2 pp. 12–17
RI.3	Explain the relationships or interactions between two or more individuals, events, ideas, or concepts in a text, based on specific information in the text	R3 pp. 18–23
RI.4	Determine the meaning of general academic and domain-specific words and phrases in a text	R4 pp. 24–29
RI.5	Compare and contrast the overall structure of events, ideas, concepts, or information in two or more texts	R5 pp. 30–35
RI.6	Analyze multiple accounts of the same event or topic, noting important similarities and differences in the point of view they represent	R6 pp. 36–41
RI.7	Draw on information from multiple sources, demonstrating the ability to locate an answer to a question quickly or solve a problem efficiently	R7 pp. 42–47
RI.8	Explain how an author uses reasons and evidence to support particular points in a text	R8 pp. 48–53
RI.9	Integrate information from several texts on the same topic in order to write or speak about the subject	R9 pp. 54–59
RI.10	Read and comprehend appropriately complex informational texts independently and proficiently	R10 pp. 60–65
Reading Foundational Skills		
RF.3	Phonics: Know and apply grade-level phonics and word analysis skills in decoding words	RF3 pp. 214–219
RF.4	Fluency: Read grade-level texts with sufficient accuracy and fluency to support comprehension	RF4 pp. 220–225
Writing		
W.1	Write opinion pieces on topics or texts, supporting a point of view with reasons and information	W1 pp. 70–75
W.2	Write informative/explanatory texts to examine a topic and convey ideas and information clearly	W2 pp. 76–81
W.3	Write narratives to develop real or imagined experiences or events using effective technique, descriptive details, and clear event sequences	W3 pp. 82–87
W.4	Produce writing in which the development and organization are appropriate to the task, purpose, and audience	W4 pp. 88–93
W.5	Develop and strengthen writing as needed by planning, revising, editing, rewriting, or trying a new approach	W5 pp. 94–99
W.6	Use technology to produce and publish writing; demonstrate keyboarding skills	W6 pp. 100–105
W.7	Conduct short research projects that use several sources to build knowledge through investigation of different aspects of a topic	W7 pp. 106–111
W.8	Recall information from experiences or gather information from print and digital sources	W8 pp. 112–117
W.9	Draw evidence from literary or informational texts to support analysis, reflection, and research	W9 pp. 118–123
W.10	Write routinely over shorter and extended time frames	W10 pp. 124–129
Speaking and Listening		
SL.1	Engage effectively in a range of collaborative discussions with diverse partners, building on others' ideas and expressing their own clearly	SL1 pp. 134–139
SL.2	Summarize a written text read aloud or information presented in diverse media and formats	SL2 pp. 140–145
SL.3	Summarize points a speaker makes and explain how each claim is supported by reasons and evidence	SL3 pp. 146–151
SL.4	Report on a topic or text or present an opinion, using appropriate facts and details to support main ideas and themes	SL4 pp. 152–157

Mississippi Strand/Standard	Focus of Mississippi Standard	For More Information
Speaking and Listening		
SL.5	Include multimedia components and visual displays in presentations when appropriate to enhance the development of main ideas or themes	SL5 pp. 158–163
SL.6	Adapt speech to a variety of contexts, using formal English when appropriate to task and situation	SL6 pp. 164–169
Language		
L.1	Demonstrate command of the conventions of standard English grammar and usage when writing or speaking	L1 pp. 174–179
L.2	Demonstrate command of the conventions of standard English capitalization, punctuation, and spelling when writing	L2 pp. 180–185
L.3	Use knowledge of language and its conventions when writing, speaking, reading, or listening	L3 pp. 186–191
L.4	Determine or clarify the meaning of unknown and multiple-meaning words and phrases, choosing flexibly from an array of strategies	L4 pp. 192–197
L.5	Demonstrate understanding of figurative language, word relationships, and nuances in word meanings	L5 pp. 198–203
L.6	Acquire and use accurately general academic and domain-specific words and phrases	L6 pp. 204–209

Missouri, Grade 3

Missouri Strand/Standard	Focus of Missouri Standard	For More Information
Reading		
R.1	Develop and apply skills to the reading process	
R.1.A	Comprehension: Draw conclusions and support with textual evidence; summarize a text's beginning, middle, and end; monitor comprehension, making corrections and adjustments as necessary	R1 pp. 6–11 R2 pp. 12–17 R4 pp. 24–29
R.1.B	Vocabulary: Use affixes and root words to determine word meaning; use context to determine word meaning; use homographs and homophones; use a dictionary; recognize literal and non-literal meanings; understand similes and metaphors; use conversational, domain-specific, and academic words and phrases	R4 pp. 24–29 RF3 pp. 214–219 L4 pp. 192–197 L5 pp. 198–203 L6 pp. 204–209
R.1.C	Making Connections: Make text-to-text and text-to-world connections	R9 pp. 54–59
R.1.D	Independent Text: Read independently for sustained periods of time by engaging with text that is developmentally appropriate; produce evidence of reading	R10 pp. 60–65
R.2	Develop and apply skills and strategies to comprehend, analyze, and evaluate fiction, poetry, and drama from a variety of cultures and times	
R.2.A	Fiction: Summarize and sequence plot and explain how past events impact future ones; use textual evidence to describe characters and their interactions; paraphrase main idea and supporting details; compare and contrast key elements presented in two texts; explain cause and effect relationships; distinguish own point of view from that of the narrator or characters	R2 pp. 12–17 R3 pp. 18–23 R6 pp. 36–41 R9 pp. 54–59
R.2.B	Poetry: Use alliteration; identify basic forms of poetry	R4 pp. 24–29 R5 pp. 30–35
R.2.C	Drama: Explain elements of plot, setting, and character as presented through dialogue; describe language that appeals to the senses	R4 pp. 24–29 R5 pp. 30–35
R.3	Develop and apply skills and strategies to comprehend, analyze, and evaluate nonfiction (e.g., narrative, information/explanatory, opinion, persuasive, argumentative) from a variety of cultures and times	
R.3.A	Text Features: Explain author's purpose; use supporting details to explain the main idea; use text and graphic features to locate information and to make and verify predictions; follow written multi-step directions; describe connections between events, ideas, concepts	R2 pp. 12–17 R3 pp. 18–23 R5 pp. 30–35 R6 pp. 36–41

(Continued)

Missouri Strand/Standard	Focus of Missouri Standard	For More Information
Reading		
R.3.B	Literary Techniques: Distinguish between biography and autobiography; distinguish fact from opinion; distinguish author's point of view from own; explain examples of literal and nonliteral meanings	R4 pp. 24–29 R6 pp. 36–41
R.3.C	Text Structures: Describe the connections between events, concepts, problem and solution, and cause and effect; explain author's purpose; compare and contrast two texts on the same topic	R3 pp. 18–23 R7 pp. 42–47 R9 pp. 54–59
R.4	Comprehend and analyze words, images, graphics, and sounds in various media and digital forms to impact meaning	
R.4.A	Digital and Media Literacy: Understand how communication changes when moving from one genre of media to another; explain how media techniques influence the message; identify text structures and graphic features of a web page	R5 pp. 30–35
Reading Foundations		
RF.1	Understand how English is written and read	
RF.1.A	Print Awareness: No expectations	
RF.2.A	Phonemic Awareness: No expectations	
RF.3	Understand how English is written and read	
RF.3.A	Phonics: Decode multisyllabic words in context by applying common spelling patterns; use the meaning of common affixes; use the meaning of homophones; read irregularly spelled high-frequency words	RF3 pp. 214–219
RF.4	Understand how English is written and read	
RF.4.A	Fluency: Read appropriate texts with fluency and purpose and understanding; use context to confirm or self-correct	RF4 pp. 220–225
Writing		
W.1	Apply a writing process to develop a text for audience and purpose	
W.1.A	Prewriting: Plan a first draft using a simple pre-writing strategy	W4 pp. 88–93 W5 pp. 94–99
W.1.B	Draft: Generate a main idea to support a multi-paragraph text; support the topic sentence of each paragraph with details; organize and sequence writing; address appropriate audience	W4 pp. 88–93 W5 pp. 94–99
W.1.C	Revise/Edit: Develop and strengthen writing by revising; edit for language conventions	W5 pp. 94–99
W.1.D	Produce/Publish and Share Writing: Use a variety of conventional/digital tools to produce and publish writing	W6 pp. 100–105
W.2	Compose well-developed writing texts for audience and purpose	
W.2.A	Opinion/Argumentative: Introduce a topic, state an opinion, provide reasons; use topic-specific words; use student's original language; use transitions to connect opinions and reasons; provide concluding statement	W1 pp. 70–75
W.2.B	Informative/Explanatory: Introduce a topic and use facts, details, and definitions to develop points; use topic-specific words; use linking words and phrases; provide a closing	W2 pp. 76–81
W.2.C	Narrative/Literary: Establish a setting and introduce a main character; develop sensory details; use dialogue and descriptions; follow a logical sequence of events and use transition words to signal order; use topic-related language	W3 pp. 82–87
W.3	Gather, analyze, evaluate, and use information from a variety of sources	
W.3.A	Research Process: Generate a list of topics; create a question and use sources to find information; gather evidence from sources and determine relevancy and accuracy; take notes; visually organize information; present and evaluate information	W7 pp. 106–111 W8 pp. 112–117
Language		
L.1	Communicate using conventions of English language	
L.1.A	Grammar: Use regular and irregular verbs, helping verbs; use complete subject and predicate and subject-verb agreement; use comparative, declarative, and superlative adjectives; produce declarative, imperative, exclamatory, and interrogative sentences	L1 pp. 174–179
L.1.B	Punctuation, Capitalization, Spelling; Write legibly; use apostrophes and quotation marks appropriately; capitalize places and titles; use spelling patterns and generalizations and consult reference materials to check spelling; arrange words in alphabetical order to the third letter	L2 pp. 180–185

Missouri Strand/Standard	Focus of Missouri Standard	For More Information
Speaking/Listening		
SL.1	Listen for a purpose	
SL.1.A	Purpose: Follow classroom listening rules; ask questions to check understanding of information presented, staying on topic, and linking their comments to the remarks of others; follow three-step instructions	SL1 pp. 134–139
SL.2	Listen for entertainment	
SL.2.A	Entertainment: Demonstrate active listening	SL1 pp. 134–139
SL.3	Speak effectively in collaborative discussions	
SL.3.A	Collaborative Discussions: Come to discussions prepared having read or studies required material; explicitly draw on that preparation and other information known about the topic to explore ideas under discussion; express opinion of reading topics	SL1 pp. 134–139 SL2 pp. 140–145
SL.4	Speak effectively when presenting	
SL.4.A	Presenting: Present information with clear ideas and details; speak clearly; use a variety of media; use academic language and conventions	SL4 pp. 152–157 SL5 pp. 158–163 SL6 pp. 164–169

Missouri, Grade 4

Missouri Strand/Standard	Focus of Missouri Standard	For More Information
Reading		
R.1	Develop and apply skills to the reading process	
R.1.A	Comprehension: Draw conclusions and make inferences, supporting with textual evidence; monitor comprehension, making corrections and adjustments as necessary	R1 pp. 6–11 R4 pp. 24–29
R.1.B	Vocabulary: Use affixes and root words to determine word meaning; use context to determine word meaning; use homographs and homophones; use a dictionary; identify meaning of common idioms and figurative language; use conversational, domain-specific, and academic words and phrases	R4 pp. 24–29 RF3 pp. 214–219 L4 pp. 192–197 L5 pp. 198–203 L6 pp. 204–209
R.1.C	Making Connections: Make text-to-text and text-to-world connections	R9 pp. 54–59
R.1.D	Independent Text: Read independently for sustained periods of time by engaging with text that is developmentally appropriate; produce evidence of reading	R10 pp. 60–65
R.2	Develop and apply skills and strategies to comprehend, analyze and evaluate fiction, poetry, and drama from a variety of cultures and times	
R.2.A	Fiction: Summarize and sequence plot and explain how past events impact future ones; use textual evidence to describe characters and their interactions; compare and contrast characters; compare and contrast the point of view from which stories are narrated, explain whether the narrator or speaker of a story is first or third person	R2 pp. 12–17 R3 pp. 18–23 R6 pp. 36–41 R9 pp. 54–59
R.2.B	Poetry: Explain structural elements of poetry	R4 pp. 24–29 R5 pp. 30–35
R.2.C	Drama: Analyze how characters change from the beginning to the end of a drama; explain structural elements of drama	R3 pp. 18–23 R5 pp. 30–35
R.3	Develop and apply skills and strategies to comprehend, analyze, and evaluate nonfiction (e.g., narrative, information/explanatory, opinion, persuasive, argumentative) from a variety of cultures and times	
R.3.A	Text Features: Use multiple text features to locate information and gain an overview of the contents of text; describe the sequence of events, ideas, concepts, or steps needed to carry out a procedure; interpret and explain factual information presented graphically	R3 pp. 18–23 R5 pp. 30–35 R7 pp. 42–47
R.3.B	Literary Techniques: Analyze, make inferences, and draw conclusions about persuasive text and use evidence from the text to explain the author's purpose and support the analysis; explain how an author uses language to present information to influence what the reader thinks or does	R1 pp. 6–11 R5 pp. 30–35 R8 pp. 48–53

(Continued)

Missouri Strand/Standard	Focus of Missouri Standard	For More Information
Reading		
R.3.C	Text Structures: Explain explicit and implicit relationships among ideas in texts; explain author's purpose; compare and contrast a firsthand and secondhand account of the same event or topic	R3 pp. 18–23 R6 pp. 36–41 R8 pp. 48–53
R.4	Comprehend and analyze words, images, graphics, and sounds in various media and digital forms to impact meaning	
R.4.A	Digital and Media Literacy: Explain how media techniques influence the message; identify text structures and graphic features of a web page	R7 pp. 42–47
Reading Foundations		
RF.1	Understand how English is written and read	
RF.1.A	Print Awareness: No expectations	
RF.2	Understand how English is written and read	
Rf.2.A	Phonemic Awareness: No expectations	
RF.3	Understand how English is written and read	
RF.3.A	Phonics: Decode words using knowledge of all letter-sound correspondences, syllabication patterns, and morphology to read unfamiliar multi-syllabic words in context; read root words, prefixes, and suffixes and important words from specific content curricula	RF3 pp. 214–219 L4 pp. 192–197
RF.4	Understand how English is written and read	
RF.4.A	Fluency: Read appropriate texts with fluency and purpose and understanding; use context to confirm or self-correct	RF4 pp. 220–225
Writing		
W.1	Apply a writing process to develop a text for audience and purpose	
W.1.A	Prewriting: Select a genre appropriate for conveying the purpose to an intended audience; plan a first draft using a simple pre-writing strategy	W4 pp. 88–93 W5 pp. 94–99
W.1.B	Draft: Generate a main idea to support a multi-paragraph text; support the topic sentence of each paragraph with details; organize and sequence writing; address appropriate audience	W4 pp. 88–93 W5 pp. 94–99
W.1.C	Revise/Edit: Develop and strengthen writing by revising; edit for language conventions	W5 pp. 94–99
W.1.D	Produce/Publish and Share Writing: Use technology to produce and publish writing	W6 pp. 100–105
W.2	Compose well-developed writing texts for audience and purpose	
W.2.A	Opinion/Argumentative: Introduce a topic, state an opinion, provide reasons; use topic-specific words; use student's original language except when using direct quotes; use transitions to connect opinions and reasons; organize the supporting details/reasons into introductory, supporting, and concluding paragraphs	W1 pp. 70–75 W8 pp. 112–117
W.2.B	Informative/Explanatory: Introduce a topic and use facts, details, definitions, and quotations to develop points; use topic-specific words appropriate to the audience; use linking words and phrases; provide a closing	W2 pp. 76–81 W8 pp. 112–117
W.2.C	Narrative/Literary: Establish a setting and introduce a main character; develop sensory details; use dialogue and descriptions; follow a logical sequence of events and use transition words to signal order; use topic-related language	W3 pp. 82–87
W.3	Gather, analyze, evaluate, and use information from a variety of sources	
W.3.A	Research Process: Generate a list of topics; create a question and use sources to find information; gather evidence from sources and determine relevancy and accuracy; take notes; visually organize information; present and evaluate information	W7 pp. 106–111 W8 pp. 112–117 W9 pp. 118–123

Missouri Strand/Standard	Focus of Missouri Standard	For More Information
Language		
L.1	Communicate using conventions of English language	
L.1.A	Grammar: Use the "be" helping verbs with "ing" verbs; use progressive verbs to show past, present, and future; use subject/verb agreement with first-, second-, and third-person pronouns; use and order adjectives within sentences to conventional patterns; use adverbs and prepositions; recognize the difference between and use coordinating conjunctions and subordinating conjunctions; produce complete sentences and correct sentence fragments and run-ons	L1 pp. 174–179
L.1.B	Punctuation, Capitalization, Spelling; Write legibly; punctuate dialogue; capitalize proper adjectives; spell grade-appropriate words correctly; use combined knowledge of all letter-sound correspondences, syllabication patterns, and morphology (roots, affixes) to read and spell accurately unfamiliar multisyllabic words in context	L2 pp. 180–185 RF3 pp. 214–219
Speaking/Listening		
SL.1	Listen for a purpose	
SL.1.A	Purpose: Follow, generate classroom listening rules; ask questions to check understanding of information presented, staying on topic, and linking their comments to the remarks of others; follow and restate multi-step instructions	SL1 pp. 134–139
SL.2	Listen for entertainment	
SL.2.A	Entertainment: Demonstrate active listening	SL1 pp. 134–139
SL.3	Speak effectively in collaborative discussions	
SL.3.A	Collaborative Discussions: Contribute to discussion after listening to others' ideas; express opinions of reading	SL1 pp. 134–139 SL2 pp. 140–145
SL.4	Speak effectively when presenting	
SL.4.A	Presenting: Paraphrase portions of a text read aloud or information presented in diverse media and formats; use efficient presentation skills with available resources; incorporate descriptive and sequential details; give a formal presentation using a variety of media; speak with expression and fluency; adjust language according to context and topic	SL2 pp. 140–145 SL4 pp. 152–157 SL5 pp. 158–163 SL6 pp. 164–169

Missouri, Grade 5

Missouri Strand/Standard	Focus of Missouri Standard	For More Information
Reading		
R.1	Develop and apply skills to the reading process	
R.1.A	Comprehension: Draw conclusions and make inferences, supporting with textual evidence; monitor comprehension, making corrections and adjustments as necessary	R1 pp. 6–11 R4 pp. 24–29
R.1.B	Vocabulary: Use affixes and root words to determine word meaning; use context to determine word meaning; use a dictionary; explain meaning of common idioms and figurative language; use words and phrases that signal contrast, addition, and other logical relationships; use a dictionary, glossary, or thesaurus to determine pronunciations, parts of speech, meanings, and alternative word choices; use academic and domain-specific words and phrases	L4 pp. 192–197 L5 pp. 198–203 L6 pp. 204–209
R.1.C	Making Connections: Make text-to-text and text-to-world connections	R9 pp. 54–59
R.1.D	Independent Text: Read independently for sustained periods of time by engaging with text that is developmentally appropriate; produce evidence of reading	R10 pp. 60–65
R.2	Develop and apply skills and strategies to comprehend, analyze, and evaluate fiction, poetry, and drama from a variety of cultures and times	

(Continued)

Missouri Strand/Standard	Focus of Missouri Standard	For More Information
Reading		
R.2.A	Fiction: Compare and contrast characters' roles, relationships, and conflicts; describe how a narrator's point of view influences events; recognize foreshadowing; explain the effect of a historical event on a work of literature; introduce different forms of third-person point of view	R2 pp. 12–17 R3 pp. 18–23 R6 pp. 36–41
R.2.B	Poetry: Explain how poets use sound and visual elements; identify forms of poems	R4 pp. 24–29 R5 pp. 30–35
R.2.C	Drama: Analyze the similarities between an original text and its dramatic adaptation; explain structural elements of drama; evaluate the impact of sensory language	R4 pp. 24–29 R5 pp. 30–35 R7 pp. 42–47
R.3	Develop and apply skills and strategies to comprehend, analyze, and evaluate nonfiction (e.g., narrative, information/explanatory, opinion, persuasive, argumentative) from a variety of cultures and times	
R.3.A	Text Features: Use multiple text features to locate information and gain an overview of the contents of text; interpret details from procedural text to complete a task or procedure; interpret factual or quantitative information	R3 pp. 18–23 R6 pp. 36–41 R7 pp. 42–47
R.3.B	Literary Techniques: Evaluate how well the author's purpose was achieved, and provide evidence; analyze multiple accounts of the same event; identify the author's viewpoint, evidence, and conclusion; use reasoning to determine the logic of an author's conclusion, providing evidence	R5 pp. 30–35 R8 pp. 48–53
R.3.C	Text Structures: Explain the difference between a stated and implied purpose; explain how organization influences relationships in a text; analyze multiple accounts of the same event or topic; integrate information from several texts on the same topic in order to communicate knowledgeably	R1 pp. 6–11 R3 pp. 18–23 R6 pp. 36–41 R9 pp. 54–59
R.4	Comprehend and analyze words, images, graphics, and sounds in various media and digital forms to impact meaning	
R.4.A	Digital and Media Literacy: Explain textual and graphics features of a web page and how they support readers	R7 pp. 42–47
Reading Foundations		
RF.1	Understand how English is written and read	
RF.1.A	Print Awareness: No expectations	
RF.2	Understand how English is written and read	
RF.2.A	Phonemic Awareness: No expectations	
RF.3	Understand how English is written and read	
RF.3.A	Phonics: Decode words using knowledge of all letter-sound correspondences, syllabication patterns, and morphology to read unfamiliar multi-syllabic words in context; read root words, prefixes, and suffixes and important words from specific content curricula	RF3 pp. 214–219 L4 pp. 192–197
RF.4	Understand how English is written and read	
RF.4.A	Fluency: Read appropriate texts with fluency and purpose and understanding; use context to confirm or self-correct	RF4 pp. 220–225
Writing		
W.1	Apply a writing process to develop a text for audience and purpose	
W.1.A	Prewriting: Select a genre appropriate for conveying the purpose to an intended audience; formulate questions and access prior knowledge related to the topic	W4 pp. 88–93 W5 pp. 94–99
W.1.B	Draft: Choose an appropriate organizational structure and build on a main idea; establish main idea with a topic sentence; sequence facts and details into introductory, supporting, and concluding paragraphs, restating the main idea in the concluding statement; address an appropriate audience and purpose	W4 pp. 88–93 W5 pp. 94–99
W.1.C	Revise/Edit: Develop and strengthen writing by revising; edit for language conventions	W5 pp. 94–99

Missouri Strand/Standard	Focus of Missouri Standard	For More Information
Writing		
W.1.D	Produce/Publish and Share Writing: Use technology to produce and publish writing	W6 pp. 100–105
W.2	Compose well-developed writing texts for audience and purpose	
W.2.A	Opinion/Argumentative: Introduce a topic, state an opinion, provide reasons; use topic-specific words; use student's original language except when using direct quotes; use transitions to connect opinions and reasons; organize the supporting details/reasons into introductory, supporting, and concluding paragraphs	W1 pp. 70–75 W8 pp. 112–117
W.2.B	Informative/Explanatory: Introduce a topic and use facts, details, definitions, and quotations to develop points; use an organizational format that suits the topic; use topic-specific words appropriate to the audience; use linking words and phrases; provide a closing	W2 pp. 76–81 W8 pp. 112–117
W.2.C	Narrative/Literary: Establish a setting and introduce a main character; develop sensory details; use dialogue and descriptions; follow a logical sequence of events and use transition words to signal order; use language suited to the topic, audience, and purpose	W3 pp. 82–87
W.3	Gather, analyze, evaluate and use information from a variety of sources	
W.3.A	Research Process: Generate a list of topics; formulate and refine a research question and use sources to find information; gather evidence from sources and determine relevancy and accuracy; convert visual data into written notes; visually organize information; differentiate between paraphrasing and plagiarism; present and evaluate	W7 pp. 106–111 W8 pp. 112–117 W9 pp. 118–123
Language		
L.1	Communicate using conventions of English language	
L.1.A	Grammar: Explain and use the eight parts of speech; use relative pronouns and adverbs; use pronouns consistently; use correct verb tenses	L1 pp. 174–179
L.1.B	Punctuation, Capitalization, Spelling; Write legibly; use commas in complex and compound sentences and to set off the words *yes* and *no*; use underlining, italics, or quotation marks to indicate titles; form and use possessives; use combined knowledge of all letter-sound correspondences, syllabication patterns, and morphology (roots, affixes) to read and spell accurately unfamiliar multisyllabic words in context	L2 pp. 180–185 L3 pp. 186–191
Speaking/Listening		
SL.1	Listen for a purpose	
SL.1.A	Purpose: Follow classroom discussion rules; ask questions to check understanding of information presented, staying on topic, and linking comments to the remarks of others; follow, restate, and give multi-step instructions	SL1 pp. 134–139
SL.2	Listen for entertainment	
SL.2.A	Entertainment: Evaluate and modify own active listening skills	SL1 pp. 134–139
SL.3	Speak effectively in collaborative discussions	
SL.3.A	Collaborative Discussions: Summarize points made by others before presenting own ideas; provide evidence to support opinion	SL1 pp. 134–139 SL3 pp. 146–151
SL.4	Speak effectively when presenting	
SL.4.A	Presenting: Plan an appropriate presentation, based on audience; use a variety of media; employ appropriate pacing, vocabulary, and gestures	SL4 pp. 152–157 SL5 pp. 158–163 SL6 pp. 164–169

Nebraska, Grade 3

Nebraska Strand/Standard	Focus of Nebraska Standard	For More Information
LA3.1	**Reading:** Students will learn and apply reading skills and strategies to comprehend text	
LA3.1.1	Concepts of Print: Mastered in Grade 1	NA
LA3.1.2	Phonological Awareness: Mastered in Grade 1	NA
LA3.1.3	Word Analysis: Students will use phonetic analysis to read and write grade-level text	RF3 pp. 214–219
LA3.1.4	Fluency: Students will develop accuracy, appropriate pace, phrasing, and expression while reading a variety of grade-level text to support comprehension	RF4 pp. 220–225
LA3.1.5	Vocabulary: Students will build and use conversational, academic, and content-specific grade-level vocabulary	L3 pp. 186–191 L4 pp. 192–197 L5 pp. 198–203 L6 pp. 204–209
LA3.1.6	Comprehension: Students will construct meaning by using prior knowledge and text information while reading grade-level literary and informational text	R1 pp. 6–11 R2 pp. 12–17 R3 pp. 18–23 R5 pp. 30–35 R6 pp. 36–41 R7 pp. 42–47 R8 pp. 48–53 R9 pp. 54–59 R10 pp. 60–65
LA3.2	**Writing:** Students will learn and apply writing skills and strategies to communicate	
LA3.2.1	Writing Process: Students will apply the writing process to plan, draft, revise, edit, and publish writing using correct spelling, grammar, punctuation, and other conventions of standard English appropriate for grade-level	W4 pp. 88–93 W5 pp. 94–99 W6 pp. 100–105 W8 pp. 112–117 L1 pp. 174–179 L2 pp. 180–185
LA3.2.2	Writing Modes: Students will write in multiple modes for a variety of purposes and audiences across disciplines	W1 pp. 70–75 W2 pp. 76–81 W3 pp. 82–87 W7 pp. 106–111
LA3.3	**Speaking and Listening:** Students will develop end apply speaking and listening skills and strategies to communicate for a variety of purposes	
LA3.3.1	Speaking: Students will develop, refine, and apply speaking skills and strategies to communicate for a variety of situations	SL4 pp. 152–157 SL5 pp. 158–163 SL6 pp. 164–169
LA3.3.2	Listening: Students will develop and demonstrate active listening skills across a variety of situations	SL2 pp. 140–145 SL3 pp. 146–151
LA3.3.3	Reciprocal Communication: Students will develop, apply, and adapt reciprocal communication skills	SL1 pp. 134–139 SL2 pp. 140–145 SL3 pp. 146–151
LA3.4	**Multiple Literacies:** Students will apply information fluency and practice digital citizenship	
LA3.4.1	Information Fluency: Students will evaluate, create, and communicate information in a variety of media and formats	R7 pp. 42–47 R8 pp. 48–53 W6 pp. 100–105 SL5 pp. 158–163
LA3.4.2	Digital Citizenship: Students will practice the norms of appropriate and responsible technology use	W6 pp. 100–105

Nebraska, Grade 4

Nebraska Strand/Standard	Focus of Nebraska Standard	For More Information
LA4.1	**Reading:** Students will learn and apply reading skills and strategies to comprehend text	
LA4.1.1	Concepts of Print: Mastered in Grade 1	NA
LA4.1.2	Phonological Awareness: Mastered in Grade 1	NA
LA4.1.3	Word Analysis: Students will use phonetic analysis to read and write grade-level text	RF3 pp. 214–219
LA4.1.4	Fluency: Students will develop accuracy, appropriate pace, phrasing, and expression while reading a variety of grade-level text to support comprehension	RF4 pp. 220–225
LA4.1.5	Vocabulary: Students will build and use conversational, academic, and content-specific grade-level vocabulary	L3 pp. 186–191 L4 pp. 192–197 L5 pp. 198–203 L6 pp. 204–209
LA4.1.6	Comprehension: Students will construct meaning by using prior knowledge and text information while reading grade-level literary and informational text	R1 pp. 6–11 R2 pp. 12–17 R3 pp. 18–23 R5 pp. 30–35 R6 pp. 36–41 R7 pp. 42–47 R8 pp. 48–53 R9 pp. 54–59 R10 pp. 60–65
LA4.2	**Writing:** Students will learn and apply writing skills and strategies to communicate	
LA4.2.1	Writing Process: Students will apply the writing process to plan, draft, revise, edit, and publish writing using correct spelling, grammar, punctuation, and other conventions of standard English appropriate for grade-level	W4 pp. 88–93 W5 pp. 94–99 W6 pp. 100–105 W8 pp. 112–117 L1 pp. 174–179 L2 pp. 180–185
LA4.2.2	Writing Modes: Students will write in multiple modes for a variety of purposes and audiences across disciplines	W1 pp. 70–75 W2 pp. 76–81 W3 pp. 82–87 W7 pp. 106–111
LA4.3	**Speaking and Listening:** Students will develop end apply speaking and listening skills and strategies to communicate for a variety of purposes	
LA4.3.1	Speaking: Students will develop, refine, and apply speaking skills and strategies to communicate for a variety of situations	SL4 pp. 152–157 SL5 pp. 158–163 SL6 pp. 164–169
LA4.3.2	Listening: Students will develop and demonstrate active listening skills across a variety of situations	SL2 pp. 140–145 SL3 pp. 146–151
LA4.3.3	Reciprocal Communication: Students will develop, apply, and adapt reciprocal communication skills	SL1 pp. 134–139 SL2 pp. 140–145 SL3 pp. 146–151
LA4.4	**Multiple Literacies:** Students will apply information fluency and practice digital citizenship	
LA4.4.1	Information Fluency: Students will evaluate, create, and communicate information in a variety of media and formats	R7 pp. 42–47 R8 pp. 48–53 W6 pp. 100–105 SL5 pp. 158–163
LA4.4.2	Digital Citizenship: Students will practice the norms of appropriate and responsible technology use	W6 pp. 100–105

Nebraska, Grade 5

Nebraska Strand/Standard	Focus of Nebraska Standard	For More Information
LA5.1	**Reading:** Students will learn and apply reading skills and strategies to comprehend text	
LA5.1.1	Concepts of Print: Mastered in Grade 1	NA
LA5.1.2	Phonological Awareness: Mastered in Grade 1	NA
LA5.1.3	Word Analysis: Students will use phonetic analysis to read and write grade-level text	RF3 pp. 214–219
LA5.1.4	Fluency: Students will develop accuracy, appropriate pace, phrasing, and expression while reading a variety of grade-level text to support comprehension	RF4 pp. 220–225
LA5.1.5	Vocabulary: Students will build and use conversational, academic, and content-specific grade-level vocabulary	L3 pp. 186–191 L4 pp. 192–197 L5 pp. 198–203 L6 pp. 204–209
LA5.1.6	Comprehension: Students will construct meaning by using prior knowledge and text information while reading grade-level literary and informational text	R1 pp. 6–11 R2 pp. 12–17 R3 pp. 18–23 R5 pp. 30–35 R6 pp. 36–41 R7 pp. 42–47 R8 pp. 48–53 R9 pp. 54–59 R10 pp. 60–65
LA5.2	**Writing:** Students will learn and apply writing skills and strategies to communicate	
LA5.2.1	Writing Process: Students will apply the writing process to plan, draft, revise, edit, and publish writing using correct spelling, grammar, punctuation, and other conventions of standard English appropriate for grade-level	W4 pp. 88–93 W5 pp. 94–99 W6 pp. 100–105 W8 pp. 112–117 L1 pp. 174–179 L2 pp. 180–185
LA5.2.2	Writing Modes: Students will write in multiple modes for a variety of purposes and audiences across disciplines	W1 pp. 70–75 W2 pp. 76–81 W3 pp. 82–87 W7 pp. 106–111
LA5.3	**Speaking and Listening:** Students will develop end apply speaking and listening skills and strategies to communicate for a variety of purposes	
LA5.3.1	Speaking: Students will develop, refine, and apply speaking skills and strategies to communicate for a variety of situations	SL4 pp. 152–157 SL5 pp. 158–163 SL6 pp. 164–169
LA5.3.2	Listening: Students will develop and demonstrate active listening skills across a variety of situations	SL2 pp. 140–145 SL3 pp. 146–151
LA5.3.3	Reciprocal Communication: Students will develop, apply, and adapt reciprocal communication skills	SL1 pp. 134–139 SL2 pp. 140–145 SL3 pp. 146–151
LA5.4	**Multiple Literacies:** Students will apply information fluency and practice digital citizenship	
LA5.4.1	Information Fluency: Students will evaluate, create, and communicate information in a variety of media and formats	R7 pp. 42–47 R8 pp. 48–53 W6 pp. 100–105 SL5 pp. 158–163
LA5.4.2	Digital Citizenship: Students will practice the norms of appropriate and responsible technology use	W6 pp. 100–105

New Jersey, Grade 3

New Jersey Strand/Standard	Focus of New Jersey Standard	For More Information
Reading Literature		
RL.1	Ask and answer questions to demonstrate understanding of a text, referring explicitly to the text as the basis for the answers	R1 pp. 6–11
RL.2	Recount stories from diverse cultures, determine their central message, lesson, or moral, and explain how it is conveyed	R2 pp. 12–17
RL.3	Describe characters in a story and explain how their actions contribute to the sequence of events	R3 pp. 18–23
RL.4	Determine the meaning of words and phrases as they are used in a text, distinguishing literal from nonliteral language	R4 pp. 24–29
RL.5	Refer to parts of stories, dramas, and poems when writing or speaking about a text, using terms such as chapter, scene, and stanza; describe how each successive part builds on earlier sections	R5 pp. 30–35
RL.6	Distinguish their own point of view from that of the narrator or those of the characters	R6 pp. 36–41
RL.7	Explain how specific elements of a text's illustrations contribute to what is conveyed by the words in a story	R7 pp. 42–47
RL.8	NA	
RL.9	Compare and contrast the themes, settings, and plots of stories written by the same author about the same or similar characters	R9 pp. 54–59
RL.10	Read literature of appropriate complexity independently with proficiency	R10 pp. 60–65
Reading Informational Text		
RI.1	Ask and answer questions to demonstrate understanding of a text, referring explicitly to the text as the basis for the answers	R1 pp. 6–11
RI.2	Determine the main idea of a text; recount the key details and explain how they support the main idea	R2 pp. 12–17
RI.3	Describe the relationship between a series of historical events, scientific ideas or concepts, or steps in technical procedures in a text	R3 pp. 18–23
RI.4	Determine the meaning of general academic and domain-specific words and phrases in a text	R4 pp. 24–29
RI.5	Use text features and search tools to locate information on a topic efficiently	R5 pp. 30–35
RI.6	Distinguish own point of view from that of the author of a text	R6 pp. 36–41
RI.7	Use information from illustrations and the words in a text to demonstrate understanding of the text	R7 pp. 42–47
RI.8	Describe the logical connection between particular sentences and paragraphs in a text	R8 pp. 48–53
RI.9	Compare and contrast the most important points and key details presented by two texts on the same topic	R9 pp. 54–59
RI.10	Read and comprehend appropriately complex informational texts independently and proficiently	R10 pp. 60–65
Reading Foundational Skills		
RF.3	Phonics: Know and apply grade-level phonics and word analysis skills in decoding words	RF3 pp. 214–219
RF.4	Fluency: Read grade-level texts with sufficient accuracy and fluency to support comprehension	RF4 pp. 220–225

(Continued)

New Jersey Strand/Standard	Focus of New Jersey Standard	For More Information
Writing		
W.1	Write opinion pieces on topics or texts, supporting a point of view with reasons	W1 pp. 70–75
W.2	Write informative/explanatory texts to examine a topic and convey ideas and information clearly	W2 pp. 76–81
W.3	Write narratives to develop real or imagined experiences or events using effective technique, descriptive details, and clear event sequences	W3 pp. 82–87
W.4	Produce writing in which the development and organization are appropriate to the task and purpose	W4 pp. 88–93
W.5	Develop and strengthen writing as needed by planning, revising, and editing	W5 pp. 94–99
W.6	Use technology to produce and publish writing	W6 pp. 100–105
W.7	Conduct short research projects that build knowledge about a topic	W7 pp. 106–111
W.8	Recall information from experiences or gather information from print and digital sources	W8 pp. 112–117
W.9	NA	
W.10	Write routinely over shorter and extended time frames	W10 pp. 124–129
Speaking and Listening		
SL.1	Engage effectively in a range of collaborative discussions with diverse partners, building on others' ideas and expressing their own clearly	SL1 pp. 134–139
SL.2	Determine the main ideas and supporting details of a text read aloud or information presented in diverse media and formats	SL2 pp. 140–145
SL.3	Ask and answer questions about information from a speaker, offering appropriate elaboration and detail	SL3 pp. 146–151
SL.4	Report on a topic or text, tell a story, or recount an experience with appropriate facts and relevant details	SL4 pp. 152–157
SL.5	Create audio recordings of stories or poems, demonstrating fluent reading; add visual displays when appropriate	SL5 pp. 158–163
SL.6	Speak in complete sentences when appropriate to task and situation in order to provide requested detail or clarification	SL6 pp. 164–169
Language		
L.1	Demonstrate command of the conventions of standard English grammar and usage when writing or speaking	L1 pp. 174–179
L.2	Demonstrate command of the conventions of standard English capitalization, punctuation, and spelling when writing	L2 pp. 180–185
L.3	Use knowledge of language and its conventions when writing, speaking, reading, or listening	L3 pp. 186–191
L.4	Determine or clarify the meaning of unknown and multiple-meaning words and phrases, choosing flexibly from an array of strategies	L4 pp. 192–197
L.5	Demonstrate understanding of word relationships and nuances in word meanings	L5 pp. 198–203
L.6	Acquire and use accurately conversational, general academic, and domain-specific words and phrases	L6 pp. 204–209

New Jersey, Grade 4

New Jersey Strand/Standard	Focus of New Jersey Standard	For More Information
Reading Literature		
RL.1	Refer to details and examples in a text when explaining what the text says explicitly and when drawing inferences	R1 pp. 6–11
RL.2	Determine a theme of a story, drama, or poem from details in the text; summarize the text	R2 pp. 12–17
RL.3	Describe in depth a character, setting, or event in a story or drama, drawing on specific details in the text	R3 pp. 18–23
RL.4	Determine the meaning of words and phrases as they are used in a text	R4 pp. 24–29
RL.5	Explain the major differences between poems, drama, and prose; refer to structural elements when writing or speaking about a text	R5 pp. 30–35
RL.6	Compare and contrast the point of view from which different stories are narrated, including the difference between first- and third-person narratives	R6 pp. 36–41
RL.7	Make connections between the text of a story or drama and a visual or oral representation of the text	R7 pp. 42–47
RL.8	NA	
RL.9	Compare and contrast the treatment of similar themes and topics and patterns of events in stories and traditional literature from different cultures	R9 pp. 54–59
RL.10	Read literature of appropriate complexity independently with proficiency	R10 pp. 60–65
Reading Informational Text		
RI.1	Refer to details and examples in a text when explaining what the text says explicitly and when drawing inferences from the text	R1 pp. 6–11
RI.2	Determine the main idea of a text and explain how it is supported by key details; summarize the text	R2 pp. 12–17
RI.3	Explain events, procedures, ideas, or concepts in a historical, scientific, or technical text	R3 pp. 18–23
RI.4	Determine the meaning of general academic and domain-specific words and phrases in a text	R4 pp. 24–29
RI.5	Describe the overall structure of events, ideas, concepts, or information in a text	R5 pp. 30–35
RI.6	Compare and contrast a firsthand and secondhand account of the same event or topic	R6 pp. 36–41
RI.7	Interpret information presented visually, orally, or quantitatively, and explain how it contributes to an understanding of the text	R7 pp. 42–47
RI.8	Explain how an author uses reasons and evidence to support particular points in a text	R8 pp. 48–53
RI.9	Integrate information from two texts on the same topic in order to write or speak about the subject	R9 pp. 54–59
RI.10	Read and comprehend appropriately complex informational texts independently and proficiently	R10 pp. 60–65
Reading Foundational Skills		
RF.3	Phonics: Know and apply grade-level phonics and word analysis skills in decoding words	RF3 pp. 214–219
RF.4	Fluency: Read grade-level texts with sufficient accuracy and fluency to support comprehension	RF4 pp. 220–225

(Continued)

New Jersey Strand/Standard	Focus of New Jersey Standard	For More Information
Writing		
W.1	Write opinion pieces on topics or texts, supporting a point of view with reasons and information	W1 pp. 70–75
W.2	Write informative/explanatory texts to examine a topic and convey ideas and information clearly	W2 pp. 76–81
W.3	Write narratives to develop real or imagined experiences or events using effective technique, descriptive details, and clear event sequences	W3 pp. 82–87
W.4	Produce writing in which the development and organization are appropriate to the task, purpose, and audience	W4 pp. 88–93
W.5	Develop and strengthen writing as needed by planning, revising, and editing	W5 pp. 94–99
W.6	Use technology to produce and publish writing; demonstrate keyboarding skills	W6 pp. 100–105
W.7	Conduct short research projects that build knowledge through investigation of different aspects of a topic	W7 pp. 106–111
W.8	Recall information from experiences or gather information from print and digital sources	W8 pp. 112–117
W.9	Draw evidence from literary or informational texts to support analysis, reflection, and research	W9 pp. 118–123
W.10	Write routinely over shorter and extended time frames	W10 pp. 124–129
Speaking and Listening		
SL.1	Engage effectively in a range of collaborative discussions with diverse partners, building on others' ideas and expressing their own clearly	SL1 pp. 134–139
SL.2	Paraphrase portions of a text read aloud or information presented in diverse media and formats	SL2 pp. 140–145
SL.3	Identify the reasons and evidence a speaker provides to support particular points	SL3 pp. 146–151
SL.4	Report on a topic or text, tell a story, or recount an experience with appropriate facts and details to support main ideas or themes	SL4 pp. 152–157
SL.5	Add audio recordings and visual displays to presentations when appropriate to enhance the development of main ideas or themes	SL5 pp. 158–163
SL.6	Differentiate between contexts that call for formal English and situations where informal discourse is appropriate; use formal English when appropriate to task and situation	SL6 pp. 164–169
Language		
L.1	Demonstrate command of the conventions of standard English grammar and usage when writing or speaking	L1 pp. 174–179
L.2	Demonstrate command of the conventions of standard English capitalization, punctuation, and spelling when writing	L2 pp. 180–185
L.3	Use knowledge of language and its conventions when writing, speaking, reading, or listening	L3 pp. 186–191
L.4	Determine or clarify the meaning of unknown and multiple-meaning words and phrases, choosing flexibly from an array of strategies	L4 pp. 192–197
L.5	Demonstrate understanding of figurative language, word relationships, and nuances in word meanings	L5 pp. 198–203
L.6	Acquire and use accurately general academic and domain-specific words and phrases	L6 pp. 204–209

New Jersey, Grade 5

New Jersey Strand/Standard	Focus of New Jersey Standard	For More Information
Reading Literature		
RL.1	Quote accurately from a text when explaining what the text says explicitly and when drawing inferences from the text	R1 pp. 6–11
RL.2	Determine a theme of a story, drama, or poem from details in the text; summarize the text	R2 pp. 12–17
RL.3	Compare and contrast two or more characters, settings, or events in a story or drama, drawing on specific details in the text	R3 pp. 18–23
RL.4	Determine the meaning of words and phrases as they are used in a text, including figurative language	R4 pp. 24–29
RL.5	Explain how a series of chapters, scenes, or stanzas fits together to provide the overall structure of a story, drama, or poem	R5 pp. 30–35
RL.6	Describe how a narrator's or speaker's point of view influences how events are described	R6 pp. 36–41
RL.7	Analyze how visual and multimedia elements contribute to the meaning, tone, or beauty of a text	R7 pp. 42–47
RL.8	NA	
RL.9	Compare and contrast stories in the same genre on their approaches to similar themes and topics	R9 pp. 54–59
RL.10	Read literature of appropriate complexity independently with proficiency	R10 pp. 60–65
Reading Informational Text		
RI.1	Quote accurately from a text when explaining what the text says explicitly and when drawing inferences from the text	R1 pp. 6–11
RI.2	Determine two or more main ideas of a text and explain how they are supported by key details; summarize the text	R2 pp. 12–17
RI.3	Explain the relationships or interactions between two or more individuals, events, ideas, or concepts in a text, based on specific information in the text	R3 pp. 18–23
RI.4	Determine the meaning of general academic and domain-specific words and phrases in a text	R4 pp. 24–29
RI.5	Compare and contrast the overall structure of events, ideas, concepts, or information in two or more texts	R5 pp. 30–35
RI.6	Analyze multiple accounts of the same event or topic, noting important similarities and differences in the point of view they represent	R6 pp. 36–41
RI.7	Draw on information from multiple sources, demonstrating the ability to locate an answer to a question quickly or solve a problem efficiently	R7 pp. 42–47
RI.8	Explain how an author uses reasons and evidence to support particular points in a text	R8 pp. 48–53
RI.9	Integrate information from several texts on the same topic in order to write or speak about the subject	R9 pp. 54–59
RI.10	Read and comprehend appropriately complex informational texts independently and proficiently	R10 pp. 60–65
Reading Foundational Skills		
RF.3	Phonics: Know and apply grade-level phonics and word analysis skills in decoding words	RF3 pp. 214–219
RF.4	Fluency: Read grade-level texts with sufficient accuracy and fluency to support comprehension	RF4 pp. 220–225

(Continued)

New Jersey Strand/Standard	Focus of New Jersey Standard	For More Information
Writing		
W.1	Write opinion pieces on topics or texts, supporting a point of view with reasons and information	W1 pp. 70–75
W.2	Write informative/explanatory texts to examine a topic and convey ideas and information clearly	W2 pp. 76–81
W.3	Write narratives to develop real or imagined experiences or events using effective technique, descriptive details, and clear event sequences	W3 pp. 82–87
W.4	Produce writing in which the development and organization are appropriate to the task, purpose, and audience	W4 pp. 88–93
W.5	Develop and strengthen writing as needed by planning, revising, editing, rewriting, or trying a new approach	W5 pp. 94–99
W.6	Use technology to produce and publish writing; demonstrate keyboarding skills	W6 pp. 100–105
W.7	Conduct short research projects that use several sources to build knowledge through investigation of different aspects of a topic	W7 pp. 106–111
W.8	Recall information from experiences or gather information from print and digital sources	W8 pp. 112–117
W.9	Draw evidence from literary or informational texts to support analysis, reflection, and research	W9 pp. 118–123
W.10	Write routinely over shorter and extended time frames	W10 pp. 124–129
Speaking and Listening		
SL.1	Engage effectively in a range of collaborative discussions with diverse partners, building on others' ideas and expressing their own clearly	SL1 pp. 134–139
SL.2	Summarize a written text read aloud or information presented in diverse media and formats	SL2 pp. 140–145
SL.3	Summarize points a speaker makes and explain how each claim is supported by reasons and evidence	SL3 pp. 146–151
SL.4	Report on a topic or text or present an opinion, using appropriate facts and details to support main ideas and themes	SL4 pp. 152–157
SL.5	Include multimedia components and visual displays in presentations when appropriate to enhance the development of main ideas or themes	SL5 pp. 158–163
SL.6	Adapt speech to a variety of contexts, using formal English when appropriate to task and situation	SL6 pp. 164–169
Language		
L.1	Demonstrate command of the conventions of standard English grammar and usage when writing or speaking	L1 pp. 174–179
L.2	Demonstrate command of the conventions of standard English capitalization, punctuation, and spelling when writing	L2 pp. 180–185
L.3	Use knowledge of language and its conventions when writing, speaking, reading, or listening	L3 pp. 186–191
L.4	Determine or clarify the meaning of unknown and multiple-meaning words and phrases, choosing flexibly from an array of strategies	L4 pp. 192–197
L.5	Demonstrate understanding of figurative language, word relationships, and nuances in word meanings	L5 pp. 198–203
L.6	Acquire and use accurately general academic and domain-specific words and phrases	L6 pp. 204–209

Oklahoma, Grade 3

Oklahoma Strand/Standard	Focus of Oklahoma Standard	For More Information
Speaking and Listening		
1.R.1	Actively listen and speak clearly using appropriate discussion rules	SL1 pp. 134–139
1.R.2	Ask and answer questions to seek help, get information, or clarify information presented orally	SL3 pp. 146–151
1.R.3	Engage in collaborative discussions	SL1 pp. 134–139
1.W.1	Report on a topic or text, tell a story, or recount an experience with appropriate facts and descriptive details	SL4 pp. 152–157
1.W.2	Work in groups respectfully, valuing contributions by group members	SL1 pp. 134–139
Reading Foundations		
2.PWS.1–3	Phonics: Know and apply grade-level phonics and word analysis skills in decoding words	RF3 pp. 214–219
2.F.1	Read common high-frequency words	RF3 pp. 214–219
2.F.2	Orally read level-appropriate text smoothly and accurately	RF4 pp. 220–225
Reading and Writing Process		
2.R.1	Locate the main idea and supporting details of a text	R2 pp. 12–17
2.R.2	Compare and contrast details to discriminate genres	R9 pp. 54–59
2.R.3	Summarize the events of a story	R2 pp. 12–17
2.W.1–2	Develop, sequence, and edit first drafts	W5 pp. 94–99
2.W.3–4	Correctly spell level-appropriate words while editing; use resources to find correct spellings	L2 pp. 180–185
Critical Reading and Writing		
3.R.1	Determine the author's stated and implied purpose	R6 pp. 36–41
3.R.2	Infer whether a story is narrated in first or third person	R6 pp. 36–41
3.R.3	Find examples of literary elements and organization (setting, plot, characters, characterization, theme) in a story	R2 pp. 12–17 R3 pp. 18–23
3.R.4	Find examples of literary devices (i.e., simile, metaphor)	R4 pp. 24–29
3.R.5	Distinguish fact from opinion in a text	R8 pp. 48–53
3.R.6	Describe the structure of a text	R5 pp. 30–35
3.R.7	Ask and answer inferential questions	R1 pp. 6–11
3.W.1	Write narratives incorporating plot, setting, characters, point of view, and conflict	W3 pp. 82–87
3.W.2	Write facts about a subject, including main idea and supporting details	W2 pp. 76–81
3.W.3	Express an opinion in writing about a topic and provide reasons as support	W1 pp. 70–75
Vocabulary		
4.R.1	Increase knowledge of academic, domain-appropriate, grade-level vocabulary to infer meaning of text	L6 pp. 204–209
4.R.2	Use word parts to define and determine meaning of unfamiliar words	L4 pp. 192–197
4.R.3	Use context clues to determine word meaning	L4 pp. 192–197
4.R.4	Infer relationships among words, including synonyms, antonyms, and multiple meaning words	L5 pp. 198–203
4.R.5	Use a dictionary or glossary to find words	L4 pp. 192–197
4.W.1	Use domain-appropriate vocabulary to communicate ideas in writing	L6 pp. 204–209
4.W.2	Select appropriate language according to purpose in writing	L6 pp. 204–209

(Continued)

Oklahoma Strand/Standard	Focus of Oklahoma Standard	For More Information
Language		
5.R.1–5	Recognize pronouns and possessive nouns; recognize irregular and past-participle verbs; recognize adjectives and adverbs; recognize prepositions and conjunctions; recognize subject-verb agreement	L1 pp. 174–179
5.W.1–4	Capitalize and appropriately punctuate; use complex contractions; compose grammatically correct sentences; compose a simple, compound, and complex sentences	L1 pp. 174–179 L2 pp. 180–185 L3 pp. 186–191
Research		
6.R.1–4	Use own questions to find information on a topic of interest; use graphic features to define a text; consult visual and text reference sources; determine relevance and reliability of information	R7 pp. 42–47 W7 pp. 106–111
6.W.1–2	Generate questions about topics of interest; organize information found during research	W7 pp. 106–111 W8 pp. 112–117
6.W.3	Summarize and present information in a report	SL4 pp. 152–157
Multimodal Literacies		
7.R.1	Locate, organize, and use information from a variety of texts to generate and answer questions	R5 pp. 30–35 R7 pp. 42–47
7.R.2	Compare how ideas and topics are depicted in a variety of media and formats	R9 pp. 54–59
7.W.1	Create multimodal content that communicates an idea	W6 pp. 100–105
7.W.2	Create presentations using multimedia elements to support communication	SL5 pp. 158–163
Independent Reading and Writing		
8.R	Select and read independently level-appropriate texts for academic and personal purposes	R10 pp. 60–65
8.W	Write independently for extended and shorter periods of time	W10 pp. 124–129

Oklahoma, Grade 4

Oklahoma Strand/Standard	Focus of Oklahoma Standard	For More Information
Speaking and Listening		
1.R.1	Actively listen and speak clearly using appropriate discussion rules	SL1 pp. 134–139
1.R.2	Ask and answer questions to seek help, get information, or clarify information presented orally	SL3 pp. 146–151
1.R.3	Engage in collaborative discussions	SL1 pp. 134–139
1.W.1	Report on a topic or text, tell a story, or recount an experience with appropriate facts and descriptive details	SL4 pp. 152–157
1.W.2	Work in groups respectfully, valuing contributions by group members	SL1 pp. 134–139
Reading Foundations		
2.PWS.1	Phonics: Know and apply grade-level phonics and word analysis skills in decoding words	RF3 pp. 214–219
2.F.1	Read common high-frequency words	RF3 pp. 214–219
2.F.2	Orally read level-appropriate text smoothly and accurately	RF4 pp. 220–225
Reading and Writing Process		
2.R.1	Distinguish how key details support the main idea of a passage	R2 pp. 12–17
2.R.2	Compare and contrast details in literary and informational texts to discriminate genres	R6 pp. 36–41 R9 pp. 54–59
2.R.3	Summarize the events of a story	R2 pp. 12–17

Oklahoma Strand/Standard	Focus of Oklahoma Standard	For More Information
Reading and Writing Process		
2.R.4	Begin to paraphrase main ideas with supporting details	R2 pp. 12–17
2.W.1–2	Develop, organize, and edit first drafts	W5 pp. 94–99
2.W.3–4	Correctly spell level-appropriate words while editing; use resources to find correct spellings	L2 pp. 180–185
Critical Reading and Writing		
3.R.1	Determine the author's purpose and infer the difference between stated and implied purpose	R8 pp. 48–53
3.R.2	Infer whether a story is narrated in first or third person	R6 pp. 36–41
3.R.3	Describe key literary elements (setting, plot, characters, characterization, theme)	R2 pp. 12–17 R3 pp. 18–23
3.R.4	Find examples of literary devices (i.e., simile, metaphor)	R4 pp. 24–29
3.R.5	Distinguish fact from opinion in a text	R8 pp. 48–53
3.R.6	Describe the structure of a text	R5 pp. 30–35
3.R.7	Ask and answer inferential questions using the text to support answers	R1 pp. 6–11
3.W.1	Write narratives incorporating plot, setting, characters, point of view, and conflict	W3 pp. 82–87
3.W.2	Write facts about a subject, including main idea and supporting details	W2 pp. 76–81
3.W.3	Express an opinion in writing about a topic and provide reasons as support	W1 pp. 70–75
Vocabulary		
4.R.1	Increase knowledge of academic, domain-appropriate, grade-level vocabulary to infer meaning of text	L6 pp. 204–209
4.R.2	Use word parts to define and determine meaning of unfamiliar words	L4 pp. 192–197
4.R.3	Use context clues to determine word meaning	L4 pp. 192–197
4.R.4	Infer relationships among words, including synonyms, antonyms, and multiple meaning words	L5 pp. 198–203
4.R.5	Use a dictionary or glossary to find words	L4 pp. 192–197
4.W.1	Use domain-appropriate vocabulary to communicate ideas in writing	L6 pp. 204–209
4.W.2	Select appropriate language according to purpose in writing	L6 pp. 204–209
Language		
5.R.1–5	Recognize pronouns and possessive nouns; recognize present and perfect verbs and verb tense; recognize comparatives and superlatives; recognize prepositions and conjunctions; recognize subject-verb agreement	L1 pp. 174–179
5.W.1–4	Capitalize appropriately; compose and expand grammatically correct sentences; compose a simple, compound, and complex sentences; correct fragments and run-on sentences	L1 pp. 174–179 L2 pp. 180–185 L3 pp. 186–191
Research		
6.R.1–4	Use own questions to find information on a topic of interest; use graphic features to interpret a text; consult visual and text reference sources; determine relevance and reliability of information	R7 pp. 42–47 W7 pp. 106–111
6.W.1–2	Generate a viable research question; organize information found during research	W7 pp. 106–111 W8 pp. 112–117 W9 pp. 118–123
6.W.3	Summarize and present information in a report	SL4 pp. 152–157

(Continued)

Oklahoma Strand/Standard	Focus of Oklahoma Standard	For More Information
Multimodal Literacies		
7.R.1	Locate, organize, and analyze information from a variety of texts to generate and answer literal and interpretive questions	R5 pp. 30–35 R7 pp. 42–47
7.R.2	Compare how ideas and topics are depicted in a variety of media and formats	R9 pp. 54–59
7.W.1	Create multimodal content that communicates an idea	W6 pp. 100–105
7.W.2	Create presentations using multimedia elements to support communication	SL5 pp. 158–163
Independent Reading and Writing		
8.R	Select and read independently level-appropriate texts for academic and personal purposes	R10 pp. 60–65
8.W	Write independently for extended and shorter periods of time	W10 pp. 124–129

Oklahoma, Grade 5

Oklahoma Strand/Standard	Focus of Oklahoma Standard	For More Information
Speaking and Listening		
1.R.1	Actively listen and speak clearly using appropriate discussion rules	SL1 pp. 134–139
1.R.2	Ask and answer questions to seek help, get information, or clarify information presented orally	SL3 pp. 146–151
1.R.3	Engage in collaborative discussions	SL1 pp. 134–139
1.W.1	Give formal and informal presentations, organizing information and determining appropriate content for audience	SL4 pp. 152–157
1.W.2	Work in groups effectively and respectfully, valuing contributions by group members	SL1 pp. 134–139
Reading and Writing Process		
2.R.1	Create an objective summary, including main idea and supporting details, while maintaining meaning and sequence of events	R2 pp. 12–17
2.R.2	Compare and contrast details in literary and informational texts to discriminate genres	R6 pp. 36–41 R9 pp. 54–59
2.R.3	Begin to paraphrase main ideas with supporting details	R2 pp. 12–17
2.W.1	Apply components of a recursive writing process to create a focused, organized, coherent piece of writing	W4 pp. 88–93
2.W.2–3	Plan, prewrite, and develop drafts; choose organizational structure, building on ideas in multi-paragraph essays	W4 pp. 88–93
2.W.4	Edit and revise multiple drafts for purpose, organization, and coherence	W5 pp. 94–99
2.W.5	Use resources to find correct spellings	L2 pp. 180–185
Critical Reading and Writing		
3.R.1	Determine the author's stated or implied purpose and evaluate how well it was achieved	R8 pp. 48–53
3.R.2	Determine the point of view and describe how it affects the text	R6 pp. 36–41
3.R.3	Describe and find evidence of key literary elements (setting, plot, characters, characterization, theme)	R2 pp. 12–17 R3 pp. 18–23
3.R.4	Evaluate literary devices (i.e., simile, metaphor) to support interpretations of text	R4 pp. 24–29

Oklahoma Strand/Standard	Focus of Oklahoma Standard	For More Information
Critical Reading and Writing		
3.R.5	Distinguish fact from opinion in a text and investigate facts for accuracy	R8 pp. 48–53
3.R.6	Distinguish the structures of texts and content by making inferences and use textual evidence to support understanding	R1 pp. 6–11 R5 pp. 30–35
3.R.7	Compare and contrast texts and ideas within and between texts	R9 pp. 54–59
3.W.1	Write narratives incorporating plot, setting, characters, point of view, and conflict	W3 pp. 82–87
3.W.2	Introduce and develop a topic, incorporating evidence and maintaining an organized structure	W2 pp. 76–81
3.W.3–4	Clearly state an opinion supported with facts and details; show relationships among facts, opinions, and supporting details	W1 pp. 70–75
Vocabulary		
4.R.1	Increase knowledge of academic, domain-appropriate, grade-level vocabulary to infer meaning of text	L6 pp. 204–209
4.R.2	Use word parts to define and determine meaning of new words	L4 pp. 192–197
4.R.3	Use context clues to determine or clarify word meaning	L4 pp. 192–197
4.R.4	Infer relationships among words with multiple meanings, including synonyms, antonyms, and multiple meaning words	L5 pp. 198–203
4.R.5	Use a dictionary, glossary, or thesaurus to find words	L4 pp. 192–197
4.W.1	Use domain-appropriate vocabulary to communicate ideas in writing clearly	L6 pp. 204–209
4.W.2	Select appropriate language to create a specific effect in writing	L6 pp. 204–209
Language		
5.R.1–5	Recognize conjunctions, prepositions, and interjections; recognize verb tense to signify times, sequences, states, and conditions; recognize subject-verb agreement	L1 pp. 174–179
5.W.1–5	Write using correct mechanics; compose simple, compound, and complex sentences; form and use present and past verb tenses; recognize and correct inappropriate shifts in verb tense	L1 pp. 174–179 L2 pp. 180–185 L3 pp. 186–191
Research		
6.R.1–3	Use own questions to find information on a topic of interest; record and organize information from sources; determine relevance and reliability of information	R7 pp. 42–47 W7 pp. 106–111
6.W.1–3	Write research papers; form a viable research question; organize information found during research	W7 pp. 106–111 W8 pp. 112–117 W9 pp. 118–123
6.W.3	Summarize and present information in a report	SL4 pp. 152–157
Multimodal Literacies		
7.R.1	Analyze the characteristics and effectiveness of a variety of texts to generate and answer literal and interpretive questions	R5 pp. 30–35 R7 pp. 42–47
7.R.2	Compare and contrast how ideas and topics are depicted in a variety of media and formats	R9 pp. 54–59
7.W.1	Create multimodal content that communicates an idea	W6 pp. 100–105
7.W.2	Create presentations using multimedia elements to enrich the presentation	SL5 pp. 158–163
Independent Reading and Writing		
8.R	Select and read independently level-appropriate texts for academic and personal purposes	R10 pp. 60–65
8.W	Write independently for extended and shorter periods of time	W10 pp. 124–129

Pennsylvania, Grade 3

Pennsylvania Strand/Standard	Focus of Pennsylvania Standard	For More Information
Foundational Skills		
CC.1.1.D	Phonics: Know and apply grade-level phonics and word analysis skills in decoding words	RF3 pp. 214–219
CC.1.1.E	Fluency: Read level-appropriate texts with purpose and understanding	RF4 pp. 220–225
Reading Informational Text		
CC.1.2.A	Determine the main idea of a text; recount the key details and explain how they support the main idea	R2 pp. 12–17
CC.1.2.B	Ask and answer questions about the text and make inferences, refer to the text to support responses	R1 pp. 6–11
CC.1.2.C	Explain how a series of events, concepts, or steps in a procedure is connected within a text	R3 pp. 18–23
CC.1.2.D	Explain the point of view of the author	R6 pp. 36–41
CC1.2.E	Use text features to locate and interpret information	R5 pp. 30–35
CC1.2.F	Determine the meaning of words and phrases as they are used in a grade-level text	R4 pp. 24–29
CC1.2.G	Use information from illustrations and the words in a text to demonstrate understanding of the text	R7 pp. 42–47
CC1.2.H	Describe how an author connects sentences a paragraphs in a text to support particular points	R8 pp. 48–53
CC1.2.I	Compare and contrast the most important points and key details in two texts on the same topic	R9 pp. 54–59
CC1.2.J	Acquire and use accurately conversational, general academic, and domain-specific words and phrases	L6 pp. 204–209
CC1.2.K	Determine or clarify the meaning of unknown and multiple-meaning words and phrases, choosing flexibly from an array of strategies	L4 pp. 192–197
CC1.2.l	Read and comprehend level-appropriate informational text	R10 pp. 60–65
Reading Literature		
CC1.3.A	Determine the central message, lesson, or moral in literary text, and explain how it is conveyed	R2 pp. 12–17
CC1.3.B	Ask and answer questions about text and make inferences from text, referring to text to support responses	R1 pp. 6–11
CC1.3.C	Describe characters in a story and explain how their actions contribute to the sequence of events	R3 pp. 18–23
CC1.3.D	Explain the point of view of the author	R6 pp. 36–41
CC1.3.E	Refer to parts of texts when writing or speaking about a text, using terms such as chapter, scene, and stanza; describe how each successive part builds on earlier sections	R5 pp. 30–35
CC1.3.F	Determine the meaning of words and phrases as they are used in a text, distinguishing literal from nonliteral language	R4 pp. 24–29
CC1.3.G	Explain how specific elements of a text's illustrations contribute to what is conveyed by the words in a story	R7 pp. 42–47
CC1.3.H	Compare and contrast the themes, settings, and plots of stories written by the same author about the same or similar characters	R9 pp. 54–59
CC1.3.I	Determine or clarify the meaning of unknown and multiple-meaning words and phrases, choosing flexibly from an array of strategies	L4 pp. 192–197
CC1.3.J	Acquire and use accurately conversational, general academic, and domain-specific words and phrases	L6 pp. 204–209
CC1.3.K	Read and comprehend level-appropriate literature	R10 pp. 60–65
Writing		
CC1.4.A-F	Write Informative/Explanatory Texts: Name a topic, use facts to develop points, create an organizational structure, choose words and phrases for effect; demonstrate command of the conventions of standard English capitalization, punctuation, and spelling when writing	W2 pp. 76–81 W4 pp. 88–93 L2 pp. 180–185
CC1.4.G-L	Write Opinion Pieces: Introduce the topic, state an opinion and support it with reasons, provide an organizational structure with a concluding statement; use a variety of sentence types; demonstrate command of the conventions of standard English capitalization, punctuation, and spelling when writing	W1 pp. 70–75 W4 pp. 88–93 L2 pp. 180–185

Pennsylvania Strand/Standard	Focus of Pennsylvania Standard	For More Information
Writing		
CC1.4.M-R	Write Narratives: Establish a situation, introduce a narrator or characters, use dialogue and description, sequence events; choose words and phrases for effect; demonstrate command of the conventions of standard English capitalization, punctuation, and spelling when writing	W3 pp. 82–87 W4 pp. 88–93 L2 pp. 180–185
CC1.4.S	Draw evidence from literary or informational texts to support analysis, reflection, and research	W9 pp. 118–123
CC1.4.T	Develop and strengthen writing as needed by planning, revising, and editing	W5 pp. 94–99
CC1.4.U	Use technology to produce and publish writing	W6 pp. 100–105
CC1.4.V	Conduct short research projects that build knowledge about a topic	W7 pp. 106–111
CC1.4.W	Recall information from experiences or gather information from print and digital sources	W8 pp. 112–117
CC1.4.X	Write routinely over extended time frames	W10 pp. 124–129
Speaking and Listening		
CC1.5.A	Engage effectively in a range of collaborative discussions with diverse partners, building on others' ideas and expressing their own clearly	SL1 pp. 134–139
CC1.5.B	Determine the main ideas and supporting details of a text read aloud or information presented in diverse media and formats	SL2 pp. 140–145
CC1.5.C	Ask and answer questions about information from a speaker, offering appropriate elaboration and detail	SL3 pp. 146–151
CC1.5.D	Report on a topic or text, tell a story, or recount an experience with appropriate facts and relevant details	SL4 pp. 152–157
CC1.5.E	Speak in complete sentences when appropriate to task and situation in order to provide requested detail or clarification	SL6 pp. 164–169
CC1.5.F	Create audio recordings of stories or poems, demonstrating fluent reading; add visual displays when appropriate	SL5 pp. 158–163
CC1.5.G	Demonstrate command of the conventions of standard English grammar and usage when speaking	L1 pp. 174–179

Pennsylvania, Grade 4

Pennsylvania Strand/Standard	Focus of Pennsylvania Standard	For More Information
Foundational Skills		
CC.1.1.D	Phonics: Know and apply grade-level phonics and word analysis skills in decoding words	RF3 pp. 214–219
CC.1.1.E	Fluency: Read level-appropriate texts with purpose and understanding	RF4 pp. 220–225
Reading Informational Text		
CC.1.2.A	Determine the main idea of a text and explain how it is supported by key details; summarize the text	R2 pp. 12–17
CC.1.2.B	Refer to details and examples in a text when explaining what the text says explicitly and when drawing inferences from the text	R1 pp. 6–11
CC.1.2.C	Explain events, procedures, ideas, or concepts in a text, including what happened and why, based on specific information in the text	R3 pp. 18–23
CC.1.2.D	Compare and contrast an event or topic told from two different points of view	R6 pp. 36–41
CC.1.2.E	Use text structure to interpret information	R5 pp. 30–35
CC.1.2.F	Determine the meaning of words and phrases as they are used in a text	R4 pp. 24–29
CC.1.2.G	Interpret various presentations of information within a text and explain how it contributes to an understanding of the text	R7 pp. 42–47

(Continued)

Pennsylvania Strand/Standard	Focus of Pennsylvania Standard	For More Information
Reading Informational Text		
CC1.2.H	Explain how an author uses reasons and evidence to support particular points in a text	R8 pp. 48–53
CC1.2.I	Integrate information from two texts on the same topic in order to write or speak about the subject	R9 pp. 54–59
CC1.2.J	Acquire and use accurately conversational, general academic, and domain-specific words and phrases	L6 pp. 204–209
CC1.2.K	Determine or clarify the meaning of unknown and multiple-meaning words and phrases, choosing flexibly from an array of strategies	L4 pp. 192–197
CC1.2.L	Read and comprehend level-appropriate informational text	R10 pp. 60–65
Reading Literature		
CC1.3.A	Determine a theme of a text from details in the text; summarize the text	R2 pp. 12–17
CC1.3.B	Cite relevant details form text to support what the text says explicitly and make inferences	R1 pp. 6–11
CC1.3.C	Describe in depth a character, setting, or event in a story or drama, drawing on specific details in the text	R3 pp. 18–23
CC1.3.D	Compare and contrast an event or topic told from two different points of view	R6 pp. 36–41
CC1.3.E	Explain the major differences between poems, drama, and prose; refer to structural elements when writing or speaking about a text	R5 pp. 30–35
CC1.3.F	Determine the meaning of words and phrases as they are used in a text	R4 pp. 24–29
CC1.3.G	Make connections between the text of a story or drama and a visual or oral representation of the text	R7 pp. 42–47
CC1.3.H	Compare and contrast similar themes and topics and patterns of events in literature including texts from different cultures	R9 pp. 54–59
CC1.3.I	Determine or clarify the meaning of unknown and multiple-meaning words and phrases, choosing flexibly from an array of strategies	L4 pp. 192–197
CC1.3.J	Acquire and use accurately conversational, general academic, and domain-specific words and phrases	L6 pp. 204–209
CC1.3.K	Read and comprehend level-appropriate literature	R10 pp. 60–65
Writing		
CC1.4.A-F	Write Informative/Explanatory Texts: Name a topic, use facts to develop points, create an organizational structure, choose words and phrases for effect; demonstrate command of the conventions of standard English capitalization, punctuation, and spelling when writing	W2 pp. 76–81 W4 pp. 88–93 L2 pp. 180–185
CC1.4.G-L	Write Opinion Pieces: Introduce the topic, state an opinion and support it with reasons, provide an organizational structure with a concluding statement; use a variety of sentence types; demonstrate command of the conventions of standard English capitalization, punctuation, and spelling when writing	W1 pp. 70–75 W4 pp. 88–93 L2 pp. 180–185
CC1.4.M-R	Write Narratives: Establish a situation, introduce a narrator or characters, use dialogue and description, sequence events; choose words and phrases for effect; demonstrate command of the conventions of standard English capitalization, punctuation, and spelling when writing	W3 pp. 82–87 W4 pp. 88–93 L2 pp. 180–185
CC1.4.S	Draw evidence from literary or informational texts to support analysis, reflection, and research	W9 pp. 118–123
CC1.4.T	Develop and strengthen writing as needed by planning, revising, and editing	W5 pp. 94–99
CC1.4.U	Use technology to produce and publish writing; demonstrate keyboarding skills	W6 pp. 100–105
CC1.4.V	Conduct short research projects that build knowledge about a topic	W7 pp. 106–111
CC1.4.W	Recall information from experiences or gather information from print and digital sources	W8 pp. 112–117
CC1.4.X	Write routinely over extended time frames	W10 pp. 124–129

Pennsylvania Strand/Standard	Focus of Pennsylvania Standard	For More Information
Speaking and Listening		
CC1.5.A	Engage effectively in a range of collaborative discussions with diverse partners, building on others' ideas and expressing their own clearly	SL1 pp. 134–139
CC1.5.B	Paraphrase portions of a text read aloud or information presented in diverse media and formats	SL2 pp. 140–145
CC1.5.C	Identify the reasons and evidence a speaker provides to support particular points	SL3 pp. 146–151
CC1.5.D	Report on a topic or text, tell a story, or recount an experience with appropriate facts and details to support main ideas or themes	SL4 pp. 152–157
CC1.5.E	Differentiate between contexts that call for formal English versus informal situations	SL6 pp. 164–169
CC1.5.F	Add audio recordings and visual displays to presentations when appropriate to enhance the development of main ideas or themes	SL5 pp. 158–163
CC1.5.G	Demonstrate command of the conventions of standard English grammar and usage when speaking	L1 pp. 174–179

Pennsylvania, Grade 5

Pennsylvania Strand/Standard	Focus of Pennsylvania Standard	For More Information
Foundational Skills		
CC.1.1.D	Phonics: Know and apply grade-level phonics and word analysis skills in decoding words	RF3 pp. 214–219
CC.1.1.E	Fluency: Read level-appropriate texts with purpose and understanding	RF4 pp. 220–225
Reading Informational Text		
CC.1.2.A	Determine two or more main ideas of a text and explain how they are supported by key details; summarize the text	R2 pp. 12–17
CC.1.2.B	Cite textual evidence by quoting accurately from the text to explain what it says explicitly and to make inferences	R1 pp. 6–11
CC.1.2.C	Explain the relationships or interactions between two or more individuals, events, ideas, or concepts in a text, based on specific information in the text	R3 pp. 18–23
CC.1.2.D	Analyze multiple accounts of the same event or topic, noting important similarities and differences in the point of view they represent	R6 pp. 36–41
CC1.2.E	Use text structure, in and among texts, to interpret information	R5 pp. 30–35
CC1.2.F	Determine the meaning of words and phrases as they are used in a text	R4 pp. 24–29
CC1.2.G	Draw on information from multiple sources, demonstrating the ability to locate an answer to a question quickly or solve a problem efficiently	R7 pp. 42–47
CC1.2.H	Determine how an author uses reasons and evidence to support particular points in a text	R8 pp. 48–53
CC1.2.I	Integrate information from several texts on the same topic in order to write or speak about the subject	R9 pp. 54–59
CC1.2.J	Acquire and use accurately conversational, general academic, and domain-specific words and phrases	L6 pp. 204–209
CC1.2.K	Determine or clarify the meaning of unknown and multiple-meaning words and phrases, choosing flexibly from an array of strategies	L4 pp. 192–197
CC1.2.L	Read and comprehend level-appropriate informational text	R10 pp. 60–65

(Continued)

Pennsylvania Strand/Standard	Focus of Pennsylvania Standard	For More Information
Reading Literature		
CC1.3.A	Determine a theme of a story, drama, or poem from details in the text; summarize the text	R2 pp. 12–17
CC1.3.B	Cite textual evidence by quoting accurately from the text to explain what the text says explicitly and make inferences	R1 pp. 6–11
CC1.3.C	Compare and contrast two or more characters, settings, or events in a story or drama, drawing on specific details in the text	R3 pp. 18–23
CC1.3.D	Analyze multiple accounts of the same event or topic	R6 pp. 36–41
CC1.3.E	Explain how a series of chapters, scenes, or stanzas fits together to provide the overall structure of a story, drama, or poem	R5 pp. 30–35
CC1.3.F	Determine the meaning of words and phrases as they are used in a text	R4 pp. 24–29
CC1.3.G	Analyze how visual and multimedia elements contribute to the meaning, tone, or beauty of a text	R7 pp. 42–47
CC1.3.H	Compare and contrast stories in the same genre on their approaches to similar themes and topics	R9 pp. 54–59
CC1.3.I	Determine or clarify the meaning of unknown and multiple-meaning words and phrases, choosing flexibly from an array of strategies	L4 pp. 192–197
CC1.3.J	Acquire and use accurately conversational, general academic, and domain-specific words and phrases	L6 pp. 204–209
CC1.3.K	Read and comprehend level-appropriate literature	R10 pp. 60–65
Writing		
CC1.4.A-F	Write Informative/Explanatory Texts: Name a topic, use facts to develop points, create an organizational structure, choose words and phrases for effect; demonstrate command of the conventions of standard English capitalization, punctuation, and spelling when writing	W2 pp. 76–81 W4 pp. 88–93 L2 pp. 180–185
CC1.4.G-L	Write Opinion Pieces: Introduce the topic, state an opinion and support it with reasons, provide an organizational structure with a concluding statement; use a variety of sentence types; demonstrate command of the conventions of standard English capitalization, punctuation, and spelling when writing	W1 pp. 70–75 W4 pp. 88–93 L2 pp. 180–185
CC1.4.M-R	Write Narratives: Establish a situation, introduce a narrator or characters, use dialogue and description, sequence events; choose words and phrases for effect; demonstrate command of the conventions of standard English capitalization, punctuation, and spelling when writing	W3 pp. 82–87 W4 pp. 88–93 L2 pp. 180–185
CC1.4.S	Draw evidence from literary or informational texts to support analysis, reflection, and research	W9 pp. 118–123
CC1.4.T	Develop and strengthen writing as needed by planning, revising, and editing	W5 pp. 94–99
CC1.4.U	Use technology to produce and publish writing; demonstrate keyboarding skills	W6 pp. 100–105
CC1.4.V	Conduct short research projects that build knowledge about a topic	W7 pp. 106–111
CC1.4.W	Recall information from experiences or gather information from print and digital sources	W8 pp. 112–117
CC1.4.X	Write routinely over extended time frames	W10 pp. 124–129
Speaking and Listening		
CC1.5.A	Engage effectively in a range of collaborative discussions with diverse partners, building on others' ideas and expressing their own clearly	SL1 pp. 134–139
CC1.5.B	Summarize a written text read aloud or information presented in diverse media and formats	SL2 pp. 140–145
CC1.5.C	Summarize points a speaker makes and explain how each claim is supported by reasons and evidence	SL3 pp. 146–151
CC1.5.D	Report on a topic or text or present an opinion, using appropriate facts and details to support main ideas and themes	SL4 pp. 152–157
CC1.5.E	Adapt speech to a variety of contexts, using formal English when appropriate to task and situation	SL6 pp. 164–169
CC1.5.F	Include multimedia components and visual displays in presentations when appropriate to enhance the development of main ideas or themes	SL5 pp. 158–163
CC1.5.G	Demonstrate command of the conventions of standard English grammar and usage when speaking	L1 pp. 174–179

South Carolina, Grade 3

South Carolina Strand/Standard	Focus of South Carolina Standard	For More Information
Reading Literary Text		
	Principles of Reading	
3	Phonics: Know and apply grade-level phonics and word analysis skills in decoding words; read grade-appropriate irregularly spelled words	RF3 pp. 214–219 L2 pp. 180–185
4	Fluency: Read grade-level texts with sufficient accuracy and fluency to support comprehension	RF4 pp. 220–225
	Meaning and Context	
5.1	Ask and answer questions to determine meaning; refer explicitly to the text to support inferences and conclusions	R1 pp. 6–11
6.1	Determine the theme by recalling details that support the theme	R2 pp. 12–17
7.1	Explain how illustrations contribute to create mood or emphasize aspects of a character or setting	R7 pp. 42–47
7.2	Compare and contrast how an author uses characters to develop theme and plot in different texts within a series	R9 pp. 54–59
8.1	Use text evidence to describe characters' traits, motivations, and feelings, and explain how their actions contribute to the plot; explain the influence of cultural and historical context on the characters, setting, and plot	R3 pp. 18–23
	Language, Craft, and Structure	
9.1	Identify and explain how the author uses language to shape meaning and style	R4 pp. 24–29 L5 pp. 198–203
10.1	Use paragraph-level context to determine the meaning of words and phrases	R4 pp. 24–29
10.2	Determine the meaning of a word when an affix is added to a base word	L2 pp. 180–185
10.5	Consult print and multimedia resources to find the pronunciation and determine the meaning of words	L2 pp. 180–185
10.6	Acquire and use general academic and domain-specific words and phrases	L6 pp. 204–209
11.1	Explain the difference between the first- and third-person points of view	R6 pp. 36–41
11.2	Compare and contrast the reader's point of view to that of the narrator or a character	R6 pp. 36–41
12.1	Identify text structures of various genres using the terms paragraph, chapter, scene, and stanza	R5 pp. 30–35
	Range and Complexity	
13.1–3	Read independently and comprehend a variety of texts for a variety of purposes	R10 pp. 60–65
Reading Informational Text		
	Principles of Reading	
3.1–6	Phonics: Know and apply grade-level phonics and word analysis skills in decoding words	RF3 pp. 214–219 L2 pp. 180–185
4.1–3	Fluency: Read grade-level texts with sufficient accuracy and fluency to support comprehension	RF4 pp. 220–225
5.1	Ask literal and inferential questions to demonstrate understanding of a text, referring explicitly to the text as the basis for the answers	R1 pp. 6–11
6.1	Summarize multi-paragraph texts using key details to support the central idea	R2 pp. 12–17
7.1	Compare and contrast diverse texts on the same topic, idea, or concept	R9 pp. 54–59
	Language, Craft, and Structure	
8.1	Explain how an author uses words and phrases to inform, explain, or describe	R4 pp. 24–29

(Continued)

South Carolina Strand/Standard	Focus of South Carolina Standard	For More Information
Reading Informational Text		
8.2	Use knowledge of appendices, timeline, maps, and charts to locate information and gain meaning	R5 pp. 30–35
9.1	Use paragraph-level context to determine the meaning of words and phrases	R4 pp. 24–29
9.2	Determine the meaning of a word when an affix is added to a base word	L2 pp. 180–185
9.4	Consult print and multimedia resources to find the pronunciation and determine the meaning of words	L2 pp. 180–185
9.5	Acquire and use general academic and domain-specific words and phrases	L6 pp. 204–209
10.1	State the author's purpose; distinguish one's own perspective from that of the author	R6 pp. 36–41
11.1–2	Identify text structures to locate information and gain meaning; describe the structures an author uses to support specific points	R8 pp. 48–53
12.1–3	Read independently and comprehend a variety of texts for a variety of purposes	R10 pp. 60–65
Writing		
	Meaning, Context, and Craft	
1.1	Write arguments to support claims with clear reasons and relevant evidence; strengthen writing as needed by planning, revising, and editing	W1 pp. 70–75 W5 pp. 94–99
2.1	Write informative/explanatory texts to examine and convey complex ideas and information clearly and accurately; strengthen writing as needed by planning, revising, and editing	W2 pp. 76–81 W5 pp. 94–99
3.1	Write narratives to develop real or imagined experiences or events using effective technique, descriptive details, and clear event sequences; strengthen writing as needed by planning, revising, and editing	W3 pp. 82–87 W5 pp. 94–99
	Language	
4.1	Demonstrate command of the conventions of standard English grammar and usage when writing or speaking	L1 pp. 174–179
5.1–5	Demonstrate command of the conventions of standard English capitalization, punctuation, and spelling when writing	L2 pp. 180–185
	Range and Complexity	
6.1–5	Write independently, legibly, and routinely for a variety of tasks, purposes, and audiences over short and extended time frames	W10 pp. 124–129
Communication		
	Meaning and Context	
1.1–5	Interact with others to explore ideas and concepts, communicate meaning, and develop logical interpretations through collaborative conversations; build upon the ideas of others to clearly express one's own views while respecting diverse perspectives	SL1 pp. 134–139 SL3 pp. 146–151
2.1	Recall information from experiences and gather information from print and multimedia sources; take notes, categorize, and organize	W8 pp. 112–117
2.2	Report on a topic or text, tell a story, or recount an experience with detail	SL4 pp. 152–157
2.4	Speak clearly, adapting speech to a variety of contexts; use standard English when indicated or appropriate	SL6 pp. 164–169
3.1–2	Communicate information through strategic use of multiple modalities and multimedia to enrich understanding when presenting ideas or information	SL5 pp. 158–163
	Language, Craft, and Structure	
4.1–3	Critique how a speaker addresses content and uses stylistic and structural craft techniques to inform, engage, and impact audiences	SL3 pp. 146–151
5.1–2	Incorporate craft techniques to engage and impact audience and convey messages	SL4 pp. 152–157 SL5 pp. 158–163 SL6 pp. 164–169

South Carolina, Grade 4

South Carolina Strand/Standard	Focus of South Carolina Standard	For More Information
Reading Literary Text		
	Principles of Reading	
3	Phonics: Know and apply grade-level phonics and word analysis skills in decoding words; read grade-appropriate irregularly spelled words	RF3 pp. 214–219 L2 pp. 180–185
4	Fluency: Read grade-level texts with sufficient accuracy and fluency to support comprehension	RF4 pp. 220–225
	Meaning and Context	
5.1	Ask and answer inferential questions to analyze meaning beyond the text; refer to details and examples to support inferences and conclusions	R1 pp. 6–11
6.1	Determine the development of a theme within a text; summarize using key details	R2 pp. 12–17
7.1	Explore similarities and differences among textual, dramatic, visual, or oral presentations	R7 pp. 42–47
7.2	Compare and contrast the treatment of similar themes, topics, and patterns of events in texts and diverse media	R9 pp. 54–59
8.1	Use text evidence to explain how conflicts cause characters to change; explain the influence of cultural, historical, and social context on characters, setting, and plot development	R3 pp. 18–23
	Language, Craft, and Structure	
9.1–2	Identify and explain how the author uses language to shape meaning and style	R4 pp. 24–29 L5 pp. 198–203
10.1	Use definitions, examples, and restatements to determine the meaning of words or phrases	R4 pp. 24–29
10.2	Determine the meaning of an unknown word using knowledge of base words and affixes	L2 pp. 180–185
10.5	Consult print and multimedia resources to find the pronunciation and determine the meaning of words	L2 pp. 180–185
10.6	Acquire and use general academic and domain-specific words and phrases	L6 pp. 204–209
11.1	Compare and contrast first- and third-person points of view; determine how an author's choice of point of view influences the content and meaning	R6 pp. 36–41
11.2	Compare and contrast the reader's point of view to that of the narrator or a character	R6 pp. 36–41
12.1–2	Explain how a series of chapters, scenes, or stanzas fit together to provide the overall structure of a text; determine the structures of a text and describe why an author uses them	R5 pp. 30–35
	Range and Complexity	
13.1–3	Read independently and comprehend a variety of texts for a variety of purposes	R10 pp. 60–65
Reading Informational Text		
	Principles of Reading	
3.1–6	Phonics: Know and apply grade-level phonics and word analysis skills in decoding words	RF3 pp. 214–219 L2 pp. 180–185
4.1–3	Fluency: Read grade-level texts with sufficient accuracy and fluency to support comprehension	RF4 pp. 220–225
5.1	Ask and answer inferential questions to analyze meaning beyond the text; refer to details and examples to support inferences and conclusions	R1 pp. 6–11
6.1	Summarize multi-paragraph texts using key details to support the central idea	R2 pp. 12–17
7.1	Compare and contrast how events, topics, concepts, and ideas are depicted in primary and secondary sources	R9 pp. 54–59
	Language, Craft, and Structure	
8.1	Determine how an author uses words and phrases to inform, explain, or describe	R4 pp. 24–29
8.2	Apply knowledge of text features to gain meaning	R5 pp. 30–35

(Continued)

South Carolina Strand/Standard	Focus of South Carolina Standard	For More Information
Reading Informational Text		
9.1	Use definitions, examples, and restatements to determine the meaning of words and phrases	R4 pp. 24–29
9.2	Determine the meaning of a word using knowledge of base words and affixes	L2 pp. 180–185
9.4	Consult print and multimedia resources to find the pronunciation and determine the meaning of words	L2 pp. 180–185
9.5	Acquire and use general academic and domain-specific words and phrases	L6 pp. 204–209
10.1	Identify and describe the difference between a primary and secondary account of the same topic	R6 pp. 36–41
11.1–2	Apply knowledge of text structures to describe how they contribute to meaning; explain how an author uses reasons and evidence to support particular points	R8 pp. 48–53
12.1–3	Read independently and comprehend a variety of texts for a variety of purposes	R10 pp. 60–65
Writing		
	Meaning, Context, and Craft	
1.1	Write arguments to support claims with clear reasons and relevant evidence; strengthen writing as needed by planning, revising, and editing	W1 pp. 70–75 W5 pp. 94–99
2.1	Write informative/explanatory texts to examine and convey complex ideas and information clearly and accurately; strengthen writing as needed by planning, revising, and editing	W2 pp. 76–81 W5 pp. 94–99
3.1	Write narratives to develop real or imagined experiences or events using effective technique, descriptive details, and clear event sequences; strengthen writing as needed by planning, revising, and editing	W3 pp. 82–87 W5 pp. 94–99
	Language	
4.1	Demonstrate command of the conventions of standard English grammar and usage when writing or speaking	L1 pp. 174–179
5.1–5	Demonstrate command of the conventions of standard English capitalization, punctuation, and spelling when writing	L2 pp. 180–185
	Range and Complexity	
6.1–5	Write independently, legibly, and routinely for a variety of tasks, purposes, and audiences over short and extended time frames	W10 pp. 124–129
Communication		
	Meaning and Context	
1.1–5	Interact with others to explore ideas and concepts, communicate meaning, and develop logical interpretations through collaborative conversations; build upon the ideas of others to clearly express one's own views while respecting diverse perspectives	SL1 pp. 134–139
2.1	Articulate ideas, perspectives, and information with details and supporting evidence in a logical sequence	W8 pp. 112–117
2.2	Discuss the purpose and credibility of information presented in diverse media and formats	SL2 pp. 140–145
2.4	Speak clearly, adapting speech to a variety of contexts; use standard English when indicated or appropriate	SL6 pp. 164–169
3.1–2	Communicate information through strategic use of multiple modalities and multimedia to enrich understanding when presenting ideas or information	SL5 pp. 158–163
	Language, Craft, and Structure	
4.1–3	Critique how a speaker addresses content and uses stylistic and structural craft techniques to inform, engage, and impact audiences	SL3 pp. 146–151
5.1–2	Incorporate craft techniques to engage and impact audience and convey messages	SL4 pp. 152–157 SL5 pp. 158–163 SL6 pp. 164–169

South Carolina, Grade 5

South Carolina Strand/Standard	Focus of South Carolina Standard	For More Information
Reading Literary Text		
	Principles of Reading	
3	Phonics: Know and apply grade-level phonics and word analysis skills in decoding words; read grade-appropriate irregularly spelled words	RF3 pp. 214–219 L2 pp. 180–185
4	Fluency: Read grade-level texts with sufficient accuracy and fluency to support comprehension	RF4 pp. 220–225
	Meaning and Context	
5.1	Quote accurately to analyze the meaning of and beyond the text to support inferences and conclusions	R1 pp. 6–11
6.1	Determine and analyze the development of a theme within a text; summarize using key details	R2 pp. 12–17
7.1	Compare and contrast textual, dramatic, visual, or oral presentations to identify similarities and differences	R7 pp. 42–47
7.2	Compare and contrast the treatment of similar themes, topics, and patterns of events depicted in diverse modalities	R9 pp. 54–59
8.1	Cite evidence within text to analyze two or more characters, events, or settings in a text; explain the influence of cultural, historical, social, and political context on characters, setting, and plot development	R3 pp. 18–23
	Language, Craft, and Structure	
9.1–2	Cite examples of how the author uses language to shape meaning and tone; analyze how word choice and conventions combine to create mood, shape meaning, and emphasize aspects of a character or setting	R4 pp. 24–29 L5 pp. 198–203
10.1	Use cause-effect relationships and comparisons to determine the meaning of words or phrases	R4 pp. 24–29
10.2	Determine the meaning of an unknown word using knowledge of base words and affixes	L2 pp. 180–185
10.5	Consult print and multimedia resources to find the pronunciation and determine the meaning of words	L2 pp. 180–185
10.6	Acquire and use general academic and domain-specific words and phrases	L6 pp. 204–209
11.1	Explain how the author's choice of the point of view od a narrator or character impacts content, meaning, and how events are described	R6 pp. 36–41
11.2	Compare and contrast the reader's point of view to that of the narrator or a character	R6 pp. 36–41
12.1–2	Explain how text structures in prose, drama, or poetry differ; compare how different text structures contribute to meaning and impact the reader	R5 pp. 30–35
	Range and Complexity	
13.1–3	Read independently and comprehend a variety of texts for a variety of purposes	R10 pp. 60–65
Reading Informational Text		
	Principles of Reading	
3.1–6	Phonics: Know and apply grade-level phonics and word analysis skills in decoding words	RF3 pp. 214–219 L2 pp. 180–185
4.1–3	Fluency: Read grade-level texts with sufficient accuracy and fluency to support comprehension	RF4 pp. 220–225
5.1	Quote accurately from a text to analyze meaning in and beyond the text	R1 pp. 6–11
6.1	Summarize a text with two or more central ideas; cite supporting details	R2 pp. 12–17
7.1	Compare and contrast how events, topics, concepts, and ideas are depicted in primary and secondary sources	R9 pp. 54–59

(Continued)

South Carolina Strand/Standard	Focus of South Carolina Standard	For More Information
Reading Informational Text		
	Language, Craft, and Structure	
8.1	Determine how an author uses words and phrases to inform, explain, or describe	R4 pp. 24–29
8.2	Apply knowledge of text features to gain meaning	R5 pp. 30–35
9.1	Use the overall meaning of a text or word's position or function to determine the meaning	R4 pp. 24–29
9.2	Determine the meaning of a word using knowledge of base words and affixes	L2 pp. 180–185
9.4	Consult print and multimedia resources to find the pronunciation and determine the meaning of words	L2 pp. 180–185
9.5	Acquire and use general academic and domain-specific words and phrases	L6 pp. 204–209
10.1	Compare and contrast a primary and secondary account of the same topic	R6 pp. 36–41
11.1–2	Apply knowledge of text structures across multiple texts to locate information and gain meaning; explain how an author uses reasons and evidence to support particular points	R8 pp. 48–53
12.1–3	Read independently and comprehend a variety of texts for a variety of purposes	R10 pp. 60–65
Writing		
	Meaning, Context, and Craft	
1.1	Write arguments to support claims with clear reasons and relevant evidence; strengthen writing as needed by planning, revising, and editing	W1 pp. 70–75 W5 pp. 94–99
2.1	Write informative/explanatory texts to examine and convey complex ideas and information clearly and accurately; strengthen writing as needed by planning, revising, and editing	W2 pp. 76–81 W5 pp. 94–99
3.1	Write narratives to develop real or imagined experiences or events using effective technique, descriptive details, and clear event sequences; strengthen writing as needed by planning, revising, and editing	W3 pp. 82–87 W5 pp. 94–99
	Language	
4.1	Demonstrate command of the conventions of standard English grammar and usage when writing or speaking	L1 pp. 174–179
5.1–5	Demonstrate command of the conventions of standard English capitalization, punctuation, and spelling when writing	L2 pp. 180–185
	Range and Complexity	
6.1–5	Write independently, legibly, and routinely for a variety of tasks, purposes, and audiences over short and extended time frames	W10 pp. 124–129
Communication		
	Meaning and Context	
1.1–5	Interact with others to explore ideas and concepts, communicate meaning, and develop logical interpretations through collaborative conversations; build upon the ideas of others to clearly express one's own views while respecting diverse perspectives	SL1 pp. 134–139
2.1	Analyze ideas, perspectives, and information using examples and supporting evidence	W8 pp. 112–117
2.2	Analyze the credibility of information presented in diverse media and formats	SL3 pp. 146–151
2.4	Speak clearly, adapting speech to a variety of contexts; use standard English when indicated or appropriate	SL6 pp. 164–169
3.1–2	Communicate information through strategic use of multiple modalities and multimedia to enrich understanding when presenting ideas or information	SL5 pp. 158–163
	Language, Craft, and Structure	
4.1–3	Critique how a speaker addresses content and uses stylistic and structural craft techniques to inform, engage, and impact audiences	SL3 pp. 146–151
5.1–2	Incorporate craft techniques to engage and impact audience and convey messages	SL4 pp. 152–157 SL5 pp. 158–163 SL6 pp. 164–169

Tennessee, Grade 3

Tennessee Strand/Standard	Focus of Tennessee Standard	For More Information
Reading Literature		
RL.1	Ask and answer questions to demonstrate understanding of a text, referring explicitly to the text as the basis for the answers	R1 pp. 6–11
RL.2	Recount stories from diverse cultures, determine their central message, lesson, or moral, and explain how it is conveyed	R2 pp. 12–17
RL.3	Describe characters in a story and explain how their actions contribute to the sequence of events	R3 pp. 18–23
RL.4	Determine the meaning of words and phrases as they are used in a text, distinguishing literal from nonliteral language	R4 pp. 24–29
RL.5	Refer to parts of stories, dramas, and poems when writing or speaking about a text, using terms such as chapter, scene, and stanza; describe how each successive part builds on earlier sections	R5 pp. 30–35
RL.6	Distinguish their own point of view from that of the narrator or those of the characters	R6 pp. 36–41
RL.7	Explain how specific elements of a text's illustrations contribute to what is conveyed by the words in a story	R7 pp. 42–47
RL.8	NA	
RL.9	Compare and contrast the themes, settings, and plots of stories written by the same author about the same or similar characters	R9 pp. 54–59
RL.10	Read literature of appropriate complexity independently with proficiency	R10 pp. 60–65
Reading Informational Text		
RI.1	Ask and answer questions to demonstrate understanding of a text, referring explicitly to the text as the basis for the answers	R1 pp. 6–11
RI.2	Determine the main idea of a text; recount the key details and explain how they support the main idea	R2 pp. 12–17
RI.3	Describe the relationship between a series of historical events, scientific ideas or concepts, or steps in technical procedures in a text	R3 pp. 18–23
RI.4	Determine the meaning of general academic and domain-specific words and phrases in a text	R4 pp. 24–29
RI.5	Use text features and search tools to locate information on a topic efficiently	R5 pp. 30–35
RI.6	Distinguish own point of view from that of the author of a text	R6 pp. 36–41
RI.7	Use information from illustrations and the words in a text to demonstrate understanding of the text	R7 pp. 42–47
RI.8	Describe the logical connection between particular sentences and paragraphs in a text	R8 pp. 48–53
RI.9	Compare and contrast the most important points and key details presented by two texts on the same topic	R9 pp. 54–59
RI.10	Read and comprehend appropriately complex informational texts independently and proficiently	R10 pp. 60–65
Reading Foundational Skills		
RF.3	Phonics: Know and apply grade-level phonics and word analysis skills in decoding words	RF3 pp. 214–219
RF.4	Fluency: Read grade-level texts with sufficient accuracy and fluency to support comprehension	RF4 pp. 220–225

(Continued)

Tennessee Strand/Standard	Focus of Tennessee Standard	For More Information
Writing		
W.1	Write opinion pieces on topics or texts, supporting a point of view with reasons	W1 pp. 70–75
W.2	Write informative/explanatory texts to examine a topic and convey ideas and information clearly	W2 pp. 76–81
W.3	Write narratives to develop real or imagined experiences or events using effective technique, descriptive details, and clear event sequences	W3 pp. 82–87
W.4	Produce writing in which the development and organization are appropriate to the task and purpose	W4 pp. 88–93
W.5	Develop and strengthen writing as needed by planning, revising, and editing	W5 pp. 94–99
W.6	Use technology to produce and publish writing	W6 pp. 100–105
W.7	Conduct short research projects that build knowledge about a topic	W7 pp. 106–111
W.8	Recall information from experiences or gather information from print and digital sources	W8 pp. 112–117
W.9	NA	
W.10	Write routinely over shorter and extended time frames	W10 pp. 124–129
Speaking and Listening		
SL.1	Engage effectively in a range of collaborative discussions with diverse partners, building on others' ideas and expressing their own clearly	SL1 pp. 134–139
SL.2	Determine the main ideas and supporting details of a text read aloud or information presented in diverse media and formats	SL2 pp. 140–145
SL.3	Ask and answer questions about information from a speaker, offering appropriate elaboration and detail	SL3 pp. 146–151
SL.4	Report on a topic or text, tell a story, or recount an experience with appropriate facts and relevant details	SL4 pp. 152–157
SL.5	Create audio recordings of stories or poems, demonstrating fluent reading; add visual displays when appropriate	SL5 pp. 158–163
SL.6	Speak in complete sentences when appropriate to task and situation in order to provide requested detail or clarification	SL6 pp. 164–169
Language		
L.1	Demonstrate command of the conventions of standard English grammar and usage when writing or speaking	L1 pp. 174–179
L.2	Demonstrate command of the conventions of standard English capitalization, punctuation, and spelling when writing	L2 pp. 180–185
L.3	Use knowledge of language and its conventions when writing, speaking, reading, or listening	L3 pp. 186–191
L.4	Determine or clarify the meaning of unknown and multiple-meaning words and phrases, choosing flexibly from an array of strategies	L4 pp. 192–197
L.5	Demonstrate understanding of word relationships and nuances in word meanings	L5 pp. 198–203
L.6	Acquire and use accurately conversational, general academic, and domain-specific words and phrases	L6 pp. 204–209

Tennessee, Grade 4

Tennessee Strand/Standard	Focus of Tennessee Standard	For More Information
Reading Literature		
RL.1	Refer to details and examples in a text when explaining what the text says explicitly and when drawing inferences	R1 pp. 6–11
RL.2	Determine a theme of a story, drama, or poem from details in the text; summarize the text	R2 pp. 12–17
RL.3	Describe in depth a character, setting, or event in a story or drama, drawing on specific details in the text	R3 pp. 18–23
RL.4	Determine the meaning of words and phrases as they are used in a text	R4 pp. 24–29
RL.5	Explain the major differences between poems, drama, and prose; refer to structural elements when writing or speaking about a text	R5 pp. 30–35
RL.6	Compare and contrast the point of view from which different stories are narrated, including the difference between first- and third-person narratives	R6 pp. 36–41
RL.7	Make connections between the text of a story or drama and a visual or oral representation of the text	R7 pp. 42–47
RL.8	NA	
RL.9	Compare and contrast the treatment of similar themes and topics and patterns of events in stories and traditional literature from different cultures	R9 pp. 54–59
RL.10	Read literature of appropriate complexity independently with proficiency	R10 pp. 60–65
Reading Informational Text		
RI.1	Refer to details and examples in a text when explaining what the text says explicitly and when drawing inferences from the text	R1 pp. 6–11
RI.2	Determine the main idea of a text and explain how it is supported by key details; summarize the text	R2 pp. 12–17
RI.3	Explain events, procedures, ideas, or concepts in a historical, scientific, or technical text	R3 pp. 18–23
RI.4	Determine the meaning of general academic and domain-specific words and phrases in a text	R4 pp. 24–29
RI.5	Describe the overall structure of events, ideas, concepts, or information in a text	R5 pp. 30–35
RI.6	Compare and contrast a firsthand and secondhand account of the same event or topic	R6 pp. 36–41
RI.7	Interpret information presented visually, orally, or quantitatively, and explain how it contributes to an understanding of the text	R7 pp. 42–47
RI.8	Explain how an author uses reasons and evidence to support particular points in a text	R8 pp. 48–53
RI.9	Integrate information from two texts on the same topic in order to write or speak about the subject	R9 pp. 54–59
RI.10	Read and comprehend appropriately complex informational texts independently and proficiently	R10 pp. 60–65
Reading Foundational Skills		
RF.3	Phonics: Know and apply grade-level phonics and word analysis skills in decoding words	RF3 pp. 214–219
RF.4	Fluency: Read grade-level texts with sufficient accuracy and fluency to support comprehension	RF4 pp. 220–225

(Continued)

Tennessee Strand/Standard	Focus of Tennessee Standard	For More Information
Writing		
W.1	Write opinion pieces on topics or texts, supporting a point of view with reasons and information	W1 pp. 70–75
W.2	Write informative/explanatory texts to examine a topic and convey ideas and information clearly	W2 pp. 76–81
W.3	Write narratives to develop real or imagined experiences or events using effective technique, descriptive details, and clear event sequences	W3 pp. 82–87
W.4	Produce writing in which the development and organization are appropriate to the task, purpose, and audience	W4 pp. 88–93
W.5	Develop and strengthen writing as needed by planning, revising, and editing	W5 pp. 94–99
W.6	Use technology to produce and publish writing; demonstrate keyboarding skills	W6 pp. 100–105
W.7	Conduct short research projects that build knowledge through investigation of different aspects of a topic	W7 pp. 106–111
W.8	Recall information from experiences or gather information from print and digital sources	W8 pp. 112–117
W.9	Draw evidence from literary or informational texts to support analysis, reflection, and research	W9 pp. 118–123
W.10	Write routinely over shorter and extended time frames	W10 pp. 124–129
Speaking and Listening		
SL.1	Engage effectively in a range of collaborative discussions with diverse partners, building on others' ideas and expressing their own clearly	SL1 pp. 134–139
SL.2	Paraphrase portions of a text read aloud or information presented in diverse media and formats	SL2 pp. 140–145
SL.3	Identify the reasons and evidence a speaker provides to support particular points	SL3 pp. 146–151
SL.4	Report on a topic or text, tell a story, or recount an experience with appropriate facts and details to support main ideas or themes	SL4 pp. 152–157
SL.5	Add audio recordings and visual displays to presentations when appropriate to enhance the development of main ideas or themes	SL5 pp. 158–163
SL.6	Differentiate between contexts that call for formal English and situations where informal discourse is appropriate; use formal English when appropriate to task and situation	SL6 pp. 164–169
Language		
L.1	Demonstrate command of the conventions of standard English grammar and usage when writing or speaking	L1 pp. 174–179
L.2	Demonstrate command of the conventions of standard English capitalization, punctuation, and spelling when writing	L2 pp. 180–185
L.3	Use knowledge of language and its conventions when writing, speaking, reading, or listening	L3 pp. 186–191
L.4	Determine or clarify the meaning of unknown and multiple-meaning words and phrases, choosing flexibly from an array of strategies	L4 pp. 192–197
L.5	Demonstrate understanding of figurative language, word relationships, and nuances in word meanings	L5 pp. 198–203
L.6	Acquire and use accurately general academic and domain-specific words and phrases	L6 pp. 204–209

Tennessee, Grade 5

Tennessee Strand/Standard	Focus of Tennessee Standard	For More Information
Reading Literature		
RL.1	Quote accurately from a text when explaining what the text says explicitly and when drawing inferences from the text	R1 pp. 6–11
RL.2	Determine a theme of a story, drama, or poem from details in the text; summarize the text	R2 pp. 12–17
RL.3	Compare and contrast two or more characters, settings, or events in a story or drama, drawing on specific details in the text	R3 pp. 18–23
RL.4	Determine the meaning of words and phrases as they are used in a text, including figurative language	R4 pp. 24–29
RL.5	Explain how a series of chapters, scenes, or stanzas fits together to provide the overall structure of a story, drama, or poem	R5 pp. 30–35
RL.6	Describe how a narrator's or speaker's point of view influences how events are described	R6 pp. 36–41
RL.7	Analyze how visual and multimedia elements contribute to the meaning, tone, or beauty of a text	R7 pp. 42–47
RL.8	NA	
RL.9	Compare and contrast stories in the same genre on their approaches to similar themes and topics	R9 pp. 54–59
RL.10	Read literature of appropriate complexity independently with proficiency	R10 pp. 60–65
Reading Informational Text		
RI.1	Quote accurately from a text when explaining what the text says explicitly and when drawing inferences from the text	R1 pp. 6–11
RI.2	Determine two or more main ideas of a text and explain how they are supported by key details; summarize the text	R2 pp. 12–17
RI.3	Explain the relationships or interactions between two or more individuals, events, ideas, or concepts in a text, based on specific information in the text	R3 pp. 18–23
RI.4	Determine the meaning of general academic and domain-specific words and phrases in a text	R4 pp. 24–29
RI.5	Compare and contrast the overall structure of events, ideas, concepts, or information in two or more texts	R5 pp. 30–35
RI.6	Analyze multiple accounts of the same event or topic, noting important similarities and differences in the point of view they represent	R6 pp. 36–41
RI.7	Draw on information from multiple sources, demonstrating the ability to locate an answer to a question quickly or solve a problem efficiently	R7 pp. 42–47
RI.8	Explain how an author uses reasons and evidence to support particular points in a text	R8 pp. 48–53
RI.9	Integrate information from several texts on the same topic in order to write or speak about the subject	R9 pp. 54–59
RI.10	Read and comprehend appropriately complex informational texts independently and proficiently	R10 pp. 60–65

(Continued)

Tennessee Strand/Standard	Focus of Tennessee Standard	For More Information
Reading Foundational Skills		
RF.3	Phonics: Know and apply grade-level phonics and word analysis skills in decoding words	RF3 pp. 214–219
RF.4	Fluency: Read grade-level texts with sufficient accuracy and fluency to support comprehension	RF4 pp. 220–225
Writing		
W.1	Write opinion pieces on topics or texts, supporting a point of view with reasons and information	W1 pp. 70–75
W.2	Write informative/explanatory texts to examine a topic and convey ideas and information clearly	W2 pp. 76–81
W.3	Write narratives to develop real or imagined experiences or events using effective technique, descriptive details, and clear event sequences	W3 pp. 82–87
W.4	Produce writing in which the development and organization are appropriate to the task, purpose, and audience	W4 pp. 88–93
W.5	Develop and strengthen writing as needed by planning, revising, editing, rewriting, or trying a new approach	W5 pp. 94–99
W.6	Use technology to produce and publish writing; demonstrate keyboarding skills	W6 pp. 100–105
W.7	Conduct short research projects that use several sources to build knowledge through investigation of different aspects of a topic	W7 pp. 106–111
W.8	Recall information from experiences or gather information from print and digital sources	W8 pp. 112–117
W.9	Draw evidence from literary or informational texts to support analysis, reflection, and research	W9 pp. 118–123
W.10	Write routinely over shorter and extended time frames	W10 pp. 124–129
Speaking and Listening		
SL.1	Engage effectively in a range of collaborative discussions with diverse partners, building on others' ideas and expressing their own clearly	SL1 pp. 134–139
SL.2	Summarize a written text read aloud or information presented in diverse media and formats	SL2 pp. 140–145
SL.3	Summarize points a speaker makes and explain how each claim is supported by reasons and evidence	SL3 pp. 146–151
SL.4	Report on a topic or text or present an opinion, using appropriate facts and details to support main ideas and themes	SL4 pp. 152–157
SL.5	Include multimedia components and visual displays in presentations when appropriate to enhance the development of main ideas or themes	SL5 pp. 158–163
SL.6	Adapt speech to a variety of contexts, using formal English when appropriate to task and situation	SL6 pp. 164–169
Language		
L.1	Demonstrate command of the conventions of standard English grammar and usage when writing or speaking	L1 pp. 174–179
L.2	Demonstrate command of the conventions of standard English capitalization, punctuation, and spelling when writing	L2 pp. 180–185
L.3	Use knowledge of language and its conventions when writing, speaking, reading, or listening	L3 pp. 186–191
L.4	Determine or clarify the meaning of unknown and multiple-meaning words and phrases, choosing flexibly from an array of strategies	L4 pp. 192–197
L.5	Demonstrate understanding of figurative language, word relationships, and nuances in word meanings	L5 pp. 198–203
L.6	Acquire and use accurately general academic and domain-specific words and phrases	L6 pp. 204–209

Utah, Grade 3

Utah Strand/Standard	Focus of Utah Standard	For More Information
Reading Literature		
RL.1	Ask and answer questions to demonstrate understanding of a text, referring explicitly to the text as the basis for the answers	R1 pp. 6–11
RL.2	Recount stories from diverse cultures, determine their central message, lesson, or moral, and explain how it is conveyed	R2 pp. 12–17
RL.3	Describe characters in a story and explain how their actions contribute to the sequence of events	R3 pp. 18–23
RL.4	Determine the meaning of words and phrases as they are used in a text, distinguishing literal from nonliteral language	R4 pp. 24–29
RL.5	Refer to parts of stories, dramas, and poems when writing or speaking about a text, using terms such as chapter, scene, and stanza; describe how each successive part builds on earlier sections	R5 pp. 30–35
RL.6	Distinguish their own point of view from that of the narrator or those of the characters	R6 pp. 36–41
RL.7	Explain how specific elements of a text's illustrations contribute to what is conveyed by the words in a story	R7 pp. 42–47
RL.8	NA	
RL.9	Compare and contrast the themes, settings, and plots of stories written by the same author about the same or similar characters	R9 pp. 54–59
RL.10	Read literature of appropriate complexity independently with proficiency	R10 pp. 60–65
Reading Informational Text		
RI.1	Ask and answer questions to demonstrate understanding of a text, referring explicitly to the text as the basis for the answers	R1 pp. 6–11
RI.2	Determine the main idea of a text; recount the key details and explain how they support the main idea	R2 pp. 12–17
RI.3	Describe the relationship between a series of historical events, scientific ideas or concepts, or steps in technical procedures in a text	R3 pp. 18–23
RI.4	Determine the meaning of general academic and domain-specific words and phrases in a text	R4 pp. 24–29
RI.5	Use text features and search tools to locate information on a topic efficiently	R5 pp. 30–35
RI.6	Distinguish own point of view from that of the author of a text	R6 pp. 36–41
RI.7	Use information from illustrations and the words in a text to demonstrate understanding of the text	R7 pp. 42–47
RI.8	Describe the logical connection between particular sentences and paragraphs in a text	R8 pp. 48–53
RI.9	Compare and contrast the most important points and key details presented by two texts on the same topic	R9 pp. 54–59
RI.10	Read and comprehend appropriately complex informational texts independently and proficiently	R10 pp. 60–65
Reading Foundational Skills		
RF.3	Phonics: Know and apply grade-level phonics and word analysis skills in decoding words	RF3 pp. 214–219
RF.4	Fluency: Read grade-level texts with sufficient accuracy and fluency to support comprehension	RF4 pp. 220–225
Writing		
W.1	Write opinion pieces on topics or texts, supporting a point of view with reasons	W1 pp. 70–75
W.2	Write informative/explanatory texts to examine a topic and convey ideas and information clearly	W2 pp. 76–81
W.3	Write narratives to develop real or imagined experiences or events using effective technique, descriptive details, and clear event sequences	W3 pp. 82–87
W.4	Produce writing in which the development and organization are appropriate to the task and purpose	W4 pp. 88–93
W.5	Develop and strengthen writing as needed by planning, revising, and editing	W5 pp. 94–99
W.6	Use technology to produce and publish writing	W6 pp. 100–105
W.7	Conduct short research projects that build knowledge about a topic	W7 pp. 106–111

(Continued)

Utah Strand/Standard	Focus of Utah Standard	For More Information
Writing		
W.8	Recall information from experiences or gather information from print and digital sources	W8 pp. 112–117
W.9	NA	
W.10	Write routinely over shorter and extended time frames	W10 pp. 124–129
Speaking and Listening		
SL.1	Engage effectively in a range of collaborative discussions with diverse partners, building on others' ideas and expressing their own clearly	SL1 pp. 134–139
SL.2	Determine the main ideas and supporting details of a text read aloud or information presented in diverse media and formats	SL2 pp. 140–145
SL.3	Ask and answer questions about information from a speaker, offering appropriate elaboration and detail	SL3 pp. 146–151
SL.4	Report on a topic or text, tell a story, or recount an experience with appropriate facts and relevant details	SL4 pp. 152–157
SL.5	Create audio recordings of stories or poems, demonstrating fluent reading; add visual displays when appropriate	SL5 pp. 158–163
SL.6	Speak in complete sentences when appropriate to task and situation in order to provide requested detail or clarification	SL6 pp. 164–169
Language		
L.1	Demonstrate command of the conventions of standard English grammar and usage when writing or speaking	L1 pp. 174–179
L.2	Demonstrate command of the conventions of standard English capitalization, punctuation, and spelling when writing	L2 pp. 180–185
L.3	Use knowledge of language and its conventions when writing, speaking, reading, or listening	L3 pp. 186–191
L.4	Determine or clarify the meaning of unknown and multiple-meaning words and phrases, choosing flexibly from an array of strategies	L4 pp. 192–197
L.5	Demonstrate understanding of word relationships and nuances in word meanings	L5 pp. 198–203
L.6	Acquire and use accurately conversational, general academic, and domain-specific words and phrases	L6 pp. 204–209

Utah, Grade 4

Utah Strand/Standard	Focus of Utah Standard	For More Information
Reading Literature		
RL.1	Refer to details and examples in a text when explaining what the text says explicitly and when drawing inferences	R1 pp. 6–11
RL.2	Determine a theme of a story, drama, or poem from details in the text; summarize the text	R2 pp. 12–17
RL.3	Describe in depth a character, setting, or event in a story or drama, drawing on specific details in the text	R3 pp. 18–23
RL.4	Determine the meaning of words and phrases as they are used in a text	R4 pp. 24–29
RL.5	Explain the major differences between poems, drama, and prose; refer to structural elements when writing or speaking about a text	R5 pp. 30–35
RL.6	Compare and contrast the point of view from which different stories are narrated, including the difference between first- and third-person narratives	R6 pp. 36–41
RL.7	Make connections between the text of a story or drama and a visual or oral representation of the text	R7 pp. 42–47
RL.8	NA	
RL.9	Compare and contrast the treatment of similar themes and topics and patterns of events in stories and traditional literature from different cultures	R9 pp. 54–59
RL.10	Read literature of appropriate complexity independently with proficiency	R10 pp. 60–65

Utah Strand/Standard	Focus of Utah Standard	For More Information
Reading Informational Text		
RI.1	Refer to details and examples in a text when explaining what the text says explicitly and when drawing inferences from the text	R1 pp. 6–11
RI.2	Determine the main idea of a text and explain how it is supported by key details; summarize the text	R2 pp. 12–17
RI.3	Explain events, procedures, ideas, or concepts in a historical, scientific, or technical text	R3 pp. 18–23
RI.4	Determine the meaning of general academic and domain-specific words and phrases in a text	R4 pp. 24–29
RI.5	Describe the overall structure of events, ideas, concepts, or information in a text	R5 pp. 30–35
RI.6	Compare and contrast a firsthand and secondhand account of the same event or topic	R6 pp. 36–41
RI.7	Interpret information presented visually, orally, or quantitatively, and explain how it contributes to an understanding of the text	R7 pp. 42–47
RI.8	Explain how an author uses reasons and evidence to support particular points in a text	R8 pp. 48–53
RI.9	Integrate information from two texts on the same topic in order to write or speak about the subject	R9 pp. 54–59
RI.10	Read and comprehend appropriately complex informational texts independently and proficiently	R10 pp. 60–65
Reading Foundational Skills		
RF.3	Phonics: Know and apply grade-level phonics and word analysis skills in decoding words	RF3 pp. 214–219
RF.4	Fluency: Read grade-level texts with sufficient accuracy and fluency to support comprehension	RF4 pp. 220–225
Writing		
W.1	Write opinion pieces on topics or texts, supporting a point of view with reasons and information	W1 pp. 70–75
W.2	Write informative/explanatory texts to examine a topic and convey ideas and information clearly	W2 pp. 76–81
W.3	Write narratives to develop real or imagined experiences or events using effective technique, descriptive details, and clear event sequences	W3 pp. 82–87
W.4	Produce writing in which the development and organization are appropriate to the task, purpose, and audience	W4 pp. 88–93
W.5	Develop and strengthen writing as needed by planning, revising, and editing	W5 pp. 94–99
W.6	Use technology to produce and publish writing; demonstrate keyboarding skills	W6 pp. 100–105
W.7	Conduct short research projects that build knowledge through investigation of different aspects of a topic	W7 pp. 106–111
W.8	Recall information from experiences or gather information from print and digital sources	W8 pp. 112–117
W.9	Draw evidence from literary or informational texts to support analysis, reflection, and research	W9 pp. 118–123
W.10	Write routinely over shorter and extended time frames	W10 pp. 124–129
Speaking and Listening		
SL.1	Engage effectively in a range of collaborative discussions with diverse partners, building on others' ideas and expressing their own clearly	SL1 pp. 134–139
SL.2	Paraphrase portions of a text read aloud or information presented in diverse media and formats	SL2 pp. 140–145
SL.3	Identify the reasons and evidence a speaker provides to support particular points	SL3 pp. 146–151
SL.4	Report on a topic or text, tell a story, or recount an experience with appropriate facts and details to support main ideas or themes	SL4 pp. 152–157
SL.5	Add audio recordings and visual displays to presentations when appropriate to enhance the development of main ideas or themes	SL5 pp. 158–163
SL.6	Differentiate between contexts that call for formal English and situations where informal discourse is appropriate; use formal English when appropriate to task and situation	SL6 pp. 164–169
Language		
L.1	Demonstrate command of the conventions of standard English grammar and usage when writing or speaking	L1 pp. 174–179
L.2	Demonstrate command of the conventions of standard English capitalization, punctuation, and spelling when writing	L2 pp. 180–185
L.3	Use knowledge of language and its conventions when writing, speaking, reading, or listening	L3 pp. 186–191
L.4	Determine or clarify the meaning of unknown and multiple-meaning words and phrases, choosing flexibly from an array of strategies	L4 pp. 192–197
L.5	Demonstrate understanding of figurative language, word relationships, and nuances in word meanings	L5 pp. 198–203
L.6	Acquire and use accurately general academic and domain-specific words and phrases	L6 pp. 204–209

Utah, Grade 5

Utah Strand/Standard	Focus of Utah Standard	For More Information
Reading Literature		
RL.1	Quote accurately from a text when explaining what the text says explicitly and when drawing inferences from the text	R1 pp. 6–11
RL.2	Determine a theme of a story, drama, or poem from details in the text; summarize the text	R2 pp. 12–17
RL.3	Compare and contrast two or more characters, settings, or events in a story or drama, drawing on specific details in the text	R3 pp. 18–23
RL.4	Determine the meaning of words and phrases as they are used in a text, including figurative language	R4 pp. 24–29
RL.5	Explain how a series of chapters, scenes, or stanzas fits together to provide the overall structure of a story, drama, or poem	R5 pp. 30–35
RL.6	Describe how a narrator's or speaker's point of view influences how events are described	R6 pp. 36–41
RL.7	Analyze how visual and multimedia elements contribute to the meaning, tone, or beauty of a text	R7 pp. 42–47
RL.8	NA	
RL.9	Compare and contrast stories in the same genre on their approaches to similar themes and topics	R9 pp. 54–59
RL.10	Read literature of appropriate complexity independently with proficiency	R10 pp. 60–65
Reading Informational Text		
RI.1	Quote accurately from a text when explaining what the text says explicitly and when drawing inferences from the text	R1 pp. 6–11
RI.2	Determine two or more main ideas of a text and explain how they are supported by key details; summarize the text	R2 pp. 12–17
RI.3	Explain the relationships or interactions between two or more individuals, events, ideas, or concepts in a text, based on specific information in the text	R3 pp. 18–23
RI.4	Determine the meaning of general academic and domain-specific words and phrases in a text	R4 pp. 24–29
RI.5	Compare and contrast the overall structure of events, ideas, concepts, or information in two or more texts	R5 pp. 30–35
RI.6	Analyze multiple accounts of the same event or topic, noting important similarities and differences in the point of view they represent	R6 pp. 36–41
RI.7	Draw on information from multiple sources, demonstrating the ability to locate an answer to a question quickly or solve a problem efficiently	R7 pp. 42–47
RI.8	Explain how an author uses reasons and evidence to support particular points in a text	R8 pp. 48–53
RI.9	Integrate information from several texts on the same topic in order to write or speak about the subject	R9 pp. 54–59
RI.10	Read and comprehend appropriately complex informational texts independently and proficiently	R10 pp. 60–65
Reading Foundational Skills		
RF.3	Phonics: Know and apply grade-level phonics and word analysis skills in decoding words	RF3 pp. 214–219
RF.4	Fluency: Read grade-level texts with sufficient accuracy and fluency to support comprehension	RF4 pp. 220–225

Utah Strand/Standard	Focus of Utah Standard	For More Information
Writing		
W.1	Write opinion pieces on topics or texts, supporting a point of view with reasons and information	W1 pp. 70–75
W.2	Write informative/explanatory texts to examine a topic and convey ideas and information clearly	W2 pp. 76–81
W.3	Write narratives to develop real or imagined experiences or events using effective technique, descriptive details, and clear event sequences	W3 pp. 82–87
W.4	Produce writing in which the development and organization are appropriate to the task, purpose, and audience	W4 pp. 88–93
W.5	Develop and strengthen writing as needed by planning, revising, editing, rewriting, or trying a new approach	W5 pp. 94–99
W.6	Use technology to produce and publish writing; demonstrate keyboarding skills	W6 pp. 100–105
W.7	Conduct short research projects that use several sources to build knowledge through investigation of different aspects of a topic	W7 pp. 106–111
W.8	Recall information from experiences or gather information from print and digital sources	W8 pp. 112–117
W.9	Draw evidence from literary or informational texts to support analysis, reflection, and research	W9 pp. 118–123
W.10	Write routinely over shorter and extended time frames	W10 pp. 124–129
Speaking and Listening		
SL.1	Engage effectively in a range of collaborative discussions with diverse partners, building on others' ideas and expressing their own clearly	SL1 pp. 134–139
SL.2	Summarize a written text read aloud or information presented in diverse media and formats	SL2 pp. 140–145
SL.3	Summarize points a speaker makes and explain how each claim is supported by reasons and evidence	SL3 pp. 146–151
SL.4	Report on a topic or text or present an opinion, using appropriate facts and details to support main ideas and themes	SL4 pp. 152–157
SL.5	Include multimedia components and visual displays in presentations when appropriate to enhance the development of main ideas or themes	SL5 pp. 158–163
SL.6	Adapt speech to a variety of contexts, using formal English when appropriate to task and situation	SL6 pp. 164–169
Language		
L.1	Demonstrate command of the conventions of standard English grammar and usage when writing or speaking	L1 pp. 174–179
L.2	Demonstrate command of the conventions of standard English capitalization, punctuation, and spelling when writing	L2 pp. 180–185
L.3	Use knowledge of language and its conventions when writing, speaking, reading, or listening	L3 pp. 186–191
L.4	Determine or clarify the meaning of unknown and multiple-meaning words and phrases, choosing flexibly from an array of strategies	L4 pp. 192–197
L.5	Demonstrate understanding of figurative language, word relationships, and nuances in word meanings	L5 pp. 198–203
L.6	Acquire and use accurately general academic and domain-specific words and phrases	L6 pp. 204–209

Virginia, Grade 3

Virginia Strand/Standard	Focus of Virginia Standard	For More Information
Oral Language		
3.1	Use effective communication skills in group activities	SL1 pp. 134–139 SL3 pp. 146–151 SL6 pp. 164–169 L6 pp. 204–209
3.2	Present brief oral reports using visual media	SL4 pp. 152–157 SL5 pp. 158–163 SL6 pp. 164–169
Reading		
3.3	Apply word-analysis skills when reading	RF3 pp. 214–219
3.4	Expand vocabulary when reading	L4 pp. 192–197 L5 pp. 198–203 L6 pp. 204–209
3.5	Read and demonstrate comprehension of fictional texts and poetry	
	• Ask and answer questions about what is read	R1 pp. 6–11
	• Identify main idea and supporting details; identify problem and solution	R2 pp. 12–17
	• Compare and contrast characters, setting, and important events	R3 pp. 18–23 R9 pp. 54–59
	• Draw conclusions about text	R2 pp. 12–17
	• Make connections between experiences and reading selections	R6 pp. 36–41
	• Use reading strategies to monitor comprehension throughout the reading process	R10 pp. 60–65
	• Read with fluency and accuracy	RF4 pp. 220–225
3.6	Read and demonstrate comprehension of nonfiction texts	
	• Preview and use text features	R5 pp. 30–35
	• Ask and answer questions about what is read	R1 pp. 6–11
	• Identify the main idea and supporting details	R2 pp. 12–17
	• Draw conclusions based on text; summarize major points found in text	R2 pp. 12–17
	• Use reading strategies to monitor comprehension throughout the reading process	R10 pp. 60–65
	• Read with fluency and accuracy	RF4 pp. 220–225
3.7	Demonstrate comprehension of information from a variety of print and electronic resources	R7 pp. 42–47 L4 pp. 192–197
Writing		
3.8	Write legibly in cursive	NA
3.9	Write for a variety of purposes	W1 pp. 70–75 W2 pp. 76–81 W3 pp. 82–87 W4 pp. 88–93 W5 pp. 94–99
3.10	Edit writing for correct grammar, capitalization, punctuation, and spelling	L1 pp. 174–179 L2 pp. 180–185
3.11	Write a short report	W7 pp. 106–111 W8 pp. 112–117
3.14	Use available technology for reading and writing	W6 pp. 100–105

Virginia, Grade 4

Virginia Strand/Standard	Focus of Virginia Standard	For More Information
Speaking, Listening, Media Literacy		
4.1	Use effective oral communication skills in a variety of settings	SL1 pp. 134–139 SL4 pp. 152–157
4.2	Make and listen to oral presentations and reports	SL4 pp. 152–157 SL6 pp. 164–169 L6 pp. 204–209
4.3	Learn how media messages are constructed and for what purposes	SL2 pp. 140–145 SL3 pp. 146–151
Reading		
4.4	Expand vocabulary when reading	L4 pp. 192–197 L5 pp. 198–203 L6 pp. 204–209
4.5	Read and demonstrate comprehension of fictional texts, narrative nonfiction, and poetry	
	• Explain author's purpose; describe how the choice of language, setting, characters, and information contributes to the author's purpose	R1 pp. 6–11
	• Identify main idea, summarize supporting details, identify problem and solution	R2 pp. 12–17
	• Draw conclusions and make inferences about text	R1 pp. 6–11 R2 pp. 12–17
	• Describe the relationship between text and previously read materials	R9 pp. 54–59
	• Identify sensory words	R4 pp. 24–29
	• Use reading strategies throughout the reading process to monitor comprehension	R10 pp. 60–65
	• Read with fluency and accuracy	RF4 pp. 220–225
4.6	Read and demonstrate comprehension of nonfiction texts	
	• Use text structures to predict and categorize information in texts	R5 pp. 30–35
	• Explain the author's purpose	R8 pp. 48–53
	• Identify the main idea and summarize supporting details	R2 pp. 12–17
	• Draw conclusions and make simple inferences based on textual information	R1 pp. 6–11 R2 pp. 12–17 R3 pp. 18–23
	• Use reading strategies to monitor comprehension throughout the reading process	R10 pp. 60–65
	• Read with fluency and accuracy	RF4 pp. 220–225
Writing		
4.7	Write cohesively for a variety of purposes	W1 pp. 70–75 W2 pp. 76–81 W3 pp. 82–87 W4 pp. 88–93 W5 pp. 94–99
4.8	Edit writing for correct grammar, capitalization, spelling, punctuation, sentence structure, and paragraphing	L1 pp. 174–179 L2 pp. 180–185
Research		
4.9	Demonstrate comprehension of information resources to research a topic	W6 pp. 100–105 W7 pp. 106–111 W8 pp. 112–117

Virginia Strand/Standard	Focus of Virginia Standard	For More Information
Speaking, Listening, Media Literacy		
5.1	Listen, draw conclusions, and share responses in subject-related group learning activities	SL1 pp. 134–139 SL2 pp. 140–145 SL3 pp. 146–151 SL4 pp. 152–157
5.2	Use effective verbal and nonverbal communication skills to deliver planned oral presentations	SL4 pp. 152–157 SL5 pp. 158–163 SL6 pp. 164–169
5.3	Learn how media messages are constructed and for what purposes	SL2 pp. 140–145 SL3 pp. 146–151
Reading		
5.4	Expand vocabulary when reading	R4 pp. 24–29 L4 pp. 192–197 L5 pp. 198–203 L6 pp. 204–209
5.5	Read and demonstrate comprehension of fictional texts, narrative nonfiction, and poetry	
	• Describe character development; describe plot development and explain the resolution of conflict	R2 pp. 12–17 R3 pp. 18–23
	• Identify main idea, summarize supporting details, identify problem and solution	R2 pp. 12–17
	• Draw conclusions and make inferences about text	R1 pp. 6–11 R2 pp. 12–17
	• Describe the relationship between text and previously read materials	R9 pp. 54–59
	• Describe how vocabulary choice contributes to author's style	R4 pp. 24–29
	• Identify and ask questions about various points of view	R6 pp. 36–41
	• Use reading strategies throughout the reading process to monitor comprehension	R10 pp. 60–65
	• Read with fluency and accuracy	RF4 pp. 220–225
5.6	Read and demonstrate comprehension of nonfiction texts	
	• Use text organizers such as type, headings, and graphics to predict and categorize information in texts	R7 pp. 42–47
	• Identify the main idea and summarize supporting details	R2 pp. 12–17
	• Locate information to support opinions, predictions, and conclusions	R1 pp. 6–11
	• Identify structural patterns found in nonfiction	R5 pp. 30–35
	• Use reading strategies to monitor comprehension throughout the reading process	R10 pp. 60–65
	• Read with fluency and accuracy	RF4 pp. 220–225
Writing		
5.7	Write cohesively for a variety of purposes: to describe, to inform, to entertain, to explain, and to persuade	W1 pp. 70–75 W2 pp. 76–81 W3 pp. 82–87 W4 pp. 88–93 W5 pp. 94–99
5.8	Edit writing for correct grammar, capitalization, spelling, punctuation, sentence structure, and paragraphing	L1 pp. 174–179 L2 pp. 180–185
Research		
5.9	Find, evaluate, and select appropriate resources for a research project	W6 pp. 100–105 W7 pp. 106–111 W8 pp. 112–117

West Virginia Strand/Standard	Focus of West Virginia Standard	For More Information
Reading Literature		
R.C1.1	Ask and answer questions to demonstrate understanding of a text, referring explicitly to the text as the basis for the answers	R1 pp. 6–11
R.C1.2	Recount stories from diverse cultures, determine their central message, lesson, or moral, and explain how it is conveyed	R2 pp. 12–17
R.C1.3	Describe characters in a story and explain how their actions contribute to the sequence of events	R3 pp. 18–23
RC2.1	Determine the meaning of words and phrases as they are used in a text, distinguishing literal from nonliteral language	R4 pp. 24–29
R.C2.2	Refer to parts of stories, dramas, and poems when writing or speaking about a text, using terms such as chapter, scene, and stanza; describe how each successive part builds on earlier sections	R5 pp. 30–35
R.C2.3	Distinguish the student's point of view from that of the narrator or those of the characters	R6 pp. 36–41
R.C3.1	Explain how specific aspects of a text's illustrations contribute to what is conveyed by the words in a story	R7 pp. 42–47
R.C3.2	Compare and contrast the themes, settings, and plots of stories written by the same author about the same or similar characters	R9 pp. 54–59
R.C4.1	Read literature of appropriate complexity independently with proficiency	R10 pp. 60–65
Reading Informational Text		
R.C1.4	Ask and answer questions to demonstrate understanding of a text, referring explicitly to the text as the basis for the answers	R1 pp. 6–11
R.C1.5	Determine the main idea of a text; recount the key details and explain how they support the main idea	R2 pp. 12–17
R.C1.6	Describe the relationship between a series of historical events, scientific ideas or concepts, or steps in technical procedures in a text	R3 pp. 18–23
R.C2.4	Determine the meaning of general academic and domain-specific words and phrases in a text	R4 pp. 24–29
R.C2.5	Use text features and search tools to locate information on a topic efficiently	R5 pp. 30–35
R.C2.6	Distinguish the student's point of view from that of the author of a text	R6 pp. 36–41
R.C3.3	Use information from illustrations and the words in a text to demonstrate understanding of the text	R7 pp. 42–47
R.C3.4	Describe the logical connection between particular sentences and paragraphs in a text	R8 pp. 48–53
R.C3.5	Compare and contrast the most important points and key details presented by two texts on the same topic	R9 pp. 54–59
R.C4.2	Read and comprehend appropriately complex informational texts independently and proficiently	R10 pp. 60–65
Reading Foundational Skills		
R.C7.1	Phonics: Know and apply grade-level phonics and word analysis skills in decoding words	RF3 pp. 214–219
R.C8.1	Fluency: Read grade-level texts with sufficient accuracy and fluency to support comprehension	RF4 pp. 220–225
Writing		
W.C9.1	Write opinion pieces on topics or texts, supporting a point of view with reasons	W1 pp. 70–75
W.C9.2	Write informative/explanatory texts to examine a topic and convey ideas and information clearly	W2 pp. 76–81
W.C9.3	Write narratives to develop real or imagined experiences or events using effective technique, descriptive details, and clear event sequences	W3 pp. 82–87
W.C10.1	Produce writing in which the development and organization are appropriate to the task and purpose	W4 pp. 88–93
W.C10.2	Develop and strengthen writing as needed by planning, revising, and editing	W5 pp. 94–99

(Continued)

West Virginia Strand/Standard	Focus of West Virginia Standard	For More Information
Writing		
W.C10.3	Use technology to produce and publish writing	W6 pp. 100–105
W.C11.1	Conduct short research projects that build knowledge about a topic	W7 pp. 106–111
W.C11.2	Recall information from experiences or gather information from print and digital sources	W8 pp. 112–117
W.C11.3	NA	
W.C12.1	Write routinely over shorter and extended time frames	W10 pp. 124–129
Speaking and Listening		
SL.C13.1	Engage effectively in a range of collaborative discussions with diverse partners, building on others' ideas and expressing their own clearly	SL1 pp. 134–139
SL.C13.2	Determine the main ideas and supporting details of a text read aloud or information presented in diverse media and formats	SL2 pp. 140–145
SL.C13.3	Ask and answer questions about information from a speaker, offering appropriate elaboration and detail	SL3 pp. 146–151
SL.C14.1	Report on a topic or text, tell a story, or recount an experience with appropriate facts and relevant details	SL4 pp. 152–157
SL.C14.2	Create audio recordings of stories or poems, demonstrating fluent reading; add visual displays when appropriate	SL5 pp. 158–163
SL.C14.3	Speak in complete sentences when appropriate to task and situation in order to provide requested detail or clarification	SL6 pp. 164–169
Language		
L.C15.1	Demonstrate command of the conventions of standard English grammar and usage when writing or speaking	L1 pp. 174–179
L.C15.2	Demonstrate command of the conventions of standard English capitalization, punctuation, and spelling when writing	L2 pp. 180–185
L.C16.1	Use knowledge of language and its conventions when writing, speaking, reading, or listening	L3 pp. 186–191
L.C17.1	Determine or clarify the meaning of unknown and multiple-meaning words and phrases, choosing flexibly from an array of strategies	L4 pp. 192–197
L.C17.2	Demonstrate understanding of word relationships and nuances in word meanings	L5 pp. 198–203
L.C17.3	Acquire and use accurately conversational, general academic, and domain-specific words and phrases	L6 pp. 204–209

West Virginia, Grade 4

West Virginia Strand/Standard	Focus of West Virginia Standard	For More Information
Reading Literature		
R.C1.1	Refer to details and examples in a text when explaining what the text says explicitly and when drawing inferences	R1 pp. 6–11
R.C1.2	Determine a theme of a story, drama, or poem from details in the text; summarize the text	R2 pp. 12–17
R.C1.3	Describe in depth a character, setting, or event in a story or drama, drawing on specific details in the text	R3 pp. 18–23
RC2.1	Determine the meaning of words and phrases as they are used in a text	R4 pp. 24–29
R.C2.2	Explain the major differences between poems, drama, and prose; refer to structural elements when writing or speaking about a text	R5 pp. 30–35
R.C2.3	Compare and contrast the point of view from which different stories are narrated, including the difference between first- and third-person narratives	R6 pp. 36–41

West Virginia Strand/Standard	Focus of West Virginia Standard	For More Information
Reading Literature		
R.C3.1	Make connections between the text of a story or drama and a visual or oral representation of the text	R7 pp. 42–47
R.C3.2	Compare and contrast the treatment of similar themes and topics and patterns of events in stories and traditional literature from different cultures	R9 pp. 54–59
R.C4.1	Read literature of appropriate complexity independently with proficiency	R10 pp. 60–65
Reading Informational Text		
R.C1.4	Refer to details and examples in a text when explaining what the text says explicitly and when drawing inferences from the text	R1 pp. 6–11
R.C1.5	Determine the main idea of a text and explain how it is supported by key details; summarize the text	R2 pp. 12–17
R.C1.6	Explain events, procedures, ideas, or concepts in a historical, scientific, or technical text	R3 pp. 18–23
R.C2.4	Determine the meaning of general academic and domain-specific words and phrases in a text	R4 pp. 24–29
R.C2.5	Describe the overall structure of events, ideas, concepts, or information in a text	R5 pp. 30–35
R.C2.6	Compare and contrast a firsthand and secondhand account of the same event or topic	R6 pp. 36–41
R.C3.3	Interpret information presented visually, orally, or quantitatively, and explain how it contributes to an understanding of the text	R7 pp. 42–47
R.C3.4	Explain how an author uses reasons and evidence to support particular points in a text	R8 pp. 48–53
R.C3.5	Integrate information from two texts on the same topic in order to write or speak about the subject	R9 pp. 54–59
R.C4.2	Read and comprehend appropriately complex informational texts independently and proficiently	R10 pp. 60–65
Reading Foundational Skills		
R.C7.1	Phonics: Know and apply grade-level phonics and word analysis skills in decoding words	RF3 pp. 214–219
R.C8.1	Fluency: Read grade-level texts with sufficient accuracy and fluency to support comprehension	RF4 pp. 220–225
Writing		
W.C9.1	Write opinion pieces on topics or texts, supporting a point of view with reasons and information	W1 pp. 70–75
W.C9.2	Write informative/explanatory texts to examine a topic and convey ideas and information clearly	W2 pp. 76–81
W.C9.3	Write narratives to develop real or imagined experiences or events using effective technique, descriptive details, and clear event sequences	W3 pp. 82–87
W.C10.1	Produce writing in which the development and organization are appropriate to the task, purpose, and audience	W4 pp. 88–93
W.C10.2	Develop and strengthen writing as needed by planning, revising, and editing	W5 pp. 94–99
W.C10.3	Use technology to produce and publish writing; demonstrate keyboarding skills	W6 pp. 100–105
W.C11.1	Conduct short research projects that build knowledge through investigation of different aspects of a topic	W7 pp. 106–111
W.C11.2	Recall information from experiences or gather information from print and digital sources	W8 pp. 112–117
W.C11.3	Draw evidence from literary or informational texts to support analysis, reflection, and research	W9 pp. 118–123
W.C12.1	Write routinely over shorter and extended time frames	W10 pp. 124–129
Speaking and Listening		
SL.C13.1	Engage effectively in a range of collaborative discussions with diverse partners, building on others' ideas and expressing their own clearly	SL1 pp. 134–139
SL.C13.2	Paraphrase portions of a text read aloud or information presented in diverse media and formats	SL2 pp. 140–145
SL.C13.3	Identify the reasons and evidence a speaker provides to support particular points	SL3 pp. 146–151
SL.C14.1	Report on a topic or text, tell a story, or recount an experience with appropriate facts and details to support main ideas or themes	SL4 pp. 152–157

(Continued)

West Virginia Strand/Standard	Focus of West Virginia Standard	For More Information
Speaking and Listening		
SL.C14.2	Add audio recordings and visual displays to presentations when appropriate to enhance the development of main ideas or themes	SL5 pp. 158–163
SL.C14.3	Differentiate between contexts that call for formal English and situations where informal discourse is appropriate; use formal English when appropriate to task and situation	SL6 pp. 164–169
Language		
L.C15.1	Demonstrate command of the conventions of standard English grammar and usage when writing or speaking	L1 pp. 174–179
L.C15.2	Demonstrate command of the conventions of standard English capitalization, punctuation, and spelling when writing	L2 pp. 180–185
L.C16.1	Use knowledge of language and its conventions when writing, speaking, reading, or listening	L3 pp. 186–191
L.C17.1	Determine or clarify the meaning of unknown and multiple-meaning words and phrases, choosing flexibly from an array of strategies	L4 pp. 192–197
L.C17.2	Demonstrate understanding of figurative language, word relationships, and nuances in word meanings	L5 pp. 198–203
L.C17.3	Acquire and use accurately general academic and domain-specific words and phrases	L6 pp. 204–209

West Virginia, Grade 5

West Virginia Strand/Standard	Focus of West Virginia Standard	For More Information
Reading Literature		
R.C1.1	Quote accurately from a text when explaining what the text says explicitly and when drawing inferences from the text	R1 pp. 6–11
R.C1.2	Determine a theme of a story, drama, or poem from details in the text; summarize the text	R2 pp. 12–17
R.C1.3	Compare and contrast two or more characters, settings, or events in a story or drama, drawing on specific details in the text	R3 pp. 18–23
RC2.1	Determine the meaning of words and phrases as they are used in a text, including figurative language	R4 pp. 24–29
R.C2.2	Explain how a series of chapters, scenes, or stanzas fits together to provide the overall structure of a story, drama, or poem	R5 pp. 30–35
R.C2.3	Describe how a narrator's or speaker's point of view influences how events are described	R6 pp. 36–41
R.C3.1	Analyze how visual and multimedia elements contribute to the meaning, tone, or beauty of a text	R7 pp. 42–47
R.C3.2	Compare and contrast stories in the same genre on their approaches to similar themes and topics	R9 pp. 54–59
R.C4.1	Read literature of appropriate complexity independently with proficiency	R10 pp. 60–65
Reading Informational Text		
R.C1.4	Quote accurately from a text when explaining what the text says explicitly and when drawing inferences from the text	R1 pp. 6–11
R.C1.5	Determine two or more main ideas of a text and explain how they are supported by key details; summarize the text	R2 pp. 12–17
R.C1.6	Explain the relationships or interactions between two or more individuals, events, ideas, or concepts in a text, based on specific information in the text	R3 pp. 18–23
R.C2.4	Determine the meaning of general academic and domain-specific words and phrases in a text	R4 pp. 24–29
R.C2.5	Compare and contrast the overall structure of events, ideas, concepts, or information in two or more texts	R5 pp. 30–35
R.C2.6	Analyze multiple accounts of the same event or topic, noting important similarities and differences in the point of view they represent	R6 pp. 36–41

West Virginia Strand/Standard	Focus of West Virginia Standard	For More Information
Reading Informational Text		
R.C3.3	Draw on information from multiple sources, demonstrating the ability to locate an answer to a question quickly or solve a problem efficiently	R7 pp. 42–47
R.C3.4	Explain how an author uses reasons and evidence to support particular points in a text	R8 pp. 48–53
R.C3.5	Integrate information from several texts on the same topic in order to write or speak about the subject	R9 pp. 54–59
R.C4.2	Read and comprehend appropriately complex informational texts independently and proficiently	R10 pp. 60–65
Reading Foundational Skills		
R.C7.1	Phonics: Know and apply grade-level phonics and word analysis skills in decoding words	RF3 pp. 214–219
R.C8.1	Fluency: Read grade-level texts with sufficient accuracy and fluency to support comprehension	RF4 pp. 220–225
Writing		
W.C9.1	Write opinion pieces on topics or texts, supporting a point of view with reasons and information	W1 pp. 70–75
W.C9.2	Write informative/explanatory texts to examine a topic and convey ideas and information clearly	W2 pp. 76–81
W.C9.3	Write narratives to develop real or imagined experiences or events using effective technique, descriptive details, and clear event sequences	W3 pp. 82–87
W.C10.1	Produce writing in which the development and organization are appropriate to the task, purpose, and audience	W4 pp. 88–93
W.C10.2	Develop and strengthen writing as needed by planning, revising, editing, rewriting, or trying a new approach	W5 pp. 94–99
W.C10.3	Use technology to produce and publish writing; demonstrate keyboarding skills	W6 pp. 100–105
W.C11.1	Conduct short research projects that use several sources to build knowledge through investigation of different aspects of a topic	W7 pp. 106–111
W.C11.2	Recall information from experiences or gather information from print and digital sources	W8 pp. 112–117
W.C11.3	Draw evidence from literary or informational texts to support analysis, reflection, and research	W9 pp. 118–123
W.C12.1	Write routinely over shorter and extended time frames	W10 pp. 124–129
Speaking and Listening		
SL.C13.1	Engage effectively in a range of collaborative discussions with diverse partners, building on others' ideas and expressing their own clearly	SL1 pp. 134–139
SL.C13.2	Summarize a written text read aloud or information presented in diverse media and formats	SL2 pp. 140–145
SL.C13.3	Summarize points a speaker makes and explain how each claim is supported by reasons and evidence	SL3 pp. 146–151
SL.C14.1	Report on a topic or text or present an opinion, using appropriate facts and details to support main ideas and themes	SL4 pp. 152–157
SL.C14.2	Include multimedia components and visual displays in presentations when appropriate to enhance the development of main ideas or themes	SL5 pp. 158–163
SL.C14.3	Adapt speech to a variety of contexts, using formal English when appropriate to task and situation	SL6 pp. 164–169
Language		
L.C15.1	Demonstrate command of the conventions of standard English grammar and usage when writing or speaking	L1 pp. 174–179
L.C15.2	Demonstrate command of the conventions of standard English capitalization, punctuation, and spelling when writing	L2 pp. 180–185
L.C16.1	Use knowledge of language and its conventions when writing, speaking, reading, or listening	L3 pp. 186–191
L.C17.1	Determine or clarify the meaning of unknown and multiple-meaning words and phrases, choosing flexibly from an array of strategies	L4 pp. 192–197
L.C17.2	Demonstrate understanding of figurative language, word relationships, and nuances in word meanings	L5 pp. 198–203
L.C17.3	Acquire and use accurately general academic and domain-specific words and phrases	L6 pp. 204–209

The Complete Common Core State Standards: Decoded

The Common Core State Standards

Reading

College and Career Readiness Anchor Standards for
Reading K–12

Source:
Common Core
State Standards

The 3–5 Reading Standards outlined on the following pages define what students should understand and be able to do by the end of each grade. Here on this page we present the College and Career Readiness (CCR) anchor standards for K–12 so you can see how students in grades 3–5 work toward the same goals as a high school senior: it's a universal, K–12 vision. The CCR anchor standards and the grade-specific standards correspond to one another by numbers 1–10. They are necessary complements: the former providing broad standards, the latter providing additional specificity. Together, they define the skills and understandings that all students must eventually demonstrate.

Key Ideas and Details

1. Read closely to determine what the text says explicitly and to make logical inferences from it; cite specific textual evidence when writing or speaking to support conclusions drawn from the text.
2. Determine central ideas or themes of a text and analyze their development; summarize the key supporting details and ideas.
3. Analyze how and why individuals, events, and ideas develop and interact over the course of a text.

Craft and Structure

4. Interpret words and phrases as they are used in a text, including determining technical, connotative, and figurative meanings, and analyze how specific word choices shape meaning or tone.
5. Analyze the structure of texts, including how specific sentences, paragraphs, and larger portions of the text (e.g., a section, chapter, scene, or stanza) relate to each other and the whole.
6. Assess how point of view or purpose shapes the content and style of a text.

Integration of Knowledge and Ideas

7. Integrate and evaluate content presented in diverse media and formats, including visually and quantitatively, as well as in words.*
8. Delineate and evaluate the argument and specific claims in a text, including the validity of the reasoning as well as the relevance and sufficiency of the evidence.
9. Analyze how two or more texts address similar themes or topics in order to build knowledge or to compare the approaches the authors take.

Range of Reading and Level of Text Complexity

10. Read and comprehend complex literary and informational texts independently and proficiently.

Note on Range and Content of Student Reading

To build a foundation for college and career readiness, students must read widely and deeply from among a broad range of high-quality, increasingly challenging literary and informational texts. Through extensive reading of stories, dramas, poems, and myths from diverse cultures and different time periods, students gain literary and cultural knowledge as well as familiarity with various text structures and elements. By reading texts in history/social studies, science, and other disciplines, students build a foundation of knowledge in these fields that will also give them the background to be better readers in all content areas. Students can only gain this foundation when the curriculum is intentionally and coherently structured to develop rich content knowledge within and across grades. Students also acquire the habits of reading independently and closely, which are essential to their future success.

Source: © Copyright 2010. National Governors Association Center for Best Practices and Council of Chief State School Officers. All rights reserved.

*Please consult the full Common Core State Standards document (and all updates and appendices) at http://www.corestandards.org/ELA-Literacy. See "Research to Build Knowledge" in the Writing section and "Comprehension and Collaboration" in the Speaking and Listening section for additional standards relevant to gathering, assessing, and applying information from print and digital sources.

College and Career Readiness Anchor Standards for
Reading K–12

The College and Career Readiness (CCR) anchor standards are the same for K–12. The guiding principle here is that the core reading skills should not change as students advance; rather, the level at which they learn and can perform these skills should increase in complexity as students move from one grade to the next. However, for grades 3–5, we have to recognize that the standards were back mapped from the secondary grades—the authors envisioned what college students needed and then wrote standards, working their way down the grades. Thus, as you use this book remember that children in grades 3–5 can't just "jump over" developmental milestones in an ambitious attempt toward an anchor standard. There are certain life and learning experiences they need to have, and certain concepts they need to learn, before they are capable of handling many complex academic skills in a meaningful way. The anchor standards nonetheless are goal posts to work toward. As you read the "gist" of the standards on the following pages, remember they represent what our 3–5 students will *grow into* during each year and deepen later in middle school and high school.

Key Ideas and Details   *What does the text say?*

This first strand of reading standards emphasizes students' ability to identify key ideas and themes in a text, whether literary, informational, primary, or foundational; whether print, graphic, quantitative, or mixed media. The focus of this first set of standards in on *reading to understand*, during which students focus on *what the text says*. The premise is that students cannot delve into the deeper (implicit) meaning of any text if they cannot first grasp the surface (explicit) meaning of that text. Beyond merely identifying these ideas, readers must learn to see how these ideas and themes, or the story's characters and events, develop and evolve over the course of a text. Such reading demands that students know how to identify, evaluate, assess, and analyze the elements of a text for their importance, function, and meaning within the text.

Craft and Structure   *How the text says what it says?*

The second set of standards builds on the first, focusing not on *what* the text says but *how* it says it, the emphasis here being on analyzing how texts are made to serve a function or achieve a purpose. These standards ask readers to examine the choices the author makes in terms of words, sentence, and paragraph structure and how these choices contribute to the meaning of the text and the author's larger purpose. Inherent in the study of craft and structure is how these items interact with and influence the ideas and details outlined in the first three standards.

Integration of Knowledge and Ideas   *Using what is written and how it is written and the chosen medium, how can I analyze the validity of the claims and the evidence provided*

This third strand might be summed up as: *reading to extend or deepen one's knowledge* of a subject by comparing what a range of sources have said about it over time and across different media. In addition, these standards emphasize the importance of being able to read the arguments; that is, they look at how to identify the claims the texts make and evaluate the evidence used to support those claims regardless of the media. Finally, these standards ask students to analyze the choice of means and medium the author chooses and the effect those choices have on ideas and details. Thus, if a writer integrates words, images, and video in a mixed-media text, readers should be able to examine how and why the author did that in terms of stylistic and rhetorical purposes.

Range of Reading and Level of Text Complexity

The Common Core State Standards document itself offers the most useful explanation of what this last standard means in a footnote titled "Note of range and content of student reading," which accompanies the reading standards:

> To become college and career ready, students must grapple with works of exceptional craft and thought whose range extends across genres, cultures, and centuries. Such works offer profound insights into the human condition and serve as models for students' own thinking and writing. Along with high-quality contemporary works, these texts should be chosen from among seminal U.S. documents, the classics of American literature, and the timeless dramas of Shakespeare. Through wide and deep reading of literature and literary nonfiction of steadily increasing sophistication, students gain a reservoir of literary and cultural knowledge, references, and images; the ability to evaluate intricate arguments; and the capacity to surmount the challenges posed by complex texts. (CCSS, 2010, p. 35)

Source: Adapted from Burke, J. (2013). *The Common Core Companion: The Standards Decoded, Grades 6–8: What They Say, What They Mean, How to Teach Them*. Thousand Oaks, CA: Corwin.

Reading 1: Read closely to determine what the text says explicitly and to make logical inferences from it; cite specific textual evidence when writing or speaking to support conclusions drawn from the text.

Literature

3 Ask and answer questions to demonstrate understanding of a text, referring explicitly to the text as the basis for the answers.

4 Refer to details and examples in a text when explaining what the text says explicitly and when drawing inferences from the text.

5 Quote accurately from a text when explaining what the text says explicitly and when drawing inferences from the text.

Informational Text

3 Ask and answer questions to demonstrate understanding of a text, referring explicitly to the text as the basis for the answers.

4 Refer to details and examples in a text when explaining what the text says explicitly and when drawing inferences from the text.

5 Quote accurately from a text when explaining what the text says explicitly and when drawing inferences from the text.

What the **Student** Does

Literature

3 **Gist:** Students say what happens in the story or what the poem is about based on evidence from the text. They ask and answer questions of the text to build literal understanding before, during, and after reading.

They consider:

- What happens in the story, play, or poem?
- What is the setting?
- Which words, pictures, and sentences help me know this?
- How can I find the answer to words and sentences that confuse me?
- Which details from the text can I point to in supporting my ideas?

4 **Gist:** Students explain—either verbally or in written form— the events of the story or what the poem says based on details and examples from the text. They provide specific examples from the text when making inferences.

They consider:

- What happens in this story, play, or poem?
- What is the setting? (time and place)
- What is the author's central message?
- As I read, which details help me understand what is happening to these characters?
- What inferences can I make and what specific details from the text led me to make each one?

5 **Gist:** Students explain—either verbally or in written form— the events of the story or what the poem says using specific, accurate quotes directly from the text. Provide quotes from the text to support inferences.

They consider:

- What happens in this story, play, or poem?
- Which specific details are most important?
- What is the setting? (time and place)
- What are the main events in the story or poem?
- What direct, explicit quotes from the text support my understanding of the author's meaning?
- What direct quotes from the text support my inferences from the text?

Informational Text

3 **Gist:** Students say what happens in the text or what it's about based on evidence from the text. Ask and answer questions of the text to build literal understanding before, during, and after.

They consider:

- What happens or is said in this text?
- Which specific details help me understand the main topic?
- How can I look at words, pictures, and headings to help me understand?
- Can I read more slowly, reread, or skim the text to find specific details that support my ideas about the text?

4 **Gist:** Students explain—either verbally or in written form— what the text is about, providing specific details and examples from the text. Provide specific examples from the text when making inferences.

They consider:

- What is the purpose for reading?
- What is the topic/subject—and what does the text say about that?
- Which specific details are most important?
- What is the setting? (time and place)
- What evidence or examples support what I understand about the text?
- What inferences can I make and what specific details from the text led me to make each one?

5 **Gist:** Students explain—either verbally or in written form— what the text is about, using specific, accurate quotes directly from the text. Provide quotes from the text to support inferences.

They consider:

- What is the purpose for reading?
- What is the topic/subject—and what does the text say about that?
- Which specific details are most important?
- What is the setting (time and place)?
- What textual evidence supports my account of what the text says?
- What evidence—a detail, quotations, or example—can I cite to support my inference or explanation of the literal meaning of the text?

What the **Teacher** Does

To teach students how to "read closely":

- Think aloud your close reading process as you share fiction and informational short texts and picture books. When reading shared novels as a class, plan ahead a chapter opening or passage you want to model with. Track thinking with sticky notes placed directly on the text, big chart paper and/or highlighting, displaying text on a screen.
- Pose questions about the text's words, actions, and details that require students to look closely. Don't do the answering for them!
- Display a text via tablet or computer and ask students to select specific words, sentences, or paragraphs they think are essential; ask students to explain how it contributes to the meaning of the larger text.
- Draw students' attention to text features and structures, and think aloud how you combine information in these elements to understand the page/section/text as a whole.
- Provide short pieces of text for students to practice "reading closely" for specific purposes.
- Have students respond to their reading and their thinking about texts. This could be accomplished in response journals or other reading notebooks.

To teach students how to ask and answer questions to demonstrate understanding:

- Using picture books, ask a question and think aloud how it helped you understand. For example, when a fiction reader muses, *"I wonder why she acted that way towards him?"* it puts the reader on high alert, looking for the answer in the text. Readers of nonfiction also pose questions when their comprehension falters or as a way to cement understandings, sentence by sentence. For example, *"What does hibernation mean? I sort of think it has something to do with winter, but I'll read on to see if the author explains it."*
- Use chart paper to record students' questions about a shared text as you read. Then, after reading, go back and answer these questions. Encourage students to pose analytical (how, why) questions along with literal (who, what, where, when) questions. Code if questions were answered literally (L), inferentially (I), or not answered at all (NA).
- Over time, help students grasp that readers pose questions before reading (What's my purpose for reading this?), during reading (What's with all the descriptions

of sunlight in each chapter?), and after reading (What did the main character finally learn?).
- Have students practice posing questions on their own (independently). Students can annotate on the text where they have questions. Have students share them with a partner or the class.

To develop students' ability to determine "what the text says explicitly, "refer to details and examples in a text," and "quote accurately from a text":

- In a series of lessons and using various texts, write *text-dependent* questions on sticky notes or annotate in the margins. Model how to find the answers to the questions posed. Annotate in the margins the exact words where questions are answered.
- Provide students with a copy of a sample text and circulate, coaching as they highlight *specific* details and annotate their thinking. Remind them to "say what it says"—not what they think it means.
- Photocopy and distribute short pieces of text and highlighter markers, and instruct students to highlight sections of the text to show where questions you pose are answered explicitly (or literally). Compare findings as a class.
- Using whiteboards, have students highlight quotes from a text to use as evidence when explaining what the text is about.
- Provide graphic organizers for students to write their questions and then record details, examples, and quotes.

To teach students how to "draw inferences from the text":

- Choose texts to read aloud and plan where you will model inferring. Think aloud how you make inferences, and tie these inferences back to specific words and phrases in the text.
- Have students use two different colored highlighters to code where information in the text is answered literally or explicitly and another color to show where it's answered inferentially. Annotate how the text led to inferences.

To help your English language learners, try this:

- Confer with students and have them read aloud a portion of the text. Then stop and have them tell you what questions they have about what they've read.

 For graphic organizer templates, see online resources at **resources.corwin.com/literacycompanion3-5**.

Preparing to Teach

Standard: _____

Preparing the Classroom

Preparing the Mindset

Preparing the Texts to Use

Preparing to Differentiate

Connections to Other Standards:

Academic Vocabulary: Key Words and Phrases

Cite specific textual evidence: Students should be able to quote a specific passage from the text to support all claims, assertions, or arguments about what a text means or says. Evidence comes from within the text itself, not from the reader's opinion or experience.

Demonstrate understanding of a text: Readers take a group of details (different findings, series of events, related examples) and draw from them an insight or understanding about their meaning or importance within the passage of the text as a whole.

Drawing inferences: To understand the text by generalizing, deducing, and concluding from reasoning and evidence that is not presented literally or explicitly. These conclusions are based on textual clues.

Explicitly: Clearly stated in great or precise detail; may pertain to factual information or literal meaning, though this is not necessarily always the case.

Informational text: These include nonfiction texts from a range of sources and written for a variety of purposes; everything from essays to advertisements, historical documents to op-ed pieces. Informational texts include written arguments as well as infographics.

Key details: Parts of a text that support the main idea, and enable the reader to draw conclusions and infer what the text or a portion of a text is about.

Literature: Fiction, poetry, drama, graphic stories, but also artworks by distinguished painters, sculptors, or photographers.

Logical inferences (drawn from the text): To infer, readers add what they *learned* from the text to what they already *know* about the subject; however, for an inference to be "logical," it must be based on evidence *from the text*.

Quote accurately: "Lifting lines" directly from the text or copying specific sections of the text to demonstrate understanding. All claims, assertions, or arguments about what a text means or says require specific examples from the text.

Read closely (aka close reading): Reading that emphasizes not only surface details but the deeper meanings and larger connotations between words, sentences, and the full text; also demands scrutiny of craft, including arguments and style used by the author.

Text: In its broadest meaning, a text is whatever one is trying to read: a poem, essay, drama, story, or article; in its most modern sense, a text can also be an image, an artwork, speech, or multimedia format such as a website, film, or social media message such as a tweet.

Textual evidence: Not all evidence is created equal; students need to choose those pieces of evidence (words, phrases, passages illustrations) that provide the best proof of what they are asserting about the text.

Notes

Planning to Teach

Standard: _____

Whole Class

_____
_____
_____
_____
_____
_____
_____
_____

Small Group

_____
_____
_____
_____
_____
_____
_____

Individual Practice/Conferring

_____
_____
_____
_____
_____
_____
_____

Reading 2: Determine central ideas or themes of a text and analyze their development; summarize the key supporting details and ideas.

Literature

3 Recount stories, including fables, folktales, and myths from diverse cultures; determine the central message, lesson, or moral and explain how it is conveyed through key details in the text.

4 **Determine a theme of a story, drama, or poem from details in the text; summarize the text.**

5 Determine a theme of a story, drama, or poem from details in the text, **including how characters in a story or drama respond to challenges or how the speaker in a poem reflects upon a topic;** summarize the text.

Informational Text

3 Determine the main idea of a text, recount the key details and explain how they support the main idea.

4 Determine the main idea of a text **and explain how it is supported by key details; summarize the text.**

5 Determine **two or more main ideas** of a text, and explain how they are supported by key details; summarize the text.

What the **Student** Does

| Literature | Informational Text |

Literature

3 **Gist:** After establishing the text's explicit meaning, students identify the central message of the text and determine how key details convey the message, lesson, or moral. Students recount or retell stories, fables, folktales, and myths.

They consider:

- Is this a fable? A folktale? A myth?
- What message, lesson, or moral do the characters learn by the end of the story?
- What specific details am I basing this understanding on?
- What happens in the story?
- What can I say about the beginning, middle, and end so that someone who doesn't know the story could understand it?

4 **Gist:** After establishing the text's explicit meaning, students identify a theme. They examine how an author introduces and develops this theme through details. Students summarize the text.

They consider:

- What is the theme of this text?
- What specific details led me to determine this?
- Where in the text might I look? (High drama scenes? Chapter openings? Final pages of book?)
- Does the author use symbols or repeating language to hint at a theme?
- What does the narrator say that helps me understand a theme?
- What details from the beginning, middle, and end would I include when summarizing this story?

5 **Gist:** After establishing the text's explicit meaning, students determine the theme, identifying key ideas, especially how characters respond to challenges in stories and dramas, or how the speaker in a poem reflects upon a topic. Students summarize the text.

They consider:

- What is the theme of this text?
- Where in the text might I look? (High drama scenes? Chapter openings? Final pages of book?)
- Does the author use symbols or repeating language to hint at a theme?
- What key ideas does the author develop throughout the chapters of this text?
- How do characters respond to the challenges they face?
- How might I look at what the main character finally understands for clues?
- What details from the beginning, middle, and end would I include in a summary on this text?

Informational Text

3 **Gist:** After establishing the text's explicit meaning, students identify the main idea. They examine how the main idea is supported through key details. Students recount the key details.

They consider:

- What is the main idea of this text?
- What key ideas, specific details, and events help me determine this?
- What details and facts from the text would I include when recounting what the text is about?

4 **Gist:** After establishing the text's explicit meaning, students identify the main idea. They examine how an author introduces and develops this idea through key details. Students summarize the text.

They consider:

- What is the main idea of this text?
- What key ideas, specific details, and events help me determine this?
- What details and facts from the text would I include when summarizing what the text is about?

5 **Gist:** After establishing the text's explicit meaning, students identify two or more central ideas in a text, examining how they are supported through specific details. Students summarize the text.

They consider:

- What are the main ideas of this text?
- What key ideas does the author develop throughout the text?
- What specific details help me determine this?
- What details and facts from the text would I include when summarizing what the text is about?

What the **Teacher** Does

To determine the main idea, central message, lesson, or moral, or theme of a story, drama, or poem:

- Point out common spots for identifying main idea/theme in a text and how you scrutinize specifics (TOC, headings, topic sentences, key events, recurring vocabulary, illustrations) to infer ideas throughout the text. Have students turn and talk whenever you want them to work through a key part where an important idea can be inferred.
- Pose questions that get students looking for theme via the following avenues:
  - Naming a lesson in the story (What lesson did _____ learn by the end? What lesson or message did you get from reading this book?)
  - Identifying a social issue in a story (What have you learned about _____ from reading this book? What are you learning about the issue of _____ here?)
- Keep a classroom chart of themes that students discover in texts (with love and understanding, families can overcome loss; accept who you are; bullies lose out; perseverance pays off, and so on).
- After skimming and scanning an informational text, ask students to generate all possible ideas and then determine which of them the text most fully develops.
- Turn topic statements into questions that spur students to read the section for answers (Grey Wolf Habitat to "What is the Grey Wolf's habitat?"). This will help students learn to "add up" subtopics toward a main idea.

To explain how it is conveyed through key details in the text:

- Model for students how to code specific details in the text that support the central idea or theme.
- Model for students using a shared text which words, phrases, or images recur throughout the text that might signal they are the main idea or central message. Mark, highlight, or annotate these words. After modeling, have students work in groups or independently using the same strategy.

To recount stories, including fables, folktales, and myths, from diverse cultures:

- As you read aloud, introduce students to different types of stories, such as realistic stories, adventure stories, fantasy, folktales, fables, and myths. Compare and contrast, and chart their attributes.
- Provide students with a variety of fables, folktales, and myths. Have students work in small groups to study a type in depth and share knowledge with class (e.g., Cinderella stories, Greek myths, American tall tales).
- Model how to recount the story. First, explain that a retell/recount involves an opening statement, followed by key events listed in sequential or chronological order, and a conclusion; have students recount stories to a partner or with the class.

To summarize the text:

- Create a shared summary with the class. Include an opening statement, key details in chronological order from the text, and a conclusion. Post on chart paper for students to refer to.
- Model explaining the story by writing a summary. Refer back to text to "lift" specific words, phrases, or sentences and embed these into the explanation.
- Have students write their own summaries, highlighting where they have used specific details and examples from the text.

To determine how characters in a story or drama respond to challenges, or how the speaker in a poem reflects upon a topic:

- Have students use graphic organizers or flow charts to monitor how characters respond to challenges over the course of a text.
- Model reading poetry and think aloud how the narrator reflects on the topic. Highlight or annotate places in the text where that is supported.
- Have students practice by annotating poetry either on tablets or on photocopies or using sticky notes.

To help your English language learners, try this:

- Have students draw pictures to reinforce setting, characters, and plot. Make certain that students understand the meaning of the academic vocabulary you're using, such as "main character" or "main idea."

 For graphic organizer templates, see online resources at **resources.corwin.com/literacycompanion3-5**.

Preparing to Teach

Standard: _____

Preparing the Classroom

_____
_____
_____
_____
_____
_____
_____

Preparing the Mindset

_____
_____
_____
_____
_____
_____

Preparing the Texts to Use

_____
_____
_____
_____
_____
_____

Preparing to Differentiate

_____
_____
_____
_____
_____
_____

Connections to Other Standards:

_____
_____
_____

Academic Vocabulary: Key Words and Phrases

Analyze their development over the course of the text: Refers to the careful and close examination of the parts or elements from which something is made and how those parts affect or function within the whole to create meaning.

Central ideas or messages: Some ideas are more important to a work than others; these are the ideas you could not cut out without fundamentally changing the meaning or quality of the text. Think of the "central" ideas of a text as you would the beams in a building: They are the main elements that make up the text and that all the supporting details help to develop.

Characters respond to challenge: In literature, characters are faced with problems and they respond or react to these problems or challenges. The way they react moves the story along and adds to the event sequence.

Conveyed through particular details: This refers to the way authors might explore an idea (e.g., the sense of isolation that often appears throughout dystopian novels) by referring to it directly or indirectly through details that evoke the idea (such as isolation).

Determine central message: Some ideas are more important to a work than others; these are the ideas you could not cut out without fundamentally changing the meaning or quality of the text. Think of the "central message" of a text as you would the beams in a building: they are the main elements that make up the text and which all the supporting details help to develop.

Development: Think of a grain of rice added to others one at a time to form a pile; this is how writers develop their ideas—by adding imagery, details, examples, and other information over the course of a text. Thus when one "analyzes (the) development" of an idea or theme, for example, they look at how the author does this and what effect such development has on the meaning of the text.

Diverse cultures: The United Nations has defined cultural as follows: "Culture should be regarded as the set of distinctive spiritual, material, intellectual and emotional features of society or a social group, and that it encompasses, in addition to art and literature, lifestyles, ways of living together, value systems, traditions and beliefs." Taking that into account, *diverse cultures* are ones with cultural variety and cultural differences that exist throughout the world or within a society.

Fables: A legendary story of supernatural happenings or a narrative that attempts to impart a truth (often through a moral)—especially in stories where animals speak and have human characteristics. A fable can also be about legendary people and their tales.

Folktales: These started as an oral tradition—short stories or legends passed down by word of mouth through the generations. These tales or legends were part of a common group of people or folk, and may include supernatural elements. Folktales generally reflect or validate certain aspects of the culture or group. Fairy tales are a subgenre of folktales.

Key supporting details and ideas: Important details and ideas support the larger ideas the text develops over time and are used to advance the author's claim(s). Not all details and ideas are equally important, however, so students must learn to identify those that matter the most in the context of the text.

Main idea: The most important or central idea of a paragraph or of a larger part of a text. The main idea tells the reader what the text is about and is what the author wants you to remember most.

Moral: Used in Standard 2, a moral is a lesson that concerns what is the right or the correct thing to do and can be derived or inferred (or in some cases stated literally) from a story—usually a fable.

Myth: A traditional or legendary story, usually with supernatural beings, ancestors, and heroes. These stories serve to explain the worldview of a people by explaining customs, society, or phenomenon of nature. Perhaps the most common are Greek and Roman myths, which have deities and demigods.

Objective summary: Describes key ideas, details, or events in the text and reports them without adding any commentary or outside description; it is similar to an evening "recap" of the news, which attempts to answer the reporter's essential questions: who, what, where, when, why, and how.

Retelling and recounting stories, including key details: Retelling and recounting involve students giving an oral account of the key details of a story. They typically include an opening statement, key events listed chronologically, and a concluding statement. (Even though "retelling" and "recount" have slightly different meanings, we use them interchangeably throughout this volume.)

Summary: Identifies the key ideas, details, or events in the text and reports them with an emphasis on who did what to whom and when; in other words, the emphasis is on retelling what happened or what the text says with the utmost fidelity to the text itself, thus requiring students to check what they say against what the text says happened.

Themes: The ideas the text explains, develops, and explores; there can be more than one, but themes are what the text is actually *about*. Themes can be the central message, the lesson, or what the author wants you to come away with. Common themes are survival, good versus evil, showing respect for others, adventure, love and friendship, and so on.

Planning to Teach

Standard: _____

Whole Class

_____
_____
_____
_____
_____
_____
_____

Small Group

_____
_____
_____
_____
_____
_____
_____

Individual Practice/Conferring

_____
_____
_____
_____
_____
_____

Reading 3: Analyze how and why individuals, events, and ideas develop and interact over the course of a text.

Literature

3 Describe characters in a story (e.g., their traits, motivations, or feelings) and explain how their actions contribute to the sequence of events.

4 Describe **in depth a character, setting, or event in a story or drama, drawing on specific details in the text** (e.g., a character's thoughts, words or actions).

5 Compare and contrast two or more **characters, setting, or events** in a story or drama, **drawing on specific details in the text** (e.g., how **characters interact).**

Informational Text

3 Describe the relationship between a series of historical events, scientific ideas or concepts, or steps in technical procedures in a text, using language that pertains to time, sequence, and cause/effect.

4 Explain events, procedures, ideas, or concepts in a historical, scientific, or technical text, including what happened and why, based on specific information in the text.

5 Explain **the relationships or interactions between two or more individuals, events, ideas, or concepts in a historical, scientific, or technical text** based on specific information in the text.

What the **Student** Does

Literature

3 **Gist:** Students reading *for the characters* describe traits, feelings, and motivations, noting how characters' actions add to the plot and move along the sequence of events toward the ending.

They consider:

- What is the main character's most important personality trait?
- What does the main character need or want at the beginning of the story?
- How does the main character try to solve her problem?
- How do the other characters respond?
- What is the sequence of important events in the story?

4 **Gist:** Students reading *for the elements* use specific details from the text, such as a character's thoughts or words or actions, and descriptions of place to describe in depth a character, setting, or event in a story or drama.

They consider:

- How does the main character behave at the beginning of the story? Why?
- What bothers her most of all? Which details tell me this in these chapters?
- How does the setting play a role in the story or the characters' actions?
- Why does the character's behavior change from the beginning of the story to the end? What has she learned?
- What are the important events that lead up to the resolution?
- How do other characters help the main character or make the problem worse?

5 **Gist:** Students reading *for interactions* between characters, settings, or events in a story or drama compare and contrast two or more of the above, using key details from the text.

They consider:

- What happens to the main characters in each chapter? By novel's end? Why?
- What does the main character have in common with another?
- How are characters not alike?
- Where and when is there the most tension? Why?
- How can I use details to explain how the character is changing?
- When I visualize the settings of important scenes, what does that reveal about the characters?

Informational Text

3 **Gist:** Students reading *for information* to describe the relationship between a series of events, ideas, concepts, or steps requires them to understand and use technical language. Having established this, students focus on time, sequences, and cause/effect to determine importance.

They consider:

- Does this text describe people and events in history?
- Does it outline steps in a process like a recipe?
- Does this text explain animals, nature, or another science topic?
- What vocabulary words help me understand the topic?
- How can I skim headings, photos, captions, and graphics to deepen my understanding of these pages?
- Does the author use language and key words that identify time, sequence, or cause/effect?

4 **Gist:** Students reading *for information* in historical, scientific, or technical texts use specific information directly from the text to recount what happened and why as they explain events, procedures, ideas, or concepts.

They consider:

- How is this text organized? Does the author tell about a topic in a chronological sequence?
- How can I "outsmart" the text by using features like the index, TOC, glossary, illustrations and photographs, bolded words, and headings to help me understand?
- What happens in the text?
- What specific information or key ideas explain why the event happened?
- If I had to choose one specific piece of information from each page that best explains what or why something happens, what would it be?

5 **Gist:** Students reading *for information* about the relationships between two or more people, events, ideas, or concepts first determine which people, events, ideas, or concepts play an influential role. Students then read the text almost like a scientist would observe an experiment, observing how various people, events, ideas, or concepts influence each other over time.

They consider:

- What type of text is this?
- Which people, events, ideas, or concepts does the author treat as important in the text?
- How would I explain their relationships or interactions?
- What examples or key details help me support my explanation?
- How do people, events, or ideas connect together?
- What are the connections and relationships between procedures, steps, and so on?

What the **Teacher** Does

To describe in depth characters, settings, or events in a story:

- As you read aloud books, get students to notice how the character drives the plot. Teach students to hit the pause button at major shifts in setting/scene, time periods, and chapter endings and ask themselves, *What does the author want me to notice as new here? How is this helping—or hindering—the character resolve the problem she is trying to solve?*
- Have students make a list of all the characters in a story, and chart what they're like (both externally and internally) and what causes them to be that way/feel that way. Discuss that characters, just like people in real life, have contradictory aspects of their personality.
- Create class charts depicting the sequence of important events, and then have students work in groups to consider an event from *each* character's POV.
- Build a plot map—individually, in groups, or as a class—noting specific events in a story.
- Think aloud how you would use the specific details to describe in detail the characters, settings, or events. Model orally and also in written form for the students.
- Have students write in-depth descriptions of characters, setting, or events from the text using specific details.

To explain how actions contribute to the sequence of events:

- Create a graphic chart or plot diagram and ask students to analyze the plot for moments when characters do something that affects the plot—increases tension, causes change—in a measurable, discernable way. Sometimes called a "fever chart" to represent the rising and falling action of events in the story.

To compare/contrast two or more characters, settings, or events in a story or drama, and to explain the relationships or interactions between two or more individuals, events, procedures, ideas, or concepts:

- Have students identify the wants or needs of key characters and parts of the story where their different wants and needs conflict.
- Have students create graphic organizers (Venn diagrams, two-column notes, double-bubble Thinking Maps) to record information about what is similar and different about characters and their families, their communities, and their beliefs. Look at settings and major events through the same bifocals: What might the author want us to notice through these sharp contrasts?

- Model how to write a comparison piece and then model how to write contrast using graphic organizers. Co-construct a comparison/contrast piece with students using a shared text.
- Help students determine *why* something happened as it did. This will help them begin to identify cause and effect relationships between concepts, people, and events in informational texts.
- Gather a few texts (informational) that each offer a different and clear example of signal words. Read the texts and chart the signal words (timelines, dates, numbered steps, and words like *first, second, next, last, most importantly,* and *years ago*).

To draw from specific details and key details in the text and to summarize:

- Model summarizing the text by thinking aloud and using specific words, phrases, and sentences.
- Have students write their own summaries, highlighting where they have used specific text details.

To use language that pertains to time, sequence, and cause/effect:

- Using a shared text, model how to discern if the text is organized in time, sequence, or cause/effect. Highlight key terms in the text and discuss how these are specific to that technique.
- Create a chart of key language that lets students know that two pieces of information, ideas, concepts, or events are being compared (e.g., *but, however, in contrast*).
- Teach students how to use highlighting or color-coding to identify and delineate the different key language.

To explain events, scientific ideas, or concepts or steps in technical procedures in a text:

- Using a shared text, model how to determine key words that are important to the main idea of the text.
- Think aloud to demonstrate how to take these key details and formulate "what happened." Create graphic organizers (e.g., cause/effect charts) to demonstrate the "why" of what happened.

To help your English language learners, try this:

- Guide a small group of students through a text and discuss setting and characters. Students should each have their own copy of the book or text. Help students use vocabulary to describe and explain. Provide students with graphic organizers. Talk thorough the task first, then fill in the organizers with labels and pictures.

 For graphic organizer templates, see online resources at **resources.corwin.com/literacycompanion3-5**.

Preparing to Teach

Standard: _____

Preparing the Classroom

Preparing the Mindset

Preparing the Texts to Use

Preparing to Differentiate

Connections to Other Standards:

Academic Vocabulary: Key Words and Phrases

Actions or events: "Actions" refer to what happens, what people *do*; in English Language Arts it is the actions of the characters we study; in history, of the people who *rebel*, *discover*, or *invent*; in science, what we must do in the context of a procedure. "Events" are those moments in a story or history or any other field when things change that merit the time we spend studying them (war, social movements).

Analyze: This means to look closely at something for the key parts and how they work together.

Cause/effect relationship: The reasons something happens and the consequences of that action. The *cause* is why something happens. The *effect* is what happens because of the cause.

Character traits: How a character is—both what they look like and who they are, which is revealed by what they do. Their motivations and feelings, thoughts, words, and actions.

Characters: Characters can be simple (flat, static) or complex (round, dynamic); only characters who change, who have a rich inner life that interacts with people and its environment, can be considered "complex." Often represented as an arc: what they are like or where they are when the story *begins* and when it *ends*.

Compare/contrast: This requires students to identify and analyze what is similar (compare) and what is different (contrast).

Develop and interact: As stories unfold, events and characters change; these changes are the consequence of interactions that take place between people, events, and ideas within a story or an actual event such as "the Twitter Revolution" in Iran, where events, people, and ideas all resulted in a variety of changes and developments as a result of multiple interactions between people, events, and ideas like social media. To "develop" is to otherwise change, increasing or decreasing in importance, growing more complex or evolving into something different altogether.

Key details: In the context of literature, key details relate to story grammar elements, that is, character, setting, problem, major events, and resolution, and how they interact.

Key steps in technical procedures: Whether in social studies or science, the idea here is that some steps or stages are more crucial in any series of steps or stages than others; one must be able to discern this so they can understand why they are so important and how they affect other people or events or experiments.

Major events: These are the most important events in a story and typically relate to how the main character resolves a problem or handles a challenge.

Sequence of events: The order that events in a story or text occur or the order that specific tasks are performed.

Setting: The place or time that a story, novel, or drama takes place. Usually students answer and can describe *where* it takes place (there may be more than one setting in texts) and *when* it takes place—this can be a specific time period or can be the *past*, *present*, or *future*.

Steps in technical procedures: Whether in social studies or science, the idea here is that some steps or stages are more crucial in any series of steps or stages than others; one must be able to discern this so they can understand why they are so important and how they affect other people or events.

Notes

Standard: _____

Whole Class

_____

_____

_____

_____

_____

_____

_____

Small Group

_____

_____

_____

_____

_____

_____

Individual Practice/Conferring

_____

_____

_____

_____

_____

_____

Reading 4: Interpret words and phrases as they are used in a text, including determining technical, connotative, and figurative meanings, and analyze how specific word choices shape meaning or tone.

Literature

3 Determine the meanings of words and phrases as they are used in a text, distinguishing literal from nonliteral language.

4 Determine the meaning of words and phrases as they are used in a text, **including those that allude to significant characters found in mythology (e.g., Herculean).**

5 Determine the meaning of words and phrases as they are used in a text, **including figurative language such as metaphors and similes.**

Informational Text

3 Determine the meaning of general academic and domain-specific words and phrases in a text relevant to a **grade 3 topic or subject area.**

4 Determine the meaning of general academic and domain-specific words or phrases in a text relevant to a **grade 4 topic or subject area.**

5 Determine the meaning of general academic and domain-specific words and phrases in a text relevant to a **grade 5 topic or subject area.**

What the **Student** Does

Literature

3 **Gist:** Students determine what words and phrases mean in text. They discern if the language is literal or nonliteral.

They consider:

- Which words or phrases on this page (in this chapter) seem most important?
- What does the author's word choice here make me think of?
- Which words or phrases help me understand what's happening?
- Which words or phrases get me to "read between the lines" and infer meaning?
- How can I use words I do know to figure out the meaning of words I don't know?

4 **Gist:** Students determine what words and phrases mean in text. They recognize that specific words refer to significant characters in mythology (e.g., Herculean, Trojan Horse, Achilles' Heel); these words often provide insight into characters or descriptions.

They consider:

- Which words or phrases on this page(s) seem most important?
- What does the author's word choice here make me think of? How can I connect that to the event here?
- Which words or phrases help me understand the literal action?
- Which words or phrases get me to "read between the lines" and infer meaning?
- How does the language in this section set a tone? How does the tone help me understand what the characters are thinking right now?
- Are there any words from Greek mythology that are used to describe characters?
- What do these mythological words mean in the context of this text?

5 **Gist:** Students figure out what words mean and how context affects the meaning of words and phrases, by examining if meaning is literal or figurative, especially metaphors and similes.

They consider:

- What words or phrases tell me the most about characters, actions, events, or the setting?
- Which words or phrases help me understand the meaning of this portion or the text as a whole?
- Which words or phrase are figurative language and why is the author using them?
- What types of figurative language are used?
- How can I use the surrounding sentences to help me determine the meaning of the figurative language (especially similes and metaphors)?
- How does the language in this section set a tone? How does the tone help me understand what the characters are thinking right now?

Informational Text

3 **Gist:** Students determine what words and phrases mean in texts relevant to third-grade topics or subject areas.

They consider:

- What is the topic of this text? How does knowing the main topic help me figure out the meaning of this sentence or section?
- How can I use the text and surrounding photos and caption to figure out what this word or phrase means?
- How can I look at text features (titles, bolded words, headings, captions) or illustrations to help me figure out what is being explained on this page?
- Is there a glossary or other feature to help me figure out the meaning of a word?
- Are there words the author uses repeatedly or did the author use a synonym to define this topic-specific word?

4 **Gist:** Students determine what words and phrases mean in texts relevant to fourth-grade topics or subject areas.

They consider:

- What is the topic of this text?
- What do I know about the topic that can help me figure out the meaning of this sentence/section?
- How can I use the text and surrounding photos and caption to figure out what this word or phrase means?
- How can I look at text features (titles, glossary, bolded words, headings, captions) or illustrations to help me figure out what is being explained on this page?
- Are there words the author uses repeatedly or did the author use a synonym to define this topic-specific word?

5 **Gist:** Students determine what words and phrases mean in texts relevant to fifth-grade topics or subject areas.

They consider:

- What is the topic of this text?
- What do I know about the topic that can help me figure out the meaning of this sentence/section?
- How can I use the text and surrounding photos and caption to figure out what this word or phrase means?
- How can I look at text features (titles, glossary, bolded words, headings, captions) or illustrations to help me figure out what is being explained on this page?
- Are there words the author uses repeatedly or did the author use a synonym to define this topic-specific word?
- When I read aloud the word or sentence, does that help me figure out the challenging word?

What the **Teacher** Does

To determine the meaning of words and phrases as they are used in a text:

- Generate a vocabulary chart at the outset of a new nonfiction unit or chapter. Don't be afraid to explicitly teach key words up front, with the idea that students will take ownership of figuring out plenty of challenging words in the subsequent reading.
- Think aloud while reading to the class to show how you puzzle out a word or phrase using syntactic, semantic, typographic, etymological, and other types of information to decipher words. Invite students to try a word.
- Teach students to look all around the words phrase as though they're hunting for something on their closet floor! Is there a word part they know? What about the other words in the sentence—is the challenging word part of a series of like things (e.g., *Lions eat deer, zebras, mice, and* _____)? What clues are on the page (captions, diagrams, images)? Does the author define it a sentence or two later?
- Point out the way authors use explanations, synonyms, restatement (e.g., *in other words . . .*), contrast, or antonyms, which can help you know a challenging word.
- Encourage students to mark unknown words in their texts with sticky notes as they are reading independently and then to go back and determine meaning. Check in with students in small group or in conferences on how they are using this strategy.
- Use a shared text to have students highlight unknown words and annotate in the margins.
- When working with the whole class or small groups or conferring one-on-one with students, encourage them to acknowledge when they don't know a word or phrase.

To determine the meaning of words and phrases as they allude to significant characters found in mythology:

- Brainstorm a list of words that harken back to mythology (e.g., Herculean, Trojan Horse, Phoenix, to Harp, fate, fury, leave no stone unturned, Achilles' Heel, Midas Touch, Mentor, Nemesis, Phobia). Read or discuss the myths where these are referenced and discuss what they mean, especially in the context of character description or events in a text.
- Keep a class list or illustrated chart of famous characters in mythology.
- Invite students to find words or phrases in their own reading that allude to significant characters in mythology and share these with the class.

To determine the meaning of figurative language such as metaphors and similes:

- Choose texts rich with figurative language and discuss the language as you read aloud to the class.
- Teach explicitly the different types of figurative language (simile, metaphor, analogy, personification, etc.) and why they are used in text. Keep class charts of examples of figurative language from shared texts or have students record examples in their writing notebooks or journals.
- Use shared texts of poetry under a document camera or projected on an interactive whiteboard to find examples of figurative language, name them, and annotate how they lead to meaning of the text or create visual and sensory images.

To distinguish between literal and nonliteral language:

- Think aloud using a shared text (or screen or under a document camera) to highlight in one color literal language—and in another color nonliteral language, discussing how they are different and how they lead to overall understanding of the text.
- Identify nonliteral language and discuss what it means within the text; then determine the literal meaning of those words; then model, or ask students, to determine, in light of how they are used, the figurative or nonliteral meaning.
- Continue to explicitly draw attention to literal and nonliteral language in shared texts.

To determine the meaning of general academic and domain-specific words in a text:

- Show students how to make use of any textual features—sidebars, captions, typography (is the word in **bold** and thus in the glossary), diagrams, footers, or glossaries in the chapter or in the appendix.
- Teach students, when appropriate, the root words or etymology of certain subject-specific words (*bio = life, ology = study of*) as part of the study of any discipline.

To help your English language learners, try this:

- Create pictures for words and visual representations for figurative language. Use these words as often as possible, speaking them aloud so students hear them used in context and pronounced correctly. Write words, model pronunciation, and provide opportunities for students to use it often in context.

 For graphic organizer templates, see online resources at **resources.corwin.com/literacycompanion3-5.**

Standard: _____

Preparing the Classroom

_____
_____
_____
_____
_____
_____
_____

Preparing the Mindset

_____
_____
_____
_____
_____

Preparing the Texts to Use

_____
_____
_____
_____
_____
_____

Preparing to Differentiate

_____
_____
_____
_____
_____
_____

Connections to Other Standards:

_____
_____
_____

Academic Vocabulary: Key Words and Phrases

Allude to significant characters found in mythology: Allude means to make an indirect reference or to hint at. By alluding to characters found in mythology, the writer wants the reader to infer their key points. For example, Hercules was beyond the mortal man as far as strength. Therefore a *Herculean task* alludes to an enormous task—something beyond the ordinary—similarly, *Achilles' Heel* alludes to a fatal weakness.

Connotative meanings: Words have primary or literal meaning; some also have a secondary or connotative meaning, which implies an additional idea or feeling related to the word or phrase.

Domain specific: Within each discipline or branch of that discipline, certain words (*cell, division*) have a domain-specific use in, for example, biology; other words, however, are unique to that discipline and are thus essential for students to know in order to read, discuss, and write about complex texts in that subject.

Figurative meanings: Figures of speech (or figurative language) are those often colorful ways we develop of saying something; they include euphemism, hyperbole, irony, understatement, metaphor, simile, personification, and paradox, among others. Some of them are specific to an era, region, or social group and thus can confuse readers.

General academic: In the CCSS, these are considered "tier 2" words—they are found in written texts and are vocabulary shared between teachers and students. These words lead to a "rich" vocabulary and are often words found in the thesaurus that students can substitute for common words. These words are more precise or subtle forms of familiar words and include multiple meaning words.

Interpret: This is best understood as a way a reader explains to himself—or another—his understanding of a piece or whole of a text; it's the act of putting an author's text into more accessible familiar language.

Literal from nonliteral language: Literal language is factual and explicit, the reader does not need to infer to glean the meaning. Nonliteral language implies figurative language—often similes, metaphors, personification, and also abstract words.

Metaphor: A figure of speech that *does not* use the words *like* or *as* to compare two unrelated objects. Rather, a metaphor states that the subject is the same as an unrelated object. For example, "the lake was a mirror"; although a lake cannot be glass or a mirror, this metaphor creates the visual that the lake was smooth and reflective in the same manner that a mirror is.

Simile: A figure of speech comparing two unlike things. Similes generally use *like* or *as* to create or link the comparison. For example "cute *as* a kitten" or "his eyes twinkled *like* stars."

Technical meaning: In general this term relates to words with specialized meanings that are specific to a topic or subject being investigated. This can often be narrowed down to mean domain-specific words that typically occur in texts related to a specific content area such as rocks and minerals (*igneous, metamorphic*) or weather (*cumulous, precipitation*).

Tone: When thinking of tone, think *tone of voice*. The formal tone of the Constitution matches its importance and subject; the tone of a literary text may be formal or informal; the tone often reveals something about the dynamics between characters.

Notes

Standard: _____

Whole Class

_____

_____

_____

_____

_____

_____

_____

Small Group

_____

_____

_____

_____

_____

_____

_____

Individual Practice/Conferring

_____

_____

_____

_____

_____

_____

_____

Craft and Structure

Reading 5: Analyze the structure of texts, including how specific sentences, paragraphs, and larger portions of the text (e.g., a section, chapter, scene, or stanza) relate to each other and the whole.

Literature

3 Refer to parts of stories, dramas, and poems when writing or speaking about a text, using terms such as chapter, scene, and stanza; describe how each successive part builds on earlier sections.

4 Explain major differences between poems, drama, and prose, and refer to the structural elements of poems (e.g., verse, rhythm, meter) and drama (e.g., casts of characters, settings, descriptions dialogue, stage directions) when writing or speaking about a text.

5 Explain how a series of chapters, scenes, or stanzas fits together to provide the overall structure of a particular story, drama, or poem.

Informational Text

3 Use text features and search tools (e.g., key words, sidebars, hyperlinks) to locate information relevant to a given topic efficiently.

4 Describe the overall structure (e.g., chronology, comparison, cause/effect, problem/solution) of events, ideas, concepts, or information in a text or part of a text.

5 Compare and contrast the overall structure (e.g., chronology, comparison, cause/effect, problem/solution) of events, ideas, concepts, or information in **two or more texts**.

Source: © Copyright 2010. National Governors Association Center for Best Practices and Council of Chief State School Officers. All rights reserved.

What the **Student** Does

Literature

3 **Gist:** Students know the function of parts of a text (stories, dramas, and poems) and can use this knowledge to help them see how each progressive part builds on previous sections. In stories, they have a concept of beginning, middle, and end; they have a sense of chapters; and they are familiar with the function of stanzas in poetry and scenes in drama.

They consider:

- What type of text is this?
- What is the story about?
- If I were to recount the story, which parts or chapters would I point to in describing the beginning, the middle, and the end?
- What happens in the first scene (drama)? How does each scene build on the one(s) before it?
- How do the scenes move the action in the drama forward?
- In poetry what is the main idea of the first stanza? How do the stanzas build on another to create meaning in the text?

4 **Gist:** Students break down the structure of a text and explain the major differences between poems, drama, and prose. Students use specific terms to differentiate (poetry-verse, rhythm, meter; drama-casts of characters, settings, descriptions, dialogue, stage directions) between texts.

They consider:

- What type of text is this? (poetry, drama, or prose)?
- When I work to understand poetry, can I apply concepts like *stanza, rhyme, rhythm,* and *alliteration* to help me?
- When I read a play, how can I use my understanding of *casts of characters, settings, dialogue,* and *stage directions* to help me comprehend each scene?
- When I read prose, how can I use my understanding of *introductions, flow of paragraphs, conclusions, word choice,* and *voice* to enhance my understanding?
- Can I explain how poetry is different from drama or from prose using these terms? Can I explain how drama is different from the others?

5 **Gist:** Students break down the structure of a text to explain how a series of chapters, scenes, or stanzas are organized and contribute to the development of the text.

They consider:

- What type of text is this (poetry, drama, or prose)?
- How does the author build her story in each chapter to help me understand?
- What happens in the beginning chapters? How do they set up what happens in the next chapters and how do these develop the story for the chapters at the end?
- If this is drama, how do the scenes build on one another? What happens in the first scenes to set up the drama? How are the following scenes sequenced?
- If this is poetry, what is the main idea of the first stanza? How do the following stanzas help to develop the text? Why do I think they're written in that particular sequence?

Informational Text

3 **Gist:** Students locate information on a specific topic by using text features and search tools—key words, sidebars, hyperlinks—in an efficient manner.

They consider:

- What specific information do I need to determine (purpose)?
- What key words are important for me to know in order to locate that information?
- What are captions? How do they help me understand the pictures and words on this page?
- How can I use words in bold, headings, and other features in the text to find information quickly?
- How can I use the glossary to help me locate information?
- How can I use the indices to help me get information?
- How can I use electronic menus, hyperlinks, sidebars, and icons to get information?
- What other search tools can I use?

4 **Gist:** Students break down the structure of a text to explain events, ideas, concepts, or information in a text; noting patterns such as chronology, cause/effect, or problem/solution.

They consider:

- How are the main sections of the text organized?
- What organizational pattern does the author use?
- How does this pattern help me understand the meaning of the text?
- How does this pattern help me explain events, ideas, or information in the text?
- How can I identify and use key words to help me explain the organization and structure of the text?
- Is the text organized chronologically?
- Do I notice cause/effect in the text?
- Is the text organized by problem/solution?

5 **Gist:** Students break down the structure of a text to compare and contrast events, ideas, concepts, or information in two or more texts, noting patterns such as chronology, cause/effect, or problem/solution.

They consider:

- What is the main idea of the texts?
- Can I find the important events, ideas, or information in each text?
- Can I identify key words that help me find patterns such as chronology, cause/effect, or problem/solution in each text?
- How are the texts and the information similar?
- How are the texts and the information different? Can I contrast the structure and the information?
- How does the structure of these texts affect their meaning and style?

What the **Teacher** Does

To teach students to refer to parts of stories, dramas, and poems and to describe how each successive part builds on earlier sections:

- Read aloud, read aloud, read aloud—students' minds are in a sense freed up to see the beauty of the structure, and how structure builds meaning, when they can hear the author's language.
- Explicitly teach elements of stories (beginning, middle, and end; chapters); dramas (scene, casts of characters, setting, descriptions, dialogue, stage directions); and poetry (stanza, verse, rhythm, meter).
- Provide text sets for each genre so students will be familiar with them. Have specific sections of the classroom library for each.
- Using the display screen or a shared text under the document camera, have students highlight a stanza, part of a scene, and so on, and explain how it builds on the previous one used.
- Create flow charts or plot charts to show how successive parts build on earlier ones.
- Have students work in small groups to look at a favorite text and pool understandings about its structure. Give them hints to look at first and last lines, first and last paragraphs.
- Use a variety of story structure graphic organizers to help students understand how stories, poetry, and drama are organized.
- Ensure that students read texts in all these genres during independent reading time.

To refer to the structural elements of poems and drama and to explain major differences between poems, drama, and prose:

- After teaching the elements of all three types, create a three-column chart with the headings *Stories, Poetry, Drama* and co-construct by filling in the columns and then discussing the major differences.
- Provide students with graphic organizers on structural elements to be completed when students read two different types of texts.

To explain how a series of chapters, scenes, or stanzas fit together to provide the overall structure:

- With a shared text (a novel, drama, or poem), co-construct with students a flow chart of the main idea of chapters, scenes, or stanzas. When finished, summarize how these all fit together to create the overall structure.
- Teach students about rising action in literature and have them chart this in their own reading.

- Provide sequencing charts for students to do as they read independently.

To use text features and search tools to locate information:

- Teach students the surface features of text structure (e.g., headings, table of contents, index).
- Bring in numerous examples of informational texts and have students work in groups (or independently) to notice text features and then to share them with the class. Record on a class chart.
- Have students take I-books or other technology to mark with sticky notes or highlight text features. Model first using your tablet or the whiteboard.

To describe the overall structure of events, ideas, concepts, or information in a text:

- Model from a shared text the organizational structure of a text. Begin to create a classroom chart of *structures* that students can refer to. Add to this chart with successive books—or have students place sticky notes on the chart when they notice a new structure. Some examples of organizational structures are sequential (e.g., chronological description or step-by-step, cause/effect, and problem/solution) and descriptive (e.g., attributes of an object, list of items or attributes, and a comparison of more than one object).
- Provide students with a variety of informational texts and have them identify the organizational structure.
- Provide graphic organizers for each of these structures for students to complete as they read a variety of informational texts.

To compare and contrast the overall structure of events, ideas, concepts, or information in two or more texts:

- Model how you determine the overall structure of each of the texts. Complete a chart with similarities and differences. Delineate events, ideas, concepts, and information. Discuss the similarities in both and the differences. Discuss the meaning of the differences between the two.
- Provide graphic organizers so that students can replicate this as they read independently or work in groups.

To help your English language learners, try this:

- Have students read through the text completely, then with your help define terms and structures and with your guidance go back into the text and find examples of those structures.

 For graphic organizer templates, see online resources at **resources.corwin.com/literacycompanion3-5**.

Preparing to Teach

Standard: _____

Preparing the Classroom

_____
_____
_____
_____
_____
_____
_____

Preparing the Mindset

_____
_____
_____
_____
_____
_____

Preparing the Texts to Use

_____
_____
_____
_____
_____
_____
_____

Preparing to Differentiate

_____
_____
_____
_____
_____
_____

Connections to Other Standards:

_____
_____
_____

Academic Vocabulary: Key Words and Phrases

Analyze the structure of a specific paragraph or . . . sentences: Considering how information in general and sentences in particular are arranged within a paragraph, particularly as it relates to the author's purpose; the sequence or arrangement of sentences within that paragraph, especially as they express cause or otherwise serve to develop an idea.

Analyze the structure of texts: This refers to how authors organize their ideas and the text as a whole. Through structural patterns—at the sentence, paragraph, and whole-text level—authors emphasize certain ideas and create such effects as tension, mystery, and humor.

Compare and contrast the . . . differing structure of each text: This asks students to identify and analyze what is similar (compare) and different (contrast), focusing on the *differences* between the two structures and how those affect the meaning of the text.

Electronic menu and icons: These are the drop-down menus on computer applications and programs or icons on a digital device users activate to get information.

How a particular sentence . . . fits into the overall structure: Think of such a sentence or single component as a *keystone* or *cornerstone* that bears the weight of an arch or wall; in other words, these elements "fit" into the overall structure in ways that add real substance to the text in which they are used and support it. Look for them as points of emphasis.

Overall structure: Authors use devices such as transitions, organizational patterns (compare/contrast, cause/effect, problem/solution), and strategies (chronological order, order of importance) that allow them to emphasize certain ideas, events, concepts, or information.

Relate to each other and the whole: Throughout this standard, students are being asked to consider the part in its relation to the whole; this then refers to how the sentence relates to the paragraph of which it is a part, or the paragraph in relation to the whole, the scene in relation to the act—or the whole play. These smaller parts might be compared to cells in a larger organism

of the text or studs that hold up the walls in a larger structure.

Scene: In drama, the place where the action occurs; a setting.

Specific sentences, paragraphs, or larger portions of a text: This refers to the levels at which writers introduce, develop, and connect ideas throughout the text.

Stanza: In poetry, the stanza is a smaller unit, usually a grouping of two or more lines separated by a space. These groupings are generally characterized by a common pattern of meter, rhyme, and number of lines. A stanza in poetry is analogous to a paragraph in prose.

Structural elements of drama: Unlike fiction and poetry, drama is written primarily to be performed. The elements of drama are characters, setting, descriptions, dialogue, stage directions, and theme. In addition to these elements there is a structure to drama that includes plot and additional stages and sets and scenes.

Structural elements of poems—verse, rhythm, meter: There are many structural elements in poems. A verse is one line in a poem. Verses are separated by line breaks and groups of verses or lines create stanzas. The meter of the poem is the number of syllables in a line and how they are accented. The meter helps to create a rhythm to the poem. In addition to these elements, poetry has rhyme schemes and themes.

Structure of texts: This refers to how authors organize their ideas and the text as a whole. Through structural patterns such as problem/resolution and cause/effect, authors emphasize certain ideas, events, concepts, or information.

Text features: These are features of an informational text that help the reader get information. Readers need to understand that they can use text features such as a table of contents, headings, and an index to access information. They can also gain information about a topic that's not expressly stated in the text (words) itself from maps, illustrations, scale drawings, and charts and graphs.

Planning to Teach

Standard: _____

Whole Class

_____

_____

_____

_____

_____

_____

_____

Small Group

_____

_____

_____

_____

_____

_____

_____

Individual Practice/Conferring

_____

_____

_____

_____

_____

_____

_____

Reading 6: Assess how point of view or purpose shapes the content and style of a text.

Literature

3 Distinguish their own point of view from that of the narrator or those of the characters.

4 Compare and contrast the point of view from which different stories are narrated, including the difference between first- and third-person narrations.

5 Describe how a narrator's or speaker's point of view influences how events are described.

Informational Text

3 Distinguish their own point of view from that of the author of a text.

4 Compare and contrast a firsthand and secondhand account of the same event or topic; describe the differences in focus and the information provided.

5 Analyze multiple accounts of the same event or topic, noting important similarities and differences in the point of view they represent.

What the **Student** Does

Literature

3 **Gist:** Students identify the point of view of the narrator or characters in the text and distinguish this from their own point of view.

They consider:

- Who is telling the story and *why?*
- What is the main character's attitude or point of view about things in scene/chapter/whole text?
- What details help me know this?
- As I follow the main character's story, what is he like as a person? What ideas do I have about him?
- Do I find I agree or disagree with how he behaves?
- Is there another character I agree with more?
- What do I think about things in the end?

4 **Gist:** Identify the point of view of the narration of different stories in order to compare and contrast them. Students determine if narration is first person or third person and how this affects point of view.

They consider:

- Is the text written in first-person or third-person?
- How does this affect the narration and the point of view?
- Who is telling the story in each text and *why?*
- What point of view does the narrator take in each text?
- How are these stories similar?
- How are they different?

5 **Gist:** Identify the point of view of the narrator or speaker in the text and describe how this point of view influences the description of the events.

They consider:

- Who is telling the story or speaking and *why?*
- How does the narrator's or speaker's point of view affect the description of events in the text?
- What effect does this text have on me? Why?

Informational Text

3 **Gist:** Students establish the author's point of view and distinguish that from their own point of view.

They consider:

- What is the topic/subject? What is the author's attitude toward it? How does the author weave in her angle or point of view about the topic?
- What do I think about this topic as I begin to read this text?
- Has the author provided information and ideas to change my attitude about the topic by the end?

4 **Gist:** Identify the differences between a firsthand and secondhand account of the same event in order to compare and contrast them, noticing the differences in focus and information that is provided in the texts.

They consider:

- Is this a firsthand or secondhand account of the event or topic?
- How do I know?
- How does the point of view differ between firsthand and secondhand accounts?
- What are the similarities between the two?
- What are the differences in the focus of the two?
- What are the differences in the information provided in each text?

5 **Gist:** Identify the point of view of multiple accounts of the same event or topic and analyze the similarities and differences they represent.

They consider:

- What is the point of view in each of the accounts?
- How do I know this?
- What words and phrases signal the author's angle on the topic?
- Do headings, photos, and captions also contribute to my sense of the author's own ideas about the topic?
- How are these accounts similar?
- How are these accounts different?

What the **Teacher** Does

To distinguish their own point of view from that of the narrator or those of the characters and to distinguish their own point of view from that of the author:

- Define and discuss with students just what point of view (POV) means and entails, providing not just written and spoken definitions but also visual illustrations with drawings, images, artworks, or film clips.
- Think aloud your POV as you read and then model how you determine the POV from the characters or narrator.
- Model how you distinguish your POV from the POV of the text.
- Use graphic organizers (Venn diagrams, two-column notes) to chart personal POV with textual POV.

To compare and contrast the POV from which different stories are narrated:

- Model by reading familiar stories told from another POV (e.g., fairy tales—a few titles are *Honestly, Red Riding Hood Was Rotten! The Story of Little Red Riding Hood as Told by the Wolf* and *Seriously, Cinderella Is SO ANNOYING! The Story of Cinderella as Told by the Wicked Stepmother* by Trisha Speed Shaskan), then discuss how the different POV changes the meaning.
- Teach that students should determine POV first. Who is telling the story? Share books and read aloud books that are written from many different characters' POV.
- Create charts or graphic organizers to compare and contrast the POV of different stories.

To compare and contrast first- and third-person narrations:

- Define and discuss with students the different types of first- and third-person POV, and how this notion of POV relates to the narrator or characters. To clarify these elements of POV, students could apply the ideas to previously read stories to show what they know before moving onto new ones.
- Have students determine who wrote the text, what did they teach or explain, and how does the student think the author feels about the topic.
- Have students identify first- or third- (or second-) person POV whenever they read independently.
- Use a variety of websites on the same topic to model compare/contrast of POV.

To describe how a narrator's or speaker's POV influences how events are described:

- Generate different reasons *why* an author would explain, describe, or discuss scientific procedures and how such explanations relate to questions the author tries to answer.
- Model by using a text for discussion. Read the text and then ask students about topic, narration, author's intent, the POV, and whether they agree with it. Continue to ask questions and then determine how the answers and the POV influence how events are described.

To compare and contrast a firsthand and secondhand account of the same event or topic and the differences in focus and information provided:

- Define and discuss firsthand and secondhand accounts of the same topic. Using examples of each, model how you determine the POV in a firsthand account and discuss the focus and then do the same with a secondhand account on the same topic (this may be a multiple-day lesson). Use graphic organizers to organize the similarities and differences between the two accounts.
- Continue with the lesson by modeling for students how to write a compare and contrast on the two accounts.
- Provide students with firsthand and secondhand accounts and have them highlight and annotate key details and what the focus is.
- Use graphic organizers to record this information and then to compare and contrast the two accounts.

To analyze multiple accounts of the same event or topic:

- Model for students what is entailed in comparing multiple accounts on the same topic. Think aloud why and how you use key details to analyze the different accounts.
- Demonstrate use of three-column organizers (claims, reasons, and evidence) to analyze different accounts on the same event or topic.
- Put a list of words, sentences, or an extended passage on the display, asking students to find those words, structures, figures of speech, or other elements that imply a certain perspective or indicate the author's purpose; as an alternative, give students the same examples or an extended passage on a handout and ask them to annotate all words that reveal POV or purpose, then explain in the margins how they do this.

To help your English language learners, try this:

- Make connections to students' cultures or experiences to help explain their different POV about some subjects so they get a more personal, concrete grasp of subject.

 For graphic organizer templates, see online resources at **resources.corwin.com/literacycompanion3-5.**

Standard: _____

Preparing the Classroom

Preparing the Mindset

Preparing the Texts to Use

Preparing to Differentiate

Connections to Other Standards:

Academic Vocabulary: Key Words and Phrases

Analyze multiple accounts of the same event or topic: Readers must analyze different perspectives from various accounts to gain an understanding or position about the subject.

Assess: In this instance, *assess* means to evaluate what the point of view is and how it shapes the story.

Content and style of a text: The perspective from which you tell a story limits what content you can include and the style you use when you write about it. Point of view determines what the narrator sees, knows, hears, and can say—and how he can say it.

Develops the point of view: Applies to those efforts the author makes to fully realize or bring to life a fictional character or speaker in a poem by establishing and "developing" the character's or a narrator's point of view.

Firsthand/secondhand: Firsthand accounts are those that come from direct observation or firsthand experience. A secondhand account comes from an "intermediary," in other words, someone who didn't directly experience it. Journals, diaries, and newspaper accounts can be firsthand, and are beneficial when discerning point of view from time periods in history. Secondhand accounts are those written about the event by people who didn't actually experience it.

Narrator or speaker: A narrator is traditionally the one telling the story in a novel or work of short fiction (think of a voice-over in a film as a variation); a speaker, on the other hand, is what one generally calls the voice of a poem, which one should *not* assume is the poet.

Point of view (POV): The place, vantage point, or consciousness through which we hear or see someone describe a situation, tell a story, or make an argument. Different POVs are distinguished by how much the narrator or reporter knows: first person (I/me); third person (she/they); an *omniscient* POV knows what everyone thinks and feels; a *limited* POV knows only so much about a character or knows only what one (out of many) character thinks; and an *unreliable* narrator is not trustworthy. In some cases multiple POVs can be used or represented within one text.

Purpose: People want to accomplish one of four purposes when they write or speak: to persuade, inform, express, or entertain. One could add others—to explain or inspire, for example—but these four account for most situations.

Notes

Standard: _____

Whole Class

_____
_____
_____
_____
_____
_____
_____
_____

Small Group

_____
_____
_____
_____
_____
_____
_____
_____

Individual Practice/Conferring

_____
_____
_____
_____
_____
_____
_____

Reading 7: Integrate and evaluate content presented in diverse media and formats, including visually and quantitatively, as well as in words.*

Literature

3 Explain how specific aspects of a text's illustrations contribute to what is conveyed by the words in a story (e.g., create mood, emphasize aspects of a character or setting).

4 Make connections between the text of a story or drama and a visual or oral presentation of the text, identifying where each version reflects specific descriptions and directions in the text.

5 Analyze how visual and multimedia elements contribute to the meaning, tone, or beauty of a text (e.g., graphic novel, multimedia presentation of fiction, folktale, myth, poem).

Informational Text

3 Use information gained from illustrations (e.g., maps, photographs) and the words in a text to demonstrate understanding of the text (e.g., where, when, why, and how key events occur).

4 Interpret information presented visually, orally, or quantitatively (e.g., in charts, graphs, diagrams, time lines, animations, or interactive elements on Web pages) and explain how the information contributes to an understanding of the text in which it appears.

5 Draw on information from multiple print or digital sources, demonstrating the ability to locate an answer to a question quickly or to solve a problem efficiently.

* Please see "Research to Build and Present Knowledge" in Writing and "Comprehension and Collaboration" in Speaking and Listening for additional standards relevant to gathering, assessing, and applying information from print and digital sources.

Source: © Copyright 2010. National Governors Association Center for Best Practices and Council of Chief State School Officers. All rights reserved.

What the **Student** Does

Literature

3 **Gist:** Students examine how the illustrations in a text enhance the meaning conveyed by the words. Students explain how the illustrations contribute to the mood in the text or reveal aspects of characters, plot, and setting.

They consider:

- What is this story about?
- What role do the words play in describing the characters, setting, and plot?
- How do the illustrations add to my understanding of the characters? The setting? The plot?
- How do the illustrations create mood?
- What do the illustrations in this book give me that the words don't?

4 **Gist:** Students make connections between reading a story or drama and listening to or watching the same text on audio, video, or performed live. They notice when descriptions from the story or directions from a drama are used verbatim.

They consider:

- What was the same in both the written text and the other version?
- What was different in the two versions?
- How did viewing or listening to the text help me understand the subject better?
- What specific descriptions from the written text did I see in the visual or oral presentation?
- Which directions from the written text of the play were evident in the visual or oral presentation?

5 **Gist:** Students examine visual presentations or multimedia elements—animations, videos, graphic novels, multimedia presentations of a written piece of fiction, folktale, myth, or poem. They analyze how the presentations change or enhance the meaning, tone, or beauty of the written text.

They consider:

- What is the main idea of the written text?
- What genre is it?
- How does the written story differ from the visual or multimedia presentation?
- How is it the same?
- How does the visual or multimedia presentation affect the tone of the written text?
- How does the visual or multimedia presentation help me appreciate the beauty of the written text?

Informational Text

3 **Gist:** Students combine visual information such as illustrations, maps, and photographs with the words in a text to demonstrate understanding. Students identify where, when, why, and how key events occur.

They consider:

- What is the topic/subject of the written text?
- What is the main idea?
- What visual information is used?
- How do the picture and captions, diagrams, and charts help me understand the main idea?
- Does the visual information help me understand the key events in the text?
- Does the visual information help me understand key concepts?

4 **Gist:** Students interpret information gained by listening to or watching the same text on audio or video or performed live, or through quantitative means—charts, graphs, diagrams, timelines, animations, or interactive elements on webpages. Students notice and explain how this visual information helps them understand the text in which it appears.

They consider:

- What is the topic/subject of the written text?
- What is the main idea?
- What visual information is used?
- How do the pictures and captions, diagrams and charts, timelines, and so on help me understand what the text says?
- How do animations or interactive elements on webpages help me understand?
- How does the oral format (recording or performance) help me understand?

5 **Gist:** Students locate the answer to a question or find the solution to a problem by drawing on information from multiple print or digital sources and their knowledge of how to locate what they need efficiently.

They consider:

- What is the topic, question, or problem I am researching?
- What information is available in different forms and formats—both print and digital?
- Which format shall I look at first in order to locate information quickly?
- Are there specific places in the various sources that can quickly point me toward the answers?

What the **Teacher** Does

To have students explain how specific aspects of a text's illustrations contribute to what is conveyed by the words in a story or informational text:

- Explicitly teach the term *mood*. Peruse novels for passages that provide palpable examples and read them aloud. Challenge students to describe the atmosphere, or mood, and cite specific words and phrases.
- Show a piece of artwork (famous painting or children's book) and challenge students to decide which aspects of the illustration create mood and explain why.
- Have students illustrate a favorite or important part of a story or informational text and write a detailed caption describing what's happening, such as, for example, "This is the part when . . ." or "The spider is making a web."

To have students make connections between the text and a visual or oral presentation:

- Read aloud a novel or drama for students. Then watch a film version of it. Have students discern the similarities and differences in how they convey the author's message.
- As you read aloud a short story or poem, have students jot down one side of a paper visual words, visual images, colors—what they see in their mind's eye. Then have them listen to a professional recording of the text, preferably by the author herself. As they listen, have them jot down when/what words conjure visual images on the other side.
- Select a scientific process of some kind for which a good short video clip is available. Find a high-quality description of the process in a written text. As a class or in small groups, have students analyze each presentation and discuss how information is conveyed in each.

To teach students to analyze how visual and multimedia elements contribute to the meaning, tone, or beauty of a text:

- Demonstrate for students how you "read" visual and multimedia elements in the context of reading. Think aloud your behaviors (e.g., glancing at images before reading; gazing at one in particular after reading the part it depicts; analyzing a photograph like a detective to discover every bit of information it imparts). Think aloud your responses (e.g., "Wow, I pictured the character's face differently" or "When I read about the Comanche migration in the 1700s, I didn't really grasp its import, but seeing this map of all the Southern Plains helps me get it.").

To use information gained from illustrations and words in a text (e.g., maps and photographs) to demonstrate understanding:

- Provide students with informational text. Pose questions for them that can be answered by drawing on information from the text and the illustrations, maps, and graphs.
- Collect a wide assortment of informational texts with photographs, maps, and other visuals. Have students write on sticky notes how the illustration or map adds meaning, and then place their sticky note directly on the illustration. Share their thinking in groups, with partners, or with you in a conference.
- Provide students with a key question or topic and then identify a set of websites to browse. Working independently or in groups, students determine which website had the best illustrations, maps, or photographs (or oral).

To interpret information presented visually, orally, or quantitatively (e.g., in charts, graphs, diagrams, timelines, animations, or interactive elements on webpages) and explain how the information contributes to an understanding of the text:

- Explicitly teach what visual elements are in informational text and how they help the reader build meaning. Start a class chart that names text features—with pictures and examples attached.
- After reading a text on a particular subject, have students use digital sources—websites, blogs, podcasts, videos, and so on about the same topic and then explain how the information presented in this different format helps to understand the text at a deeper level.

To draw on information from multiple print or digital sources:

- Give a question to students and then provide them with a graphic organizer divided into two columns—one for "print" and one for "digital source." Have students find the answer to the question using both print and digital sources and recording their answers on the organizer.

To help your English language learners, try this:

- Have students use sticky notes to place on illustrations where the illustrations help them understand a vocabulary word. Confer with individual students so they can explain their thinking.

 For graphic organizer templates, see online resources at **resources.corwin.com/literacycompanion3-5**.

Preparing to Teach

Standard: _____

Preparing the Classroom

Preparing the Mindset

Preparing the Texts to Use

Preparing to Differentiate

Connections to Other Standards:

Academic Vocabulary: Key Words and Phrases

Digital text: Any document of any sort created or reformatted to be read, viewed, or experienced on a computer, tablet, smartphone, or other digital technology that is interactive, multiple-media, Web-enabled, or otherwise incorporates digital technology.

Diverse formats: Consider the same information presented in alternative ways—numbers, narrative, images, graphic, written, mixed media, or spoken—to allow the reader to consider a subject from multiple perspectives, but also to know and see why and how others communicate this information differently through these diverse formats.

Diverse media: This includes print, pictures and illustrations, and electronic and new-age media (e.g., Internet).

Information expressed visually or quantitatively: The emphasis here is on how the same ideas are expressed in different ways or to different effect in one form or another.

Integrate: Readers must combine different perspectives from various media into a coherent understanding or position about the subject.

Mood: The atmosphere in the text that evokes a certain emotion or feeling. Basically it's the way a reader feels when reading a scene, chapter, or story. Writers use diction, sentence style, setting, tone, and other devices that result in mood.

Plot: This is the story line or sequence of actions built around a conflict or problem the main character in a fictional text is experiencing. Even an expository text has a "plot" of sorts. The plot is like a road map that gets the reader, in a logically organized way, from point A (which in an informational text is typically an introduction) to point B (the conclusion). For example, it would make little sense to begin a book about raptors by explaining how they build their nests. That type of information would come later in the text.

Visual form/visually: Visual explanations, often called "infographics," may include the traditional pie chart or bar graph but may also incorporate many other features that make these visual or graphic forms much more complex than the previous generation of such texts. To read these visuals, students must be able to read them as arguments, explanations, or even narratives expressed through numbers and signs, patterns, colors, and shapes; they must learn to restate the information in words.

Visual information: While related to the entry above, in the context of the standard, it refers more specifically to visual displays of information such as charts, graphs, diagrams, timelines, maps, images, animations, or interactive elements on webpages.

Visually or quantitatively: The emphasis here is on how the same ideas are expressed in different ways, that is, through images or an expression of how much there is of something. Pie charts and bar graphs, for example, are effective ways of showing how much there is of something.

Notes

Standard: _____

Whole Class

_____
_____
_____
_____
_____
_____
_____
_____

Small Group

_____
_____
_____
_____
_____
_____
_____
_____

Individual Practice/Conferring

_____
_____
_____
_____
_____
_____
_____
_____

Reading 8: Delineate and evaluate the argument and specific claims in a text, including the validity of the reasoning as well as the relevance and sufficiency of the evidence.

Literature	Informational Text
3 (Not applicable to literature)	**3** Describe the logical connection between particular sentences and paragraphs in a text (e.g., comparison, cause/effect, first/second/third in a sequence).
4 (Not applicable to literature)	**4** Explain how an author uses reasons and evidence to support particular points in a text.
5 (Not applicable to literature)	**5** Explain how an author uses reasons and evidence to support particular points in a text, **identifying which reasons and evidence support which point(s).**

What the **Student** Does

| Literature | Informational Text |

Literature

3 **Gist:** The K–5 Common Core Standards claim this standard is "not applicable to literature."

4 **Gist:** The K–5 Common Core Standards claim this standard is "not applicable to literature."

5 **Gist:** The K–5 Common Core Standards claim this standard is "not applicable to literature."

Informational Text

3 **Gist:** Students follow the connections between particular sentences that hold key details to the meaning of the text and paragraphs in the text, noting patterns such as comparison, cause/effect, and first/second/third in order to describe the connections between sentences and paragraphs.

They consider:

- What is the topic?
- What is the most important idea about topic the author wants me to learn?
- What details in this section seem to support a main idea?
- How does this detail fit with the one I just read?
- How has the author organized his piece?
- Is the text organized using cause/effect? What words in the text help me know that?
- Is the text organized using comparison? What words in the text help me know that?
- Is the text organized sequentially? What words help me know that?
- Is there a different organizational pattern?
- How do the sentences connect to the paragraphs?

4 **Gist:** Students examine how an author uses reasons and evidence to support key points in written text.

They consider:

- What is the topic of this text?
- What is the main idea/key point the author is making about the topic?
- Does the introduction and conclusion help me?
- What seem the supporting reasons and details?
- Do the topic sentences give clues?
- How can I use headings to help me locate the author's reasons for the main idea?

5 **Gist:** Students examine how an author provides reasons and evidence to support key points in a text, then identify which reasons or evidence support which ideas or points.

They consider:

- What is the topic of this text?
- What is the main idea/key point the author is making about the topic?
- How do headings, topic sentences, repeating words help me decide it?
- Are there subtopics?
- Might the subtopics help me know which reasons support each key point?
- What evidence does the author provide to support each key idea?

What the **Teacher** Does

To have students describe the logical connection between particular sentences and paragraphs in a text:

- Explicitly teach different organizational patterns (cause/effect, comparison and sequence) and key words by sharing a variety of informational texts with students.
- Using an array of nonfiction articles and books, develop lessons that give students practice with comprehending small chunks of text. For example, take two paragraphs on great white sharks, and model how you list out the facts on paper before deciding the author's main point. Invite students to do the same kind of listing/bulleting as they see how details relate and add up. Use chart paper to make the process more understandable.
- Take apart a shared text—either by sentences or paragraphs—and have students put it back together in logical order.
- Use the whiteboard to rearrange a paragraph out of order and have students reassemble it. After, have students explain how and why they determined the order.
- In a shared text, have students highlight key words or linking words that signal order or organization in a text.

To teach students to explain how an author uses reasons and evidence to support particular points in a text and to identify which reasons and evidence support which point:

- Model for students how you decide what the main idea (key point/conclusion) of the text is. Think aloud all your questioning strategies (e.g., What is the author trying to convey in this section? The next? What is this mostly about? Are there words that repeat? What does the author say first? What does he say last? What do all the details seem to be about?), then highlight or mark reasons and evidence in the text that support that main idea.
- Provide students with a short piece of informational text and have them determine the author's main idea, using the strategies you've modeled. After they have determined that, read through the text again as a class and highlight the reasons and evidence and annotate in the margins how this supports the main idea.
- Have students use note cards to record the main idea or key points in a text and then sticky notes to record

reasons and evidence. Place sticky notes on the note cards their reasons support.
- Provide graphic organizers for students to record key points and reasons and evidence. An open-hand graphic could have a key point in the palm and the supporting reasons on five fingers.
- After gathering the reasons and evidence in support of a main idea, have students evaluate and explain if the author has provided adequate reasons and evidence to support the point.
- To help students understand what you mean by "key points" and "reasons," explain these terms using examples that are closer to their life experiences. For example, you might make the statement (key point) that "Julia is a top-notch soccer player." To prove that point, you might say 1. She was the highest scoring player last season, 2. She was selected to be part of a traveling team, 3. She practices every night after school and on weekends. Have students provide statements of their own and reasons to back them up.
- In a shared text, have students highlight the key point the author is making. (This is often written as the topic sentence.) Then guide students to reread the text to look for evidence in the text that backs up the author's key point. Mark the evidence with highlighting tape or sticky notes, or annotate in the margins.
- Have students examine the illustrations and text features in a shared text, such as, for example, pictures and captions, scale drawings, and diagrams for evidence that supports the key point.
- As you read aloud or share a text, identify one key point. Make a "statement/evidence chart" where you write out the full statement at the top of the chart and then list in each line below the evidence you found to support the statement (with page numbers when applicable) and/or the text feature that provided the evidence.

To help your English language learners, try this:

- Work with them to make sure they understand the concept of main idea. Discuss what they think the author wants them to learn from a text that they're reading. Then have them show you a reason in the text that supports this.

 For graphic organizer templates, see online resources at **resources.corwin.com/literacycompanion3-5.**

Standard: _____

Preparing the Classroom

Preparing the Mindset

Preparing the Texts to Use

Preparing to Differentiate

Connections to Other Standards:

Academic Vocabulary: Key Words and Phrases

Argument: The writer or speaker adopts a position, about which they attempt to persuade others to think or feel differently about an issue, to change how they act, or to resolve disagreements between themselves and other parties about an issue. They accomplish these ends by presenting claims supported with reasons, evidence, and appeals. Arguments are related to but different from claims, propositions, thesis statements, or assertions.

Claims: A claim is what an author wants readers to accept as true and act on; the author's thesis is the *primary* claim he or she will make, develop, and support with evidence throughout the paper. Because a claim is debatable, it requires supporting evidence to counter inevitable challenges the critical reader will make as they assess the validity of the claims, logic, and evidence.

Delineate: The reader must be able to describe or represent in precise detail the author's argument, as well as his or her claims, reasoning, and evidence; to delineate is to draw a line between what is and is *not* the exact argument, claim, reasoning, or evidence.

Evidence (relevance and sufficiency of): It is the reader's job to determine if the evidence is, in fact, related to the claim and does, indeed, provide adequate support. If the evidence is from an unreliable source or is limited to a few details, the reader should consider the evidence insufficient.

Validity of the reasoning: Readers determine if the writer's logic is based on valid, reliable evidence from current and credible sources or one or more fallacies that are false or misleading, connected as they are by dubious links between the claim and the evidence.

Notes

Standard: _____

Whole Class

_____
_____
_____
_____
_____
_____
_____
_____

Small Group

_____
_____
_____
_____
_____
_____
_____
_____

Individual Practice/Conferring

_____
_____
_____
_____
_____
_____
_____
_____

Reading 9: Analyze how two or more texts that address similar themes or topics in order to build knowledge or to compare the approaches the authors take.

Literature

3 Compare and contrast the themes, settings, and plots of stories written by the same author about the same or similar characters (e.g., in books from a series).

4 Compare and contrast **the treatment of similar themes and topics (e.g., opposition of good and evil) and patterns of events (e.g., the quest) in stories, myths, and traditional literature from different cultures.**

5 Compare and contrast **stories in the same genre (e.g., mysteries and adventure stories) on their approaches to similar themes and topics.**

Informational Text

3 Compare and contrast the most important points and key details presented in two texts on the same topic.

4 Integrate information from two texts on the same topic in order to write or speak about the subject knowledgeably.

5 Integrate information from **several texts** on the same topic in order to write or speak about the subject knowledgeably.

What the **Student** Does

Literature

3 **Gist:** Students read various stories by the same author or books in a series, with the same or similar characters comparing and contrasting the themes, settings, and plots.

They consider:

- How are the themes similar in the books?
- How are the themes different in the books?
- Does this author always leave me with a similar feeling about people and life in each book?
- How are settings and plots similar in the books?
- How are settings and plots different in the books?

4 **Gist:** Students read various stories, myths, and traditional literature from different cultures, comparing and contrasting how themes and topics—such as the opposition of good versus evil—and the pattern of events—for example, the quest or hero journey—are treated in the text.

They consider:

- What type of text is this and what culture does it represent?
- When is the story set?
- What is it about?
- When I finish it, how would I put its theme into words?
- How is this similar to another version of this story?
- How is it different?
- Do the similarities and differences give me any clues about the culture it's from?

5 **Gist:** Students read various stories in the same genre—mysteries, adventures, fantasy—in order to compare and contrast their approaches to themes and topics that are similar.

They consider:

- What is the genre of the book?
- What is its theme?
- How is it similar to another book in the same genre?
- How does it differ?
- How do the authors approach their topics?
- Do I have a favorite genre? If so, what is it about this type of text that makes it enjoyable to read?

Informational Text

3 **Gist:** Students compare and contrast two texts on the same topic, focusing on the most important points and key details.

They consider:

- What is the topic/subject of these texts?
- What are the important points in each text?
- Where can I look to confirm my ideas about what's important, e.g., headings, first sentences of paragraphs, table of contents?
- How are the important points in each text similar?
- How are the important points in each text different?

4 **Gist:** Students examine two texts on the same topic in order to integrate the information and apply it in written or spoken form to demonstrate knowledge.

They consider:

- What is the subject of these texts?
- What are the important points in each text?
- Where can I look to confirm my ideas about what's important, such as, for example, headings, first sentences of paragraphs, table of contents?
- How can I combine—or integrate—the information from both texts into one written piece or speech?

5 **Gist:** Students examine several texts on the same topic in order to integrate the information and apply it in written or spoken form to demonstrate knowledge.

They consider:

- What is the subject of these texts?
- What are the important points in each text?
- Where can I look to confirm my ideas about what's important, such as, for example, headings, first sentences of paragraphs, table of contents?
- How can I combine—or integrate—the information from each text into one written piece or speech?

What the **Teacher** Does

To have students compare and contrast the themes, settings, and plots of stories written by the same author about the same or similar characters:

- Read aloud to the class at least two books (these could be picture books) written by the same author with the same character in each. After reading each book, record on chart paper the theme, setting, and plot. Also record character traits for the main characters in that book. After reading and charting both books, create a Venn diagram (or Thinking Map)—either for *one* of the elements or a Venn diagram for each.
- Have students discuss the major problems in both books.
- Provide students access to books by the same author or books in a series so they can replicate this independently or in small groups, or in book clubs or literature circles.

To have students compare and contrast the treatment of similar themes and topics and patterns of events in stories, myths, and traditional literature from different cultures:

- Choose either stories, myths, or traditional literature with similar themes or topics, but find books from different cultures. Model reading at least two books from different cultures. Record on chart paper the theme or topic and how it was treated—and also record setting, the problem(s) characters faced, responses of characters to each other, and how the stories ended. After reading two or more stories, discuss how they were similar and different.
- Create sequence charts to record the pattern of events.
- Discuss how culture affects how the story was told.

To have students compare/contrast stories in the same genre on their approaches to similar themes and topics:

- Model for students by reading two books in the same genre with similar themes or the same topic and discussing the theme and topic. What is the theme? How are they similar or different? How did the different authors convey the theme?
- Create Venn diagrams (or other Thinking Maps) to complete on theme after reading books in the same genre.

- Provide students with text sets in order to read and practice independently.
- Read aloud a traditional folktale/fairy tale, such as *Cinderella* by Marcia Brown, and a fractured version of the same tale, such as Frances Minters' *Cinder-Elly*, a modern, urban, rap-based tale. Have students compare the two. How are they alike and different, in terms of the basic story elements? Language? Illustrations? After working with several of such traditional/fractured pairs, have partners write their own version of a traditional folktale or fairy tale.

To have students compare and contrast the most important points and key details presented in two texts on the same topic:

- Have students read two different texts on the same topic and take notes in a two-column format, drawing arrows and lines to connect the information that is the same.
- Refer to the table of contents in two books on the same topic to identify the topics each addresses. Guide students to notice the similarities and differences, and discuss what may have led each author to include or leave out certain information.

To integrate information from two texts on the same topic:

- Assign students a topic (or they can self-select). Students read one text on that topic, taking notes or annotating important information. Then they read a second text on the same topic (this may take a couple of days to complete), again taking notes. After reading both, students write what they now know about the topic.
- Use two content-area texts and students take notes on each (on a graphic organizer, etc.) After reading both, have students make a key statement and then back it up with reasons and details from their notes.

To help your English language learners, try this:

- Have students draw pictures of one element (setting, character, etc.) from two different texts and then place them side by side and either verbally explain or label how they are the same and how they are different. If possible, allow English learners to work with native English speakers in group activities comparing and contrasting texts.

 For graphic organizer templates, see online resources at **resources.corwin.com/literacycompanion3-5**.

Preparing to Teach

Standard: _____

Preparing the Classroom

_____
_____
_____
_____
_____
_____
_____

Preparing the Mindset

_____
_____
_____
_____
_____
_____

Preparing the Texts to Use

_____
_____
_____
_____
_____
_____

Preparing to Differentiate

_____
_____
_____
_____
_____
_____

Connections to Other Standards:

_____
_____
_____

Academic Vocabulary: Key Words and Phrases

Approaches: This refers to the ways different authors approach their subject matter, through stylistic elements such as voice, imagery, or format. Approach can also refer to point of view or genre.

Approaches to similar themes and topics: As it applies to several of the standards here, this phrase refers to the act of comparing and contrasting the "approaches" to same topic used by different authors, different texts, and different types of texts.

Build knowledge: This refers to the author's efforts to build the reader's knowledge about the subject of the text; the ways in which the author provides for the reader the necessary information to understand the story or text.

Compare and contrast two texts (themes, topics, stories, genres): Look at the similarities (*compare*) and differences (*contrast*) when examining how two different books present themes, topics, stories, or genres.

Draws on themes, patterns of events, or character types: This pertains to noticing *archetypes*; the idea is that these themes, patterns, and types are found across cultures and eras going back to our very beginnings and thus represent enduring ideas or patterns we can use today to express those ideas. Authors adapt these stories for our modern tastes, transforming them in the process so they seem new but add depth to the text through the resonant echoes of older, familiar stories.

Theme: For the purpose of several standards here, the theme is the central meaning, message, or idea in a literary text that the author wants to communicate. Themes are never stated explicitly, but must be inferred by the reader from the evidence in the text. (One exception is fables, where the theme is clearly stated either at the very beginning or end of the tale.)

Topic: When referring to informational texts, the topic is the main subject or content at hand—migration, animal habitats, machines, farm life, outer space, and so on.

Notes

Standard: _____

Whole Class

_____
_____
_____
_____
_____
_____
_____
_____

Small Group

_____
_____
_____
_____
_____
_____
_____
_____

Individual Practice/Conferring

_____
_____
_____
_____
_____
_____
_____
_____

Reading 10: Read and comprehend complex literary and informational texts independently and proficiently.

Literature

3 By the end of the year, read and comprehend literature, including stories, dramas, and poetry, at the high end of the grades 2–3 text complexity band independently and proficiently.

4 By the end of the year, read and comprehend literature, including stories, dramas, and poetry in the **grades 4–5 text complexity band proficiently, with scaffolding as needed at the high end of the range.**

5 By the end of the year, read and comprehend literature, including stories, dramas, and poetry, **at the high end of the grades 4–5 text complexity band independently and proficiently.**

Informational Text

3 By the end of the year, read and comprehend informational texts, including history/social studies, science, and technical texts, at the high end of the grades 2–3 text complexity band independently and proficiently.

4 By the end of year, read and comprehend informational texts, including history/social studies, science, and technical texts, in the **grades 4–5 text complexity band proficiently, with scaffolding as needed at the high end of the range.**

5 By the end of the year, read and comprehend informational texts, including history/social studies, science, and technical texts, **at high end of the grades 4–5 text complexity band independently and proficiently.**

What the **Student** Does

Literature

3 **Gist:** Students read a range of literary text—fiction, poetry, and drama—appropriate for grades 2–3 text complexity band, including texts that make progressively greater demands in terms of cognitive, linguistic, and conceptual complexity. Students work toward becoming resilient and independent readers, receiving help only when needed as they reach the high end of the grade 2–3 complexity band.

They consider:

- How easy or difficult is this text (complex)?
- Will I need help reading it?
- What type of support, if any, will I need?
- Can I read it independently?
- Am I reading a range of texts?

4 **Gist:** Students read a range of literary text—fiction, poetry, and drama—appropriate for grades 4–5 text complexity band, including texts that make progressively greater demands in terms of cognitive, linguistic, and conceptual complexity. Students work toward becoming resilient and independent readers, receiving help only when needed as they reach the high end of the grade 4–5 complexity band.

They consider:

- How easy or difficult is this text (complex)?
- Will I need help reading it?
- What type of support, if any, will I need?
- Can I read it independently?
- Am I reading a range of texts?

5 **Gist:** Students read a range of literary text—fiction, poetry, and drama—appropriate for grades 3–5 text complexity band, including texts that make progressively greater demands in terms of cognitive, linguistic, and conceptual complexity. Students work toward becoming resilient and independent readers, receiving help only when needed as they reach the high end of the grade 3–5 complexity band.

They consider:

- How easy or difficult is this text (complex)?
- Will I need help reading it?
- What type of support, if any, will I need?
- Can I read it independently?
- Am I reading a range of texts?

Informational Text

3 **Gist:** Students read a range of nonfiction appropriate for grades 2–3 text complexity band, including texts that make progressively greater demands in terms of cognitive, linguistic, and conceptual complexity. Students work toward becoming resilient and independent readers, receiving help only when needed as they reach the high end of the grade 2–3 complexity band.

They consider:

- How easy or difficult is this text (complex)?
- Will I need help reading it?
- What type of support, if any, will I need?
- Can I read it independently?

4 **Gist:** Students read a range of nonfiction appropriate for grades 4–5 text complexity band, including texts that make progressively greater demands in terms of cognitive, linguistic, and conceptual complexity. Students work toward becoming resilient and independent readers, receiving help only when needed as they reach the high end of the grade 4–5 complexity band.

They consider:

- How easy or difficult is this text (complex)?
- Will I need help reading it?
- What type of support, if any, will I need?
- Can I read it independently?

5 **Gist:** Students read a range of nonfiction appropriate for grades 3–5 text complexity band, including texts that make progressively greater demands in terms of cognitive, linguistic, and conceptual complexity. Students work toward becoming resilient and independent readers, receiving help only when needed as they reach the high end of the grade 3–5 complexity band.

They consider:

- How easy or difficult is this text (complex)?
- Will I need help reading it?
- What type of support, if any, will I need?
- Can I read it independently?
- Am I reading a range of texts?

What the **Teacher** Does

To have students comprehend complex texts independently and proficiently:

- Assign an array of literary (novels, plays, and poems) and informational texts (literary nonfiction, essays, biographies, historical accounts) to be read in class and outside, so students can build their stamina, speed, and confidence with longer and more complex texts.
- Build in opportunities for students to choose among the texts you recommend/require, and provide reading time for students to read independently with books of their choice. Give students plenty of time and opportunities to practice reading, and process and incorporate new skills and strategies into their repertoire. This processing time involves talking and writing in response to texts and also voluminous amounts of time each day spent actually reading—just reading.
- Organize students into groups (inquiry circles, literature circles, book clubs); each group reads a different book or the same as others, using the discussion within the group to help them work through the challenges the book presents.
- Engage in full-class close reading periodically, modeling what such close reading looks like and discussing how you do it as you go; then let students take on more of the responsibility for reading and discussing.
- Teach students a range of questions to ask when they read different types of texts and techniques they can use throughout their reading process as needed with different types of texts.
- Assign a series of reading, both informational and literary, about the same subject (e.g., survival, being different from others, the environment) in order to understand it in depth from different perspectives.
- Provide opportunities for students to write in response to reading to help them determine the author's message and integrate it into what they already know. However, reading responses should not be assigned every time students read.
- Work with students in small reading groups to differentiate the instruction you provide. Most often the groups will involve guiding students through a text that would be too difficult for them to read on their own. However, you might also gather students for interactive read-alouds or shared reading, oral language intervention, skill and strategy groups, and literature circles.
- Confer with students to learn what they do well and need to learn; address a skill or strategy you observe students needing help with.

To provide scaffolding as needed at the high end of the range:

- Frequently assess students and help them choose books at the appropriate level.
- Provide targeted questions or directions students can use to guide them when engaging in close reading of any type of text; such questions might direct their attention to stylistic elements, nuances of plot or character, or how these elements interact with each other.
- Encourage students to consult annotated versions of the texts they are studying in their textbooks or which you provide (or find available online) as students develop their capacity to read closely, gradually phasing out such support as they develop their own independence.
- Understand that your goal, in addition to challenging readers to work harder and figure things out on their own, is to scaffold and support their efforts. Continually monitor the experience for evidence that the task is too hard or that students are at their frustration level. Students who act out or who can't attend for even a minimal amount of time to the task at hand are often sending signals that what we're asking of them is too difficult. To be helpful in the long run and to instill a love of reading, make sure the task we assign is not only challenging, but doable. Only then can it inspire students to want more.

To develop students' ability to read complex history and science texts:

- Expose students to an array of texts written by experts in the field and other sources (blogs, reports, news articles) where the quality of the writing will challenge them and, due to the often shorter nature of the articles, require students to consider the subject from a range of perspectives, sources, or fields.
- Include in the history, social science, science, or technical subjects longer texts. Students might read these longer works as part of an ongoing inquiry into the environment, historical events, or cultures, giving a presentation or writing a report when they finish.

To help your English language learners, try this:

- Help them find books and other texts appropriate to their current reading level but that challenge them with ideas, language, and other elements that are new or more complex than previous texts they have read.
- Make sure students understand the task you're asking them to do. They need to understand the meaning of the academic vocabulary we use but take for granted. For example, while English language users understand (at least at the surface level) the meaning of words like describe, compare, and explain, English language learners need more explicit and repeated instruction regarding what these words are asking them to do.
- Whenever possible, meet with English language learners before or after a whole group lesson to prepare them for what they'll be doing or to process what happened.
- Use picture and realia (pictures and artifacts) to make concepts they meet in texts more concrete and accessible.

 For graphic organizer templates, see online resources at **resources.corwin.com/literacycompanion3-5**.

Preparing to Teach

Standard: _____

Preparing the Classroom

_____
_____
_____
_____
_____
_____
_____

Preparing the Mindset

_____
_____
_____
_____
_____
_____
_____

Preparing the Texts to Use

_____
_____
_____
_____
_____
_____
_____

Preparing to Differentiate

_____
_____
_____
_____
_____
_____
_____

Connections to Other Standards:

_____
_____
_____

Academic Vocabulary: Key Words and Phrases

Complex literary and informational texts: *Complex* is not the same as *difficult*; literary and informational texts are complex for different reasons, as they are written for different reasons and are written for different purposes. Texts can be complex due to sentence structure, syntax, and other structural factors. But they can also be complex in content and ideas, despite short, simple sentences. In the context of the standards, complexity is one measure of a work's quality but is at the heart of the CCSS when it comes to reading.

Group reading activities: These are activities that students do as a whole class, such as read-aloud and shared reading, or when working in small groups, such as guided reading groups.

High end of the range: For intermediate grades, this means third grade (for grades 2 and 3) and fifth grade (for grades 4 and 5). Students reading at their grade level at the end of the year should be able to read independently, with little, less, or no teachers' guidance.

Independently: One is able to read whatever texts are assigned without the aid of a teacher or, when challenged by the teacher with a complex text, is able to do the work as assigned without the aid of scaffolding or guided instruction.

Informational: Texts designed to inform, though this can include argument, a range of expository texts, also a range of media and formats, including infographics and videos.

Literary nonfiction: Informational texts, often books or essays, that use novelistic and other literary techniques to engage readers, then use the story to convey information.

Proficiently: Describes the way and level at which the individual student is able to read complex texts; proficiency is equated with skill, though not mastery.

Scaffolding: Support from teachers, aides, or other students that helps a student read text or complete a task; examples include providing background knowledge, reading aloud, or any other strategy designed to help students become independent readers or writers.

Text complexity band: Indicates the text difficulty associated with the grade levels around which the Common Core standards are organized: grades 2–3, 4–5, 6–8, 9–10, 11–CCR (college and career readiness). The individual text complexity bands correspond with associated grade levels, that is, grades 2–3. The levels themselves are determined by the three-part model of text complexity discussed in Appendix A of the complete CCSS document. The three factors in text complexity are *qualitative dimensions* (levels of meaning, language complexity as determined by an attentive reader); *quantitative dimensions* (word length and frequency, sentence length, and cohesion); and *reader and task considerations* (factors related to a specific reader such as motivation, background knowledge, or persistence; others associated with the task itself such as purpose or demands of the task).

Notes

Standard: _____

Whole Class

_____
_____
_____
_____
_____
_____
_____

Small Group

_____
_____
_____
_____
_____
_____
_____

Individual Practice/Conferring

_____
_____
_____
_____
_____
_____
_____

The Common Core State Standards

Writing

College and Career Readiness Anchor Standards for
Writing K–12

Source: Common Core State Standards

The 3–5 Writing Standards outlined on the following pages define what students should understand and be able to do by the end of each grade. Here on this page we present the College and Career Readiness (CCR) anchor standards for K–12 so you can see how students in grades 3–5 work toward the same goals as a high school senior: it's a universal, K–12 vision. The CCR anchor standards and the grade-specific standards correspond to one another by numbers 1–10. They are necessary complements: the former providing broad standards, the latter providing additional specificity. Together, they define the skills and understandings that all students must eventually demonstrate.

Text Types and Purposes*

1. Write arguments to support claims in an analysis of substantive topics or texts, using valid reasoning and relevant and sufficient evidence.
2. Write informative/explanatory texts to examine and convey complex ideas and information clearly and accurately through the effective selection, organization, and analysis of content.
3. Write narratives to develop real or imagined experiences or events using effective technique, well-chosen details, and well-structured event sequences.

Production and Distribution of Writing

4. Produce clear and coherent writing in which the development, organization, and style are appropriate to task, purpose, and audience.
5. Develop and strengthen writing as needed by planning, revising, editing, rewriting, or trying a new approach.
6. Use technology, including the Internet, to produce and publish writing and to interact and collaborate with others.

Research to Build and Present Knowledge

7. Conduct short as well as more sustained research projects based on focused questions, demonstrating understanding of the subject under investigation.
8. Gather relevant information from multiple print and digital sources, assess the credibility and accuracy of each source, and integrate the information while avoiding plagiarism.
9. Draw evidence from literary or informational texts to support analysis, reflection, and research.

Range of Writing

10. Write routinely over extended time frames (time for research, reflection, and revision) and shorter time frames (a single sitting or a day or two) for a range of tasks, purposes, and audiences.

Note on Range and Content of Student Writing

For students, writing is a key means of asserting and defending claims, showing what they know about a subject, and conveying what they have experiences, imagined, thought, and felt. To be college- and career-ready writers, students must take task, purpose and audience into careful considerations, choosing words, information, structures, and formats deliberately. They need to know how to combine elements for different kinds of writing—for example, to use narrative strategies within argument and explanation within narrative—to produce complex and nuanced writing. They need to be able to use technology strategically when creating, refining, and collaborating on writing. They have to become adept at gathering information, evaluating sources, and citing material accurately, reporting findings from their research and analysis of sources in a clear and cogent manner. They must have the flexibility, concentration, and fluency to produce high-quality first draft text under a tight deadline as well as the capacity to revisit and make improvements to a piece of writing over multiple drafts when circumstances encourage or require it.

* These broad types of writing include many subgenres. See Appendix A in the Common Core State Standards for definitions of key writing types.

College and Career Readiness Anchor Standards for
Writing K–12

The College and Career Readiness (CCR) anchor standards are the same for K–12. The guiding principle here is that the core writing skills should not change as students advance; rather, the level at which they learn and can perform these skills should increase in complexity as students move from one grade to the next. However, for grades 3–5, we have to recognize that the standards were back mapped from the secondary grades—the authors envisioned what college students needed and then wrote standards, working their way down the grades. Thus, as you use this book, remember that children in grades 3–5 can't just "jump over" developmental milestones in an ambitious attempt toward an anchor standard. There are certain life and learning experiences they need to have, and certain concepts they need to learn, before they are capable of handling many complex academic skills in a meaningful way. The anchor standards nonetheless are goal posts to work toward. As you read the "gist" of the standards on the following pages, remember they represent what our grades 3–5 students will *grow into* during each year and deepen later in middle school and high school.

Text Types and Purposes*

Argument appears first as it is essential to success in college and develops the critical faculties needed in the adult world. Crafting arguments requires students to analyze texts or topics and to determine which evidence best supports your arguments. Informational/explanatory writing conveys ideas, events, and finding by choosing and explaining the behavior, meaning, or importance of key details. Students draw from a range of sources, including primary and secondary sources. Narrative writing includes not just stories but also accounts of historical events and lab procedures. Students write to change minds, hearts, and actions (argument); to extend readers' knowledge or acceptance of ideas and procedures (informational/explanatory); and to inform, inspire, persuade, or entertain (narrative).

Production and Distribution of Writing

This set of anchor standards involves the stages of the writing process. These standards also highlight the importance of knowing who the audience is and the style and format the writer should use to achieve a purpose. Students also learn the skills needed throughout the writing process: generating ideas, trying other styles, structures, perspectives, or processes as they bring their ideas into focus and some final form. Finally, these standards call for writers to use technology not only to publish but also to collaborate throughout the writing process with others.

Research to Build and Present Knowledge

These standards focus on inquiry processes of varying lengths, all of which should develop students' knowledge of the subject they are investigating and the skills needed to conduct that investigation. Students acquire and refine the ability to find, evaluate, and use a range of sources during these research projects, which can take from a class period to as much as a month. Such inquiries demand students correctly cite the source of all information to ensure they learn what plagiarism is and how to avoid it.

Range of Writing

This standard emphasizes not only what students write but also how often and for what purposes they write over the course of the school year. Writing, as this standard makes clear, is something students should be doing constantly and for substantial lengths of time. Also, they should write for an array of reasons and audiences, and in response to a mix of topics and tasks.

Source: Adapted from Burke, J. (2013). *The Common Core Companion: The Standards Decoded, Grades 6–8: What They Say, What They Mean, How to Teach Them.* Thousand Oaks, CA: Corwin.

* These broad types of writing include many subgenres. See Appendix A in the Common Core State Standards for definitions of key writing types.

Writing 1: Write arguments to support claims in an analysis of substantive topics or texts, using valid reasoning and relevant and sufficient evidence.

English Language Arts

3 Write opinion pieces on topics or texts, supporting a point of view with reasons.
   a. Introduce the topic or text they are writing about, state an opinion, and create an organizational structure that lists reasons.
   b. Provide reasons that support the opinion.
   c. Use linking words and phrases (e.g., *because, therefore, since, for example*) to connect opinion and reasons.
   d. Provide a concluding statement or section.

4 Write opinion pieces on topics or texts, supporting a point of view with reasons **and information.**
   a. Introduce a topic or text **clearly,** state an opinion, and create an organizational structure **in which related ideas are grouped to support the writer's purpose.**
   b. Provide reasons that **are supported by facts and details.**
   c. Link opinion and reasons using words and phrases (e.g., *for instance, in order to, in addition*).
   d. Provide a concluding statement or section **related to the opinion presented.**

5 Write opinion pieces on topics or texts, supporting a point of view with reasons and information.
   a. Introduce a topic to text clearly, state an opinion, and create an organizational structure in which ideas are **logically** grouped to support the writer's purpose.
   b. Provide **logically ordered** reasons that are supported by facts and details.
   c. Link opinion and reasons using words, phrases, and **clauses (e.g., *consequently, specifically*).**
   d. Provide a concluding statement or section related to the opinion presented.

Source: © Copyright 2010. National Governors Association Center for Best Practices and Council of Chief State School Officers. All rights reserved.

* These broad types of writing include many subgenres. See Appendix A in the Common Core State Standards for definitions of key writing types.

What the **Student** Does

English Language Arts

3 **Gist:** Students write opinion pieces supporting a point of view on topics or texts that, when introduced, state the opinion about the topic or text and provide a list of strong reasons to support the opinion. The organizational structure enhances the list of reasons, and students use linking words and phrases, such as *because, therefore, since,* and *for example,* to connect the reasons. Students end the piece with a concluding statement or section.

They consider:

- What is the topic or text I am writing about?
- What is my opinion or my point of view, and have I explained *why?*
- What reasons do I have to support that opinion?
- Have I connected my opinion with linking words such as *because, therefore, since,* and *for example?*
- How can I end my writing with sentences, a concluding statement, or section?

4 **Gist:** Students write opinion pieces supporting a point of view on topics or texts that, when introduced clearly, say *what* the opinion is and *why* by providing reasons supported by facts and details. Supporting reasons are grouped to support the writer's purpose, and students choose words or phrases to link the opinion and reason, using words such as *for instance, in order to,* and *in addition.* The conclusion is a statement or section that is related to the opinion presented in the introduction.

They consider:

- What is the topic or text I am writing about?
- What is my opinion or my point of view and have I explained *why?*
- What are the reasons, supported by facts and details, that support my opinion?
- Have I grouped my reasons and connected them with linking words and phrases such as *for instance, in order to,* and *in addition?*
- Do I have a concluding statement that relates to the opinion I stated in the introduction?

5 **Gist:** Students write opinion pieces supporting a point of view on topics or texts that, when introduced clearly, say *what* the opinion is and *why* by providing reasons supported by facts and details. Supporting reasons are grouped to support the writer's purpose, and students choose words, phrases, or clauses to link the opinion and reason, using words such as *consequently* and *specifically.* The conclusion is a statement or section that is related to the opinion presented in the introduction.

They consider:

- What is the topic or text I am writing about?
- What is my opinion or my point of view and why do I think this?
- What are the reasons, supported by facts and details, that support my opinion?
- Have I grouped my reasons and connected them with linking words and phrases?
- Do I have a concluding statement that relates to the opinion I stated in the introduction?

What the **Teacher** Does

To help students understand and learn to write opinions:

- Share multiple examples of opinion pieces—from books, to book reviews, editorials, sports columns, persuasive letters, and so on—and discuss how opinion writing is different from narrative and informative/explanatory texts.
- List on chart paper types of opinion writing (editorials, letters to the editor, movie reviews, blogs, etc.).
- Share expectations for opinion writing. Create rubrics breaking down the requirements of this type of piece.
- Model for students how to write an opinion piece, explicitly thinking aloud what you are doing as you write the introduction, state your opinion, give reasons why for that opinion, and conclude your writing.
- Introduce persuasive letter writing (which contains the same basic elements as an opinion piece) and explain that a persuasive letter, like an opinion piece, is written to change someone's mind and effect change. Decide on an authentic topic—something students would really like to change—and write a class letter to model how it's done. Post the sample letter prominently in the classroom so that students can try writing their own letters during their writing time of day. Select recipients who may actually write a letter in response to the letter students send.

To teach students how to generate and use reasons, facts, and details:

- Select a topic that has a lot of student buy-in (adopting rescue dogs and cats, stopping poaching of elephants, etc.). Model for students how to generate a list of reasons to support an opinion.
- After generating reasons, model how to determine facts and details to support each reason, quickly consulting texts and online sources.
- Draft in front of the students by choosing one reason and thinking aloud as you add details. Continue to model, adding additional reasons.
- Provide graphic organizers to help students give an opinion and then provide a reason (My favorite sports team is _____, because _____. Another reason it is a favorite is because _____, etc.).
- Provide graphic organizers or webs to then take each reason and add facts and details in support.

To teach students to write introductions where they introduce a topic or text clearly and state an opinion:

- Read and discuss the introductions of a variety of published pieces—both in print and through technology.

- Model writing introductions.
- Have students practice writing introductions—listing the text or topic, then their opinion, followed by their reasons.

To teach students organizational structure and group related ideas and reasons to support the writer's purpose:

- Demonstrate for students by writing reasons on note cards and add facts and details to each. Organize note cards in the order they would be written.
- Have students follow this process, but have students write one reason with facts and details and check with you before moving on to the next reason so you can see that their work is sufficient.

To use linking words, phrases, or clauses:

- Brainstorm linking words to use in opinion writing and notice them in published texts. Have these words displayed or accessible for students. Specifically include the words for your grade-level expectations.
- Model and have students practice writing opinion sentences with linking words, phrases, or clauses.

To teach students how to conclude by relating to the opinion presented:

- Read the conclusions of a variety of published pieces to observe how authors conclude their opinion pieces. Create a classroom chart of different types.
- Model for students how to write a conclusion.
- Have students practice writing multiple conclusions.
- Have students highlight their opinion in the introduction and then in the conclusion to ensure that it matches.

To help your English language learners, try this:

- Meet with them and discuss their opinion. Help them to get an opinion statement written and brainstorm reasons. If they are independent enough, have them continue to write their piece; if not, provide starter sentences for the reasons you discussed together, or provide a sentence stem, such as I think that _____ because _____ when stating their opinion and reason. Make sure they understand the significance of the word "because."

 For graphic organizer templates, see online resources at **resources.corwin.com/literacycompanion3-5**.

Standard: _____

Preparing the Classroom

Preparing the Mindset

Preparing the Texts to Use

Preparing to Differentiate

Connections to Other Standards:

Academic Vocabulary: Key Words and Phrases

Analysis: This involves breaking up a complex idea or process into smaller parts (what is it, how it works, and what it is made from) to make it easier to understand.

Argument: Arguments are claims backed by reasons that are supported by evidence. Arguments have three objectives: to explain, to persuade, and to resolve conflicts between positions, readers, or ideas. Writers make their case by building their argument with reasons and supporting evidence.

Claim: This is the statement that the writer is attempting to prove is true. Effective claims are short, precise, clear, and summarize the writer's main point. They typically come near the beginning of the piece and then are bolstered by a well-reasoned chain of evidence. A thesis statement is the writer's main claim.

Concluding statement or section: This comes at the end of an opinion piece where the writer brings his or her argument (piece) to an end. Writers provide some statement or section that connects all the reasons, facts, and details (claims and evidence), and then show how they support the argument or opinion presented in the paper or speech.

Evidence: Evidence is the detail the writer provides to support an argument or opinion. It might include facts, quotations, examples, photographs, expert opinions, and, when appropriate, personal experience. Evidence supports reasons that in turn support the argument or claim. Each discipline has its own standards for evidence, but most lists would include quotations, observations, interviews, examples, facts, data, results from surveys and experiments, and, when appropriate, personal experience.

Linking words and phrases: These words or phrases connect one sentence, idea, or paragraph to another, allowing writers to express the nature or importance of the relationship between those two ideas.

Opinion: This is a belief, conclusion, or judgment based on reasoning. In this standard, students need to base opinions on reasons and evidence, which can take the form of facts and details; the important thing is they avoid relying on personal opinions to support their claim. That said, you'll find some students may need extra support to move from personal opinions to more objective reasoning; it will happen as they mature and gain experience.

Organizational structure: This is the logical progression (beginning, middle, and end or introduction, body, conclusion) and the completeness of ideas in a text.

Point of view: This is the place, vantage point, or consciousness through which we hear or see someone describe a situation, tell a story, or make an argument.

Reasons/reasoning: Writers must base their claims and ideas on more than personal preferences or opinions when constructing arguments. The reasons students give to support an opinion or argument must be based on evidence, information, and logic.

Substantive topics or texts: Writers are expected to be writing about compelling, important ideas or texts that examine big questions meant to challenge the reader. For 3–5 students, this means writing opinions and responding to texts on age-appropriate topics; students can write substantively by responding to rich, "meaty," even controversial, inquiry questions about curriculum.

Notes

Standard: _____

Whole Class

Small Group

Individual Practice/Conferring

Writing 2: Write informative/explanatory texts to examine and convey complex ideas and information clearly and accurately through the effective selection, organization, and analysis of content.

English Language Arts

3 Write informative/explanatory texts to examine a topic and convey ideas and information clearly.
   a. Introduce a topic and group related information together; include illustrations when useful to aiding comprehension.
   b. Develop the topic with facts, definitions, and details.
   c. Use linking words and phrases (e.g., *also, another, and, more, but*) to connect ideas within categories of information.
   d. Provide a concluding statement or section.

4 Write informative/explanatory texts to examine a topic and convey ideas and information clearly.
   a. Introduce a topic clearly and group related information in **paragraphs and sections, include formatting (e.g., headings), illustrations, and multimedia when useful to aiding comprehension.**
   b. Develop the topic with facts, definitions, **concrete details, quotations, or other information and examples related to the topic.**
   c. **Link ideas within categories of information using words and phrases** (e.g., *another, for example, also, because*).
   d. **Use precise language and domain-specific vocabulary to inform about or explain the topic.**
   e. Provide a concluding statement or section **related to the information or explanation presented.**

5 Write informative/explanatory texts to examine a topic and convey ideas and information clearly.
   a. Introduce a topic clearly, **provide a general observation and focus,** and group related information **logically;** include formatting (e.g., headings), illustrations, and multimedia when useful to aiding comprehension.
   b. Develop the topic with facts, definitions, concrete details, quotations, or other information and examples related to the topic.
   c. Link ideas within and **across** categories of information using words, phrases, and clauses (**e.g., *in contrast, especially***).
   d. Use precise language and domain specific vocabulary to inform about or explain the topic.
   e. Provide a concluding statement or section related to the information or explanation presented.

Source: © Copyright 2010. National Governors Association Center for Best Practices and Council of Chief State School Officers. All rights reserved.

* These broad types of writing include many subgenres. See Appendix A in the Common Core State Standards for definitions of key writing types.

What the **Student** Does

English Language Arts

3 **Gist:** Students explain or provide information about a subject or idea(s), choosing only the details and information related to the topic, which are then introduced, organized, and elaborated upon through the use of illustrations. Students further build on these ideas by including facts, definitions, and details. Students help all these details flow and reveal the links between ideas within categories of information by using linking words and phrases (e.g., *also, another, and, more, but*). Finally, students bring their paper to an end, providing a concluding statement or section.

They consider:

- What is the topic—and my purpose?
- What format will I use to write my piece?
- What information and details should I include to give my reader enough information on the topic?
- How will I organize or group the contents so they convey the information clearly?
- Have I included illustrations to explain the topic more fully?
- Have I used linking words like *also, another, and, more,* and *but* to connect my ideas?
- Do I have a concluding statement section to end the piece?

4 **Gist:** Students explain or provide information about a topic or idea(s) choosing only the details and information related to the topic, which are then introduced, organized in paragraphs and sections with headings, and elaborated upon through the use of illustrations and multimedia. Students further build on these ideas by including facts, definitions, concrete details, and evidence, usually in the form of quotations. Students help all the ideas within categories flow by using linking words and phrases (e.g., *another, for example, also, because*), along with precise vocabulary and words specific to the domain or topic, to aid the writer trying to explain the topic. Finally, students bring their paper to an end with a concluding statement or section that relates all the information or explanations presented.

They consider:

- What is the topic—and my purpose?
- What format will I use to write my piece?
- What information and details should I include to give my reader enough information on the topic?
- What definitions and quotations from books should I include?
- How will I organize or group the contents so they convey the information clearly?
- Have I included headings, illustrations, or multimedia to explain the topic more fully?
- Have I used linking words or phrases like *another, for example, also,* and *because* to connect my ideas?
- Have I used specific vocabulary to explain the topic?
- Do I have a concluding statement or section to end the piece?

5 **Gist:** Students explain or provide information about a topic or idea(s), choosing only the details and information related to the topic, which are then introduced, organized in paragraphs and sections with headings, and elaborated upon through the use of illustrations and multimedia. Students further build on these ideas by including facts, definitions, concrete details, and evidence, usually in the form of quotations. Students help all the ideas within categories flow by using linking words, phrases, and clauses (e.g., *in contrast, especially*), along with precise vocabulary and words specific to the domain or topic, to aid the writer trying to explain the topic. Finally, students bring their paper to an end with a concluding statement or section that relates all the information or explanations presented.

They consider:

- What is the topic—and my purpose?
- What format will I use to write my piece?
- What information and details should I include to give my reader enough information on the topic?
- What is the general observation or focus that I want to include in my introduction?
- What definitions and quotations should I include?
- How will I organize or group the contents so they convey the information clearly?
- Have I included headings, illustrations, or multimedia to explain the topic more fully?
- Have I used linking words or phrases like *in contrast* and *especially* to connect my ideas?
- Have I used specific vocabulary to explain the topic?
- Do I have a concluding statement or section to end the piece?

What the **Teacher** Does

To introduce students to informative/explanatory texts:

- Provide numerous examples of published informative/explanatory texts and also access via technology to informative/explanatory writing. Call attention to the introductions, key ideas or points, organization, graphics, and endings. This will give you opportunities to acquaint students with the genre and identify features of informative/explanatory text.
- Discuss the expectations of this type of writing and the different formats.
- Show students a range of writing samples so they see what it is that you want them to do.
- Give student a copy of a sample text and, if possible, display it on a screen so you can annotate portions of it while discussing the text's relevant features.
- Have students use sticky notes or annotate a sample text as they determine relevant features.
- Bring in content-area texts to use as models of informative/explanatory texts.
- As you read informative/explanatory texts aloud, ask students to try to determine the author's purpose in writing the piece. Make a chart (that you will later post in the classroom and add to throughout the year) listing what students have determined various authors' purposes for writing to be.

To format and integrate illustrations, headings, and multimedia into the texts:

- Explore examples of illustrations, headings, charts, and so on with the class. Create charts of all the options to add to their pieces.
- Offer direct instruction to the whole class or a smaller group of students who need to learn how to use those features of the word processor or other software applications.
- Provide time for students to practice these skills and share.

To develop their topic with details, examples, and information:

- Model for students how to choose a topic and add details.
- Model how to write and use categories and headings.
- Provide graphic organizers, information maps, outlines, and so on to help students organize their thinking.
- Practice together writing a topic on a sheet of chart paper, then have students generate details, examples, and information on sticky notes. Place these on the chart paper and move them to group relevant facts together.
- Have students practice doing this independently with their own topic on their own paper.
- Work directly with them to generate ideas and gather evidence, data, examples, or other content; then develop with them criteria for how to evaluate and choose the best of the bunch to work into their writing.

To have students use linking words, phrases, and clauses to link ideas and create cohesion:

- Give students a copy of a sample text and highlight the linking words, phrases, and clauses. Annotate how these help create cohesion.
- Generate with students a list of linking words, phrases, or clauses.
- Have students go through their papers once they have a complete draft and highlight their linking words.

To help students use precise language and academic vocabulary:

- Direct them to circle any words in their papers that are abstract, too general, or otherwise ineffective; then have them replace weaker words or phrases.
- Generate with the class words they might or should use when writing about a specific subject, procedure, event, or person.

To help students provide a concluding statement or section:

- Model how to write a conclusion in front of the class.
- Share published writing with students and determine how authors conclude their pieces.
- Create a list of ways authors conclude informative/explanatory texts and have students choose from that list.
- Have students practice writing a variety of conclusions for their text.

To help your English language learners, try this:

- Allow students to draw or illustrate facts and details about their topic and label these. Then provide predictable frames for the student to continue to add details (e.g., Elephants live . . . Elephants eat . . . Elephants look like . . .).

 For graphic organizer templates, see online resources at **resources.corwin.com/literacycompanion3-5**.

Standard: _____

Preparing the Classroom

Preparing the Mindset

Preparing the Texts to Use

Preparing to Differentiate

Connections to Other Standards:

Academic Vocabulary: Key Words and Phrases

Complex ideas: Complex ideas are those that are multifaceted. They require us to look at them and analyze them from different angles. To understand the noun "peace time," for example, we need to consider it in relation to war time, and to look at its "parts" (civilian, government, global politics), how the parts work together, and again, its meaning in relation to a similarly complex idea, war time. Simple ideas, on the other hand, are those we can grasp more easily and through a sensory experience. The fact that cadets' uniforms are cadet grey is a simple, concrete idea.

Concluding statement or section: Writers provide some final statement or section that connects all the ideas and information, and then relate this to the information or explanation presented. This is where writers circle back to restate their opinion and perhaps sum up their evidence in support of the argument they're making. This brings a sense of closure to the piece.

Concrete details: Specific details that refer to actual objects or places; it is the difference between Thomas Jefferson declaring the British guilty of "repeated injuries and usurpations" (general) and listing the crimes committed by the British under its "absolute Tyranny" (concrete) against the American colonies in the Declaration of Independence.

Convey ideas and information clearly: Writers choose the most important facts and details about the subject, organizing and grouping them to achieve a clear objective or focus.

Domain-specific vocabulary: The language of a discipline. To be accurate and precise, writers, when writing about any topic or text on a specific subject, use domain specific vocabulary to explain or describe.

Explanatory texts: Such texts are defined by their objective: to explain to or inform the audience about a topic using facts and an objective tone; the writer's role here is to report what they see.

Formatting: Headers, fonts (style, size, typeface), color, graphics, and spatial arrangement of a page. Formatting allows writers to emphasize ideas, connections, or other details with these tools.

Linking words, phrases, or clauses: Words or phrases that connect one sentence, idea, or paragraph to another, allowing writers to express the nature or importance of the relationship between those two ideas.

Selection, organization, and analysis of content: Writers choose the most important facts and details about the subject, organizing them to achieve a clear objective. As part of the process, the writer also analyzes how those elements relate to each other and the larger idea of the paper in general. Writers consider how each detail contributes to the meaning of that text.

Notes

Standard: _____

Whole Class

Small Group

Individual Practice/Conferring

Writing 3:   Write narratives to develop real or imagined experiences or events using effective technique, well-chosen details, and well-structured event sequences.

English Language Arts

3   Write narratives to develop real or imagined experiences or events using effective technique, descriptive details, and clear event sequences.
   a. Establish a situation and introduce a narrator and/or characters; organize an event sequence that unfolds naturally.
   b. Use dialogue and descriptions of actions, thoughts, and feelings to develop experiences and events or show the response of characters to situations.
   c. Use temporal words and phrases to signal event order.
   d. Provide a sense of closure.

4   Write narratives to develop real or imagined experiences, or events, using effective technique, descriptive details, and clear event sequences.
   a. **Orient the reader** by establishing a situation and introducing a narrator and/or characters; organize an event sequence that unfolds naturally.
   b. Use dialogue and description to develop experiences and events or show the responses of characters to situations.
   c. **Use a variety of transitional words and phrases to manage the sequence of events.**
   d. **Use concrete words and phrases and sensory details to convey experiences and events precisely.**
   e. **Provide a conclusion that follows from the narrated experiences or events.**

5   Write narratives to develop real or imagined experiences or events using effective technique, descriptive details, and clear event sequences.
   a. Orient the reader by establishing a situation and introducing a narrator and/or characters; organize an event sequence that unfolds naturally.
   b. **Use narrative techniques,** such as dialogue, description, and **pacing,** to develop experiences and events or show the responses of characters to situations.
   c. Use a variety of transitional words, phrases, **and clauses** to manage the sequence of events.
   d. Use concrete words and phrases and sensory details to convey experiences and events precisely.
   e. Provide a conclusion that follows from the narrated experiences or events.

Source: © Copyright 2010. National Governors Association Center for Best Practices and Council of Chief State School Officers. All rights reserved.

* These broad types of writing include many subgenres. See Appendix A in the Common Core State Standards for definitions of key writing types.

What the **Student** Does

English Language Arts

3 **Gist:** Students convey real or imagined experiences and events through narratives that employ appropriate methods and story structures that make clear what is happening and who is involved. Students arrange events that unfold naturally, adding dialogue, description, and thoughts and feelings of the characters to bring the story and its characters alive. Students also insert various transitional words (e.g., *after, before, while, during*) that orient readers to the event order. Finally, students give the story an ending that provides a conclusion for the narrative.

They consider:

- What am I telling here: a real or imagined event?
- What happened—and why am I telling this story about it?
- Have I described the character(s) and included dialogue and what they are thinking and feeling?
- Are the events in the story organized in order?
- Have I used words like *after, before, while, during* to help the reader understand the order of events?
- What details do I need to include to achieve my purpose by the end? Have I made it clear how one event leads to another?
- How does my story end? Does it make sense to the reader?

4 **Gist:** Students convey real or imagined experiences and events through narrative, using sensory details, and story structures that make clear what is happening and who is involved. Students arrange events into authentic sequences that unfold naturally, adding dialogue and description to bring the story and its characters alive. Students insert various transitional words and phrases that orient readers to the sequence of events. In addition, students choose words with care, evoking through these words or phrases the full range of sensory details needed to convey the experiences or events being described. Finally, students give the story an ending that makes sense in light of all that came before it and provides the narrative a satisfying conclusion.

They consider:

- What am I telling here: a real or imagined event?
- What happened—and why am I telling this story about it?
- Have I described the character(s) and included dialogue?
- Are the events in the story organized in order?
- Have I used words or phrases to help the reader understand the order of events?
- Have I included specific words and sensory details to help my reader understand the experiences and emotions in the story?
- What details do I need to include to achieve your purpose by the end? Have I made it clear how one event leads to another?
- How does my story end? Does it make sense to the reader?

5 **Gist:** Students convey real or imagined experiences and events through narratives, using sensory details, and story structures that make clear what is happening and who is involved. Students arrange events into authentic sequences that unfold naturally, adding dialogue, pacing, and description to bring the story and its characters alive. Students insert various transitional words, phrases, and clauses that orient readers to the sequence of events. In addition, students choose words with care, evoking through these words or phrases the full range of sensory details needed to convey the experiences or events being described. Finally, students give the story an ending that makes sense in light of all that came before it and provides the narrative a satisfying conclusion.

They consider:

- What am I telling here: a real or imagined event?
- What happened—and why am I telling this story about it?
- Have I described the character(s) and included dialogue?
- Are the events in the story organized in order?
- Have I used words, phrases, or clauses to help the reader understand the order of events?
- Have I included specific words and sensory details to help my reader understand the experiences and emotions in the story?
- What details do I need to include to achieve my purpose by the end? Have I made it clear how one event leads to another?
- How does my story end? Does it make sense to the reader?

What the **Teacher** Does

To write narratives about real or imagined experiences:

- Read a diverse sampling of narratives similar to and slightly different from the sort you want students to write.
- Have students generate a list of narrative topics. This list can be in their writer's notebook or wherever they keep their writing.
- Teach the difference between real experiences (personal narratives, memoir, etc.) and imagined experiences.
- Guide students through the process of creating a story map, storyboard, or other graphic form that allows them to identify, discuss, and arrange the different events or scenes in the story.
- Generate with students or provide a list of the elements of an effective narrative of the story you are assigning. Explicitly teach these elements as you read and share a variety of narratives—picture books, novels, memoir, short stories, and so on.
- Consider allowing students to incorporate images in their narrative if they complement the narrative.

To have students set out a problem or create a situation in a narrative:

- Discuss the problems in books that have been shared in class. Keep a class chart of the types of problems encountered.
- Read a short story (or stories) and discuss the problem.
- Establish a problem up front that the story will examine and the protagonist will solve after a series of scenarios richly imagined.
- Ask students to imagine a situation in rich detail (perhaps inspired by another book they have read or a subject they studied) and then describe how characters (or they, if it is a personal narrative) responded and changed over the course of the story.
- Lead students through the creation of a detailed observation about an event, process, or experience, guiding them by examples and questions that prompt them to add sensory details; then generate with them questions they should ask and apply to their narrative as they write.
- Have students use graphic organizers to identify the problem and then how that problem will affect the story and the sequence of events.

To have students introduce or develop a narrator or characters in a narrative:

- Discuss character traits in books read aloud in class. Have students examine character traits in the books they're reading independently.

- Help students develop questions that not only portray the character's physical persona but also reveal the character's personality and motivations within the context of the story (inner and outer character traits).
- Allow students to draw their characters and list specific character traits.
- Have students confer with a partner, asking questions about what the character looks like and how they act.
- Provide students with a list of archetypal characters—or discuss characters from books that have been shared in class—to help them imagine their own.
- Ask students, when writing personal narratives that involve people they know, to fill in a graphic organizer with boxes describing what the person says, does, thinks, and feels prior to writing.

To have students sequence events in a coherent way throughout a narrative:

- Have students create storyboards of the main events or episodes in their story.
- Have students fold paper into three sections and label them *beginning*, *middle*, and *ending*. Students jot notes in each section or sketch what will happen.
- Have students write on index cards key events in the narrative they are creating; then ask them to arrange them in different ways, stopping to explain to others what they are thinking, until they find the sequence that best works with the story they are trying to tell.
- Use graphic organizers or thinking maps to organize the sequence of events.
- Use a presentation software program to create the story as a series of slides, with notes and images on the slides so they can manipulate and better understand the elements of their story.

To help your English language learners, try this:

- Give students the opportunity to draw out the story first as a cartoon strip with notes and captions and speech bubbles for dialogue, in their own language if they prefer, before asking them to write the story; give them the chance to tell their story before writing it.

 For graphic organizer templates, see online resources at **resources.corwin.com/literacycompanion3-5.**

Preparing to Teach

Standard: _____

Preparing the Classroom

Preparing the Mindset

Preparing the Texts to Use

Preparing to Differentiate

Connections to Other Standards:

Academic Vocabulary: Key Words and Phrases

Conclusion: This comes at the end of narrative where the writer brings his or her piece to an end by telling the reader how things turned out. Conclusions in narrative tales are often more subtle than other forms, whose structure dictates where and how to conclude the story. One always looks for some point or ideas one can draw from a story; otherwise, why tell it?

Concrete words: These words refer to things we can touch, see, hear, smell, and taste (e.g., desk, pencil, coffee, hamburger). Good writing finds a balance between using concrete words and abstract words. Concrete words provide facts and details to the text.

Description: Stories rely on precise, detailed descriptions of people, places, and events to bring them alive in vivid ways that convey the characters' emotions and capture the reader's imagination.

Develop (experiences, events, or characters): When one "develops," for example, characters in a story, one adds specific details about what the characters did, said, and thought, which brings the characters to life; writers must develop the character(s), place(s), or event(s) as they move through time and change if they are to seem real.

Dialogue: The actual words characters say. Dialogue is written with quotation marks and is a conversation between two or more characters.

Event sequences: This is the order in which events occur in a story. Events that are well organized help the reader understand the story. How the writer arranges the events directly affects how the story affects us; some events create tension, mystery, and surprise; others create humor, nostalgia, and wonder.

Narrative: This is a story one tells, whether in prose or verse, a picture book or a play, or even a poem. A narrative can be fictional or grounded in facts, such as an autobiographical or historical narrative, or simply a recount of a personal experience in one's life.

Pacing: The speed at which the action unfolds or the story is told; pacing affects the tone, mood, and atmosphere, instilling in readers a feeling of anxiety, nostalgia, despair, or excitement.

Real or imagined experience: Narratives that are imagined are fictional (novels, plays, poems, fairy tales); those that are real are based on personal or historical records (memoirs, autobiographies).

Resolution: Also known as the falling action or dénouement, the resolution falls near the end of the story and typically resolves the major conflicts and problems explored throughout the story. Complex literary narratives involve multiple conflicts or plot lines that culminate in often surprising, unpredictable resolutions.

Sensory language: Evokes a place, person, or situation through its use of smells, sounds, textures, and other such rich details.

Technique: Literary narratives are carefully crafted to create certain emotional impacts on the reader; to study the writer's technique is to study how their work affects the reader.

Temporal words or phrases: These are words or phrases that signal the position of an event in time. They can also express duration and frequency. Examples of temporal words are *after, before, between, during, until*, and *while*. Examples of temporal phrases are *last summer, decades ago*, and *next time*.

Transitional words, phrases, and clauses: Words that connect one sentence or idea to another; allowing writers to express the passage of time or the sequence of events.

Notes

Standard: _____

Whole Class

Small Group

Individual Practice/Conferring

Writing 4: Produce clear and coherent writing in which the development, organization, and style are appropriate to task.

English Language Arts

3 With guidance and support from adults, produce writing in which the development and organization are appropriate to task and purpose. (Grade-specific expectations for writing types are defined in standards 1–3 above.)

4 **Produce clear and coherent writing** in which the development and organization are appropriate to task, purpose, **and audience.** (Grade-specific expectations for writing types are defined in standards 1–3 above.)

5 Produce clear and coherent writing in which the development and organization are appropriate to task, purpose, and audience. (Grade-specific expectations for writing types are defined in standards 1–3 above.)

What the **Student** Does

English Language Arts

3 **Gist:** Students write with support and guidance from adults, developing and organizing ideas that are appropriate for the task and the purpose when composing those types outlined in Writing Standards 1–3.

They consider:

- What is my topic and task for writing?
- What is my purpose: to inform, explain, argue, or entertain?
- What language, organization, and style is most appropriate for my writing task and purpose?
- In what format am I writing?
- Does it make sense to the reader?
- Does my writing include everything it needs?
- Does it stay on topic?
- Does it include enough details to be clear?
- Are my ideas organized in order?
- Does the voice in my writing match the audience?

4 **Gist:** Students write with clarity and coherence, developing and organizing ideas that are appropriate to the audience, purpose, and occasion when composing those types outlined in Writing Standards 1–3.

They consider:

- What is my topic and task for writing?
- What is my purpose: to inform, explain, argue, or entertain?
- What language, organization, and style is most appropriate for my writing task and purpose?
- In what format am I writing?
- Does it make sense to the reader?
- Does my writing include everything it needs?
- Does it stay on topic?
- Does it include enough details to be clear?
- Are my ideas organized in order?
- Does the voice in my writing match the audience?

5 **Gist:** Students write with clarity and coherence, developing and organizing your ideas and creating a style that is appropriate to the audience, purpose, and occasion when composing those types outlined in Writing Standards 1–3.

They consider:

- What is my topic and task for writing?
- What is my purpose: to inform, explain, argue, or entertain? What language, organization, and style is most appropriate for my writing task and purpose?
- In what format am I writing?
- Does it make sense to the reader?
- Does my writing include everything it needs?
- Does it stay on topic?
- Does it include enough details to be clear?
- Are my ideas organized in order?
- Does the voice in my writing match the audience?

What the **Teacher** Does

To have students produce writing that is clear and coherent:

- Establish for them what these terms mean and why they are important to good writing by showing them models from different writers.
- Teach explicitly what *task, purpose,* and *audience* are.
- Model in front of the students writing the same topic for different audiences and different tasks and have students notice how the pieces differ.
- Model for students how writers add and remove information in their pieces to achieve clarity. Using a tablet or document camera, write a draft and then "think aloud" what you could remove and *why.* Then find a section where you could add more and model how you would do that.
- Have students read through their writing and highlight any words or sections that could be removed.
- Explain the difference between *concrete* and *abstract* words and generate examples of both. Demonstrate how using concrete words produces clear writing.
- Direct students to underline the subject of each sentence in their text; then ask them to find all the abstract subjects and replace these with concrete subjects appropriate to the subject.
- Teach students how to determine the extent to which all the sentences in a paragraph and the larger piece itself work together to make one coherent whole; think of each sentence as a piece in a larger puzzle that should, when assembled, show us the big picture.
- Have students determine who the audience for the piece of writing will be, so you can anticipate and respond appropriately to their concerns and questions about your topic.
- Evaluate the task and all related directions to be sure students know what they must do, include, or avoid when writing.

To have students ensure that their writing is effectively organized:

- Collect a wide range of texts on the same subject but written for different audiences and purposes. Have students notice differences, including organizational structures. Chart the various organizational structures—for different genres, and so on.
- Make clear—or have students determine—the task, purpose, and occasion for this writing; then have students determine the best way to organize, present, and develop the topic in the paper.
- Model for students how to organize a paper. Write an example, or create a model with the students.
- Provide graphic organizers to students, modeling how to use them.
- Have students create some sort of map, outline, or plan before writing to improve the organization of the writing.
- Allow students to "talk it through" with a partner to ensure the organization makes sense.
- Provide students with a variety of organizational structures to choose from, helping them to evaluate each in light of their purpose, the task, and the audience.

To develop students' ideas to the fullest effect:

- Provide graphic organizers that encourage students to elaborate their ideas prior to writing.
- Provide numerous examples and mentor texts that model details and elaboration. Have students highlight and notice how these details develop and enhance the writing.
- Gather and incorporate into the writing examples, details, data, information, or quotations that illustrate or support their ideas.
- Explain what the examples, details, data, information, or quotations mean and why they are important to the main idea or claim they are developing.
- Allow students to confer with partners to ask questions and to add details.
- Consider integrating graphs, tables, charts, images, or infographics of some sort to illustrate and reinforce some point students are trying to make.

To help your English language learners, try this:

- Meet individually with your English language learner students to ensure they have time and opportunity to talk about the assignment and their needs as they try to write it. Listen to them as they read their writing and then help them revise one specific part.

 For graphic organizer templates, see online resources at **resources.corwin.com/literacycompanion3-5.**

Preparing to Teach

Standard: _____

Preparing the Classroom

Preparing the Mindset

Preparing the Texts to Use

Preparing to Differentiate

Connections to Other Standards:

Academic Vocabulary: Key Words and Phrases

Audience: This is considered an essential part of the "rhetorical situation" when writing. Key considerations include: Who is the audience? What do they already know or need to learn to understand the writer's message? How is the audience likely to respond to the piece? What biases do they have that the writer must anticipate and address to effectively advance her or his argument?

Clear: Effective writers produce clear compositions. This clarity is a fundamental quality of good writing. Writers achieve such clarity by using precise words, proper grammar, and sentence structure. Other techniques to improve clarity include using concrete or specific nouns or subjects instead of abstractions, including verbs that express action, and avoiding unnecessary use of passive voice, which often undermines clarity and precision in writing.

Coherent: Think of your words and sentences as building blocks in a larger structure such as a wall; all work together to form a strong, stable structure that serves a purpose; so it is with coherent writing where each word and sentence adds to the larger whole of the text and thereby creates a sense of clarity.

Development: Includes everything from examples and quotations, to details and other forms of evidence used to support and illustrate whatever the writer is saying about the subject. All such forms of development should extend, clarify, or otherwise enhance the writer's claims or, in narrative, advance her story. Development can also come in the form of figures, tables, dialogue, or images that add more information or further illustration.

Organization: No one approach or strategy is appropriate for organizing ideas in academic writing; what matters is that there is a clear, appropriate, logical, and effective structure to the ideas. One can arrange information from new to old, least to most important, areas of agreement to areas of disagreement, or more traditional forms such as spatial, sequential, and problem-solution, among others. Also important are the transitional phrases or words used to signal organizational shifts.

Purpose: What the writer is trying to accomplish through this piece; the writer's purpose intersects with and is shaped by the rhetorical situation (occasion, topic, audience). The most common purposes are to persuade, to inform/explain, to entertain, or to inspire.

Style: How the writing sounds, how it moves, how it feels when one reads or hears it read; it involves the words and how those words are joined to others to form patterns of sound and meaning in the service of some larger idea or purpose. The style complements and helps the writer to achieve his or her purpose.

Task: The writer's "task" is dictated by the purpose for the writing, and the genre. For example, the task of a journalist covering a local fire would be to describe the event, perhaps using the 5 Ws (who, what, when, where, and how). A poet writing a sonnet has a different task, with different criteria. In the context of school, the task might require students to write a letter to the editor in which they take a position for or against a certain controversial subject such as banning sodas in school or changing the age at which one can apply for a driver's license.

Notes

Planning to Teach

Standard: _____

Whole Class

_____

_____

_____

_____

_____

_____

_____

Small Group

_____

_____

_____

_____

_____

_____

_____

_____

_____

Individual Practice/Conferring

_____

_____

_____

_____

_____

_____

_____

Writing 5: Develop and strengthen writing as needed by planning, revising, editing, rewriting, or trying a new approach.

English Language Arts

3 With guidance and support from peers and adults, develop and strengthen writing as needed by planning, revising, and editing.

(Editing for conventions should demonstrate command of Language standards 1–3 up to and including grade 3.)

4 With guidance and support from peers and adults, develop and strengthen writing as needed by planning, revising, and editing.

(Editing for conventions should demonstrate command of Language standards 1–3 up to and including **grade 4**.)

5 With guidance and support from peers and adults, develop and strengthen writing as needed by planning, revising, and editing.

(Editing for conventions should demonstrate command of Language standards 1–3 up to and including **grade 5**.)

What the **Student** Does

English Language Arts

3 **Gist:** Generate and gather ideas about the topic with help from classmates and teachers, making a plan for how to write about and use those ideas, not only drafting what to say but deciding how best to say or organize it by choosing different formats, mixing media, or blending genres. Students then improve the writing by revising, editing, rewriting, or starting all over with a new idea.

They consider:

- What sort of guidance or support do I need—and who is best to provide it?
- Am I clear about my topic? Is it too broad? Too narrow?
- Could it improve my paper to choose a different structure, format, or medium—or shift the emphasis to a different aspect of my topic?
- How can I revise my paper to improve it? Can I change words, add to it, cut sections out, or change the sequencing?
- Have I fixed up my spelling, punctuation, grammar, etc., so that the information is clear to my reader?
- What other editing strategies should I consider besides using the spell- and grammar-check in my word processor?
- Have I used peers or teachers to help me improve my paper?
- Who can I ask to read and respond to my paper with honesty and attention to details?

4 **Gist:** Students generate and gather ideas about the topic with help from classmates and teachers, making a plan for how to write about and use those ideas, not only drafting what to say but deciding how best to say or organize it by choosing different formats, mixing media, or blending genres. Students then improve the writing by revising, editing, rewriting, or starting all over with a new idea.

They consider:

- What sort of guidance or support do I need—and who is best to provide it?
- Am I clear about my topic? Is it too broad? Too narrow?
- Could it improve my paper to choose a different structure, format, or medium—or shift the emphasis to a different aspect of my topic?
- How can I revise my paper to improve it? Can I change words, add to it, cut sections out, or change the sequencing?
- Have I fixed up my spelling, punctuation, grammar, etc., so that the information is clear to my reader?
- What other editing strategies should I consider besides using the spell- and grammar-check in my word processor?
- Have I used peers or teachers to help me improve my paper?
- Who can I ask to read and respond to my paper with honesty and attention to details?

5 **Gist:** Students generate and gather ideas about the topic with help from classmates and teachers, making a plan for how to write about and use those ideas, not only drafting what to say but deciding how best to say or organize it by choosing different formats, mixing media, or blending genres. Students then improve the writing by revising, editing, rewriting, or starting all over with a new idea.

They consider:

- What sort of guidance or support do I need—and who is best to provide it?
- Am I clear about my topic? Is it too broad? Too narrow?
- Could it improve my paper to choose a different structure, format, or medium–or shift the emphasis to a different aspect of my topic?
- How can I revise my paper to improve it? Can I change words, add to it, cut sections out, or change the sequencing?
- Have I fixed up my spelling, punctuation, grammar, and so on so that the information is clear to my reader?
- What other editing strategies should I consider besides using the spell- and grammar-check in my word processor?
- Have I used peers or teachers to help me improve my paper?
- Who can I ask to read and respond to my paper with honesty and attention to details?

What the **Teacher** Does

To improve students' ability to plan prior to beginning to write:

- Read and share books on how authors write (autobiographical), discussing their different processes with students.
- Provide opportunities for generative conversations about the text, topic, or task before they begin to write about it; if possible, have them capture all ideas on posters, whiteboards, sticky notes, or other means—then post them in the classroom or to an online site they can access later for further reference or even addition.
- Show students how you or professional writers prepare to write by either demonstrating live in front of them or providing examples of such notes and plans by major writers, many of which are available through *The Paris Review*.
- Expose them to a range of planning strategies—mapping, outlining, sticky notes or index cards, apps or features of Microsoft Word you use—then let them choose the one(s) that suit their ways of working best.
- Have students draw or sketch prior to writing as a way to help them plan.

To improve students' capacity to revise, edit, or rewrite:

- Explicitly teach what each of these things mean and how they differ in the writing process. Provide ample opportunities for students to practice each one *separately*.
- Require them to focus on one specific aspect of the writing that would lead to improved clarity and comprehension by the audience. For example, students could *add details* to help the reader understand complex ideas in greater focus, *remove details* that interfere with clarity, *move a section of text* to help with sequence of events, or *substitute words* to provide clarity and sensory details.
- Project a piece on the interactive whiteboard that needs details added and have students help annotate revision techniques—what could be added to make the piece better.

- Teach students specific goals of editing—and then model for students. At the intermediate level, editing is often capitalization, punctuation, usage, and spelling. Have students practice both independently and with peers to improve the editing in their own pieces.
- Ask them to read their paper, and after each sentence, ask of that sentence (and their ideas), "So what?" If the next sentence does not answer that question, look for ways to rewrite the sentence or paragraph so that it does explain why any idea, quotation, or claim matters or what it means.
- Using the interactive whiteboard, project texts that have editing errors and have students practice correcting them.
- After modeling for the class, have students read each other's papers, stopping at any point to jot a question in the margin about some aspect of the writing that they do not understand.
- Offer editing checklists for students to fill out prior to finalizing so that they are reflective of their own editing skills.
- Pull together "Needs-based groups" to reteach/reinforce specific editing skills.
- Teach students how to confer with each other for specific purposes—revision or editing conferences. Encourage them to ask their peers for feedback on their writing.
- Provide class time for sharing writing with peers, small groups, or whole class (author's chair) to gain feedback on writing.

To help your English language learners, try this:

- Meet with your English language learners often to teach *one thing* in a conference. Focus on revision techniques so that you are reinforcing the writing and writing for meaning versus always "getting it right"—this way, they will take more risks in their writing.

For graphic organizer templates, see online resources at **resources.corwin.com/literacycompanion3-5.**

Notes

Preparing to Teach

Standard: _____

Preparing the Classroom

_____
_____
_____
_____
_____
_____

Preparing the Mindset

_____
_____
_____
_____
_____
_____

Preparing the Texts to Use

_____
_____
_____
_____
_____
_____

Preparing to Differentiate

_____
_____
_____
_____
_____
_____

Connections to Other Standards:

_____
_____
_____

Academic Vocabulary: Key Words and Phrases

Audience: Whether the audience is known (the teacher, the class, the school, or local community) or unknown (a prospective employer, anyone who visits the class blog or wiki), students must consider who that audience is and what they do and do not know before writing.

Conventions: The rules that apply to and govern the genre, format, grammar, and other aspects of writing this paper, including spelling.

Details to strengthen writing: Specificity via details, examples, and elaboration are what readers look for and expect from both informational and literary texts, and help satisfy the reader that the writer knows what he or she is talking about. It's not enough to state broad and general ideas or events. It's also important to provide details and specifics to flesh out the larger ideas and breathe life into them.

Develop: Refers to the process one follows to improve a piece of writing before one even sets words down on paper; that is, such steps as gathering and generating ideas for the writing, taking time to outline, brainstorm, or map out one's ideas. Once those ideas are down in a rough draft, development means seeking better words, editing out unnecessary words, adding material to clarify underdeveloped points, or improving clarity and cohesion by tightening the sentences.

Editing: When students revise the paper to make it more concise, coherent, or cohesive, they are editing; when one looks for and fixes spelling and mechanics, they are proofreading. Editing can and, with more fluent writers, does take place throughout the composing process, not just at the end, as with proofreading.

New approach: At some point the writer may feel the current approach—the voice, the style, the perspective or stance—is not effective, at which point it makes sense to write the whole piece over in some new style, different format, or alternate perspective in order to better convey one's ideas to the audience on this occasion.

Planning: Writers can do many things to plan: outline ideas, gather and generate ideas, block off the main ideas before refining them into an outline, and make concept maps, mind maps, and brainstorms to generate and make connections between ideas. Some writers make lists of what they need to do, read, or include; all review throughout the planning process to make sure they include all they should.

Purpose: We always have some purpose when we write, whether it is to persuade, inform, entertain, or inspire. It is essential that students know what it is they are trying to achieve (and for whom and under what circumstances) before they even begin to write, as their purpose influences everything from the words and structures they choose to the media and formats they use. Even when the writing task is assigned or outlined on a timed writing exam, it is crucial that students learn to identify the purpose and approach the writing with that in mind as they plan, draft, edit, and revise their papers.

Revising: This does not mean, as some think, merely correcting or proofreading a paper. To revise is to re-see, to consider the paper or idea from a whole new angle or hear a different way to express an idea or emotion. Revising the paper should improve not just clarity and cohesion but also content as the writer strives to strengthen the story or the arguments, the logic, and the style.

Rewriting: Sometimes used interchangeably with revising, this phase of the writing process involves not tweaking or polishing up what is there but replacing it with new ideas or language better suited to the audience, purpose, or occasion. Student writers sometimes need to take a whole paper or some portion of it and rewrite it in light of what they learn after getting that first draft down.

Strengthen: This is what revising for concision, clarity, and coherence does to the writing: it strengthens it by tightening the wording, refining the argument, removing what is unnecessary so that key ideas, reasoning, or evidence are emphasized.

Planning to Teach

Standard: _____

Whole Class

_____

_____

_____

_____

_____

_____

_____

_____

Small Group

_____

_____

_____

_____

_____

_____

_____

_____

_____

Individual Practice/Conferring

_____

_____

_____

_____

_____

_____

_____

_____

Writing 6: Use technology, including the Internet, to produce and publish writing and to interact and collaborate with others.

English Language Arts

3 With guidance and support from adults, use technology to produce and publish writing (using keyboarding skills) as well as to interact and collaborate with others.

4 With some guidance and support from adults, use technology, **including the Internet,** to produce and publish writing as well as to interact and collaborate with others; **demonstrate sufficient command of keyboarding skills to type a minimum of one page in a single sitting.**

5 With some guidance and support from adults, use technology, including the Internet, to produce and publish writing as well as to interact and collaborate with others; demonstrate sufficient command of keyboarding skills to type a minimum of **two pages** in a single sitting.

What the **Student** Does

English Language Arts

3 **Gist:** Students compose texts using digital devices, software, websites, and other digital tools and collaborate with others (via Google Docs, chat, and other social media applications) with guidance and support from adults. Students use keyboarding skills to produce written text.

They consider:

- Do I know how to access technology?
- What is my task?
- What is my purpose?
- Who is my audience?
- What tools or technologies offer the greatest means of creating and working with others on this project?
- What opportunities should we consider for publishing writing to a larger audience?
- How do I use technology to interact with others and collaborate on my writing?

4 **Gist:** Students compose texts using digital devices, software, websites, the Internet, and other digital tools and collaborate with others (via Google Docs, chat, and other social media applications) with some guidance and support from adults. Students master the keyboard well enough to type a minimum of one page in a single sitting.

They consider:

- Do I know how to access technology?
- What is my task?
- What is my purpose?
- Who is my audience?
- What tools or technologies offer the greatest means of creating and working with others on this project?
- What opportunities should we consider for publishing writing to a larger audience?
- How do I use technology to interact with others and collaborate on my writing?
- How well and how fast can I type?

5 **Gist:** Students compose texts using digital devices, software, websites, the Internet, and other digital tools and collaborate with others (via Google Docs, chat, and other social media applications) with some guidance and support from adults. Students master the keyboard well enough to type a minimum of two pages in a single sitting.

They consider:

- Do I know how to access technology?
- What is my task?
- What is my purpose?
- Who is my audience?
- What tools or technologies offer the greatest means of creating and working with others on this project?
- What opportunities should we consider for publishing writing to a larger audience?
- How do I use technology to interact with others and collaborate on my writing?
- How well and how fast can I type?

What the **Teacher** Does

To have students use technology to produce, publish, and collaborate:

- Make digital tools a natural part of the classroom learning environment. Scaffold students' use of computers, tablets, and other technological tools by demonstrating and doing shared writing, as an entire class. This whole-class collaboration helps ensure that students who haven't had access to technology at home can learn to use various devices and tools. Likewise, have students work in small groups and pairs if you see that "tech savvy" can be peer-mentored. Be prepared to work one on one with those students who need extra support.
- Delineate the function of various writing tools so that students can choose from among them for one or more stages of writing and publishing: (1) Researching information and visual images (Internet); (2) Writing and drafting; (3) Sharing (wikis); and (4) Publishing (Keynote, PowerPoint, Google).
- Provide direct instruction as needed in the use of any devices, platforms, applications, or software for a given assignment.
- Teach one aspect of technology at a time.
- Monitor student use of technology—their usage and application and their safety and "etiquette."
- Select technology that supports and enhances student writing.
- Ensure that students can access and use the technology as you intend or expect (e.g., if you say they must collaborate through an online discussion group, do all have access and know-how?).
- Display, when possible, the contents of your own screen via a projector so they can follow along or check their work against yours if you are guiding them through a sequence of steps.
- Prepare ahead of time as needed (e.g., checking to see that the lab printer is working and loaded with paper) so that you will not lose instructional time.
- Stay abreast of new technology and new developments.

To have students use the Internet to produce writing:

- Explore different online applications designed to help students generate, organize, and develop their ideas.
- Create links to specific resources you want students to visit for content to incorporate into their paper; such content might include primary source documents, images, or applications students can use to create infographics for their papers.

- Instruct students in the use of free programs such as Google Docs or various graphics applications that they can use to produce their texts or develop content to embed in those texts.

To have students use technology to produce writing:

- Look for ways to use technology—computers, tablets, displays, interactive whiteboards, document cameras—that are efficient, effective, and appropriate to the writing task.
- Evaluate the writing assignment for small but worthwhile opportunities that allow you to teach students additional features of word processing (e.g., how to embed images, how to design the page so text flows around images, how to insert headers), graphic design (e.g., infographics, images, layout), multimedia formatting (e.g., how to embed a slideshow or video clip in a written document), or even just improved typing skills.

To have students use the Internet to publish writing:

- Consider carefully the options and implications of publishing student work (especially if it contains images or any copyrighted material) online.
- Try setting up a class blog to which all can contribute in one place so it is easier to maintain, monitor, and model how to use.
- Take those extra steps, when publishing for the world to see, that ensure that the writing is correct, appropriate, and formatted according to the platform they are using. To use technology to interact or collaborate.
- Set up a group or collaborative space online (via Google Docs, a wiki site, or any other platform that allows users to create a password-protected space) where they can meet, discuss, and respond to each other's ideas and writing in or outside of class.
- Gather useful links—to applications, primary source sites, exhibits, or other rich resources related to a paper they are writing—which they explore together in class or at home during the process of gathering and generating ideas for writing.

To help your English language learners, try this:

- Make sure students are familiar with basic technological vocabulary such as mouse, keyboard, menu, and cursor, and demonstrate with a visual prop whenever possible. Ensure they have access to and know how to use the platform, application, software, computer, or tablet you are assuming all students have at home and know how to use in the ways you have assigned.

 For graphic organizer templates, see online resources at **resources.corwin.com/literacycompanion3-5**.

Preparing to Teach

Standard: _____

Preparing the Classroom

_____
_____
_____
_____
_____
_____

Preparing the Mindset

_____
_____
_____
_____
_____
_____

Preparing the Texts to Use

_____
_____
_____
_____
_____
_____

Preparing to Differentiate

_____
_____
_____
_____
_____
_____

Connections to Other Standards:

_____
_____
_____

Academic Vocabulary: Key Words and Phrases

Collaborate: Students work together to come up with ideas for their writing or respond to one another's papers using features like Comments (Google Docs) or Track Changes (Microsoft Word). This might include comments from the teacher or classmates about writing provided through recorded voice memos, features such as Microsoft Word's track changes, or annotations of any sort offered through tablet applications that allow the reader to offer feedback via voice, digital highlighters, digital sticky notes, or annotations written on the digital document itself. Such feedback comes throughout the entire composing process. Students receive—from one or more sources—ideas about how they can improve some aspect of whatever they are writing.

Interact: Students collaborate in a written dialogue online through chat groups, social media, e-mail, and other such interactive platforms to generate ideas about a text they are analyzing, a paper they are writing, or a topic they are exploring (prior to writing). Thus, they are using technology to facilitate and extend discussions, generate ideas, provide feedback to peers' papers, or write and share their own writing with others for feedback or publication.

Produce: Students use a range of technology tools—computers, applications, digital cameras to capture images, make videos, instruments for scientific data gathering, software and advanced calculators for mathematics—to generate the content and help students write.

Publish: Students use computers to publish and distribute quality materials around school, community, or online.

Technology: This refers to using computers to compose, revise, and correct any papers; also, implies using applications to gather or generate data, evidence, or content (in the form of quantitative information, examples, graphic displays, still and video images) to incorporate into the paper itself. Technology is also an essential research tool for writers: the Internet in general, as well as specialized databases and other online resources. Using "technology" also means writing with and for a range of forms, formats, and features: essays, blogs, wikis, websites, multimedia presentations, or digital essays using the full spectrum of available digital features (color, size, hotlinks, embedded media) to communicate or publish the work for audiences to read on smartphones, tablets, computers, presentation screens—and, of course, paper.

Writing products: Given the emphasis here on the use of technology, such products would include the traditional papers students write, but also such new and emerging forms as blogs, wikis, websites, tweets, presentations, and multimedia or hybrid texts.

Notes

Planning to Teach

Standard: _____

Whole Class

_____

_____

_____

_____

_____

_____

_____

Small Group

_____

_____

_____

_____

_____

_____

_____

_____

Individual Practice/Conferring

_____

_____

_____

_____

_____

_____

_____

Writing 7: Conduct short as well as more sustained research projects based on focused questions, demonstrating understanding of the subject under investigation.

English Language Arts

3 Conduct short research projects that build knowledge about a topic.

4 Conduct short research projects that build knowledge **through investigation of different aspects of** a topic.

5 Conduct short research projects that build knowledge through investigation of different aspects of a topic.

What the **Student** Does

English Language Arts

3 **Gist:** Students gather, investigate, or observe information to conduct a short research project and build knowledge about a specific topic.

They consider:

- What is my research topic?
- What do I already know about my topic?
- What do I want to learn?
- What questions can I ask to help me get the information I need?
- How am I going to get this information? What are some different sources I should consult for this topic?
- Can I make observations to build my knowledge on the topic?
- What kind of project am I doing? What are the expectations?

4 **Gist:** Students gather information and investigate different aspects of a topic in order to conduct a short research project and build knowledge.

They consider:

- What is my research topic?
- What do I already know about my topic?
- What do I want to learn?
- What questions can I ask to help me get the information I need?
- How am I going to get this information? What are some different sources I should consult for this topic?
- What are different aspects of the topic?
- What kind of project am I doing? What are the expectations?

5 **Gist:** Students gather information from several sources and investigate different aspects of a topic in order to conduct a short research project and build knowledge.

They consider:

- What is my research topic?
- What do I already know about my topic?
- What do I want to learn?
- What questions can I ask to help me get the information I need?
- How am I going to get this information? What are some different sources I should consult for this topic?
- What are different aspects of the topic?
- What kind of project am I doing? What are the expectations?

What the **Teacher** Does

To have students conduct short research projects:

- Choose a question as a class and work collaboratively to answer it.
- Collect numerous books and other resources that will help answer this question for students to access.
- Conduct Inquiry Circles—allowing students to investigate a topic and share their learning with a small group studying the same topic. Have groups share their research in some way (a project, presentation, report, etc.) with the class.
- Model for students how to conduct a short research project or co-construct a research project with students, with the goal for them to be able to do a future research project independently.
- Teach students how to gather data or investigate a topic.
- Teach students how observations build background knowledge. Provide opportunities for students to make observations in class—especially in content areas like science.
- Organize some of your research and writing projects around science and social studies topics. With time being of the essence, it makes sense to integrate reading, writing, and content areas as often as possible.
- Have students keep a list of possible topics they would want to research.
- Model for students how to take notes when gathering information or observing. Teach them how to take notes to answer specific questions or to address specific aspects of their subject they want to learn (e.g., the *habitat* of the grizzly bear, the *appearance* of the grizzly bear). Encourage students to create "thick" questions that are answered in depth, versus "thin" questions that can be answered in one or two words to frame their research (e.g., a "thin" question would be "When did Columbus make his first journey?—1492" versus a "thick" question—"*Why* did Columbus want to go on the expedition and *why* did Queen Isabella finance him?" This question requires more research and depth and leads to a greater understanding.).

- Provide students with graphic organizers in order to take notes and gather information.
- Organize units of study around a Big Idea or Essential Question.
- Identify key questions or problems students can investigate in some depth within the constraints of a class period, using their findings when writing, speaking, or interviewing someone about that subject.
- Discuss with students the process you or respected writers, scientists, historians, and others go through to discover a subject.
- Pass out sticky notes to all in the class; ask them to list a subject on the top of the note that relates to the text or topic the class is studying; then tell them to write a question about that text or topic that could be developed into a short research project. Finally, have them stick all the notes on the front board and let the whole class examine them as part of the process of learning.

To have students use several sources to build knowledge through investigation of different aspects of a topic:

- Provide students with multiple texts and sites that provide information on the same topic.
- Gather and collect multiple sources for topics students are investigating.
- Encourage students to seek out and bring into the classroom multiple sources to use for their research projects.
- Provide multiple sources/resources around content-area topics so students have access to multiple sources across the curriculum.

To help your English language learners, try this:

- Guide students to choose a topic that they have background knowledge on and one on which they can access information that they can read and understand. (Providing them with research materials is important.) Help them generate questions to frame their research and provide graphic organizers.

 For graphic organizer templates, see online resources at **resources.corwin.com/literacycompanion3-5.**

Preparing to Teach

Standard: _____

Preparing the Classroom

Preparing the Mindset

Preparing the Texts to Use

Preparing to Differentiate

Connections to Other Standards:

Academic Vocabulary: Key Words and Phrases

Build knowledge through investigation of different aspects of a topic/Demonstrating understanding of the subject: Students show the depth of their knowledge and their research skills by gathering a range of quality information, data, evidence, and examples related to the problem, question, or topic they are investigating; they then demonstrate what they have learned by choosing the most salient details and examples and using those to support their claims in a coherent, logical manner throughout the paper.

Questions (includes self-generated): Researchers generate their own or investigate others' questions about a topic of substance; such questions are often the driving purpose of the research: We are investing x to answer the questions about why x leads to y.

Research (short and more sustained): Students and teachers are engaged in research any time they seek information about a question or subject, ask themselves or others questions about causes, types, effects, meaning, and importance of anything they find themselves studying for class or their own interests. Short or brief inquiries might involve getting some background knowledge on an author, a book, or a time period; in science, search for and consider previous findings for certain experiments; in social studies, digging up primary sources to see how people thought about an event at that time or opinion pieces in different newspapers to measure the response to an event (e.g., dropping of the atomic bomb) from different parts of the country or world. Longer, more sustained research projects demand far more depth and many more sources from different perspectives. It is a fundamental skill for success in college, one's career, and at home as a consumer who must increasingly take responsibility for researching the best health care program, insurance policy, or cell phone provider.

Subject under investigation: Refers to the topic, research question, or problem the student seeks to understand and develop an argument about after completing the research. This subject can come from students themselves or from a teacher or institution (e.g., College Board, the students' state or district) that requires students to study in depth a sustained or brief research project.

Synthesize multiple sources: Considering the subject from different and competing angles to arrive at a meaningful or significant insight. A writer must consider multiple sources, some of which offer counterarguments or alternative perspectives, if their claims and arguments are to be considered reliable, valid, and substantial. These must all be established, trustworthy sources if they are to be cited or used to support one's claims.

Notes

_____
_____
_____
_____
_____
_____
_____
_____
_____
_____

Standard: _____

Whole Class

_____

_____

_____

_____

_____

_____

_____

_____

Small Group

_____

_____

_____

_____

_____

_____

_____

_____

Individual Practice/Conferring

_____

_____

_____

_____

_____

_____

_____

_____

Writing 8: Gather relevant information from multiple print and digital sources, assess the credibility and accuracy of each source, and integrate the information while avoiding plagiarism.

English Language Arts

3 Recall information from experiences or gather information from print and digital sources; take brief notes on sources and sort evidence into provided categories.

4 Recall relevant information from experiences or gather relevant information from print and digital sources; **take notes and categorize information, and provide a list of sources.**

5 Recall relevant information from experiences or gather relevant information from print and digital sources; **summarize or paraphrase information in notes and finished work,** and provide a list of sources.

What the **Student** Does

English Language Arts

3 **Gist:** Students search for and gather information from print and digital sources or recall personal experiences. Using these resources, they take brief notes and categorize the information.

They consider:

- What is the topic I'm researching?
- What sources can I use to find information on my topic?
- What information should I include in notes?
- How will I organize or categorize the information?

4 **Gist:** Students search for and gather information from print and digital sources or recall personal experiences, provide a list of all sources used. Using these resources, they take brief notes and categorize the information.

They consider:

- What is the topic I'm researching?
- What sources can I use to find information?
- What information should I include in notes?
- How can I organize or categorize the information?
- What sources did I use for this research? How am I keeping track of these sources?
- When I use technology or digital sources, how am I marking them so that I can go back to them or share them with others?

5 **Gist:** Students search for and gather information from print and digital sources or recall personal experiences and provide a list of all sources used. They take notes from these resources—summarizing and paraphrasing in both notes and in final work.

They consider:

- What is the topic I'm researching?
- What sources can I use to find information?
- How will I take/organize my notes? How am I going to organize them?
- What information should I include in notes?
- How can I summarize and paraphrase the information?
- When I use technology or digital sources, how am I marking them so that I can go back to them or share them with others? What sources did I use for this research?

What the **Teacher** Does

To have students gather relevant information or recall information from experiences:

- Model for students or co-construct with them how to gather materials and access information on a given topic, by using a written text under a document camera or an interactive whiteboard or tablet. Model highlighting relevant information, annotating in the margins, or using sticky notes to synthesize/paraphrase information.
- Model for students how to recall and record notes on information they already know about a topic. Have them practice independently, perhaps using graphic organizers.
- Have students practice gathering relevant information from an assigned text or website.
- Begin by first asking students to define the problem they are trying to solve or the question they are investigating.
- Provide graphic organizers for students to take notes on.
- Present students with criteria you develop for—or with—them, or which are provided by other audiences for this assignment.
- Teach students how to take notes. Model first, practice together, then encourage independence.
- Give or create with your students an effective means of collecting information, details, examples, data, and all other content for subsequent integration into their paper.
- Model how to mark or annotate technical and digital sources.

To have students categorize information:

- Provide graphic organizers for students to categorize their information.

- Model and co-construct note-taking and categorizing by having students write down one important fact from a shared text. As a class, determine categories and create columns on the front board or on chart paper. Instruct students to place their sticky note in the correct category.
- Have students take notes on sticky notes and sort them into categories independently.

To help students summarize or paraphrase information in notes and finished work:

- Model using the document camera or interactive whiteboard with a shared text. Highlight or annotate important information, then using note cards summarize the highlighted information.
- Allow students to practice using a shared piece of text or website.
- Create charts and organizers delineating how to summarize text.

To help students provide a list of sources:

- Demonstrate for students how to create a bibliography.
- Provide a template for students to fill in as they access resources.
- Use websites that create bibliographies for students to record their resources.

To help your English language learners, try this:

- Provide them organizers and charts on which to take notes and draw pictures of their research. Break research into manageable topics on which that they can find appropriate resources and understand and record information.

For graphic organizer templates, see online resources at **resources.corwin.com/literacycompanion3-5.**

Notes

Preparing to Teach

Standard: _____

Preparing the Classroom

Preparing the Mindset

Preparing the Texts to Use

Preparing to Differentiate

Connections to Other Standards:

Academic Vocabulary: Key Words and Phrases

Accuracy: Correctness. The information used as evidence for a claim or support for a hypothesis is true, current, and precise; the measurements used the appropriate terms for that subject or discipline to ensure maximum clarity and correctness.

Assess: Taking stock of all the information your search yields or all the quotations and evidence you could include in your paper. Deciding which you should use based on your criteria or research question.

Credibility: A measure of the believability of the source of information, based on how current, established, and relevant the source is, as well as the ethos of the writer and of any source cited. Established sources affiliated with recognized publishers, reputable universities, or respected authors are considered credible, authoritative sources.

Gather relevant information: Information is only relevant to the degree that it answers the research question or supports an argument the writer makes; all else should be left out or dismissed as irrelevant. If students have a carefully conceived, clear, and narrow research question or problem they are reading to answer or solve, they will be better equipped to know which information is most useful or relevant.

Integrate information into the text selectively: To weave the quotations, examples, details, or evidence into the paper through paraphrase, indirect, or direct quotation. Students need not include every word of a source when quoting them directly; instead, they embed it in their own sentence in a way (by using ellipses to indicate omissions, brackets to signal additions) that maintains or enhances the flow of the text and ideas.

Multiple print and digital sources: Legitimate researchers consider an array of sources from different perspectives and media to be as thorough as possible in their analysis.

Plagiarism: Including another's words as your own (without using quotation marks); those words can be copied from a famous writer, any website, or a fellow student. It is not plagiarism to use an author's words so long as you cite them and put quotation marks around those words being quoted.

Source: This refers to the need to be mindful of the strengths and limitations of each source: some sources may have particularly good data about one issue but not another; when assessing or quoting sources, it is vital to be aware of the quality and reputation of that source on this subject. A source may, for example, offer quality data about technology and teens but be weak when it comes to looking at technology and different cultural groups. Avoid overusing or relying exclusively on any one source: when researching a subject, students cannot rely on a few select sources that conveniently offer them a wealth of quotations or evidence. They need to reference (and make use of) a variety of sources that represent different perspectives and stances on the issue or question they are researching if their observations, conclusions, and arguments are to be credible.

Notes

Standard: _____

Whole Class

Small Group

Individual Practice/Conferring

Writing 9: Draw evidence from literary or informational texts to support analysis, reflection, and research.

English Language Arts

3 (Begins in grade 4)

4 Draw evidence from literature, informational texts to support analysis, reflection, and research.
   a. Apply *grade 4 Reading standards* to literature (e.g., "Describe in depth a character setting or event in a story or drama, drawing on specific details in the text [e.g., a character's thoughts, words, or actions].").
   b. Apply *grade 4 Reading standards* to informational texts (e.g., "Explain how an author uses reasons and evidence to support particular points in a text.").

5 Draw evidence from literature, informational texts to support analysis, reflection, and research.
   a. Apply **grade 5 Reading standards** to literature (e.g., "Compare and contrast two or more characters, settings, or events in a story or a drama, drawing on specific details in the text [e.g., how characters interact].").
   b. Apply **grade 5 Reading standards** to informational texts (e.g., "Explain how an author uses reasons and evidence to support particular points in a text, identifying which reasons and evidence support which point[s].").

What the **Student** Does

English Language Arts

3 (Begins in grade 4)

4 **Gist:** Students support their interpretations, analyses, reflections, or finding with evidence found in literary or informational texts, applying grade 4 standards for reading literature and informational texts. See the "Reading Standards" sections for the full standards.

They consider:

- What is the character in the story and how can I describe him using details from the text?
- Are there thoughts, words, or actions from the character that help to describe her?
- What is the setting in the story and how can I describe it using details from the text?
- What is an important event in the story and how can I describe it using details from the text?
- What is the topic or text I am writing about? What evidence can I find in the literary or informational text(s) to support my claim(s)?
- How does this evidence support my analysis, reflection, or findings?

5 **Gist:** Students support their interpretations, analyses, reflections, or finding with evidence found in literary or informational texts, applying grade 5 standards for reading literature and informational texts. See the "Reading Standards" sections for the full standards.

They consider:

- Who are two characters from this text? How are they alike? How are they different?
- How can I use specific details from the story to compare and contrast them?
- How do they interact? How can I use that to describe them?
- Are there two settings in the story? How are they alike? How do they differ, and how can I use details from the story to explain this?
- Are there two important events in the story that I can compare and contrast using details from the text?
- What is the topic or text I am writing about—and what is my claim?
- What evidence can I find in the literary or informational text(s) to support my claim(s)?
- How does this evidence support my analysis, reflection, or findings?

What the **Teacher** Does

To have students draw evidence from literary or informational texts:

- Model for students how to draw evidence from texts. Read a shared text together and ask an important question that you want to answer or make an interpretation about the text. Then go back to the text and highlight or code where it is answered in the text. This becomes the evidence.
- Co-construct a reflection or analysis of a shared text. Model for students how to "lift" words, lines, or phrases directly from the text to use as evidence in the piece.
- Practice this skill with students using a shared text. Allow them to read and make an interpretation and then find the evidence and share with a group or partner their findings.
- Have students write reflections about their reading, citing specific evidence from the text to support their thinking.
- Define and illustrate what counts as "evidence" for students so they know what it looks like and thus what to search for; this is particularly important for students learning to assess primary sources and other text types such as multimedia and infographics.
- Require students to annotate or code the texts they read with an eye toward using different elements as evidence in a subsequent paper; thus, for example, the teacher might show them how to put a Q in the margin to indicate, upon rereading later, the location of a possible quotation worth using; those using tablets can teach students how to use digital tools to annotate, search texts for specific words, and capture images for future use.

To have students draw specific details from literary texts to support description or comparison and contrast of characters, settings, or events:

- Model and discuss these elements from shared books in the classroom. Refer to books previously read. Be explicit when modeling character traits, settings, and events.
- Use shared texts to highlight and code specific details. Demonstrate to students how to "lift" these details from the text and write them into your response. Model for students or co-construct writing descriptions or comparison/contrasts.
- Practice writing in response to reading frequently. Have students write in response to characters, setting, plot, or events. Require students to include details in their responses.
- Teach students how to mark text in order to refer back to it when sharing their thinking and specific details about the text. This could be through highlighting, using sticky notes, writing on book marks, or writing notes. When using technology (e-books, Kindles, etc.), this could be marking words or passages.

- Have students share orally their thinking about texts. Literature circles, book clubs, reading groups, or peer shares are all methods for doing this. Encourage them to share details from the text and to refer back to the text in their discussions.
- Teach compare/contrast writing. Provide students with graphic organizers or other ways to hold on to the similarities and differences of their topic.
- Have students practice using a shared text. Encourage students to highlight or somehow code the text and the specific details that they will use to support the comparison or contrast.
- Help students first learn what and how much of a passage to quote by illustrating the difference between using a full quotation (too long) and one that only uses the relevant portion (just right) and is written in the literary present tense.
- Clarify and illustrate for your students when, how, and why to use direct, indirect, and block quotations to support their description or explanation.

To have students explain how an author uses reasons and evidence to support particular points in a text:

- Introduce them to a wide range of sources of evidence, including examples, statistics, expert opinions, interviews, surveys, observations, experiments, primary source documents, and quotations. Have available a wide assortment of books and resources for students to investigate independently.
- Establish with students—or apply from another source—specific criteria for selecting evidence, demonstrating how to assess the degree to which all evidence is valid, reliable, relevant, and sufficient.
- Show students how to find and use evidence in different forms—graphs, images, charts, tables, even videos—then integrate and comment upon it to support their claims.

To have students use evidence to support particular points in a text:

- Display (on a projection screen and/or a handout) contrasting examples of evidence used to support a writer's ideas, ensuring a continuum of quality; have students evaluate, rank, and discuss.
- Together, analyze representative examples of how writers on the opinion page of major newspapers use evidence to support their analysis.

To help your English language learners, try this:

- Allow students access to graphic organizers to use with both written words and/or pictures to aid them in producing description and explanations.

 For graphic organizer templates, see online resources at **resources.corwin.com/literacycompanion3-5**.

Standard: _____

Preparing the Classroom

Preparing the Mindset

Preparing the Texts to Use

Preparing to Differentiate

Connections to Other Standards:

Academic Vocabulary: Key Words and Phrases

Analysis: To break down a subject, text, event, or process into its component parts to understand what it means or how it works.

Delineate and evaluate the reasoning: Separating out the different reasons and associated evidence behind any claims; to evaluate each claim apart from the others so you can determine, when writing about others' ideas, just how sound they are.

Draw evidence: The word *draw* here means to extract, as in draw water from a well; thus one draws out from all that they read, view, hear, or see about a subject the evidence that best supports their claims.

Evidence: Comes in a variety of forms: quantitative data, observation, quotation, example, and findings from surveys and such queries. The reasoning behind arguments must be based on sound premises; the connection between the claim and evidence used to support that claim should match up, agree; otherwise, you offer fallacies such as the hasty generalization.

Evidence is relevant and sufficient: The data or examples you draw from the sources must be appropriate and useful for the claim you are making; it must also be adequate (e.g., high quality, complete, thorough) if it is to be effective, reliable, and credible.

Literary and informational texts: Literary: fiction, drama, poetry, literary nonfiction, art, graphic novels; informational: essays, articles, infographics, mixed-media texts; primary source documents: seminal and foundational documents.

Literary nonfiction (creative nonfiction): Essays, books, or other nonfiction texts such as biographies, memoirs, histories, or narrative accounts of events that use literary or novelistic techniques such as plot, characterization, and point of view in ways that bring the story, its events, and characters alive.

Reasoning: The logic behind why you think something; it should be based on some credible logic if the reasoning is to be considered sound.

Support analysis, reflection, and research: In short, this concerns providing evidence or examples to support and illustrate whatever analysis you offer, statement you make while reflecting, or a finding you make from your research. The key habit of mind for this standard is to support what you say with sound and relevant evidence.

Notes

Planning to Teach

Standard: _____

Whole Class

_____
_____
_____
_____
_____
_____
_____
_____

Small Group

_____
_____
_____
_____
_____
_____
_____
_____

Individual Practice/Conferring

_____
_____
_____
_____
_____
_____
_____
_____

Writing 10: Write routinely over extended time frames (time for research, reflection, and revision) and shorter time frames (a single sitting or a day or two) for a range of tasks, purposes, and audiences.

English Language Arts

3 Write routinely over extended time frames (time for research, reflection, and revision) and shorter time frames (a single sitting or a day or two) for a range of discipline-specific tasks, purposes, and audiences.

4 Write routinely over extended time frames (time for research, reflection, and revision) and shorter time frames (a single sitting or a day or two) for a range of discipline-specific tasks, purposes, and audiences.

5 Write routinely over extended time frames (time for research, reflection, and revision) and shorter time frames (a single sitting or a day or two) for a range of discipline-specific tasks, purposes, and audiences.

What the **Student** Does

English Language Arts

3 **Gist:** Students write regularly for a range of reasons (e.g., to reflect, research, and revise) in different contexts and modes (times, in-class, and extended tasks), for a variety of audiences.

They consider:

- Am I writing to entertain, to persuade, to inform, or to connect with others?
- What is the subject, purpose, occasion, and audience for my writing?
- What questions should I ask or techniques should I use when writing this type of text or about this topic?
- What conventions or other ideas should I keep in mind when writing this sort of discipline-specific task?

4 **Gist:** Students write regularly for a range of reasons (e.g., to reflect, research, and revise) in different contexts and modes (times, in-class, and extended tasks), for a variety of audiences.

They consider:

- Am I writing to entertain, to persuade, to inform, or to connect with others?
- What is the subject, purpose, occasion, and audience for my writing?
- What questions should I ask or techniques should I use when writing this type of text or about this topic?
- What conventions or other ideas should I keep in mind when writing this sort of discipline-specific task?

5 **Gist:** Students write regularly for a range of reasons (e.g., to reflect, research, and revise) in different contexts and modes (times, in-class, and extended tasks), for a variety of audiences.

They consider:

- Am I writing to entertain, to persuade, to inform, or to connect with others?
- What is the subject, purpose, occasion, and audience for my writing?
- What questions should I ask or techniques should I use when writing this type of text or about this topic?
- What conventions or other ideas should I keep in mind when writing this sort of discipline-specific task?

What the **Teacher** Does

To help students write routinely over extended time frames:

- Model how writing serves a function and keep it meaningful for students. Allowing a degree of choice and ownership to students makes writing more meaningful and brings "buy-in" from students.
- Provide students multiple ways to organize and keep their writing. This could include writer's notebooks or journals, reading response journals or logs, writing folders, and so on.
- Provide explicit feedback on student writing. This could be in the form of one-on-one conferences, rubrics, or written feedback. Teach the writer, not the writing, and keep in mind that words have power—both positive and negative. Feedback should be framed in a positive manner.
- Allow for time to talk and discuss writing. This could be whole group, small group, or peer conferences.
- Model and explicitly teach the writing process. Provide students with regular writing periods, steadily increasing the amount of time spent writing and their stamina for writing.
- Allow for ample opportunities for writing across the day and across content areas.
- Provide regular opportunities for your students to research and then write about the big ideas, questions, and problems that are central to your class and subject area; such investigations might be major research papers or shorter inquiries into a specific topic related to a unit, book, or subject they are studying in class.
- Ask students to reflect on what they learn from a process or experience, how they learn it, and why it matters; or have them reflect on their evolving understanding of ideas, drawing examples and connections from the different units or texts they have studied over the semester.
- Make room in the composing process for time to revise, thereby fostering a culture of revision, a class where students feel they can try out ideas and approaches, knowing they can make changes.

To have students write routinely over shorter time frames:

- Have students write for a single sitting; such writing includes beginning the period by analyzing a text or writing about a topic the class will examine during that period; pausing during class to write about or respond to a text, topic, or procedure the class has been studying for the period up to that point; or wrapping up the period by having students write a summary, synthesis, or response to what they have learned about a topic that day.
- Provide students with a mentor text—this could be a picture book, a short story, or short piece of text—and have students connect to the piece, expressing either what they *notice* the author doing or how they connect to the topic. These are short bursts of writing or quick-writes that provide students with practice.
- Create opportunities to write as a way of building on what they read, viewed, or learned that day in class.
- Allow writing opportunities to extend over several days, each day, for example, culminating in a paragraph of a larger paper the students write over the course of the week, then spend the following week revising.

To have students write for various discipline-specific tasks:

- Create opportunities for students to produce those forms of writing common to the content areas. For example, in science experiment write-ups, in social studies, explanatory pieces or speeches, in art class reviews, and so on.
- Incorporate the sort of writing practiced by people in a discipline as a way of thinking-within-the-discipline; examples would include having students keep field notes like Lewis and Clark; lab notes such as all scientists use to record their thoughts and procedures; jots, scribbles, and sketches by everyone from writers and scientists to designers and programmers.

To have students write for various purposes:

- Require students to write regularly to argue, inform/explain, inspire and entertain; to deepen and extend their own learning; to reflect on their own processes or progress; and to make connections across texts or ideas the class has studied lately.
- Have students write in response to reading.
- Allow students to publish their writing for a variety of audiences.

To help your English language learners, try this:

- Reinforce lessons and techniques from your class by giving all students—but especially your English language learner students—the chance to keep practicing the different types of writing you teach them so the forms and features of these different types can become familiar and these students become fluent, confident academic writers.

 For graphic organizer templates, see online resources at **resources.corwin.com/literacycompanion3-5**.

Preparing to Teach

Standard: _____

Preparing the Classroom

Preparing the Mindset

Preparing the Texts to Use

Preparing to Differentiate

Connections to Other Standards:

Academic Vocabulary: Key Words and Phrases

Audiences: The intended readers of a particular piece of writing. Students need to write for more than just their teachers; other audiences include classmates, other classes, parents, local businesses and organizations, as well as audiences found online through blogs, wikis, social media, and other venues appropriate to students.

Discipline-specific tasks, purposes, and audiences: Each subject area has its own traditional forms as well as types of writing specific to the academic work of those subjects (e.g., essays, summaries, analyses, and more). The emphasis here is on the idea that not all writing in all disciplines is written in the same way for the same reasons. The word *tasks* alludes not only the types of writing but also the ways of thinking when one writes; these are best understood through the verbs such as *summarize, synthesize, analyze, narrate, compare, contrast, evaluate, describe,* and so on.

Extended time frames: These are process papers or otherwise long-term assignments that might take anywhere from one week to more than a month. For example, students may write major research projects over such an extended period that draw from a wide array of sources, some of which might be book length and thus require such longer periods of time. The reference to "research, reflection, and revision" suggests that students should have time to research a topic, reflect on their process, and revise their work, all of which demand substantial time and instruction.

Purposes: These are the reasons a writer writes and include: to inform, explain, persuade, entertain, and inspire.

Range of tasks, purposes, and audiences: See the "Discipline-specific" entry earlier.

Reflection: When writers reflect on events and experiences, they often go beyond revisiting details of what happened but consider what something meant; what they understood then versus now; how things have changed and how they have changed.

Research: Investigating a subject in depth from a range of perspectives using different media. May be initiated by a question one seeks to answer or a problem one aspires to solve.

Revision: Changes made to a piece of writing not so much for correction of spelling, usage, or grammatical errors, but to improve the content and ideas, which may evolve as the student learns more through additional research and reflection.

Routinely: Literally to write as part of a routine in the class, for many reasons, not all of which are graded or even collected; writing is a dominant mode of the class as a performance in itself and as a means of preparing to write about a text or topic.

Shorter time frames: This refers to work that might begin in class, finish for homework, then get collected the next day; or it might be timed, in-class assignments used to assess or extend learning. It is not the same as in-class writing; writing of this sort can also be done at home.

Single sitting or a day or two: Writing that takes place in class, possibly, but not necessarily under timed conditions.

Tasks: The things students are asked to write or do when they write; examples might include asking students to read and summarize a text, or asking students to read a collection of texts about a topic, then draw conclusions about what the authors say about it; or they might be directed to contrast these competing views on the subject, then construct an argument that cites evidence from those texts.

Notes

Standard: _____

Whole Class

_____
_____
_____
_____
_____
_____
_____
_____

Small Group

_____
_____
_____
_____
_____
_____
_____
_____

Individual Practice/Conferring

_____
_____
_____
_____
_____
_____
_____

The Common Core
State Standards

Speaking and Listening

College and Career Readiness Anchor Standards for

Speaking and Listening K–12

Source: Common Core State Standards

The 3–5 Speaking and Listening Standards outlined on the following pages define what students should understand and be able to do by the end of each grade. Here on this page we present the College and Career Readiness (CCR) anchor standards for K–12 so you can see how students in grades 3–5 work toward the same goals as a high school senior: it's a universal, K–12 vision. The CCR anchor standards and the grade-specific standards correspond to one another by numbers 1–10. They are necessary complements: the former providing broad standards, the latter providing additional specificity. Together, they define the skills and understandings that all students must eventually demonstrate.

Comprehension and Collaboration

1. Prepare for and participate effectively in a range of conversations and collaborations with diverse partners, building on others' ideas and expressing their own clearly and persuasively.

2. Integrate and evaluate information presented in diverse media and formats, including visually, quantitatively, and orally.

3. Evaluate a speaker's point of view, reasoning, and use of evidence and rhetoric.

Presentation of Knowledge and Ideas

4. Present information, findings, and supporting evidence such that listeners can follow the line of reasoning and the organization, development, and style are appropriate to task, purpose, and audience.

5. Make strategic use of digital media and visual displays of data to express information and enhance understanding of presentations.

6. Adapt speech to a variety of contexts and communicative tasks, demonstrating command of formal English when indicated or appropriate.

Note on Range and Content of Student Speaking and Listening

To become college and career ready, students must have ample opportunities to take part in a variety of rich, structured conversations—as part of a whole class, in small groups, and with a partner—built around important content in various domains. They must be able to contribute appropriately to these conversations, to make comparisons and contrasts, and to analyze and synthesize a multitude of ideas in accordance with the standards of evidence appropriate to a particular discipline. Whatever their intended major or profession, high school graduates will depend heavily on their ability to listen attentively to others so that they are able to build on others' meritorious ideas while expressing their own clearly and persuasively. New technologies have broadened and expanded the role that speaking and listening play in acquiring and sharing knowledge and have tightened their link to other forms of communication. The Internet has accelerated the speed at which connections between speaking, listening, reading, and writing can be made, requiring that students be ready to use these modalities nearly simultaneously. Technology itself is changing quickly, creating a new urgency for students to be adaptable in response to change.

College and Career Readiness Anchor Standards for

Speaking and Listening K–12

The College and Career Readiness (CCR) anchor standards are the same for K–12. The guiding principle here is that the core reading skills should not change as students advance; rather, the level at which they learn and can perform these skills should increase in complexity as students move from one grade to the next. However, for grades 3–5, we have to recognize that the standards were back mapped from the secondary grades—the authors envisioned what college students needed and then wrote standards, working their way down the grades. Thus, as you use this book remember that children in grades 3–5 can't just "jump over" developmental milestones in an ambitious attempt toward an anchor standard. There are certain life and learning experiences they need to have, and certain concepts they need to learn, before they are capable of handling many complex academic skills in a meaningful way. The anchor standards nonetheless are goal posts to work toward. As you read the "gist" of the standards on the following pages, remember they represent what our grades 3–5 students will *grow into* during each year and deepen later in middle school and high school.

Comprehension and Collaboration

Discussion in one form or another is a vital, integral part of learning and classroom culture. To ensure students contribute substance, they are expected to read, write, or investigate as directed so they come to class ready to engage in the discussion of that topic or text with peers or the whole class. During these discussions, they learn to acknowledge and respond to others' ideas and incorporate those ideas, as well as others they discover through their own research, as evidence to support their conclusions or claims. Details and evidence in various forms and from different sources is first evaluated, then selected as needed by the student to use in their presentations. When listening to others speak, students learn to listen for key details and qualities in order to evaluate the perspective, logic, evidence, and use of rhetoric in their presentation or speech.

Presentation of Knowledge and Ideas

When giving a presentation, students carefully select which details and evidence to use when supporting their ideas or findings, organizing this information in a clear, concise manner that ensures the audience understands. To that end, students focus on how to best organize and develop their ideas and supporting evidence according to their purpose, audience, occasion, and appointed task. When appropriate, they use digital media to enhance, amplify, or otherwise improve their presentation, adapting their language and delivery as needed to the different contexts, tasks, or audiences.

Source: Adapted from Burke, J. (2013). *The Common Core Companion: The Standards Decoded, Grades 6–8: What They Say, What They Mean, How to Teach Them.* Thousand Oaks, CA: Corwin.

Speaking and Listening 1: Prepare for and participate effectively in a range of conversations and collaborations with diverse partners, building on others' ideas and expressing their own clearly and persuasively.

English Language Arts

3 Engage effectively in a range of collaborative discussions (one-on-one, in groups, and teacher-led) with diverse partners on *grade 3 topics and texts*, building on others' ideas and expressing their own clearly.
    a. Come to discussions prepared, having read or studied required material; explicitly draw on that preparation and other information known about the topic to explore ideas under discussion.
    b. Follow agreed-upon rules for discussions (e.g., gaining the floor in respectful ways, listening to others with care, speaking one at a time about the topics and texts under discussion).
    c. Ask questions to check understanding of information presented, stay on topic, and link their comments to the remarks of others.
    d. Explain their own ideas and understanding in light of the discussion.

4 Engage effectively in a range of collaborative discussions (one-on-one, in groups, and teacher-led) with diverse partners on *grade 4 topics and texts*, building on others' ideas and expressing their own clearly.
    a. Come to discussions prepared, having read or studied required material; explicitly draw on that preparation and other information known about the topic to explore ideas under discussion.
    b. Follow agreed-upon rules for discussions and carry out assigned roles.
    c. **Pose and respond to specific questions to clarify or follow up on information, and make comments that contribute to the discussion** and link to the remarks of others.
    d. **Review the key ideas expressed** and explain their own ideas and understanding in light of the discussion.

5 Engage effectively in a range of collaborative discussions (one-on-one, in groups, and teacher-led) with diverse partners on *grade 5 topics and texts*, building on others' ideas and expressing their own clearly.
    a. Come to discussions prepared, having read or studied required material; explicitly draw on that preparation and other information known about the topic to explore ideas under discussion.
    b. Follow agreed-upon rules for discussions and carry out assigned roles.
    c. Pose and respond to specific questions **by making comments that contribute to the discussion and elaborate** on the remarks of others.
    d. Review the key ideas expressed **and draw conclusions in light of information and knowledge gained from the discussions.**

What the **Student** Does

English Language Arts

3 **Gist:** Students participate in different discussions (pairs, groups, full class) with a range of peers about grade 3 topics and texts, adding to others' ideas while contributing their own. Arriving at these discussions prepared to discuss what they read or studied, students draw from what they learned, citing evidence in those texts or from their background knowledge during the discussion. As they participate and collaborate, students follow all guidelines for such academic discussions and their role in them. Also, when discussing or collaborating with others, students ask and answer questions and stick to the topic. Finally, students explain their ideas and show how they understand the topic after having discussed it.

They consider:

- What is the topic or text being discussed and what questions can I contribute?
- How can I prepare so that I will be ready to discuss this text or topic?
- What are the rules for this discussion or collaboration?
- What do I want to share in the discussion?
- Did I stay on topic?
- After the discussion, can I share what I learned from the members of the group?

4 **Gist:** Students participate in different discussions (pairs, groups, full class) with a range of peers about grade 4 topics and texts, adding to others' ideas while contributing their own. Arriving at these discussions prepared to discuss what they read or studied, students draw from what they learned, citing evidence in those texts or from their background knowledge during the discussion. As they participate and collaborate, students follow all guidelines for such academic discussions and their role in them, offering comments and contributions that link to the remarks of others. Also, when discussing or collaborating with others, students ask and answer questions to clarify or follow up on information already presented. Finally, students explain their ideas and understanding of the topic after having discussed it and reviewing key ideas.

They consider:

- What is the topic or text being discussed and what questions can I contribute?
- How can I prepare to discuss this text or topic?
- What are the rules for this discussion or collaboration?
- What questions do I want to ask in the discussion?
- Am I prepared to answer other's questions?
- After the discussion, what key ideas did I learn and how did my understanding of the topic deepen?

5 **Gist:** Students participate in different discussions (pairs, groups, full class) with a range of peers about grade 4 topics and texts, adding to others' ideas while contributing their own. Arriving at these discussions prepared to discuss what they read or studied, students draw from what they learned, citing evidence in those texts or from their background knowledge during the discussion. As they participate and collaborate, students follow all guidelines for such academic discussions and their role in them. Also, when discussing or collaborating with others, students ask and answer questions, elaborating in some detail about how their remarks relate to the topic or text the class is studying. Finally, students draw conclusions after having gained knowledge from the discussion and reviewing key ideas.

They consider:

- What is the topic or text being discussed and what questions can I contribute?
- How can I prepare to discuss this text or topic?
- What are the rules for this discussion or collaboration?
- During the discussion did I contribute by adding comments or elaborating on other's remarks?
- After the discussion, what key ideas did I learn and how did my understanding deepen?

What the **Teacher** Does

To prepare and help students to participate in conversations:

- Teach explicitly what it means to be a good listener—co-construct a norm chart for the class. Then discuss what leads to great conversations and create norms for students to follow when having discussions.
- Create a norm chart for what constitutes "Great Talking." Post this for students to refer to, revisit, or add new thinking.
- Model for students using books read aloud or shared texts how to hold thinking by marking text to prepare for discussions. This may mean asking questions, making predictions, noticing important information, and so on. Use sticky notes, annotations, graphic organizers, and so on. It is important for students to understand what they are doing prior to their trying it independently.
- Co-construct with students using a shared text. Model your thinking and have students also hold their thinking on sticky notes, annotations, book marks, or graphic organizers. Provide opportunities for students to "turn and talk" to share their thinking.
- Give students a short piece of text to read and prepare for a conversation, then have them share with partners.
- Model for students how to participate in the specific conversation for which you want to prepare them; for example, to discuss or respond to classmates' writing.
- Have students view a group involved in discussion. When you see a group that exemplifies strong participation, invite the rest of the class to "fishbowl." They observe what the group is doing by sitting or standing around them and watching. Observers should not talk until *after* the group is done. Then the teacher can facilitate reflections and observations, making it explicit what was working *well*.
- Provide students with sentence templates that provide them with the language needed to enter the discussion (e.g., I agree with what Maria said about _____, but disagree that _____) or generate with them the sorts of questions they should ask when discussing a particular text or topic. Or post these on a class chart for easy reference.
- Review the conventions, rules, roles, or responsibilities that apply to a specialized discussion strategy (e.g., literature circles, book clubs, Socratic dialogue).
- Track participation by keeping a record of the exchange using visual codes that indicate who initiates, responds, or extends; use this to assess and provide feedback for students.
- After discussions, have students reflect on their participation, explaining how and what they contributed.
- Provide rubrics to complete after discussions.

To participate in a range of collaborations with diverse partners:

- Create the culture of respect for other views and ideas within the class that is necessary for students to collaborate with others.
- Investigate alternative venues such as video conferencing or chat for such collaboration with classmates, community members, or people from other countries.
- Use various strategies that require students work with different people in various contexts to solve problems, develop ideas, or improve each other's work.
- Provide numerous opportunities for students to talk and share their thinking in class.

To build on others' ideas and effectively express their own:

- Try, when establishing norms for class discussion early on, requiring students first to respond to other students' comments before they can offer a new one of their own.
- Model for students what this looks and sounds like when talking to students in whole group, small group, and individual conferences.

To pose questions that elicit elaboration and connect others' ideas:

- Introduce the idea of "follow-up" or "clarification" questions. Teach students ways to respond to other people's ideas or to ways to include others' ideas in their follow-up questions, providing models that show these kinds of questions; explain how, when, and why to use them in small or full class discussions.
- List out on the board or screen a list of ideas or comments made by different students during the discussion of a topic. What are the key connections? Emphasize the importance of listening for these key connections; have students practice generating questions that show that they listened and heard the "idea behind the ideas"—the real heart of the conversation about a text or topic.
- Model for students this strategy. When students share their thinking, follow up by saying, "Can you tell me more?" "Why are you thinking that?" or "How did you figure that out?"

To help your English language learners, try this:

- Have the full class first write about a text or topic they will subsequently discuss together or in small groups; allow students to read what they wrote if they are not comfortable speaking extemporaneously in class or small groups.

 For graphic organizer templates, see online resources at **resources.corwin.com/literacycompanion3-5**.

Standard: _____

Preparing the Classroom

Preparing the Mindset

Preparing the Texts to Use

Preparing to Differentiate

Connections to Other Standards:

Academic Vocabulary: Key Words and Phrases

Collaborative discussions: This refers to discussing ideas and working jointly with others to create new thinking. Students take the remarks of others and add details or further develop the thoughts.

Diverse partners [and perspectives]: People and ideas from different backgrounds, cultures, and perspectives than the students' own; the idea is one must know and be able to converse with all people.

Draw conclusions: Using the key ideas and evidence and also the implied or inferred meaning, students synthesize the information into some sort of conclusion or "wrap-up" of the discussion.

Elaborate on the remarks of others: To take the remarks of others on a given topic or thought and to add details or to further develop that thought.

Explicitly draw on that preparation: Make use of the notes, ideas, any materials the student prepared specifically for the discussion; this shows how thoroughly the student prepared and how well they anticipated the demands and directions of the discussion.

Expressing: Students articulate and convey their own ideas instead of merely parroting back classmates' or the author's.

Pose questions: To "pose" is to ask; students ask each other—or the teacher—questions about the text, task, or topic during a discussion.

Questions that elicit elaboration and respond to others' ideas: During a legitimate, healthy conversation, all are responsible for including other views and making all in the group feel involved; sometimes a member is reluctant to join in, at which point the group or an appointed discussion leader should pose questions that help such people to join in and share or otherwise expand on their ideas.

Notes

Planning to Teach

Standard: _____

Whole Class

_____

Small Group

_____

Individual Practice/Conferring

_____

Speaking and Listening 2: Integrate and evaluate information presented in diverse media and formats, including visually, quantitatively, and orally.

English Language Arts

3 Determine the main ideas and supporting details of a text read aloud or information presented in diverse media and formats, including visually, quantitatively, and orally.

4 **Paraphrase portions** of a text read aloud or information presented in diverse media and formats, including visually, quantitatively, and orally.

5 **Summarize a written text** read aloud or information presented in diverse media and formats, including visually, quantitatively, and orally.

What the **Student** Does

English Language Arts

3 **Gist:** Students determine the main ideas and the key details in all information delivered in different media and formats (e.g., visual, oral, and quantitative) and in texts read aloud.

They consider:

- What is the topic?
- What is it mostly about?
- What is the author saying?
- What is the main idea?
- What facts go along with the main idea?

4 **Gist:** Students paraphrase all information delivered in different media and formats (e.g., visual, oral, and quantitative) and in portions of texts read aloud.

They consider:

- What is this text or discussion mostly about?
- What do I know about the topic that can help me identify the main idea?
- What details are important to include if I were helping a friend learn about this information?
- How can I restate the information in my own words?

5 **Gist:** Students summarize all information delivered in different media and formats (e.g., visual, oral, and quantitative) and in a written text read aloud.

They consider:

- What is this text mostly about?
- What is the author's message?
- How would I state the topic if I were telling a friend about it?
- What ideas and details would I want to share?
- How can I give a brief statement of the main points using my own words?

What the **Teacher** Does

To have students determine the main ideas and supporting details of a text read aloud or in information presented in diverse formats and media:

- Model for students by thinking aloud as you view, listen to, or read a text; this means pausing the video, audio, or reading to indicate to students what you notice at that point—a term, some feature, a phrase—labeling these details and how it helps to determine the main idea.
- Provide students with a graphic organizer that asks them to identify the main idea and explain why they think that is the main idea; then sort those supporting ideas into appropriate categories relative to the main ideas.
- Annotate some portion of a text to show that a text can have more than one main idea and supporting details. Use different color highlighters—one for the main idea and another for details that support it.
- Provide students with shared copies of texts to highlight and annotate main ideas and details.
- After reading a shared text, instruct students to write a brief paragraph explaining the main idea and the details that support it. Share this with a partner to see if there is agreement; if there is not, discuss why.

To have students paraphrase portions of a text read aloud or information presented in diverse formats and media:

- Begin by explicitly teaching what it means to paraphrase, then model paraphrasing for students by restating using different words. Emphasize that paraphrasing often is about putting something into your own words, and it's okay if it becomes less formal, and briefer, than the text. Give a short speech to students, show a short video, or play a short audio and have students work with a partner to paraphrase what they listened to or watched. Practice this often with diverse formats and media so that students are comfortable paraphrasing different formats.

- Provide graphic organizers for students to record main ideas and details and then have them work with a partner, paraphrasing the information on a given topic, book, and so on.
- Read aloud to students and at the end of each paragraph (or section or chapter, or the end of the class period), have students paraphrase what happened in that portion of the text.

To have students summarize a written text read aloud or information presented in diverse formats and media:

- Model for students how to summarize—either orally or in written form. Explicitly teach that a summary is different from a retelling—a summary includes the most important points. It has a beginning, the important events or ideas, and then a conclusion.
- Read aloud a text and record the main idea and details and then co-construct a written summary with students. Write the summary on chart paper and post for students. You could even write the different sections of the summary in different colors to accent the beginning, middle, and end.
- Using a shared text—with a copy for each student—have them highlight or annotate the main idea and details. Then using their annotations, have them write a summary or work with a partner and tell them their summary.
- Provide graphic organizers for students to record main ideas and details as they listen to or view diverse formats and media. After recording information, instruct students to either write a summary or share a summary with a partner or with a small group.

To help your English language learners, try this:

- Allow students to listen to or watch audio, video, or mixed media texts multiple times. Meet with the student to discuss the important points they notice. Have the student stop the audio or video at appropriate times to explain their thinking.

 For graphic organizer templates, see online resources at **resources.corwin.com/literacycompanion3-5**.

Standard: _____

Preparing the Classroom

Preparing the Mindset

Preparing the Texts to Use

Preparing to Differentiate

Connections to Other Standards:

Academic Vocabulary: Key Words and Phrases

Determine the main ideas and supporting details: Breaking down the different elements to reveal the main ideas and their relationship to the supporting details; this might include examining how structures, grammar, syntax, or more media-based features serve to emphasize the main or supporting ideas in the text you are studying.

Diverse media: All the different forms ideas and information, evidence and data come in, including print, audio, video, photograph, as well as mixed media, such as websites or presentation slides with embedded digital imagery (still photographs, videos, animations) and audio.

Evaluate: To determine the quality, value, use, or importance of data, details, or other forms of information one might include in his or her presentation as evidence to support a position.

Formats: This refers to the ways in which information can be presented—charts, slides, graphics, images, as well as multiple media, all of which allow the speaker to represent ideas more fully and effectively.

Information presented in diverse media and formats: The *content* of presentations and speeches presented in many different modes, including still and video images, colors and shapes, as well as more quantitative techniques such as charts, tables, and graphs.

Integrate: To join the different sources or data into one cohesive body of evidence used to support one's claims.

Paraphrase: A restatement of text or spoken thinking using different words than the original but maintaining the same meaning.

Summarize: Giving a brief statement of the main points.

Visually, quantitatively, orally: Images, video, art, graphics of any other sort intended to convey the ideas the speaker wants to communicate; measureable, numerical, quantifiable data that is displayed or formatted so as to suit the speaker's purpose; spoken, whether in front of a live audience or anonymous listener viewing a slideshow online with a voiceover instead.

Notes

Planning to Teach

Standard: _____

Whole Class

_____
_____
_____
_____
_____
_____
_____
_____

Small Group

_____
_____
_____
_____
_____
_____
_____
_____

Individual Practice/Conferring

_____
_____
_____
_____
_____
_____
_____

Speaking and Listening 3: Evaluate a speaker's point of view, reasoning, and use of evidence and rhetoric.

English Language Arts

3 Ask and answer questions about information from a speaker, offering appropriate elaboration and detail.

4 Identify the reasons and evidence a speaker provides to support particular points.

5 Summarize the points a speaker makes and explain how each claim is supported by reasons and evidence.

What the **Student** Does

English Language Arts

3 **Gist:** After listening to a speaker, students raise questions in order to generate recall of information presented by the speaker.

They consider:

- What was this speaker's main message?
- What was the topic?
- What questions do I have after listening to the speaker?
- Can I answer questions about the information presented using details from the speaker?

4 **Gist:** After listening to a speaker, students report back the reasons and evidence that the speaker used to support specific points.

They consider:

- What was the topic?
- What particular points was the speaker making?
- What reasons or evidence did the speaker provide to explain those points?
- Can I share with others the important reasons and evidence the speaker provided?

5 **Gist:** After listening to a speaker, students determine the main points or claims and how they are supported by reasons and evidence. Students summarize the information.

They consider:

- What are the main claims of the speaker?
- What are the reasons and evidence to support these claims?
- How can I summarize these points?

What the **Teacher** Does

To have students ask and answer questions about information from a speaker, offering appropriate elaboration and detail:

- Have students pose questions after listening to a speaker. Model first by answering student questions to show you would answer the question simply and then model answering a second time using elaboration and description.
- Practice asking questions prior to listening to a speaker. Have students work with partners. Pose a question and have one student give a simple answer and then have the partner continue to answer the question by adding details and elaboration.
- Listen to a speaker via technology. Have students record questions as they listen and then share their questions in small groups, allowing other students to answer and to continue to elaborate.
- Provide graphic organizers to students to fill out with questions when listening to a speaker.

To have students identify the reasons and evidence a speaker provides to support particular points:

- Listen to a prerecorded speech. Stop the speech at key points and model how or why you know that is a key point the speaker is attempting to make. Record these key points on chart paper or some other manner for all students to see. Under that point add reasons and evidence from the speech—continuing to stop the speech and discuss main ideas and details.

- Create a graphic organizer with spaces for students to fill in the particular points a speaker is trying to make, leaving space to add reasons and details that support it.
- Give students a printed copy of the speaker's text if possible. Have them highlight in one color the particular points made and then with another color highlight the reasons and evidence.

To have students summarize the points a speaker makes and explain how each claim is supported by reasons and evidence:

- Model for students how to write a summary by co-constructing a summary with the class after listening to a speech. Begin with a topic sentence that introduces the speech and the main points the speaker was making. In the following sentences, delineate the points and the evidence and then conclude the summary, restating the key points.
- Use graphic organizers where students have recorded particular points, reasons, and evidence. Have them write summaries based on the information they recorded.

To help your English language learners, try this:

- Use a speech that students can read (in print), hear (in audio), and watch (as a video). Use these versions in stages to help students ask and answer questions and determine the points the speaker was making.

 For graphic organizer templates, see online resources at **resources.corwin.com/literacycompanion3-5.**

Notes

Preparing to Teach

Standard: _____

Preparing the Classroom

Preparing the Mindset

Preparing the Texts to Use

Preparing to Differentiate

Connections to Other Standards:

Academic Vocabulary: Key Words and Phrases

Evaluate: In this instance, evaluate means to judge the credibility of a speaker and/or the information he or she presents.

Evidence: What data, details, quotations, or examples the speaker uses in the presentation or speech and how credible, accurate, and valid they are.

Point of view: In this instance, point of view is the position a speaker takes in relation to the subject. A speaker may be representing his or her own point of view or that of another person. Either way, the audience needs to consider the speaker's point of view, as it may reveal a bias about the subject and undermine the credibility of the information being presented.

Reasoning: The logic of the speaker as it relates to his or her ideas; refers to how well and to what end the speaker's ideas and the reasoning behind them connect with and complement each other to improve the coherence of the speech.

Rhetoric: The speaker's use of any devices, techniques, or strategies to persuade or otherwise influence how the listener or audience thinks, acts, or feels about the topic being addressed.

Summarize the points: Giving a brief statement of the main points.

Notes

Planning to Teach

Standard: _____

Whole Class

_____
_____
_____
_____
_____
_____
_____

Small Group

_____
_____
_____
_____
_____
_____
_____

Individual Practice/Conferring

_____
_____
_____
_____
_____
_____
_____

Speaking and Listening 4: Present information, findings, and supporting evidence so listeners can follow the line of reasoning and the organization, development, and style are appropriate to task, purpose, and audience.

English Language Arts

3 Report on a topic or text, tell a story, or recount an experience with appropriate facts and relevant, descriptive details, speaking clearly at an understandable pace.

4 Report on a topic or text, tell a story, or recount an experience **in an organized manner**, using appropriate facts and relevant, descriptive details to **support main ideas or themes;** speak clearly at an understandable pace.

5 Report on a topic or **text or present an opinion, sequencing ideas logically** and using appropriate facts and relevant, descriptive details to support main ideas or themes; speak clearly at an understandable pace.

What the **Student** Does

English Language Arts

3 **Gist:** Students report, tell a story, or recount an experience using appropriate facts and details with description.

They consider:

- What is my topic or what am I speaking about?
- If I'm telling a story, do I have a beginning, middle, and end?
- What facts and details do I want to include?
- Can I add to these details and make them descriptive?

4 **Gist:** Students use organization to report on a topic or text or tell a story or recount an experience, including appropriate facts and descriptive, relevant details that support the main ideas or themes, while also speaking clearly at a pace that is understandable for the audience.

They consider:

- What is my topic or what am I speaking about?
- What are the main ideas or themes I want to share?
- What are the details I should include? Are they detailed?
- How can I get feedback on the pace of my speaking?

5 **Gist:** Students present an opinion or report on a topic or text in a sequential manner, including appropriate facts and descriptive, relevant details supporting main ideas and themes, while speaking clearly at a pace that is understandable for the audience.

They consider:

- What is my topic or what am I speaking about?
- What main ideas or themes do I want to share?
- What details should I include? Are they detailed?
- How can I get feedback on the pace of my speaking?

What the **Teacher** Does

To present information and findings so that listeners can follow:

- Identify for students the key elements that they should include in the speech they will give.
- Give students a tool, such as a storyboard organizer or a graphic organizer that they can use to plan; they should use this tool, however, only after they have generated many possible ideas about what they might say about their findings or this topic.
- Introduce students to organizing patterns such as cause/effect, compare/contrast, problem/solution, chronological, and narrative; see Common Core Speaking and Listening Standard 5 for more detail about using graphic formats, including tables, charts, and graphs.

To have students report on a topic or text, tell a story, or recount an experience in an organized manner using appropriate facts and relevant, descriptive details to support main ideas or themes:

- Assign a topic about which students are already familiar. Have them choose the main ideas or themes that they would share. Students record these main ideas on graphic organizers, two column notes, or note cards.
- Share audio/video of famous speeches (and not so famous ones) that you know will resonate with your students. Select from TED Talks, YouTube, history websites, and other online resources. Ask students: What makes them compelling?
- Have students elaborate each main idea of their speech by adding facts or descriptive details. Students could record these on sticky notes and attach to note cards, or they could continue to fill in graphic organizers.
- Organize the main ideas in a sequential manner by arranging the note cards or numbering the main ideas to show the order in which they should be presented.
- Have students use this process, organizing the notes into speech form, independently when preparing to orally report, tell, or recount.
- Ask students to analyze their own speech in light of organization and development explaining why they organize their content as they do and why they think it is the most effective approach for their speech.
- Give students a printed text of a speech they can annotate and view in class, as well; after guiding students through an analysis of the speaker's organization, and once they show an acceptable mastery of the ideas, have them conduct a similar analysis of their own speech.

To have students present an opinion, sequencing ideas logically and using appropriate facts and relevant, descriptive details to support main ideas or themes:

- Practice sharing opinions about certain topics, so that students understand what an opinion is. Then share why they feel that way.
- Co-construct a script for presenting an opinion and the details that support it with the class. Then model an actual presentation. Have students add or change this script and then practice presenting with a partner or a small group.
- Model for students how to choose an opinion and then decide the strongest main points and ideas. Write these on note cards and display under a document camera. Under each note card (or heading on the tablet), record facts and details and discuss *why* you would include them and *how* they help the listener understand your point. Invite students to evaluate if the facts are elaborated enough.
- Model a speech that is not in sequential order. Show the written text of the speech on an interactive whiteboard and have students reorder the sections so that they are sequential.
- Use the note cards; rearrange them to try out different sequences (or arrange headings on tablet to sequence ideas). Ask for feedback from students on which order makes the most sense.
- Share your speech so that students can observe the entire process—from organization to presentation.

To have students speak clearly at an understandable pace:

- Have students practice with partners, giving feedback as they share.
- Record or video students practicing speeches and let them listen to their pacing.

To help your English language learners, try this:

- Meet with students in each stage of the process to help them plan and practice a speech. Provide sentence starters to help them build a speech; for example, "My topic is _____. An important idea about this is _____ because of _____ and _____. Another important point is _____ . . . ," and so on. Build on these starters depending on the student's fluency and ability to articulate in English.

 For graphic organizer templates, see online resources at **resources.corwin.com/literacycompanion3-5**.

Preparing to Teach

Standard: _____

Preparing the Classroom

_____
_____
_____
_____
_____
_____

Preparing the Mindset

_____
_____
_____
_____
_____
_____

Preparing the Texts to Use

_____
_____
_____
_____
_____
_____

Preparing to Differentiate

_____
_____
_____
_____
_____
_____

Connections to Other Standards:

_____
_____
_____

Academic Vocabulary: Key Words and Phrases

Appropriate to the task, purpose, and audience: How one organizes, develops, or speaks varies depending on the objective, the actual purpose of the presentation, and the audience to whom one is speaking.

Findings: Conclusions drawn from observations, investigations, experiments, or inquiries about questions or problems.

Line of reasoning: The building of an argument wherein the speaker connects one idea to the next in a meaningful and clear way. The listeners can thus grasp why the speaker thinks as she does and how the speaker arrived at a conclusion or argument.

Organization: An appropriate and effective structure. Common organizations in speeches and writing include cause/effect or problem/solution, from least to most important, or from past to present. A clear organizing structure allows listeners to hear and process the ideas presented.

Present: Speaking to an audience with a specific purpose such as to persuade the audience to think or act in a certain way. To achieve this outcome, the presenter often uses evidence from a range of established sources. They may use presentation software such as Keynote or PowerPoint to illustrate points in different media; when simply speaking, the presenter may be standing at a podium telling a story, explaining what a text means, or discussing what they learned from an experience.

Relevant, descriptive details: Students choose details that relate to the topic and provide description.

Supporting evidence: Data, information, quotations, examples, or other information that the speaker uses to back up whatever they are saying or presenting.

Understandable pace: Pace is the speed at which students read or speak. When reading out loud, students should demonstrate a flow or a pace that is pleasing for the listener. It should be understandable—in other words, not so fast that words run together and not so slow that it is labored and the listener can't follow.

Notes

Standard: _____

Whole Class

Small Group

Individual Practice/Conferring

Speaking and Listening 5: Make strategic use of digital media and visual displays of data to express information and enhance understanding of presentations.

English Language Arts

3 Create engaging audio recordings of stories or poems that demonstrate fluid reading at an understandable pace; add visual displays when appropriate to emphasize or enhance certain facts or details.

4 Create engaging audio recordings of stories or poems that demonstrate fluid reading at an understandable pace; add visual displays when appropriate to emphasize or enhance certain facts or details.

5 **Include multimedia components (e.g., graphics, sound) and visual displays in presentations** when appropriate to enhance the development of main ideas or themes.

What the **Student** Does

English Language Arts

3 **Gist:** Students design and deliver an audio recording of stories or poems, adding visual displays to enhance or emphasize facts or details if necessary, while reading at an understandable pace.

They consider:

- Have I practiced reading my story or poem?
- Do I need to add visual displays to make my presentation better? What can I add?
- Am I reading clearly and at a pace that is understandable for the listener?

4 **Gist:** Students design and deliver presentations that include audio recordings and visual displays to enhance development of main ideas and details.

They consider:

- What is the subject and purpose of my presentation?
- What are my main ideas and/or themes?
- What information is most important?
- What do I want to include in the audio recording?
- What type of visual displays can I include to enhance my ideas?

5 **Gist:** Students design and deliver presentations that incorporate multimedia components (e.g., graphics or sound) and visual displays of information (e.g., charts, graphs, or infographics) to enhance the development of main ideas or themes.

They consider:

- What is the subject or purpose of my presentation?
- Which elements or information are most important?
- What are my main ideas or themes?
- What multimedia components (e.g., graphics or sound) are most appropriate to enhance my presentation?
- What ideas will benefit most from the visual display of those details?

What the **Teacher** Does

To have students demonstrate fluid reading at an understandable pace:

- Read out loud often to students from a variety of materials to provide students with a strong model of fluency.
- Confer with students and listen to them read, providing feedback.
- Provide opportunities for students to read aloud in class.
- Bring drama and poetry slams into the classroom so students are exposed to and practicing a variety of oral language.
- Use Reader's Theater scripts for students to practice oral reading and drama.

To have students create engaging audio recordings of stories or poems:

- Have students practice oral reading frequently for fluency, pace, and expression. This can be partner reading, conferring, reading to buddies in a different grade or to volunteers in the classroom.
- Help students choose appropriate stories or poems to record.
- Practice using websites and technology to record on. Vocaroo allows students to record for 30 seconds. On Voki, students can record or write text while creating an animated avatar to share their words.
- Have students listen to their recordings and re-record if necessary. Share their website recordings with larger audiences so that students receive feedback.
- Provide opportunities for students to record their own writing on podcasts to have students make strategic use of digital media and visual displays of data.
- Give students access to a variety of multimedia sites; teach them how to use the sites and navigate through them.
- Create together and require students to follow a set of principles or guidelines for all presentation slides and visual displays (e.g., graphs, charts, infographics, diagrams) they incorporate into their slides; assemble in a presentation of your own a range of samples that model the principles of effective presentation design.

- Provide contrasting examples of different presentation slide designs with the same content to illustrate the effect of different fonts, layouts, colors, and content on presentations.
- Direct students to sites like Prezi, SlideRocket, or Google Presentations for examples and guidelines for effective use and creation of visual displays of information. Do not allow students to incorporate distracting animations, wacky fonts, extended video clips, degraded or otherwise lower grade images, useless sound effects, or any other elements that will detract from an effective presentation of the information; design is an ever-increasing part of effective communication and composition.

To have students enhance the development of main ideas or themes:

- Have students determine their main ideas or themes prior to working with multimedia components or visual displays.
- Emphasize to students the role and uses of story in any presentation, and how they can use different elements—images, numbers, data, their voice, gestures, storytelling itself—to convey their main ideas and themes clearly to the audience.
- Stress the importance of reducing any content that competes with or otherwise distracts from the content or point they are trying to make in their presentation.
- Encourage students to play around with audio recordings and visual explanations (graphs) and visual displays (images, video, diagrams, cartoons) as well as color, font, and composition to convey the relationships between different parts of their subject more clearly and effectively—without adding distraction and confusion through extraneous elements.

To help your English language learners, try this:

- Take time to be sure they know how to use all these digital tools and have access to them to do what you are assigning; if they do not, make time in class for all to work on this assignment.

 For graphic organizer templates, see online resources at **resources.corwin.com/literacycompanion3-5**.

Preparing to Teach

Standard: _____

Preparing the Classroom

_____
_____
_____
_____
_____
_____
_____

Preparing the Mindset

_____
_____
_____
_____
_____
_____
_____

Preparing the Texts to Use

_____
_____
_____
_____
_____
_____
_____

Preparing to Differentiate

_____
_____
_____
_____
_____
_____
_____

Connections to Other Standards:

_____
_____
_____

Academic Vocabulary: Key Words and Phrases

Audio elements: Any recorded content, including music and sound effects, embedded into the presentation such as voice-over or featured content as in an interview (e.g., image of the person interviewed shown while audio interview plays).

Digital media: This includes presentation software applications such as PowerPoint, Keynote, Google Presentations, and Prezi; also, it refers to digital images, screen captures of online material, stand-alone or embedded video, as well as audio and mixed-media formats.

Enhance understanding: Using all available media and methods—images, audio, multimedia, words, and graphs—in ways that make the abstract more concrete, more visual, more comprehensible. Through charts, images, graphs, or video, speakers illustrate the processes, concepts, or procedures they are discussing, using these as tools to clearly convey their message.

Express information: To put forth, to convey or relate data, ideas, details, and content to the audience in the clearest way possible.

Fluid reading at an understandable pace: Oral reading that "flows easily" and is at an understandable speed. Students should demonstrate a flow or a pace that is pleasing for the listener. It should be understandable—in other words, not so fast that words run together and not so slow that it is labored and the listener can't follow.

Multimedia component (e.g., graphics, sound): Media and content that use a combination for different content forms. It can also include the use of computers (or any other forms of technology) to present text, graphics, video, animation, and sound.

Visual displays to clarify information: Tables, charts, graphs, or other infographic used to visually explain or otherwise convey an idea, especially one that is complicated or abstract.

Notes

Standard: _____

Whole Class

Small Group

Individual Practice/Conferring

Speaking and Listening 6: Adapt a speech to a variety of contexts and communication tasks, demonstrating command of formal English when indicated or appropriate.

English Language Arts

3 Speak in complete sentences when appropriate to task and situation in order to provide requested detail or clarification. (See grade 3 Language standards 1 and 3 on page 28 for specific expectations.)

4 **Differentiate between contexts that call for formal English (e.g., presenting ideas) and situations where informal discourse is appropriate (e.g., small-group discussion);** use formal English when appropriate to task and situation. (See **grade 4 Language standards 1** on page 28 for specific expectations.)

5 **Adapt speech to a variety of contexts and tasks,** using formal English when appropriate to task and situation. (See **grade 5 Language standards 1 and 3** on page 28 for specific expectations.)

What the **Student** Does

English Language Arts

3 **Gist:** Students decide what to say and how to say it to provide detail or clarification, using complete sentences.

They consider:

- What is my task? What do I want to say?
- What information do I want to share?
- How do I want to say it?
- Do I have enough details?
- Am I using complete sentences?

4 **Gist:** Students decide what to say and how to say it depending on whether it is a situation such as a speech where formal English is required or an informal situation such as a small-group discussion.

They consider:

- What is the situation or task? What do I want to say?
- How do I want to say it?
- Who is the audience?
- Is this a setting where I can be informal, or just "talk like a kid"? Is formal English required in this situation?

5 **Gist:** Students decide what to say and how to say it, adjusting their voice and style to suit the occasion, purpose, and audiences, while always modeling their command of formal English when it is appropriate.

They consider:

- What is my purpose or task?
- What do I want to say?
- How do I want to say it?
- What is the reason for speaking? Is it a speech or am I talking with a small group, or am I recording myself to share on technology?
- Who is the audience?
- How do I make sure that the way I'm speaking matches my audience?
- Do I need to use formal English for this?

What the **Teacher** Does

To have students speak in complete sentences when appropriate to task and situation in order to provide requested detail or clarification:

- Provide numerous opportunities for students to answer questions orally. Ask them to add to statements or answers they've already provided to present more information and thinking. Remind them to use complete sentences and allow them to restate in complete sentences if the first answer isn't complete.
- After students present a speech, allow other students to ask questions in complete sentences and have the speaker answer in complete sentences.

To have students differentiate between contexts that call for formal English (e.g., presenting ideas) and situations where informal discourse is appropriate:

- Create a two-column chart on large chart paper. Head one column "Formal Situations" and the other "Informal Situations." View a recorded presentation on a whiteboard (or give a formal presentation yourself) and have students record in the "Formal" column formal elements such as speech, word choice, and so on. On another occasion, have a small group participate in an informal discussion—this could be a book club or a discussion around a specific topic. Have the remainder of the class observe their discussion with this purpose in mind: to notice their language and how it is different from formal English. Record their findings in "Informal" column. Note the differences between the two columns.
- Brainstorm situations when formal English is appropriate and situations when informal English is appropriate. Have students record their thinking on sticky notes and attach to the first chart or create a new chart for students to refer to. Add to this chart as students discover additional examples of formal and informal speaking situations.

To have students adapt a speech to a variety of contexts and tasks:

- Discuss with and warn students about those problems or errors most common to language when spoken on formal or otherwise important occasions (e.g., job interviews). These problems include using slang, euphemisms, stereotypes, clichés, and incorrect grammar, usage, or vocabulary.
- Identify and instruct them to also be wary of using any of the following when speaking at a formal occasion: culturally insensitive language or remarks, jokes, sarcasm, irony, and jargon (unless the audience you are addressing would be fluent in such jargon, in which case it is acceptable).

To have students demonstrate their command of formal English when appropriate:

- Have students identify before they speak any words, phrases, or parts of the speech that cause the student trouble when they speak; once identified, these portions might be replaced with words that are more familiar but no less appropriate for the occasion or audience.
- Deliver your own speech, even if it is created on the spot, in different styles, having fun with it but not being in any way disrespectful of those you might be trying to address; follow up with a chance to discuss the differences between the styles, which one is likely to be more effective and why.
- Make time to confer with students to discuss their speeches, making a special effort to identify any flaws that would undermine correctness and thus their credibility as a speaker in any situation that required a mastery of formal English.

To help your English language learners, try this:

- Meet individually with them or, if appropriate, as a small group to walk through their speech, first editing for content, then for correctness; then have them do a read-through with you so they can get feedback about words, phrases, or sections of the speech that need to be changed. During this session, you might also model for them how to say certain words or give emphasis while speaking. This sort of task, giving a speech in front of a group, is near the top of most people's list of anxieties, all the more so if you must give a speech in a language you are still learning, so it is important to do all you can to address the emotional aspect of such an assignment.

 For graphic organizer templates, see online resources at **resources.corwin.com/literacycompanion3-5.**

Preparing to Teach

Standard: _____

Preparing the Classroom

_____
_____
_____
_____
_____
_____
_____

Preparing the Mindset

_____
_____
_____
_____
_____
_____
_____

Preparing the Texts to Use

_____
_____
_____
_____
_____
_____
_____

Preparing to Differentiate

_____
_____
_____
_____
_____
_____
_____

Connections to Other Standards:

_____
_____
_____

Academic Vocabulary: Key Words and Phrases

Adapt speech: To change the language, style of delivery, tone, or format of the presentation or speech as needed to suit the audience, purpose, and occasion.

Appropriate: Each presentation or talk has its own unique audience each time one speaks, and so one must know how to speak—which words, tone, and style of address one should use when speaking on each occasion. What is appropriate on one occasion—informal, colloquial speech to a group of people you know—may be inappropriate, even offensive, the next time when the occasion is formal and the audience has completely different expectations. Certain things are never appropriate: spelling and formatting mistakes on handouts, slides, or other visual aids; slang, foul language, or otherwise rude terms or comments that undermine the speaker's credibility.

Command of formal English: The standards place a clear and consistent emphasis on a command of formal English—grammatically correct, clearly enunciated words delivered with good eye contact—as an essential ingredient in college or career success. This means knowing how to speak in ways that would be appropriate when addressing customers, colleagues, classmates or professors in college.

Communicative tasks: These "tasks" include contributing to a discussion group in class, delivering a formal speech, debating a controversial issue with others, or presenting a formal topic or argument to a group with the idea of persuading them to act, think, or believe a certain way. Increasingly, these tasks and their related contexts will include, for example, conferring with people through online audio and video (or chat) platforms in order to collaborate, confer, or communicate.

Contexts: Refers to the place as much as the purpose of any speaking event; examples include speaking in class, online, in small and larger groups, to the full class or larger groups; in the community at-large or at work with customers and colleagues; or for interviews with bosses or organizations.

Indicated: One is sometimes asked to talk in a specific way to a group on a topic or occasion; thus one looks to the prompt, directions, adviser, teacher, or other source for indications about how to speak on a given occasion to a particular audience about a particular topic. In the event that it is not indicated, one must learn to determine for oneself what is the most appropriate way to speak in a given situation.

Informal discourse: Talk and discussions between peers that is relaxed, casual, and familiar. Discourse that will not be held to the standards of formal standard English.

Notes

Planning to Teach

Standard: _____

Whole Class

_____
_____
_____
_____
_____
_____
_____
_____

Small Group

_____
_____
_____
_____
_____
_____
_____
_____

Individual Practice/Conferring

_____
_____
_____
_____
_____
_____
_____
_____

The Common Core State Standards

Language

College and Career Readiness Anchor Standards for
Language K–12

**Source:
Common Core
State Standards**

The 3–5 Language Standards outlined on the following pages define what students should understand and be able to do by the end of each grade. Here on this page we present the College and Career Readiness (CCR) anchor standards for K–12 so you can see how students in grades 3–5 work toward the same goals as a high school senior: it's a universal, K–12 vision. The CCR anchor standards and the grade-specific standards correspond to one another by numbers 1–10. They are necessary complements: the former providing broad standards, the latter providing additional specificity. Together, they define the skills and understandings that all students must eventually demonstrate.

Conventions of Standard English

1. Demonstrate command of the conventions of standard English grammar and usage when writing or speaking.
2. Demonstrate command of the conventions of standard English capitalization, punctuation, and spelling when writing.

Knowledge of Language

3. Apply knowledge of language to understand how language functions in different contexts, to make effective choices for meaning or style, and to comprehend more fully when reading or listening.

Vocabulary Acquisition and Use

4. Determine or clarify the meaning of unknown and multiple-meaning words and phrases by using context clues, analyzing meaningful word parts, and consulting general and specialized reference materials, as appropriate.
5. Demonstrate understanding of figurative language, word relationships, and nuances in word meanings.
6. Acquire and use accurately a range of general academic and domain-specific words and phrases sufficient for reading, writing, speaking, and listening at the college and career readiness level; demonstrate independence in gathering vocabulary knowledge when encountering an unknown term important to comprehension or expression.

Note on Range and Content of Student Language Use

To be college and career ready in language, students must have firm control over the conventions of standard English. At the same time, they must come to appreciate that language is as at least as much a matter of craft as of rules and be able to choose words, syntax, and punctuation to express themselves and achieve particular functions and rhetorical effects. They must also have extensive vocabularies, built through reading and study, enabling them to comprehend complex texts and engage in purposeful writing about and conversations around content. They need to become skilled in determining or clarifying the meaning of words and phrases they encounter, choosing flexibly from an array of strategies to aid them. They must learn to see an individual word as part of a network of other words—words, for example, that have similar denotations but different connotations. The inclusion of Language standards in their own strand should not be taken as an indication that skills related to conventions, effective language use, and vocabulary are unimportant to reading, writing, speaking, and listening; indeed, they are inseparable from such contexts.

College and Career Readiness Anchor Standards for
Language K–12

The College and Career Readiness (CCR) anchor standards are the same for K–12. The guiding principle here is that the core speaking and listening skills should not change as students advance; rather, the level at which they learn and can perform these skills should increase in complexity as students move from one grade to the next. However, for grades 3–5, we have to recognize that the standards were back mapped from the secondary grades—the authors envisioned what college students needed and then wrote standards, working their way down the grades. Thus, as you use this book, remember that children in grades 3–5 can't just "jump over" developmental milestones in an ambitious attempt toward an anchor standard. There are certain life and learning experiences they need to have, and certain concepts they need to learn, before they are capable of handling many complex academic skills in a meaningful way. The anchor standards nonetheless are goal posts to work toward. As you read the "gist" of the standards on the following pages, remember they represent what our grades 3–5 students will *grow into* during each year and deepen later in middle school and high school.

Conventions of Standard English

Simply put, students should know and use the proper forms of English—spelling, grammar, usage, and conventions—when speaking or writing for public purposes or audiences such as at work or school. The emphasis here is on the crucial role that such attention to correctness plays in college and the workplace, where first impressions matter and the smallest error can cost customers or money. This becomes all the more important in light of social media trends where businesses communicate more and more online, through social media, chat, and text messages.

Knowledge of Language

This standard recognizes the range of functions language plays in creating style, voice, and meaning; but also it emphasizes the importance of diction, syntax, and other factors as they relate to the writer's or speaker's ethos and general effect on the audience in a given context. One must, in other words, give serious thought to which words, which order, for which audience and purpose if one is to convey meaning effectively and for maximum effect.

Vocabulary Acquisition and Use

Vocabulary, so instrumental in reading, writing, and speaking/listening, is divided into several domains in these standards. First are those words that are unknown or have many possible meanings, the proper one(s) determined by the occasion or context in which they are used. An essential part of this standard involves using general and specialized reference materials in print or online to determine the etymology of words and learn more about their different meanings and usages. In addition to these words, students add to their word bank the way language is used figuratively, as well as through word relationships that suggest some association, connotation, or nuance depending on how it is used. Finally, students should pay most of their attention to those words that will help them understand or complete their assignments for school; this means learning those domain-specific words and phrases unique to each discipline that students routinely encounter when they read, write, speak, or listen. Over time, students should actively gather and work to grow their knowledge of and ability to use the words and phrases in each subject area to accommodate the increasing complexity of the texts and tasks they face at each subsequent grade level.

Source: Adapted from Burke, J. (2013). *The Common Core Companion: The Standards Decoded, Grades 6–8: What They Say, What They Mean, How to Teach Them.* Thousand Oaks, CA: Corwin.

Language 1: Demonstrate command of the conventions of standard English grammar and usage when writing or speaking.

English Language Arts

3 Demonstrate command of the conventions of standard English grammar and usage when writing or speaking.
    a. Explain the function of nouns, pronouns, verbs, adjectives, and adverbs in general and their functions in particular sentences.
    b. Form and use regular and irregular plural nouns.
    c. Use abstract nouns (e.g., *childhood*).
    d. Form and use regular and irregular verbs.
    e. Form and use the simple (e.g., *I walked; I walk; I will walk*) verb tenses.
    f. Ensure subject-verb and pronoun-antecedent agreement.*
    g. Form and use comparative and superlative adjectives and adverbs, and choose between them depending on what is to be modified.
    h. Use coordinating and subordinating conjunctions.
    i. Produce simple, compound, and complex sentences.

4 Demonstrate command of the conventions of standard English grammar and usage when writing or speaking.
    a. Use relative pronouns (*who, whose, whom, which, that*) and relative adverbs (*where, when, why*).
    b. Form and use the progressive (e.g., *I was walking; I am walking; I will be walking*) verb tenses.
    c. Use modal auxiliaries (e.g., *can, may, must*) to convey various conditions.
    d. Order adjectives within sentences according to conventional patterns (e.g., *a small red bag* rather than *a red small bag*).
    e. Form and use prepositional phrases.
    f. Produce complete sentences, recognizing and correcting inappropriate fragments and run-ons.*
    g. Correctly use frequently confused words (e.g., *to, too, two; there, their*).*

5 Demonstrate command of the conventions of standard English grammar and usage when writing or speaking.
    a. Explain the function of conjunctions, prepositions, and interjections in general and their function in particular sentences.
    b. Form and use the perfect (e.g., *I had walked; I have walked; I will have walked*) verb tenses.
    c. Use verb tense to convey various times, sequences, states, and conditions.
    d. Recognize and correct inappropriate shifts in verb tense.*
    e. Use correlative conjunctions (e.g., *either/or, neither/nor*).

* The following skills, marked with an asterisk (*) in Language standards 1–3, are particularly likely to require continued attention in higher grades as they are applied to increasingly sophisticated writing and speaking.

What the **Student** Does

English Language Arts

3 **Gist:** Students know the conventions of standard English grammar and usage, applying them whenever speaking or writing. Students form and use nouns, pronouns, verbs, adjectives, and adverbs and explain how they function in sentences in the following cases:

a. Regular and irregular plural nouns
b. Abstract nouns (e.g., childhood)
c. Regular and irregular verbs
d. Simple verb tenses (e.g., I walked, I walk, I will walk)
e. Subject-verb and pronoun-antecedent agreement
f. Comparative and superlative adjectives and adverbs, choosing between them depending on what is to be modified
g. Coordinating and subordinating conjunctions

In addition, students produce simple, compound, or complex sentences.

They consider:

- Are my sentences written correctly? How do I know?
- When I reread my writing out loud, does it sound right? Does it make sense?
- Have I used nouns correctly?
- Are my verbs tenses written the way I intend them?
- Is there agreement between subjects and verbs?
- Is there anything I need to repair to have correct usage?
- Have I used the correct pronouns?

4 **Gist:** Students know the conventions of standard English grammar and usage, applying them whenever speaking or writing, and doing the following with parts of speech and commonly misspelled words:

a. Use the correct pronouns (e.g., who, whom, and whose) and adjectives (e.g., where, when, why) as they refer to nouns
b. Use progressive verb tenses (e.g., I was walking, I am walking, I will be walking) correctly in sentences
c. Use modal auxiliaries or specific verbs (e.g., can, may, must) to show conditions in writing
d. Place adjectives in order within sentences (e.g., *a small red bag* rather than *a red small bag*)
e. Write prepositional phrases
f. Use and spell correctly frequently confused words (e.g., to, too, two, there, their, they're)

In addition, students produce complete sentences.

They consider:

- Are all my sentences complete sentences? Have I read my piece out loud to double-check?
- Is this a sentence fragment? How do I correct it?
- Is this a run-on sentence? How do I correct it?
- Which words, phrases, or sentences are incorrect in standard English and how can I fix them to make them correct?
- Are all my verbs in the same tense (the past, the present, or the future)?
- Have I used adjectives correctly to make my writing better?
- Have I used prepositional phrases correctly to make my writing better?
- Have I checked to make sure that I've used the correct spelling—especially of homophones like *their, there, they're* or *to, too, two*?

5 **Gist:** Students know the conventions of standard English grammar and usage, applying them whenever speaking or writing and doing the following with parts of speech:

a. Use the perfect verb tense (e.g., I had walked, I have walked, I will have walked)
b. Use verb tenses to show various times, sequences, states, and conditions
c. Correct inappropriate shifts in verb tense
d. Use correlative conjunctions (e.g., either/or, neither/nor)

In addition, explain the reasons why conjunctions, prepositions, and interjections are used in particular sentences.

They consider:

- Do I know the reasons or rules behind the construction of my sentences? Do I understand about conjunctions, prepositions, and interjections?
- Have I used words, phrases, or sentences correctly?
- If I have used words or phrases incorrectly, how can I fix them?
- Can I explain my grammatical decisions?
- Do the verb tenses agree? If not how can I correct them?

What the **Teacher** Does

To show a command of standard English grammar and usage:

- Explicitly teach parts of speech (nouns, pronouns, adjectives, etc.)—what they do, how they're used, and various rules. Share books and texts with students and have them identify different parts of speech and notice *how* and *why* they are used. Post definitions in the classroom.
- Provide students with photocopies of brief sections of texts. Instruct them to highlight a specific part of speech (e.g., verbs). Annotate in the margins explaining the function of these words.
- Use the whiteboard to project text with poorly written English and have students correct it, explaining why they made the choices they did.
- Teach students the various conventions appropriate to whatever type of writing they are doing, studying, or reading, providing a rich and varied array of examples of how these conventions are used in the world and by real writers.
- Provide mentoring texts that show how students should write certain constructions. Picture books lend themselves to this. After reading the text out loud for the class, type the text and give each student a copy to highlight and annotate for a specific purpose. In this manner, they will see how published authors use grammar and usage to the best effect.
- Confer with students to assess and teach their use of grammar.
- Collect picture books that focus specifically on grammar and usage. Read and discuss these with students and create a classroom chart.
- Cultivate an environment of respect and wonder relative to language in general and specific aspects of it in particular, one that invites students into language instead of inspiring fear of it; this can be done by bringing in real-world writing (or articles about such writing) that captures the power of language to shape our thinking and convey ideas. Invite students to share new words or to ask when they don't know a word—especially when you are reading aloud to them.

Create a culture that respects the idea that *words give us power.*

- Invest in and continually add to your own knowledge about language, grammar, and usage as these relate to the subjects you teach; share this learning with your students to establish and reinforce your own authority when working with language.
- Try always to model the virtue of correctness when writing and speaking to your students; this means seeing every handout, every e-mail to the class, and every homework assignment posted online for your students as an occasion to reinforce the importance of communicating clearly and correctly at all times.
- Use the three-step process to teach conventions: (1) Provide direct, separate instruction in the concept—what it is, how it works, why they should know and use it; (2) Create opportunities to practice and refine their knowledge of the concept through simulations and feedback; (3) Apply the knowledge and use the learning in an actual piece of writing to demonstrate a full understanding of the concept, refining their use as needed through your feedback and opportunities to apply the learning in more sophisticated ways.
- Require that students use these conventions and constructions in their writing to reinforce and further develop their knowledge of these conventions in their own writing; a necessary adjunct to this requirement to use what they learn would be that you provide targeted, constructive feedback on their use, with the opportunity to revise in light of your comments so they might refine their knowledge and use of these conventions until such actions are habits and the rules internalized.
- See books by Jeff Andersen and Michael W. Smith and Jeff Wilhelm on teaching grammar and usage.

To help your English language learners, try this:

- Provide many models and opportunities to practice, while meeting often with students to confer on their writing. Teach only *one* thing in a conference and then when you meet the next time, assess how the student is applying what was taught.

Preparing to Teach

Standard: _____

Preparing the Classroom

_____

_____

_____

_____

_____

_____

Preparing the Mindset

_____

_____

_____

_____

_____

_____

Preparing the Texts to Use

_____

_____

_____

_____

_____

Preparing to Differentiate

_____

_____

_____

_____

_____

Connections to Other Standards:

_____

_____

_____

Academic Vocabulary: Key Words and Phrases

Adjective: These are words that modify or describe another person or thing in a sentence. An adjective describes a noun and provides more information about the object signified.

Adverb: These are words that usually modify verbs, but can also modify adjectives or other adverbs. They change or qualify the meaning of these parts of speech. Adverbs often answer questions such as *how? in what way? when? where?* and *to what extent?*

Conventions: A way of doing or using something—in this case, words, punctuation, grammar—as established and endorsed by a group that has agreed to observe certain practices or rules.

Coordinating and subordinating conjunctions: And, but, for, nor, or, so, and yet. Coordinating conjunctions are used to join independent clauses to make compound sentences. These are useful to repair run-on sentences or choppy or simple sentences, joining them to create compound or complex sentences. Subordinating conjunctions also are used to join independent clauses; however, they make complex sentences. Some examples of subordinating conjunctions include the following: after, although, as, as if, before, rather, since, which.

Form and use comparative and superlative adjectives and adverbs: Comparative and superlative adjectives and adverbs are used for comparison. We use the *comparative* form when comparing two items, people, places, or ideas. *Superlatives* are used to compare more than two. An example using adjectives is the following: Tall, comparative—taller, superlative—tallest. An example for adverbs is the following: carefully; comparative—more carefully; superlative—most carefully.

Grammar: The study of words and their component parts and how they combine to form sentences; the structural relationships in language that contribute to their meaning.

Modal auxiliaries: Often known as helping verbs, these combine with the main verb to express shades of time and mood. Examples include the following: shall, will, can, could, should, would.

Noun: A noun is a word used to name a person, place, thing, animal, or abstract idea.

Prepositional phrases: These are modifying phrases consisting of a preposition and its object, which is usually a noun or pronoun and any modifiers of the object. The phrase begins with the preposition—of which there are about 150 in the English language. Some examples include about, after, by, to, and toward.

Progressive verb tense: In a nutshell, this means time. Does the verb tense show the present, the past, or the future?

Pronoun-antecedent agreement: A pronoun is a word used to stand for or take the place of a noun. An antecedent is a word for which the pronoun stands. For example, in the sentence: *The girl wore her favorite dress*, girl is the antecedent and "her" is the pronoun antecedent—it tells whose dress it is without restating the noun.

Regular and irregular plural nouns: To make the plural of a regular noun, add "s." However, rules apply when changing irregular nouns to plurals—that may mean adding "es," adding "ies," or changing the spelling (e.g., man—men).

Relative pronoun: These introduce a relative clause, which are dependent clauses. Relative clauses modify a word, phrase, or ideas in the main clause. In the sentence "The house **that** Fred built is big." *That Fred built* is the relative clause and "that" is the relative pronoun referring back to "the house."

Subject-verb agreement: In a nutshell, subject-verb agreement means that they match—the basic rule is that if it is a singular noun, then a singular verb must also be used. If it's a plural noun, then it must be a plural verb. There are additional rules to subject-verb agreement, but for the elementary grades, the basic rule is appropriate.

Types of sentences: Sentences can be described by their grammatical structure or their function. The following sentence types focus on the former:

- *Simple:* one independent clause and no dependent clause. (e.g., The story is set in the future.)

- *Complex:* one independent clause and at least one dependent clause. (e.g., The story, which takes place on Mars, is set in the future.)

- *Compound:* two or more independent clauses and no dependent clause; the independent clauses can be joined by a conjunction (for, and, nor, but, or, yet, so) and a comma or a semicolon. (e.g., The story takes place on Mars; it is set in the future.)

Usage: How one uses language—and if it is permitted, approved.

Verb: A word that names an action or state of being; verbs change form to indicate tense, number, voice, or mood.

Planning to Teach

Standard: _____

Whole Class

_____

_____

_____

_____

_____

_____

_____

_____

Small Group

_____

_____

_____

_____

_____

_____

_____

Individual Practice/Conferring

_____

_____

_____

_____

_____

_____

_____

Language 2: Demonstrate command of the conventions of standard English capitalization, punctuation, and spelling when writing.

English Language Arts

3 Demonstrate command of the conventions of standard English capitalization, punctuation, and spelling when writing.
    a. Capitalize appropriate words in titles.
    b. Use commas in addresses.
    c. Use commas and quotation marks in dialogue.
    d. Form and use possessives.
    e. Use conventional spelling for high-frequency and other studied words and for adding suffixes to base words (e.g., *sitting, smiled, cries, happiness*).
    f. Use spelling patterns and generalizations (e.g., word families, position-based spellings, syllable patterns, ending rules, meaningful word parts) in writing words.
    g. Consult reference materials, including beginning dictionaries, as needed to check and correct spellings.

4 Demonstrate command of the conventions of standard English capitalization, punctuation, and spelling when writing.
    a. Use correct capitalization.
    b. Use commas and quotation marks to mark direct speech and quotations from a text.
    c. Use a comma before a coordinating conjunction in a compound sentence.
    d. Spell grade-appropriate words correctly, consulting references as needed.

5 Demonstrate command of the conventions of standard English capitalization, punctuation, and spelling when writing.
    a. Use punctuation to separate items in a series.*
    b. Use a comma to separate an introductory element from the rest of the sentence.
    c. Use a comma to set off the words *yes* and *no* (e.g., *Yes, thank you*), to set off a tag question from the rest of the sentence (e.g., *It's true, isn't it?*), and to indicate direct address (e.g., *Is that you, Steve?*).
    d. Use underlining, quotation marks, or italics to indicate titles of works.
    e. Spell grade-appropriate words correctly, consulting references as needed.

* The following skills, marked with an asterisk (*) in Language standards 1–3, are particularly likely to require continued attention in higher grades as they are applied to increasingly sophisticated writing and speaking.

What the **Student** Does

English Language Arts

3 **Gist:** Students show their knowledge of and ability to follow the conventions of capitalization, punctuation, and spelling when writing by:
a. Capitals—capitalize appropriate words in titles
b. Commas in address (e.g., Susie, please turn in your paper.)
c. Commas and quotation marks (e.g., John said, "I love school.")
d. Conventional spelling for high frequency words
e. Conventional spelling when adding suffixes to base words (e.g., sitting, smiled, cried, happiness)
f. Spelling patterns—demonstrating basic knowledge of word families, position-based spelling (e.g., i before e except after c and in words that sound like weigh or neigh), ending rules (e.g., plurals, ed, ing), and meaningful word parts
g. Use dictionaries to correct spellings

They consider:

- Have I checked my punctuation?
- What words should—or should *not*—be capitalized?
- What words do I most often misspell, especially those that spellcheck is not likely to detect (e.g., their, there, they're) and how can I check these correctly throughout my piece?
- Can I use the dictionary to help me spell words correctly?

4 **Gist:** Students show their knowledge of and ability to follow the conventions of capitalization, punctuation, and spelling when writing by:
a. Correct capitalization
b. Commas and quotations—to mark direct speech and quotations from a text
c. Commas before a coordinating conjunction (forms a compound sentence)
d. Spell grade-level-appropriate words correctly

They consider:

- What words should—or should *not*—be capitalized?
- Have I used punctuation correctly? How have I checked?
- What words do I most often misspell, especially those that spellcheck is not likely to detect (e.g., their, there, they're) and how can I check these correctly throughout my piece?
- Have I checked the punctuation in dialogue and quotations?

5 **Gist:** Students show their knowledge of and ability to follow the conventions of capitalization, punctuation, capitalization, and spelling when writing by:
a. Punctuation to separate items in a series
b. Commas to separate introductory element from the rest of the sentence
c. Commas to set off yes and no, tag questions, and direct address (e.g., Yes, I'd love a piece of cake! It's true, isn't it? Would you like to go, Joe?)
d. Underlining, quotation marks, or italics to show titles
e. Spell grade-appropriate words correctly

They consider:

- What words should—or should *not*—be capitalized?
- What words do I most often misspell, especially those that spellcheck is not likely to detect (e.g., their, there, they're) and how can I check these correctly throughout my piece?
- Which punctuation marks have I used in my writing? How do I know they're used correctly?

What the **Teacher** Does

To develop a command of conventions of standard English:

- Emphasize, reinforce, and teach students how to capitalize, punctuate, and spell as needed within the context of your larger writing curriculum.
- Teach the punctuation marks explicitly, discussing the rules for use. Provide students with copies of texts and have students highlight the different types of punctuation and annotate in the margins *why* it's used and *how* it helps the reader make meaning.
- Use mentor texts similar to the type of writing you want your students to do. As you read, model and think aloud how the punctuation and capitalization is used and how it helps the reader. Invite students to notice punctuation and capitalization in texts they read independently—sharing rules with the class. Indicate how the writers you study apply these conventions to achieve clarity and convey relationships by using punctuation.
- Use multiple and contrasting models to show proper and incorrect use of conventions such as dashes and commas, using such models to show when, how, where, and why to use these.
- Confer with students on their writing, and, if necessary, teach a new punctuation or capitalization skill. Through conferences and informal assessments, pull together groups of students who need more instruction on specific skills. Provide targeted, constructive feedback about students' use of those conventions that have been the focus of recent instruction and the opportunity to revise in light of your comments.
- Provide editing checklists for students to check their punctuation or capitalization.

- Use the whiteboard to display text—both written correctly and those with errors. Have students identify correct use and correct the mistakes.
- Honor at all times, when writing or speaking to students, the value of correctness; treat every assignment, e-mail to students, and homework directions posted online as an opportunity to demonstrate and reiterate the importance of correctness.
- Teach conventions using this three-step approach: (1) Provide direct instruction in the concept, explaining what it is, how it works, why they should know and use it; (2) Create opportunities to practice and refine the lesson through simulations and feedback; (3) Demonstrate what they learned in an actual piece of writing that shows they understand the concept.
- Require students to keep their own lists of conventions they need to learn or improve their use of; to these, they might add samples of correct—or incorrect—usage; they might consider extending their own learning online by using sites like noredink.com to practice and improve their grammar skills.
- Limit the number of grammatical terms you actively teach so the focus remains how to write better instead of what to remember; you can reinforce the terms by routinely using them when discussing them.

To help your English language learners, try this:

- Try to limit the number of new conventions you introduce at any one time to avoid overwhelming your English language learner students. When you do introduce them, arrange your examples in a progression over time, starting with the most basic, easy-to-grasp examples you can find or create to convey the idea you are teaching.

Notes

Standard: _____

Preparing the Classroom

Preparing the Mindset

Preparing the Texts to Use

Preparing to Differentiate

Connections to Other Standards:

Academic Vocabulary: Key Words and Phrases

Capitalization: Use of uppercase letters to signal where sentences begin but also to indicate that word is a title, a person's name, a product or brand name, or some other form of proper noun. This is especially important in light of trends to ignore capitalization when texting and carry that over into the workplace or classroom when writing more formal documents.

Commas: These are hard-working punctuation marks and are used for a plethora of reasons. The basic tenet, though, is that commas are used to separate words or word groups.

Conventional spelling: This is the correct spelling of a word, the one you would find in a dictionary.

Conventions: Those rules about which punctuation marks to use, how, when, why, and where to use them when writing different types of documents in various media.

Coordinating conjunction: These connect words, phrases, or clauses. There are seven coordinating conjunctions: *and, but, for, nor, or, so, yet.*

Italics: In typography, italics is cursive typeface and serves as the equivalent of underlining.

Possessives: These show that something belongs to somebody or something. Generally, the rule is to add 's to singular words and to add s' to plurals to show possession.

Punctuation: All the marks—period, comma, colon, semicolon, dash, hyphen, quotation and question marks, parentheses, exclamation points, and others—that writers use to be clear, make connections, and create a style that suggests how the text should be read. It is, as some say, what makes the music of the writing happen in ways similar to musical notations that signal where, when, and how long to stop or speed up, where to pause and what to emphasize.

Quotation marks: The main use of quotation marks is to set off or represent exact language either spoken or written that comes from someone else.

Reference materials: A symbol placed in text to direct a reader's attention to further information, like a footnote, bibliography, or other text. These are usually represented by *, +, and dagger symbols.

Suffixes: The short and sweet definition—word endings that add a certain meaning to the word. These can be a letter or a group of letters attached to the end of a word to form a new word or to change the grammatical function of the original word.

Notes

Standard: _____

Whole Class

_____
_____
_____
_____
_____
_____
_____
_____

Small Group

_____
_____
_____
_____
_____
_____
_____

Individual Practice/Conferring

_____
_____
_____
_____
_____
_____
_____

Language 3: Apply knowledge of language to understand how language functions in different contexts, to make effective choices for meaning or style, and to comprehend more fully when reading or listening.

English Language Arts

3 Use knowledge of language and its conventions when writing, speaking, reading, or listening.
    a. Choose words and phrases for effect.*
    b. Recognize and observe differences between the conventions of spoken and written standard English.

4 Use knowledge of language and its conventions when writing, speaking, reading, or listening.
    a. **Choose words and phrases to convey ideas precisely.***
    b. **Choose punctuation for effect.***
    c. **Differentiate between contexts that call for formal English (e.g., presenting ideas) and situations where informal discourse is appropriate (e.g., small-group discussion).**

5 Use knowledge of language and its conventions when writing, speaking, reading, or listening.
    a. **Expand, combine, and reduce sentences for meaning, reader/listener interest, and style.**
    b. **Compare and contrast the varieties of English (e.g., dialects, registers) used in stories, dramas, or poems.**

* The following skills, marked with an asterisk (*) in Language standards 1–3, are particularly likely to require continued attention in higher grades as they are applied to increasingly sophisticated writing and speaking.

What the **Student** Does

English Language Arts

3 **Gist:** Students know about and use language and conventions to choose words and phrases for effect and to recognize the differences between written and spoken standard English when writing, speaking, reading, or listening.

They consider:

- What effect am I trying to achieve?
- What types of words and phrases will help me do that?
- What is the message I want to get across to the reader?
- When I read my draft aloud, are there things I want to circle to think about improving?
- Which words in my text could be changed for greater effect?
- Which phrases in my text could be changed for greater effect?
- Is my word choice appropriate for this piece or speech?
- How does written standard English differ from the spoken?

4 **Gist:** Students know about and use language and conventions to choose precise words and phrases, to use punctuation for effect, and to understand when formal English is required (e.g., presenting ideas in speeches) and when informal discourse is appropriate (e.g., small-group discussions), when writing, speaking, reading, or listening.

They consider:

- When I read my draft aloud, are there things I want to circle to think about improving?
- Which words in my text could be changed for greater precision?
- Which phrases in my text could be changed for greater precision?
- What effect am I trying to achieve?
- Have I used punctuation for effect?
- When giving a speech am I using formal standard English?

5 **Gist:** Students know about and use language and conventions to expand, combine, or reduce sentences to hold reader interest, affect meaning and style, and to compare and contrast varieties of English—dialects and registers used in dramas, stories, or poems when writing, speaking, reading, or listening.

They consider:

- When I read my draft aloud, are there things I want to circle to think about improving?
- Can I combine sentences to make them interesting?
- Can I expand my sentences or make them longer?
- Is there anything that I can reduce or cut from my sentences that doesn't need to be included?
- Do I have a variety of sentences?
- Do I hold the reader's interest?
- Do I convey meaning?
- Does the story, drama, or poem I'm reading have dialect or registers? What does that signal to me as a reader?

What the **Teacher** Does

To help students understand how language functions in different contexts:

- Find books on the same topic written in a variety of ways, and share these books with students—either by reading them aloud or having students read them. Discuss how the way the author writes and uses language affects the reader.
- Direct students to read the assigned texts closely, focusing their attention on the ways the author uses language—specifically through the mood, tone, patterns, and grammar—to create meaning or a style that contributes substance to the text; this might lead to such strategies as parsing the sentences out to help students see the spatial relationship between parts of the sentences, or using color-coding functions on the computer when displaying the passages being analyzed.
- Use a range of contrasting models that clarify and extend students' understanding of how language can function within a text; this might mean showing them examples of the same passage modified to show the effect of it written as a series of simple sentences versus more sophisticated sentences in light of the topic or their purpose.
- Expose students to a wide variety of texts and authors, styles and genres, forms and formats so they learn from these practitioners the full range of choices they can make as writers, but also so they can learn how to read for these same elements.

To help students make effective choices in word choice, phrases, and punctuation, for precision, meaning, and style:

- Have students highlight words in their drafts that they think are precise and then in another color highlight those they would like to change. Work with partners to find better choices to create meaning.
- Encourage students to confer with classmates to discuss if their drafts convey desired meaning and style and to get feedback on word choice.
- Provide feedback to their drafts throughout the process, offering them suggestions about the different choices they can make in word choice or phrases or punctuation.

To improve knowledge of and ability to vary sentence patterns:

- Instruct students on the different types of sentences and using shared texts, preferably copies they can mark up (*Story Grammar for Elementary School—A Sentence Composing Approach* by Don and Jenny Killgallon is a great resource for this), have students identify different types of sentences and how the variety affects the piece.

- Have students highlight two simple sentences in one of their drafts and then practice different ways to combine them. Conversely, have students find a long or run-on sentence in one of their drafts and practice reducing it.
- Have students highlight the first word in each of their sentences in a paragraph and notice if they have used a variety of beginnings. Then have them create a graph—with the first word of each sentence on the horizontal axis and the number of words on the vertical axis. Have them count the number of words in each sentence and graph it appropriately. This will provide them with a visual of the length and variety of their sentences. Have them share or write about what they notice, making any changes if necessary to their writing.
- Direct students to count the average length of each sentence in their paper (or, given the limits of class time, the first page in a longer paper); ask them to jot down what they notice about length, sentence patterns (do they all sound the same), the beginnings of their sentences; revise accordingly for greater variation, cohesion, and concision.

To help students differentiate between formal English and informal and to compare and contrast the varieties of English (e.g., dialects, registers) used in stories, dramas, and poems:

- Define the terms *dialects* and *registers* and discuss how and why they are used in literature.
- Have students work in small groups and read dialogue you've selected from fiction, relishing diction and what it might reveal about region, character, and so on. Is it southern? Modern? Old fashioned? British? Urban? Rural?
- Read and share stories, dramas, and poems in class. Identify when dialects and registers are used. Create comparison/contrast charts of those varieties of English with formal English used today.
- Have students work in groups to write brief sketches and perform them for classmates. They have to craft dialogue that captures a particular dialect(s) or time period clearly for their audience.

To help your English language learners, try this:

- Meet with students and focus on sentence structure. Have them read aloud a sentence and then through conferring, help them add details to it or cut out anything that doesn't make sense. Teach them that writing good sentences is like riding on a rollercoaster—the sentences go up and down in length to hold the reader's attention.

Preparing to Teach

Standard: _____

Preparing the Classroom

Preparing the Mindset

Preparing the Texts to Use

Preparing to Differentiate

Connections to Other Standards:

Academic Vocabulary: Key Words and Phrases

Compare and contrast the varieties of English (e.g., dialects, registers): Dialects are a particular form of language spoken in a particular area. This can include some of the particular area's own words, grammar, and pronunciations. Registers are any of the varieties of language that a speaker uses in a particular social context.

Effective choices for meaning or style: Drawing on such elements as syntax, rhetoric, punctuation, and diction, among others, writers choose words and arrange them to serve some purpose (meaning) or effect (style).

Expand, combine, and reduce sentences for meaning, reader/listener interest, and style: To create a variety of sentences and aid sentence fluency, students expand or lengthen sentences, combine two or more simple sentences into a more complex sentence, and shorten sentences—especially run-on sentences—to ensure reader interest and understanding.

How language functions in different contexts: We are always writing a specific type of text for an audience, on some occasion, for some purpose. Decisions about how we write, what features or format we choose, which words or sentence types we include, what tone or style we adopt—are based on the context in which that document is written and presented. In turn, the reader or listener takes both the author's context and his own into account.

Knowledge of language: In all its forms and functions, including vocabulary, grammar, usage, syntax, rhetoric, diction, and style.

Precisely/precision: Best defined by Mark Twain as the difference between the word fire and fire extinguisher; one must use the correct, precise word if one is to convey an idea as clearly as possible or achieve the desired effect.

Notes

Planning to Teach

Standard: _____

Whole Class

Small Group

Individual Practice/Conferring

Language 4: Determine or clarify the meaning of unknown and multiple-meaning words and phrases by using context clues, analyzing meaningful word parts, and consulting general and specialized reference materials, as appropriate.

English Language Arts

3 Determine or clarify the meaning of unknown and multiple-meaning words and phrases based on *grade 3 reading and content,* choosing flexibly from a range of strategies.

    a. Use sentence-level context as a clue to the meaning of a word or phrase.

    b. Determine the meaning of the new word formed when a known affix is added to a known word (e.g., *agreeable/disagreeable, comfortable/uncomfortable, care/careless, heat/preheat*).

    c. Use a known root word as a clue to the meaning of an unknown word with the same root (e.g., *company, companion*).

    d. Use glossaries or beginning dictionaries, both print and digital, to determine or clarify the precise meaning of key words and phrases.

4 Determine or clarify the meaning of unknown and multiple-meaning words and phrases based on *grade 4 reading and content*, choosing flexibly from a range of strategies.

    a. **Use context (e.g., definitions, examples, or restatements in text) as a clue to the meaning of a word or phrase.**

    b. **Use common, grade-appropriate Greek and Latin affixes and roots as clues to the meaning of a word (e.g., *telegraph, photograph, autograph*).**

    c. **Consult reference materials (e.g., dictionaries, glossaries, thesauruses), both print and digital, to find the pronunciation and determine or clarify the precise meaning of key words and phrases.**

5 Determine or clarify the meaning of unknown and multiple-meaning words and phrases based on *grade 5 reading and content*, choosing flexibly from a range of strategies.

    a. Use context (**e.g., cause/effect relationships and comparisons in text**) as a clue to the meaning of a word or phrase.

    b. Use common, grade-appropriate Greek and Latin affixes and roots as clues to the meaning of a word (**e.g., *photograph, photosynthesis***).

    c. Consult reference materials (e.g., dictionaries, glossaries, thesauruses), both print and digital, to find the pronunciation and determine or clarify the precise meaning of key words and phrases.

What the **Student** Does

English Language Arts

3 **Gist:** Students apply strategies to understand or clarify the meaning of new or polysemous words (words with multiple meanings) they encounter when reading and listening to grade 3 content. Specifically, these strategies include the following:

1. **Context clues:** Readers use the general meaning of the sentence to develop a sense of what the word or phrase means.
2. **Affixes:** Readers derive some idea about the meaning of a word by considering when a known affix is attached to a known root.
3. **Root word:** Readers derive some meaning when they use a known root to help them with an unknown word that shares the same root.
4. **Reference materials:** Readers turn to beginning dictionaries—both print and digital—to learn how to pronounce a word and to understand what it means as it is used in this context.

They consider:

- Which words or phrases in a sentence don't I understand?
- How can I figure out its meaning?
- Can I use the context, or the words around it to help me figure out the meaning?
- Can I use the root word or the affix to figure out the meaning of the unknown word?
- Can I use a dictionary to confirm the meaning of the word?

4 **Gist:** Students apply strategies to understand or clarify the meaning of new or polysemous words (words with multiple meanings) they encounter when reading and listening to grade 4 content. Specifically, these strategies include the following:

1. **Context clues:** Readers use definitions, examples, or restatements in the text to develop a sense of what the word or phrase means.
2. **Affixes and roots:** Readers derive some idea about the meaning of a word by considering those Greek and Latin affixes and roots appropriate to grade 4 reading and content.
3. **Reference materials:** Readers turn to a range of general print and digital reference works to learn how to pronounce a word and to understand what it means as it is used in this context; such works also clarify a word's meaning and its part of speech.

They consider:

- Which words or phrases in a sentence don't I understand?
- How can I figure out its meaning?
- Can I use the context or the words around it to help me figure out the meaning?
- Can I use the root word or the affix to figure out the meaning of the unknown word?
- Can I use reference materials to find the precise meaning of unknown words?

5 **Gist:** Students apply strategies that help them understand or clarify the meaning of new or polysemous words (words with multiple meanings) they encounter when reading and listening to grade 5 content. Specifically, these strategies include the following:

1. **Context clues:** Readers use context, especially cause/effect relationships or comparisons in text to develop a sense of what the word or phrase means.
2. **Affixes and roots:** Readers derives some idea about the meaning of a word by considering those Greek and Latin affixes and roots appropriate to grade 5 reading and content.
3. **Reference materials:** Readers turn to a range of general print and digital reference works to learn how to pronounce a word and to understand what it means as it is used in this context; such works also clarify a word's meaning and its part of speech.

They consider:

- Which words or phrases in a sentence don't I understand?
- How can I figure out its meaning?
- Can I use the context, or the words around it to help me figure out the meaning?
- Can I use the root word or the affix to figure out the meaning of the unknown word?
- Can I use reference materials to find the precise meaning of unknown words?

What the **Teacher** Does

To determine the meaning of unknown words and phrases:

- Teach students a range of strategies to choose from, including using context clues, word parts, reference works, and available resources such as an index, glossary, sidebar, footnotes, and other texts you may be using as part of the unit.
- Model for students by thinking aloud how you handle unknown words when reading, noting that you first acknowledge that you do not know a word and wonder if you need to know it to understand the text; having decided you do, you would then try one of the strategies listed above in an effort to infer its meaning; in the event that you cannot, you would actually turn to a dictionary to show them how you use it to decide which, of the many different definitions, is the one that best fits.
- Use this six-step procedure developed by Robert Marzano in *Building Background Knowledge for Academic Achievement* to teach words you want students to know or which they have determined they do not understand but must learn to comprehend a text: (1) You describe, explain, or provide an example of the new term in association with the specific word you want them to learn; (2) Students explain the new term, paraphrasing your description in their own words; (3) Students represent the term in some graphic way that helps them understand and remember the word; (4) Students revisit the term over time, encountering it through various activities and contexts designed to deepen their fluency with that word; (5) You ask students to return to and discuss these target words with each other periodically; (6) You engage students in activities or games that invite them to interact with these terms to reinforce and deepen their understanding and fluency.

To determine or clarify word meanings by analyzing word parts:

- Create classroom charts of grade-appropriate Greek and Latin root words, prefixes, and suffixes.
- Work with students to identify the suffixes, prefixes, and roots that make up a particular word; sometimes it is best to ask them if the root calls to mind other, more familiar, words that can help them access the word's meaning.
- Model how you go about understanding a word such as indomitable by analyzing its parts, looking to the prefix for some clue (e.g., *in-* meaning not), then the base or root (*domitare* meaning to tame, which calls to mind the word dominate), and finally the suffix (*able*, which means able to be), concluding for the class that it means unable to be controlled.

To learn to consult general and specialized reference materials:

- Have dictionaries, thesauruses, and a wide variety of reference materials out and available to students in the classroom. Teach students how to use them and provide opportunities to use them when determining definitions, finding synonyms and specific words, and so on.
- Demonstrate how to access digital reference materials—especially the dictionary and the thesaurus.
- Guide your students through different reference works related to vocabulary.

To determine words and phrases with multiple meanings:

- Help students learn to identify which words are likely to have multiple meanings in the context in which they are used; then break out the dictionary and, working in pairs, have them determine which of the possible definitions (there are eight for *fair*) apply to the passage where the author uses it repeatedly but never the same way.

To help your English language learners, try this:

- Confirm that they have access to an appropriate English language learner dictionary in their primary language at school and at home; then work with them to develop a set of the most important words for them to know in your class—words the other students are likely to know to varying degrees—and help them learn them as needed.

Standard: _____

Preparing the Classroom

Preparing the Mindset

Preparing the Texts to Use

Preparing to Differentiate

Connections to Other Standards:

Academic Vocabulary: Key Words and Phrases

Affixes: An extra element attached to the beginning, middle, or end of a word or its root that changes the word's meaning. They include prefixes and suffixes.

Consult general and specialized reference materials: Includes everything from a dictionary to usage handbooks such as Garner's Modern American Usage or other sources that focus on specialized aspects of words and phrases such as etymologies and allusions, as well as the Oxford English Dictionary to examine the word in depth.

Context clues: One makes an informed guess about the meaning of a word after looking at all the words around it, the way it is used (to determine its part of speech), how it is used in this context, and its place in the sentence or paragraph.

Determine and clarify the meaning of unknown and multiple-meaning words: Students cannot afford to ignore or not know many words in complex texts they read at this level; lacking such understanding, they cannot understand the texts read, especially when these words appear in discipline-specific texts as specialized terms related to a field of study. As for "multiple-meaning" (polysemic) words they may encounter in literary texts, they must look these up in specialized or unabridged dictionaries with etymologies and the full range of definitions available.

Glossaries: These are lists of specialized words in a text with their definitions, often found at the backs of books.

Greek and Latin affixes and roots: One way to determine meaning of words is to analyze the different parts. Greek and Latin root words have specific meanings. *Affixes* are both prefixes and suffixes, and in Greek and Latin, they too have specific meanings. When an affix is added to a root word the meaning changes (e.g., root word *pseudo* means false, the affix *nym* refers to name; therefore *pseudonym* is a false name).

Thesaurus: When looking at the etymology of this word from the Latin *thesaurus*, it means the treasury, storehouse, or book of words. For students it is a book of words and their synonyms.

Notes

Planning to Teach

Standard: _____

Whole Class

_____
_____
_____
_____
_____
_____
_____
_____

Small Group

_____
_____
_____
_____
_____
_____
_____
_____

Individual Practice/Conferring

_____
_____
_____
_____
_____
_____
_____
_____

Language 5: Demonstrate understanding of word relationships and nuances in word meanings.

English Language Arts

3 Demonstrate understanding of word relationships and nuances in word meanings.
  a. Distinguish the literal and nonliteral meanings of words and phrases in context (e.g., *take steps*).
  b. Identify real-life connections between words and their use (e.g., describe people who are *friendly* or *helpful*).
  c. Distinguish shades of meaning among related words that describe states of mind or degrees of certainty (e.g., *knew, believed, suspected, heard, wondered*).

4 Demonstrate understanding of **figurative language**, word relationships, and nuances in word meanings.
  a. **Explain the meaning of simple similes and metaphors (e.g., *as pretty as a picture*) in context.**
  b. **Recognize and explain the meaning of common idioms, adages, and proverbs.**
  c. **Demonstrate understanding of words by relating them to their opposites (antonyms) and to words with similar but not identical meanings (synonyms).**

5 Demonstrate understanding of **figurative language**, word relationships, and nuances in word meanings.
  a. **Interpret figurative language, including similes and metaphors, in context.**
  b. Recognize and explain the meaning of common idioms, adages, and proverbs.
  c. **Use the relationship between particular words (e.g., synonyms, antonyms, homographs) to better understand each of the words.**

What the **Student** Does

English Language Arts

3 **Gist:** Students show they understand the following by applying their knowledge about word relationships and nuances in word meanings in three key ways:

    a. **Literal versus nonliteral:** Readers determine from context the meanings of literal words and phrases and nonliteral or figurative words and phrases.

    b. **Connections between real life and words and their use:** Readers determine relationships between words and how they apply to real life.

    c. **Connotations:** Readers distinguish "shades of meaning" among related words that describe state of mind or degrees of certainty (e.g., *knew, believed, suspected, heard, wondered*).

They consider:

- Which words are used literally? How can I use the context to double-check that I understand them?
- Which words are nonliteral words—and what does the context suggest they mean? If I'm not sure about their meaning, how can I figure them out?
- What can I determine about the meaning of words from real-life connections?
- Which words show how a character or the writer felt?

4 **Gist:** Students show they understand the following by applying their knowledge about word relationships and nuances in word meanings in three key ways:

    a. **Figures of speech:** Readers determine from context the meanings of simple similes and metaphors.

    b. **Relationship between words:** Readers recognize and explain the meaning of common idioms, adages, and proverbs.

    c. **Connotations:** Readers demonstrate understanding by relating new words to their antonyms and synonyms.

They consider:

- Which words or phrases are similes or metaphors—and what does the context suggest they mean?
- Can I identify idioms, adages, or proverbs and what does the context suggest they mean?
- Can I use antonyms or synonyms to help determine the meaning of unknown words?

5 **Gist:** Students show they understand the following by applying their knowledge about word relationships and nuances in word meanings in three key ways:

    a. **Figures of speech:** Readers determine from context the meaning of such figures of speech as similes and metaphors.

    b. **Relationship between words:** Readers determine the meaning of common idioms, adages, and proverbs.

    c. **Connotations:** Readers distinguish between particular words (synonyms, antonyms, homonyms) to better understand the word.

They consider:

- Which words or phrases are figures of speech—and what does the context suggest they mean?
- Are there idioms, adages, or proverbs and what do they mean?
- Can I use synonyms, antonyms, or homonyms to help me understand the meaning of unfamiliar words?

What the **Teacher** Does

To help students distinguish literal and nonliteral words and explain and interpret figurative language such as similes and metaphors:

- Teach what *literal* means—that it is explicit or answered right there on the page. That literal is exact meaning. Then demonstrate how authors use nonliteral language. Create two column charts to record the literal meanings of words and the nonliteral meanings as used in the context.
- Think aloud how you puzzle out the meanings of nonliteral or figurative language.
- Teach different types of figurative language—one at a time. Use shared texts or picture books to notice and share specific types of figurative language (e.g., similes and metaphors) with students. Discuss what it means in that context and the images it evokes. Teach students that *like* or *as* when used in comparison generally denotes a simile. A metaphor does not include "like" or "as."
- Give students copies of shared texts with examples of similes or metaphors (or other figurative language). Have students highlight examples of figurative language and then annotate in the margins what it means.
- Have students use sticky notes to find figurative language in their own reading, marking the language and recording what they think it means by using the context.

To help students understand word relationships:

- Teach how words describe real-life situations. Students observe what they see and write about it using "real-life" words. Have students highlight "real-life" words in shared texts and annotate how these words are used and what they mean.

- Provide direct instruction to help students recognize idioms, adages, and proverbs by reading examples and discussing how the meaning is different from the literal meanings of the words. Have students find examples of these in their own reading and share in class.
- Provide them with a set of words from the text that are somehow related. Students reading in a social studies class about American history, for example, might get words like liberty, freedom, independence, self-determination, and license. Those reading a novel such as Lowry's *The Giver* might get a list of words such as dystopia, utopia, and eugenics. In science classes, they would study whatever words were related to the subject of their unit. The task of any such group would be to determine what the relationship is between these different words and how it relates to and affects the meaning of the text when the words are used together.

To help students demonstrate understanding of words by relating them to antonyms or synonyms or homographs:

- Teach the meaning of antonyms, synonyms, and homographs. Have students find examples and share them.
- Give students vocabulary words and have students use graphic organizers to show the synonyms or antonyms of the words. Maps, webs, and so on are beneficial for this.

To help your English language learners, try this:

- Create pictures to label with words and then show words that are the same (synonyms), such as big and large, and that are opposite (antonyms), such as big and little. Or create webs of synonyms with both the label and the pictures attached.

Notes

Preparing to Teach

Standard: _____

Preparing the Classroom

Preparing the Mindset

Preparing the Texts to Use

Preparing to Differentiate

Connections to Other Standards:

Academic Vocabulary: Key Words and Phrases

Adages: A proverb or a traditional saying expressing a common experience, which has gained credit through long use (e.g., "Out of sight, out of mind.").

Antonyms: These are words that mean the opposite of other words (e.g., *good/bad, up/down, hot/cold*).

Figurative language (aka figures of speech): The use of more visual, associative language to help readers "see" what one is saying or otherwise convey a deeper idea or emotion through such figures of speech as metaphor, simile, analogy, and allusion; clichés and mixed metaphors are also figures of speech, but they are often weak points the writer should revise or otherwise rewrite.

Homographs: These are words that share the same spelling or written form, but have different meanings (e.g., bear—*an animal*, bear—*to carry or support*). When spoken, they may have different pronunciations that identify the meaning (e.g., wind—*noun*, wind—*verb*).

Idioms: Often referred to as "figures of speech," an idiom is a combination of words that have a figurative meaning because of common usage. This figurative meaning is different than the literal meaning of both the phrase and the words within it. For example: *Sue kicked the bucket* as an idiom means that Sue died. Taken literally, Sue would be kicking (with her foot) a bucket.

Literal/nonliteral meanings of words in phrases in context: Literal meaning is the exact meanings of words. Nonliteral refers to figurative language. These meanings are determined by using the *context* or the part of the text that surrounds the particular word or passage and helps the reader determine its meaning.

Metaphor: A figure of speech that *does not* use the words *like* or *as* to compare two unrelated objects. Rather, a metaphor states that the subject is the same as an unrelated object. For example, "The lake was a mirror." Although a lake cannot be glass or a mirror, this metaphor creates the visual that the lake was smooth and reflective in the same manner that a mirror is.

Proverb: A simple and concrete saying in frequent and widespread use that states a general truth or piece of advice based on common sense. Also known as an *adage*.

Simile: A figure of speech comparing two unlike things. Similes generally use *like* or *as* to create or link the comparison. For example "cute *as* a kitten" or "his eyes twinkled *like* stars."

Synonyms: Words with the same or nearly the same meaning in a language. For example *small* and *little* are synonyms.

Word relationships: How two or more words might be related grammatically, rhetorically, conceptually, or in some other meaningful way as they are used in a text. Included in this category of words are figures of speech such as metaphors, analogies, and similes, which are based entirely on associations and relationships between words and ideas.

Notes

Planning to Teach

Standard: _____

Whole Class

Small Group

Individual Practice/Conferring

Language 6: Acquire and use accurately a range of general academic and domain-specific words and phrases sufficient for reading, writing, speaking, and listening at the college- and career-readiness level; demonstrate independence in gathering vocabulary knowledge when considering a word or phrase important to comprehension or expression.

English Language Arts

3 Acquire and use accurately grade-appropriate conversational, general academic, and domain-specific words and phrases, including those that signal spatial and temporal relationships (e.g., *After dinner that night we went looking for them*).

4 Acquire and use accurately grade-appropriate general academic and domain-specific words and phrases, including those that signal **precise actions, emotions, or states of being** (e.g., *quizzed, whined, stammered*) **and that are basic to a particular topic** (e.g., *wildlife, conservation,* and *endangered* when discussing animal preservation).

5 Acquire and use accurately grade-appropriate general academic and domain-specific words and phrases, including those that signal **contrast, addition, and other logical relationships** (e.g., *however, although, nevertheless, similarly, moreover, in addition*).

What the **Student** Does

English Language Arts

3 **Gist:** Students learn and use the language of discourse appropriate to the subject, discipline, or context when reading, writing, or speaking about it, along with specific words and phrases that signal spatial or temporal relationships (e.g., *After dinner that night we went looking for them*).

They consider:

- What are those academic words or phrases I hear most often when writing about or discussing a text or topic?
- What words do I use most in conversations?
- What works best for me to gather, learn, and remember when learning something new or a difficult subject?
- Are there certain words that I can use to signal time or relationships (like *after, before, next*)?

4 **Gist:** Students learn and use the language of discourse appropriate to the subject, discipline, or context when reading, writing, or speaking about it, along with precise words that show emotions or states of being (e.g., *quizzed, whined, stammered*).

They consider:

- What are those academic words or phrases I hear most often when writing about or discussing a text or topic?
- What are precise words that show emotions?
- What works best for me to gather, learn, and remember when learning something new or a difficult subject?

5 **Gist:** Students learn and use the language of discourse appropriate to the subject, discipline, or context when reading, writing, or speaking about it, along with those that signal contrast, addition, and other logical relationships (e.g., *however, although, nevertheless, similarly, moreover, in addition*).

They consider:

- What are those academic words or phrases I hear most often when writing about or discussing a text or topic?
- What are precise words that show emotions?
- What works best for me to gather, learn, and remember when learning something new or a difficult subject?
- Have I used words like *however, although, nevertheless,* or *in addition* to show contrast or relationships?

What the **Teacher** Does

To help students acquire and use academic and specialized words:

- Gather a list of words—academic vocabulary words—used in directions, prompts, and assignments for classes or subject areas such as yours; these are words students need to know in order to do what you assign them and which have often slight but significant differences (e.g., between *evaluate* and *analyze*). These are not the same as specialized academic words, which the Common Core document calls "Tier Three" words, such as *iambic pentameter* (English), *moral hazard* (economics), or other "domain-specific words . . . specific to a domain or field of study (*lava, carburetor, circumference, aorta*) that are key to understanding a new concept within a text" (Common Core State Standards, Appendix A, p. 33).

- Ask students at the beginning to assess their knowledge of the specialized words important to know in your class; they can do this most efficiently by taking a list of words you prepare and scoring themselves as follows: 1. Never heard or seen it; 2. Heard of it, but don't know it; 3. Recognize it as somehow related to _____; 4. Know it when I read it but not sure I can use it correctly when writing or speaking; 5. Know it and can use it as a reader, writer, speaker, and listener.

- Focus on what the Common Core calls "Tier Two" words, which it defines as, "general academic words . . . [that] are far more likely to appear in written texts than in speech, [including] informational texts (words such as *relative, vary, formulate, specificity,* and *accumulate*), technical texts (*calibrate, itemize, periphery*), and literary texts (*misfortune, dignified, faltered, unabashedly*). [These] Tier Two words often represent subtle or precise ways to say relatively simple things—*saunter* instead of *walk*, for example" (Common Core State Standards, Appendix A, p. 33).

To help students use temporal words, or words and phrases that signal precise actions, emotions, or states of being:

- Provide students with chart paper and put actions, emotions, or states of being on the headings. Working in groups, have students record words that signal these headings.

- Discuss and create a class list of temporal words that signify a position of an event in time. Post these for students to refer to.

- Have students highlight these precise words in their own writing.

To help students use words and phrases that signal contrast, addition, and other logical relationships:

- Create a class chart of these words and how and why they are used.

- Bring in texts that use these forms. Have students use sticky notes to mark where they're used and why they're used. Add these reasons to the class chart.

- Have students highlight use of these words in their own writing.

To help your English language learners, try this:

- Check that they always know the essential academic terms in order to be able to complete work independently.

Notes

Standard: _____

Preparing the Classroom

Preparing the Mindset

Preparing the Texts to Use

Preparing to Differentiate

Connections to Other Standards:

Academic Vocabulary: Key Words and Phrases

Acquire and use accurately: The emphasis here is on students adding words to their vocabularies so they are prepared for any text they might read or write about. To "acquire" words students must attend to the words they see but do not know and then make an effort both to learn and remember them for future use. The added emphasis on using words accurately reminds us that the difference between one word and another is often crucial to full and deeper comprehension.

College- and career-readiness level: Upon entering any postsecondary career or classroom, students immediately realize they are either ready to meet the demands of that situation or not. Those not ready for the demands of college-level reading most often have to take one or more remedial classes, which costs time and money—and often momentum—for those trying to pursue college degrees.

Comprehension: It means understanding what you read; but full, robust comprehension demands the reader take in all the details of a text and examine them in light of the occasion, purpose, and audience to see if there are other or deeper meanings to the text.

Expression: As it is used here, expression refers to writing; it is saying that it is important to know what a word or phrase means before students choose to include it in something they are writing.

General academic and domain-specific words: These are the general words students encounter in all subjects—analyze, evaluate, describe, compare, contrast, and so on—and the specialized vocabulary they face in specific course or subject areas—gravity, force, evolution, inflection point, and the many works specific to literature and other subject areas.

Independence in gathering vocabulary knowledge: To grow their vocabulary, students must take pains to look up words and note those meanings so they can draw on them in the future as readers and writers. This independence comes from jotting down and looking up words that either interest or confuse the reader and so merit further efforts to understand and distinguish them from others.

Words and phrases sufficient . . . for college level: This is similar to the earlier entry for college- and career-readiness level; however, the difference here is the emphasis on being able to use words and phrases appropriate to the college-level classroom. This means using refined, specific, and appropriate language when writing about or discussing a topic in a class. One must learn to master the discourse patterns common to a specific subject area or topic on which the student might be writing or doing research.

Notes

Standard: _____

Whole Class

_____

_____

_____

_____

_____

_____

_____

_____

Small Group

_____

_____

_____

_____

_____

_____

_____

_____

Individual Practice/Conferring

_____

_____

_____

_____

_____

_____

_____

_____

The Common Core State Standards

Reading Standards: Foundational Skills

College and Career Readiness Anchor Standards for

Reading Standards: Foundational Skills K–5

Source: Common Core State Standards

These standards are directed toward fostering students' understanding and working knowledge of concepts of print, the alphabetic principle, and other basic conventions of the English writing system. These foundational skills are not an end in and of themselves; rather, they are necessary and important components of an effective, comprehensive reading program designed to develop proficient readers with the capacity to comprehend texts across a range of types and disciplines. Instruction should be differentiated: good readers will need much less practice with these concepts than struggling readers will. The point is to teach students what they need to learn and not what they already know—to discern when particular children or activities warrant more or less attention.

Print Concepts

Grades K–1; not applicable to grades 3–5

Phonological Awareness

Grades K–1; not applicable to grades 3–5

Phonics and Word Recognition

3. Know and apply grade-level phonics and word analysis skills in decoding words.

Fluency

4. Read with sufficient accuracy and fluency to support comprehension.

College and Career Readiness Anchor Standards for
Reading Standards: Foundational Skills K–5

The Reading Foundational Standards are exclusive to the elementary grades. These are the print, phonological awareness, word recognition, and fluency pieces that aid in comprehension, which is the ultimate goal. As with the Reading Standards, students should be working in grade-level texts of increasing complexity as the year progresses. The first two standards, *Print Concepts* and *Phonological Awareness,* are directed to students in kindergarten and grade 1; however, students in grades 3–5 may need practice in these skills, depending on their needs.

Print Concepts

Grades K–1; not applicable to grades 3–5

Phonological Awareness

Grades K–1; not applicable to grades 3–5

Phonics and Word Recognition

This standard requires students to recognize and identify written words. Phonics is included in this standard, as well as decoding multisyllabic words and knowing syllabication patterns. Another aspect of this standard is morphology, which is the true study of how words are formed in language. When students recognize meaningful *morphological units* in unfamiliar words—specifically, prefixes, root words, and suffixes, then they can identify unfamiliar words. Teaching the meaning of common prefixes, suffixes, and root words is an integral part of this standard. In addition, students learn to read and understand unfamiliar words using the context of the text.

Fluency

The key words in this standard are *purpose* and *understanding.* Students read grade-level texts silently or orally with purpose and understanding as they learn to decode text. In addition, students become accurate and fluent readers. Students read poetry and prose orally, practicing by rereading and increasing their fluency, accuracy, and expression.

Reading: Foundational Skills 3: Know and apply grade-level phonics and word analysis skills in decoding words.

English Language Arts

3 Know and apply grade-level phonics and word analysis skills in decoding words.
    a. Identify and know the meaning of the most common prefixes and derivational suffixes.
    b. Decode words with common Latin suffixes.
    c. Decode multisyllable words.
    d. Read grade-appropriate irregularly spelled words.

4 Know and apply grade-level phonics and word analysis skills in decoding words.
    a. **Use combined knowledge of all letter-sound correspondences, syllabication patterns, and morphology (e.g., roots and affixes) to read accurately unfamiliar multisyllabic words in context and out of context.**

5 Know and apply grade-level phonics and word analysis skills in decoding words.
    a. Use combined knowledge of all letter-sound correspondences, syllabication patterns, and morphology (e.g., roots and affixes) to read accurately unfamiliar multisyllabic words in context and out of context.

What the **Student** Does

English Language Arts

3 **Gist:** Students recognize and identify grade-level written words by using phonics and word analysis skills in the following manner:
- Prefixes and suffixes: Identify and know the meaning of common prefixes and suffixes, and also common Latin suffixes.
- Multisyllabic words
- Irregularly spelled words

They consider:

- Are there prefixes attached to the word? What do they mean and how do they help me understand the word?
- Are there suffixes attached to the word? What do they mean and how do they help me understand the word?
- What is the root word? Do I know the meaning?
- Can I split the word into syllables?

4 **Gist:** Students use a range of skills to recognize and identify and read accurately grade-level written words. They do this by applying their knowledge of letter-sound correspondence, breaking the words into syllables, and identifying and knowing the meanings of prefixes, suffixes, and root words both in and out of context.

They consider:

- Do I know the meaning of the word? (out of context)
- Can I use context clues to help me figure out the meaning of the word?
- Can I sound out the word?
- Can I break the word into syllables?
- What is the prefix and its meaning?
- What is the suffix and its meaning?
- What is the root word?

5 **Gist:** Students use a range of skills to recognize and identify and read accurately grade-level written words. They do this by applying their knowledge of letter-sound correspondence, breaking the words into syllables, and identifying and knowing the meanings of prefixes, suffixes, and root words both in and out of context.

They consider:

- Do I know the meaning of the word? (out of context)
- Can I use context clues to help me figure out the meaning of the word?
- Can I sound out the word?
- Can I break the word into syllables?
- What is the prefix and its meaning?
- What is the suffix and its meaning?
- What is the root word?

What the **Teacher** Does

To have students identify and know the meaning of the most common prefixes and derivational suffixes, including common Latin suffixes:

- Instruct students on common prefixes and suffixes. Post these in the classroom.
- Have students highlight prefixes and suffixes in words to aid in determining meaning. Use sticky notes or annotate in the margin the meaning by identifying the prefix and its meaning, the root word and its meaning, and the suffix and its meaning. Use graphic organizers to show the parts of the word, their meaning, and then when put back together, the meaning of the unfamiliar word.
- Provide lists of words with common prefixes but different root words; have students determine the meaning of the prefix and then determine the meaning of the entire word.
- Do the above activity with suffixes.
- Determine specific words that are giving students difficulties and teach them explicitly by pulling apart affixes and the root word. Practice spelling these words by "chunking" them back together.
- Conduct a miscue analysis and then share with the students the types of errors they made. Discuss the miscues and have the student reflect and tell you *why* they pronounced the word the way they did. Use that as an opportunity to teach specific skills.

To have students decode multisyllable words:

- Teach students how to look for "chunks" in words (e.g., prefix, suffix, root word, or syllables) to help them decode.
- Teach students the patterns for determining syllables (e.g., closed, open, silent e, vowel teams, r-control, consonant e), and help them apply these patterns to decoding.

To have students read grade-appropriate irregularly spelled words:

- Post grade-level-appropriate words in the classroom. Practice both reading and spelling these words.
- Confer with students or work in a small group, having them read orally, and note when they read aloud if they recognize and accurately read irregularly spelled words.

To have students use combined knowledge of all letter-sound correspondence, syllabication patterns, and morphology to read accurately unfamiliar multisyllabic words in context and out of context:

- Do the strategies in the previous subheadings to teach and reinforce morphology.
- Confer with individual students to determine both miscues and comprehension by having students read orally and then do a brief retell after reading.
- Select a passage and either using the whiteboard or a shared text, read together and highlight unfamiliar words. Then use morphology and the context of the text to determine the meaning of those words.
- Conduct short exercises on the whiteboard where students "take apart" words, discuss what the parts mean, then reconstruct the word.
- Use webs and graphic organizers to record new vocabulary and how the student determined its meaning.
- Provide plenty of time for students to read independently.

To help your English language learners, try this:

- Provide sight words with pictures to help identify them. Discuss with the student the meaning and have them relate it to self. Access their background knowledge to help them identify unfamiliar words.

For graphic organizer templates, see online resources at **resources.corwin.com/literacycompanion3-5.**

Notes

Standard: _____

Preparing the Classroom

Preparing the Mindset

Preparing the Texts to Use

Preparing to Differentiate

Connections to Other Standards:

Academic Vocabulary: Key Words and Phrases

Affixes: An extra element attached to the beginning, middle, or end of a word or its root that changes the word's meaning. These are prefixes and suffixes. One way to determine meaning of words is to analyze the different parts. Latin root words have specific meanings. *Affixes* are both prefixes and suffixes, and in Latin, they too have specific meanings. When an affix is added to a root word the meaning changes (e.g., root word *pseudo* means false, the affix *nym* refers to name; therefore *pseudonym* is a false name).

Decode: This refers to applying knowledge of letter-sound relationships to a set of letters, thus making it into a meaningful word. Decoding is the opposite of encoding, which involves changing spoken words into print.

Grade-level phonics: This refers to phonics instruction that is appropriate for students at a particular age and grade level, and from which they are likely to benefit.

Irregularly spelled words: Words that are not spelled as they sound, so they cannot be sounded out or decoded. "Sight words" are included in this category; however, sight words should be recognized automatically.

Letter-sound correspondence: The understanding of the sounds represented by the letters of the alphabet *and* the letters used to represent the sounds.

Morphology: The true meaning is the study and description of how words are formed in a language. In the intermediate standards, this is delineated by the study of roots, prefixes, and suffixes.

Multisyllabic words: A word of many syllables.

Syllabication patterns: Syllables are units of pronunciation containing a single vowel sound or "sound chunks." When students learn the patterns to determine where the word is broken into syllables, this aides in decoding and pronunciation. Common syllable patterns are: *closed, open, silent e, vowel teams, r. control,* and *consonant e.*

Word analysis skills: These skills involve breaking a word down into its smaller parts—its root, prefixes, and suffixes—so it can be read and understood. This is different from phonics, which relies on matching sounds to letters and letter combinations.

Notes

Planning to Teach

Standard: _____

Whole Class

_____

_____

_____

_____

_____

_____

_____

_____

Small Group

_____

_____

_____

_____

_____

_____

_____

Individual Practice/Conferring

_____

_____

_____

_____

_____

_____

_____

Reading: Foundational Skills 4: Read with sufficient accuracy and fluency to support comprehension.

English Language Arts

3 Read with sufficient accuracy and fluency to support comprehension.
  a. Read grade-level text with purpose and understanding.
  b. Read grade-level prose and poetry orally with accuracy, appropriate rate, and expression on successive readings.
  c. Use context to confirm or self-correct word recognition and understanding, rereading as necessary.

4 Read with sufficient accuracy and fluency to support comprehension.
  a. Read grade-level text with purpose and understanding.
  b. Read grade-level prose and poetry orally with accuracy, appropriate rate, and expression on successive readings.
  c. Use context to confirm or self-correct word recognition and understanding, rereading as necessary.

5 Read with sufficient accuracy and fluency to support comprehension.
  a. Read grade-level text with purpose and understanding.
  b. Read grade-level prose and poetry orally with accuracy, appropriate rate, and expression on successive readings.
  c. Use context to confirm or self-correct word recognition and understanding, rereading as necessary.

What the **Student** Does

English Language Arts

3 **Gist:** Students read grade-level prose and poetry with purpose and for understanding, both to themselves and orally. As they practice reading these texts, their accuracy, rate of reading, and expression increase. If there are unknown words, students use context and reread to self-correct or identify these words.

They consider:

- Is this an appropriate text for me?
- Are there any words I don't know? How can I figure them out?
- Am I understanding what I read?
- How is my rate? If I were reading out loud, would my audience be able to understand?
- Do I need to reread any parts of the text?

4 **Gist:** Students read grade-level prose and poetry with purpose and for understanding, both to themselves and orally. As they practice reading these texts, their accuracy, rate of reading, and expression increase. If there are unknown words, students use context and reread to self-correct or identify these words.

They consider:

- Is this an appropriate text for me?
- Are there any words I don't know? How can I figure them out?
- Am I understanding what I read?
- How is my rate? If I were reading out loud, would my audience be able to understand?
- Do I need to reread any parts of the text?

5 **Gist:** Students read grade-level prose and poetry with purpose and for understanding, both to themselves and orally. As they practice reading these texts, their accuracy, rate of reading, and expression increase. If there are unknown words, students use context and reread to self-correct or identify these words.

They consider:

- Is this an appropriate text for me?
- Are there any words I don't know? How can I figure them out?
- Am I understanding what I read?
- How is my rate? If I were reading out loud, would my audience be able to understand?
- Do I need to reread any parts of the text?

What the **Teacher** Does

To have students read with sufficient accuracy and fluency to support comprehension:

- Read aloud often, from a variety of genres, so students hear what it sounds like to read with expression.
- Offer numerous opportunities for students to read orally. This may be reading with a partner, reading in small-group situations, or reading aloud in class. Select or have students select a passage to memorize and recite from fiction but also find narrative nonfiction and informational texts so students can practice oral, fluent reading while pronouncing content-specific vocabulary.
- Provide "buddy time" for oral reading with students in another grade level.
- Assess student reading using miscue analysis. Give feedback to students so when faced with a similar word, they will have a strategy. In addition, assess comprehension by asking for a short retell after the student has read.
- Read aloud from a shared text (either in a small-group setting, with one student, or with the whole class) and have students follow along, tracking if necessary.

To have students read grade-level text with purpose and understanding:

- Have a wide variety of grade-level texts available for students.
- Confer and assess student comprehension/understanding of text.
- Teach explicitly what reading with *purpose* means, whether it's to read for enjoyment, to read for a specific task, to read to gain new understanding, and so on.
- Conduct short retells or other comprehension assessments after students have read.
- Work with students in small groups—setting a purpose and checking for understanding as they read and discuss the shared text.
- Provide independent reading time for students to practice. Students should be reading independently and building stamina.

To have students read grade-level prose and poetry orally with accuracy, appropriate rate, and expression on successive readings:

- Model for students how to read prose and poetry orally. Choose a difficult piece of text and read through once. Discuss what you noticed about your reading and what you will do differently in the next reading. Have students listen for how your reading improves—especially in rate and expression. Read a second time and then discuss what students notice.
- Have students find poems they like and are comfortable with to read aloud; allow them ample practice before reading aloud.
- Have students record their reading and then listen and reflect and then record again.
- Provide opportunities for students to do podcasts for poetry or participate in poetry slams. Recite favorite song lyrics as poems; tie this to explorations of tone and mood.
- Have students participate in choral reading.
- Use Reader's Theatre to improve their oral reading skills. Tie this work into content-area learning too; for example, look for mythology-related Reader's Theatre scripts. Have students recite parts and wholes of famous documents, from King's "I Have a Dream" speech to the Declaration of Independence.
- Work with students in small groups to practice their oral reading, get feedback, and then practice some more.

To have students use context to confirm or self-correct word recognition and understanding, rereading as necessary:

- Model your process for using context to confirm or self-correct word recognition. Use a piece of text that is difficult for you to read, so that students can see you modeling authentically.
- Confer with students to check on word recognition and their word attack skills. Ask them to explain *how* they determined how to pronounce unfamiliar words and how they figured out the meaning.
- Have students mark unknown vocabulary words in their independent reading with sticky notes and then meet with you or check for meaning.
- Have students share unfamiliar words in their literature circles, book clubs, partner reading, or in small groups.
- Ensure that students have time to read independently.

To help your English language learners, try this:

- Create vocabulary books of unfamiliar words for the student—especially words that they will frequently encounter or words that they should use in their writing. In addition to the printed word, include a picture to help with meaning.
- Provide audio books for students to listen to or to follow along with.

 For graphic organizer templates, see online resources at **resources.corwin.com/literacycompanion3-5**.

Preparing to Teach

Standard: _____

Preparing the Classroom

_____
_____
_____
_____
_____
_____

Preparing the Mindset

_____
_____
_____
_____
_____
_____

Preparing the Texts to Use

_____
_____
_____
_____
_____
_____

Preparing to Differentiate

_____
_____
_____
_____
_____
_____

Connections to Other Standards:

_____
_____
_____

Academic Vocabulary: Key Words and Phrases

Accuracy: This refers to reading words correctly or precisely. Readers need to read accurately to get an author's intended meaning.

Confirm or self-correct word recognition and understanding: This refers to readers checking back to make sure that they've read particular words correctly. They either confirm that they've read the words correctly or they self-correct when they find that what they've read doesn't match the words in print. Readers do the same for comprehension: they confirm that they understand or they intervene with a strategy to make sense of what they're reading.

Expression: Conveying emotion or feeling when reading orally. This may include inflections, or pacing, or noticing different speakers in dialogue.

Fluency: To read easily and smoothly. To be *fluent*, a reader demonstrates fluid reading as if flowing effortlessly. Students pronounce words correctly, use punctuation cues, and read with expression.

Read grade-level text with purpose and understanding: Grade-level text indicates the text difficulty associated with the grade levels around which the Common Core State Standards are organized: grades 2–3, 4–5, 6–8, 9–10, 11–CCR (college and career readiness). To read with *purpose and understanding* is for students to have a reason to read (for enjoyment, to learn, to access information, etc.) and for them to demonstrate comprehension or understanding of the text. Writers generally have one of four purposes when they write: to persuade, inform, express, or entertain, and readers choose specific texts for particular reasons to match that purpose.

Use context to confirm or self-correct word recognition and understanding: A reader uses the *context* or the parts of a piece of writing to help determine the meaning of an unfamiliar word. The context is the word or phrases that surround the unfamiliar word that help to explain its meaning. This is often referred to as using "context cues." Context helps determine the word (i.e., confirm) and if incorrect, to self-correct the word—either in pronunciation or in meaning.

Notes

Standard: _____

Whole Class

_____

_____

_____

_____

_____

_____

_____

Small Group

_____

_____

_____

_____

_____

_____

_____

Individual Practice/Conferring

_____

_____

_____

_____

_____

_____

_____

Resources

Common Core Recommended Reading Lists

The following links take you to places that showed a commitment to building on the initial reading lists provided by the Common Core State Standards document itself. We include this short list to help you explore other sources for rich texts for your students:

Common Core Curriculum Maps

> http://commoncore.org/maps

Cooperative Children's Book Center

> http://www.education.wisc.edu/ccbc/books/commoncore.asp

North Carolina Department of Public Instruction

> http://www.dpi.state.nc.us/docs/acre/standards/common-core-tools/exemplar/ela.pdf

Official Common Core State Standards 3–5 Text Exemplars

Grades 2–3 Text Exemplars

Stories

Averill, Esther. *The Fire Cat*

Cameron, Ann. *The Stories Julian Tells*

Gannett, Ruth Stiles. *My Father's Dragon*

LaMarche, Jim. *The Raft*

MacLachlan, Patricia. *Sarah, Plain and Tall*

Osborne, Mary Pope. *The One-Eyed Giant* (Book One of *Tales From the Odyssey*)

Rylant, Cynthia. *Henry and Mudge: The First Book of Their Adventures*

Rylant, Cynthia. *Poppleton in Winter*

Rylant, Cynthia. *The Lighthouse Family: The Storm*

Shulevitz, Uri. *The Treasure*

Silverman, Erica. *Cowgirl Kate and Cocoa*

Steig, William. *Amos & Boris*

Stevens, Janet. *Tops and Bottoms*

Poetry

Dickinson, Emily. "Autumn"

Field, Rachel. "Something Told the Wild Geese"

Frost, Robert. "Stopping by Woods on a Snowy Evening"

Giovanni, Nikki. "Knoxville, Tennessee"

Hughes, Langston. "Grandpa's Stories"

Jarrell, Randall. "A Bat Is Born"

Merriam, Eve. "Weather"

Millay, Edna St. Vincent. "Afternoon on a Hill"

Rossetti, Christina. "Who Has Seen the Wind?"

Soto, Gary. "Eating While Reading"

Read-Aloud Stories

Babbitt, Natalie. *The Search for Delicious*

Curtis, Christopher Paul. *Bud, Not Buddy*

Kipling, Rudyard. "How the Camel Got His Hump"

Say, Allen. *The Sign Painter*

Selden, George. *The Cricket in Times Square*

Thurber, James. *The Thirteen Clocks*

White, E. B. *Charlotte's Web*

Read-Aloud Poetry

Browning, Robert. "The Pied Piper of Hamelin"

Eliot, T. S. "The Song of the Jellicles"

Fleischman, Paul. "Fireflies"

Johnson, Georgia Douglas. "Your World"

Lear, Edward. "The Jumblies"

Informational Texts

Aliki. *A Medieval Feast*

Beeler, Selby. *Throw Your Tooth on the Roof: Tooth Traditions Around the World*

Davies, Nicola. *Bat Loves the Night*

Einspruch, Andrew. *Crittercam*

Floca, Brian. *Moonshot: The Flight of Apollo 11*

Gibbons, Gail. *From Seed to Plant*

Kudlinski, Kathleen V. *Boy, Were We Wrong About Dinosaurs!*

Leonard, Heather. *Art Around the World*

Milton, Joyce. *Bats: Creatures of the Night*

Ruffin, Frances E. *Martin Luther King and the March on Washington*

St. George, Judith. *So You Want to Be President?*

Thomson, Sarah L. *Where Do Polar Bears Live?*

Read-Aloud Informational Texts

Aliki. *Ah, Music!*

Arnosky, Jim. *Wild Tracks! A Guide to Nature's Footprints*

Coles, Robert. *The Story of Ruby Bridges*

D'Aluisio, Faith. *What the World Eats*

Deedy, Carmen Agra. *14 Cows for America*

Freedman, Russell. *Lincoln: A Photobiography*

Mark, Jan. *The Museum Book: A Guide to Strange and Wonderful Collections*

Smith, David J. *If the World Were a Village: A Book about the World's People*

Wick, Walter. *A Drop of Water: A Book of Science and Wonder*

Grades 4–5 Text Exemplars

Stories

Babbitt, Natalie. *Tuck Everlasting*

Burnett, Frances Hodgson. *The Secret Garden*

Carroll, Lewis. *Alice's Adventures in Wonderland*

Curtis, Christopher Paul. *Bud, Not Buddy*

Erdrich, Louise. *The Birchbark House*

Farley, Walter. *The Black Stallion*

Hamilton, Virginia. *M. C. Higgins, the Great*

Lin, Grace. *Where the Mountain Meets the Moon*

Saint-Exupéry, Antoine de. *The Little Prince*

Singer, Isaac Bashevis. "Zlateh the Goat"

Poetry

Blake, William. "The Echoing Green"

Dahl, Roald. "Little Red Riding Hood and the Wolf"

Dickinson, Emily. "A Bird Came Down the Walk"

Frost, Robert. "Dust of Snow"

Lazarus, Emma. "The New Colossus"

Mora, Pat. "Words Free as Confetti"

Nichols, Grace. "They Were My People"

Sandburg, Carl. "Fog"

Thayer, Ernest Lawrence. "Casey at the Bat"

Informational Texts

Banting, Erinn. *England the Land*

Berger, Melvin. *Discovering Mars: The Amazing Story of the Red Planet*

Buckmaster, Henrietta. "Underground Railroad"

Carlisle, Madelyn Wood. *Let's Investigate Marvelously Meaningful Maps*

Cutler, Nellie Gonzalez. "Kenya's Long Dry Season"

Hakim, Joy. *A History of US*

Hall, Leslie. "Seeing Eye to Eye"

Kavash, E. Barrie. "Ancient Mound Builders"

Koscielniak, Bruce. *About Time: A First Look at Time and Clocks*

Lauber, Patricia. *Hurricanes: Earth's Mightiest Storms*

Montgomery, Sy. *Quest for the Tree Kangaroo: An Expedition to the Cloud Forest of New Guinea*

Nelson, Kadir. *We Are the Ship: The Story of Negro League Baseball*

Otfinoski, Steve. *The Kid's Guide to Money: Earning It, Saving It, Spending It, Growing It, Sharing It*

Ronan, Colin A. "Telescopes"

Ruurs, Margriet. *My Librarian Is a Camel: How Books Are Brought to Children Around the World*

Schleichert, Elizabeth. "Good Pet, Bad Pet"

Simon, Seymour. *Horses*

Simon, Seymour. *Volcanoes*

Wulffson, Don. *Toys! Amazing Stories Behind Some Great Inventions*

Source: Appendix B of the official Common Core State Standards

Text Complexity Tool

Title:		Author:		Date:	
Appropriate Grade Level:		Length:		Text Type/Genre:	
		Too Simple	**Just Right**	**Too Complex**	

	Too Simple	Just Right	Too Complex
QUANTITATIVE FACTORS			
Word Length			
☐ What is the average length of a word in this text? ☐ Do the words tend to have one or many meanings?			
Sentence Length			
☐ How long is the average sentence? ☐ Do sentences tend to be all the same length or vary as a function of style? ☐ Do the sentences have a range of syntactical complexity—or do they tend to follow the same pattern?			
Word Frequency			
☐ Which words are used frequently? ☐ Are these words known/familiar?			
Text Cohesion			
☐ How well does this text hold together or flow (thanks to signal words such as transitions)? ☐ Does the text use other techniques such as repetition or concrete language to improve cohesion? ☐ Does the text lack cohesion as a result of having no signal words?			
QUALITATIVE FACTORS			
Levels of Meaning or Purpose			
☐ If *literary*, does the text have more than one obvious meaning? ☐ If *informational*, is the purpose explicitly stated or implied? ☐ Does the text explore *more* than one substantial idea?			
Text Structure			
☐ Does the text use simple, predictable structures such as chronological order? ☐ Does the text use complex literary structures such as flashbacks or, if informational, sophisticated graphics and genre conventions? ☐ Does the text use other features—layout, color, graphics—in ways that might confuse or challenge some readers?			
Language Conventions and Clarity			
☐ Is the language literal, clear, modern, and conversational? ☐ Is the language figurative, ironic, ambiguous, archaic, specialized, or otherwise unfamiliar?			
Knowledge Demands			
☐ Does the text make few assumptions about what you have experienced or know about yourself, others, and the world? ☐ Does the text assume you know about this topic or text based on prior experience or study?			
READER AND TASK CONSIDERATIONS			
Motivation, Knowledge, and Experience			
☐ How motivated is this student to read this text? ☐ How much does this student know about this topic or text? ☐ How much experience does the student have with this task or text type?			
Purpose and Complexity of the Assigned Task			
☐ Is this student able to read and work at the assigned level? ☐ Are these questions the student will know how to answer? ☐ Is the student expected to do this work alone and without any support—or with others and guidance? ☐ Is this text or task appropriate for this student at this time? ☐ Is this text or task as, less, or more complex than the last one?			

Created by Jim Burke. Visit www.englishcompanion.com for more information.

Planning Calendar Templates

July Planning Calendar

Sunday	Monday	Tuesday	Wednesday	Thursday	Friday	Saturday

August Planning Calendar

Sunday	Monday	Tuesday	Wednesday	Thursday	Friday	Saturday

September Planning Calendar

Sunday	Monday	Tuesday	Wednesday	Thursday	Friday	Saturday

October Planning Calendar

Sunday	Monday	Tuesday	Wednesday	Thursday	Friday	Saturday

November Planning Calendar

Sunday	Monday	Tuesday	Wednesday	Thursday	Friday	Saturday

December Planning Calendar

Sunday	Monday	Tuesday	Wednesday	Thursday	Friday	Saturday

January Planning Calendar

Sunday	Monday	Tuesday	Wednesday	Thursday	Friday	Saturday

February Planning Calendar

Sunday	Monday	Tuesday	Wednesday	Thursday	Friday	Saturday

March Planning Calendar

Sunday	Monday	Tuesday	Wednesday	Thursday	Friday	Saturday

April Planning Calendar

Sunday	Monday	Tuesday	Wednesday	Thursday	Friday	Saturday

May Planning Calendar

Sunday	Monday	Tuesday	Wednesday	Thursday	Friday	Saturday

June Planning Calendar

Sunday	Monday	Tuesday	Wednesday	Thursday	Friday	Saturday

Teacher Notes

STANDARDS-BASED TEACHING

The key to raising school- and district-wide achievement is purposeful, potent, standards-based instruction—all year long in every classroom. That's where the Your Literacy Standards Companion series can help. Series creator Jim Burke and an all-star team of authors walk you step by step through what the standards mean and how to teach them. Ensure that every student in your district has the critical skills they need to succeed on test day, in school, and in life.

Grades K–2
978-1-5063-8682-9

Grades 3–5
978-1-5063-8700-0

Grades 6–8
978-1-5063-8553-2

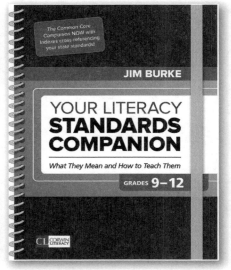

Grades 9–12
978-1-5063-8552-5

BECAUSE ALL TEACHERS ARE LEADERS

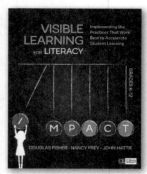

Grades K–12
978-1-5063-3235-2

**Douglas Fisher,
Nancy Frey,
John Hattie**
Ensure students demonstrate more than a year's worth of learning during a school year by implementing the right literacy practice at the right moment.

Grades K–5
978-1-5063-3236-9

**Douglas Fisher,
Nancy Frey,
John Hattie**
High-impact strategies to use for all you teach—all in one place. Deliver sustained, comprehensive literacy experiences to K–5 learners each day.

Grades K–2
978-1-5063-2688-7

Wiley Blevins
Foremost phonics expert Wiley Blevins explains the 7 ingredients that lead to the greatest student gains, and includes common pitfalls, lessons, word lists, and routines.

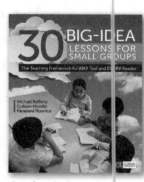

Grades 3–6
978-1-5063-3438-7

**Michael Rafferty,
Colleen Morello,
Paraskevi Rountos**
This amazing 4-part framework—Engaging, Discussing, Deep-See Thinking, and Connecting—gets students interacting with texts, developing their literal, inferential, evaluative, and analytical skills.

Grades K–8
978-1-5063-1493-8

Gravity Goldberg
Let go of the default roles of assigner, monitor, and manager, and shift to a growth mindset. The 4*M*s framework lightens your load by allowing students to direct their own reading lives.

Grades K–2, 978-1-5063-2646-7
Grades 3–6, 978-1-4833-7567-0

Nancy Boyles
Nancy Boyles delivers the playbook on close reading through lessons, assessment strategies, planning templates, online video, and more.

A SAGE Publishing Company

Helping educators make the greatest impact

CORWIN HAS ONE MISSION: to enhance education through intentional professional learning.

We build long-term relationships with our authors, educators, clients, and associations who partner with us to develop and continuously improve the best evidence-based practices that establish and support lifelong learning.